JAPAN, 1972

# Japan, 1972

VISIONS OF MASCULINITY IN
AN AGE OF MASS CONSUMERISM

Yoshikuni Igarashi

Columbia University Press
*New York*

Columbia University Press
*Publishers Since 1893*
New York   Chichester, West Sussex
cup.columbia.edu
Copyright © 2021 Columbia University Press
All rights reserved

Library of Congress Cataloging-in-Publication Data
Names: Igarashi, Yoshikuni, 1960– author.
Title: Japan, 1972 : visions of masculinity in an age of mass consumerism / Yoshikuni Igarashi, Columbia University Press.
Description: New York : Columbia University Press, [2021] | Includes bibliographical references and index.
Identifiers: LCCN 2020047647 (print) | LCCN 2020047648 (ebook) | ISBN 9780231195546 (hardback) | ISBN 9780231195553 (trade paperback) | ISBN 9780231551380 (ebook)
Subjects: LCSH: Consumer behavior—Japan. | Masculinity—Japan. | Japan—Civilization—1945– | Popular culture—Japan—History—20th century.
Classification: LCC HF5415.33.J3 I35 2021  (print) | LCC HF5415.33.J3 (ebook) | DDC 306.30811/0952—dc23
LC record available at https://lccn.loc.gov/2020047647
LC ebook record available at https://lccn.loc.gov/2020047648

Cover: TV Frame Left in a Reclamation Area, Tokyo, 1969
Cover design: Julia Kushnirsky
Cover photograph: © Ryōji Akiyama

*For Teresa, Maya, and Kaita*

# Contents

Acknowledgments  ix
List of Abbreviations  xiii
Note on Personal Names  xv

INTRODUCTION  1

PART I  Television

1  Reflections on the Consuming Subject: The High-Growth Economy and the Emergence of a New National Community  19

2  Circular Vision: The Metavisuality of Television  50

PART II  Travel

3  Japan on the Move, a Family on the Run: Yamada Yōji's Countervision of Contemporary Japan  87

4  Lost in Transition: Travel, Memory, and Nostalgia in Tsuge Yoshiharu's Travel Manga  115

5  The Ethics of Witnessing: Kaikō Takeshi's Vietnam War  144

## PART III  Violence

6  Heroes in Crisis: The Transformation of Yakuza Film   173

7  Jō and Hyūma: Kajiwara Ikki's Manga Heroes and
   Their Violent Quest for Historical Agency   199

8  Dead Bodies and Living Guns: The United Red Army and
   Its Deadly Pursuit of Revolution   228

EPILOGUE: LEGACIES OF 1972   254

Notes   267
Bibliography   325
Index   347

# Acknowledgments

Over the years that I have worked on this project, I have benefitted greatly from many people's support, guidance, and encouragement. Their timely advice and material assistance were key to pushing this project across the finish line. At the University of Hawai'i Library, Patricia Steinhoff and Tokiko Bazell helped me navigate the Takazawa Collection, an essential archive for studies of Japan's new left movements in the 1960s and 1970s. I was a beneficiary of Hamasaki Kōji's years of effort to build a TV documentary archive at the Kawasaki City Museum. He generously shared his insights into Ushiyama Jun'ichi's pioneering work in establishing Japan's TV documentary as a genre. I sincerely hope that the museum will quickly recover from the heavy damage it sustained in the October 2019 flooding. Saitō Shigeru kindly granted me access to Ritsumeikan University's school history archive and storage vault. I am also thankful to the Ōya Sōichi Library staff for their laborious work to archive and index popular Japanese weeklies. Yuh-Fen Benda always found ways to acquire the Japanese books I requested for the Vanderbilt University Library. Jim Toplon and the Interlibrary Loan staff of Vanderbilt University handled my numerous requests.

I would like to thank Alex Bates, Shawn Bender, Cynthia Bisson, Kim Brandt, Peter Eckersall, Andrew Gordon, Christine Greiner, Maki Kaneko, Jason Karlin, Kawamura Kunimitsu, Thomas Looser, Markus Nornes, Nakagawa Shigemi, Doug Slaymaker, Alan Tansman, Sharon Traweek,

Beatrice Trefalt, Tsuboi Hideto, Wesley Sakaki-Uemura, and Umemori Naoyuki for kindly inviting me to present part of this book at their home institutions. Feedback I received on each occasion was enormously helpful in shaping this project.

Taking time out of his busy schedule, Markus Nornes made me copies of some classical Yakuza film, which proved to be essential to my early writing on the topic. Igarashi Akio warmly welcomed me as a visiting researcher at Rikkyō University. Ann Walthall's and Victor Koschmann's strong endorsement was a key to securing outside funds for this project. Michael Raine, Takuya Tsunoda, and Ayako Saitō generously shared their expert knowledge on Japanese film. The comments that Noriko Aso, Gerald Figal, and Mitsuyo Wada-Marciano made on early draft chapters were essential to the subsequent evolution of the project. Just as he did with my previous book, Mark Shoenfield combed through each chapter and helped sharpen its focus. Jane Barry, Kathleen DeGuzman, Aubrey Porterfield, and Davis Winkie proofread the manuscript in part or whole at various stages, offering stylistic and substantive comments. An anonymous reader and Max Ward, who reviewed the manuscript for the press, gave it candid appraisals with encouraging words. Their detailed reports served as an invaluable guide in the final stage of this project. Christopher Benda read the manuscript at the final stage, providing concrete suggestions as to how best to fine-tune my argument.

I am grateful that Caelyn Cobb and the editorial team of Columbia University Press deemed this project worthy of their attention and guided me through the final manuscript preparation. Monique Briones deftly handled my frequent logistical inquiries. Erin Greb converted my very rough sketches into print-ready maps and images. Akiyama Ryōji generously gave me permission to use his powerful photo for the cover.

The research for and writing of this project have been supported by an Advanced Research in the Social Sciences on Japan Fellowship jointly administered by the National Endowment for the Humanities and the Japan-U.S. Friendship Commission, an Association for Asian Studies Northeast Asia Council Short-Term Travel Grant to Japan, and Vanderbilt University Central Research Scholar Grant Program's Research Scholar Fellowships and Faculty Development Grant. Vanderbilt's generous leave policy also allowed me to focus on the project for extended periods.

An earlier version of chapters 4 and 8 appeared, respectively, in *Mechademia 6: User Enhanced* (2011): 271–85 and *Japanese Studies* 27, no. 2

(September 2007): 119–37. I thank University of Minnesota Press and Taylor & Francis for their permissions to reprint this material. An earlier Japanese version of chapters 6 and 7 appeared in *Bunka/hihyō* (2009): 1–32 and *Bunka/hiyō* (Winter 2006): 361–86.

My final thanks go to my wife, Teresa, and our children, Maya and Kaita, for being my biggest source of joy and happiness. Their humor and laughter always keep me balanced. I am blessed to be a member of this wonderful team, and for that, I dedicate this book to them.

# Abbreviations

*KTZ*   Kaikō Takeshi, *Kaikō Takeshi zenshū*, 22 vols. (Tokyo: Shinchōsha, 1991–1993)

*MS*   Mizuki Shigeru, Mizuki Shigeru manga daizenshū, 109 vols. (Tokyo: Kōdansha, 2013-2019)

*SG*   Kajiwara Ikki and Kawasaki Noboru, *Kyojin no hoshi* (Star of the Giants), 19 vols. (Tokyo: Kōdansha, 1970–1972)

*TJ*   Asamori Akio and Chiba Tetsuya, *Ashita no jō* (Tomorrow's Jō), 20 vols. (Tokyo: Kōdansha, 1993)

*TYZ*   Tsuge Yoshiharu, *Tsuge Yoshiharu zenshū*, 9 vols. (Tokyo: Chikuma shobō, 1993–1994)

# Note on Personal Names

In transcribing Japanese and Korean names, I follow the local custom of placing the family name first. But when the work is written in English, the author's name (e.g., my name) is cited with the given name first.

JAPAN, 1972

# Introduction

> 1972 was "an end of the beginning" and "a beginning of the end" of the new era.
>
> —TSUBOUCHI YŪZŌ, *1972* (2003)

In June 1972 the Japanese beverage company Suntory began airing a television commercial for its new product, Delica, an inexpensive blended wine. Striving to cultivate a wine market that had hitherto been nonexistent in Japan, the ad targeted young, urban, middle-class couples, promoting wine as a perfect beverage for their new lifestyle. The advent of the five-day workweek inspired Suntory's public relations team to devise the slogan "Friday is the day to buy wine."[1] In the ad, a man clutches an oversized paper bag full of groceries to his chest. Flowers, bread, and a bottle of wine peek from the mouth of the bag, obscuring the man's face. A male singer performs a short jingle that puts the responsibility for procuring the wine on men: "Friday, I buy flowers, bread, and wine on my way home. Over the weekend, I will dine, drink wine, and talk with my wife. How tiresome" (*aa shindo*).[2] Between the first and second lines, a female voice announces the prices of the Delica products. As the song comes to an end, two lines appear on the screen: "Let's buy wine on Friday. Suntory, the leader of the wine age."

The commercial tells young Japanese men what they need to purchase and how they should behave in order to participate in an attractive and desirable consumer life. However, the last phrase of the jingle, "*aa shindo*," which best translates as "tiresome" or "bothersome," provides an interesting twist to the new middle-class image that Suntory is trying to promote. The faceless man's inner monologue punctures the rosy scenario, intimating

[ 1 ]

that wine is a necessary prop for performing a happy middle-class life. He may be nobody in the larger industrial structure of Japan, but he can be somebody in the domestic space as long as he brings home a bottle of wine. Yet the lightness of the tune and the colloquial tone of the phrase suggest that his criticism is merely a moment of self-reflection on the world that the commercial promotes. He may be a bit hesitant about embracing the wonderful world of mass consumption, but once in it, he will most likely forget about his minor misgivings. The Suntory commercial attests not only to the long reach of contemporary Japan's consumerism but also to the difficulty of escaping it: even the weary voice of consternation can effectively promote products in this world.

The poet Ōki Minoru (1913–1996) was keenly aware of this difficulty when he tried to express his discomfort about living in the material comfort of postwar society. His complaints came with the sharp realization that he was already deeply ensconced in that society. His poem "The Average" (Heikinteki), published in 1971, articulates his conflicting feelings about living a pleasant yet remarkably unremarkable life in contemporary Japan:

> My physique appears average.
> Standard store-bought suits fit me well.
> My life and everyday habits, in which store-bought suits fit well,
>     appear fairly average.
> I live happily with my wife and children, cherish my work, gently
>     smile at others, and don't get upset even when I want to be
>     angry.
> Even my mind has become average.
> Another me inside myself—
> That man constantly gets upset and sad,
> Upset with Ōki Minoru, who lives an average life,
> Sad and frustrated.[3]

Japanese society had come a long way since the dire economic hardships of the immediate postwar years.[4] In the material comfort that he now can afford, Ōki's "I" is frustrated because everything about his life has become "average." Comfortably clad in mass-produced apparel, his average body seems like that of a faceless mannequin. Even his emotions have been molded into a pleasant and predictable form. The price to maintain membership in the now-affluent society seemed extremely high: having a decent, steady job (and perhaps buying a bottle of cheap wine for Friday night dinner) meant to subject oneself to a regimented corporate lifestyle where everything was more or less predetermined. The price of affluence was a colorless, uniform future. Trapped in his average physique, "I" wishes to break away from the status quo but is fully aware that he would not dare.

Both the Suntory commercial and Ōki's poem suggest that living in a mass consumer society is accompanied by a degree of self-awareness about life as a consumer. The concept of self-reflectivity is the key to understanding the complex relations between individuals and a society dominated by consumption. The Suntory commercial is aware of consumerism's coercive power but diffuses it by prefiguring possible pushback from the audience. The skeptical "*aa shindo*" at the end disarms the viewers with its frankness, while inviting them to embrace consumerism with full knowledge of its problematic nature. Ōki discusses his ambivalent relations with mass consumer society, suggesting the difficulty of maintaining a critical voice inside the quicksand-like condition: the harder one tries to criticize it, the deeper one finds oneself tangled in it. Critical awareness alone does not guarantee a clear break from the object of criticism: consumer culture.

To put it more schematically, it is not difficult to criticize consumer society and its attendant effects, but it is far more challenging to imagine an identity other than being a consumer. Some of the critical images we will witness in the following chapters—products of desperate efforts to imagine a way out of consumer society—circulated as attractive commodities through the mass media in late 1960s and early 1970s Japan. A critical perspective could even serve as a rationalization for embracing what consumerism offered. Individuals had little choice but to accept the peace and prosperity of the postwar world, but some did so with a sense of unease, resignation, or defiance. This book is attentive to these complex and contradictory emotions as it explores what it meant to live in Japan's mass consumer society while trying to maintain a critical perspective.

## The Project: Shifting the Focus from 1968 to 1972

*Japan, 1972: Visions of Masculinity in an Age of Mass Consumerism* aims to excavate the fault lines between two Japans—the one before the high economic growth from the late 1950s to early 1970s and the one borne of those years. It analyzes the ways in which Japanese society grappled with the socioeconomic transformation that accompanied the high-growth economy, a struggle in which television and the new media played an integral part. The main ground of our inquiry is visual criticism in popular culture of contemporary social conditions. More specifically, the focus is on the explosive expansion of mass consumerism, its effects on Japanese society, and the search for counternarratives in the form of masculine drama, which valorized Japanese manhood as critical impetus. The title *Japan, 1972* signals that the volume is concerned less with the fiery political activism of 1968 and 1969 than with what ensued at the end of that political season: the somber realization that consumer culture and its attendant effects had taken a tight hold on Japanese society.[5]

To distance itself from its war legacies, particularly from the memory of its own destruction, postwar Japan struggled to establish itself as an economic power in the international community.[6] Although a mass consumer society had begun to emerge in the 1920s in Japanese cities, this socioeconomic transformation culminated in the postwar period and was farther-reaching in its effects. Technological innovation and the culture of consumption rapidly penetrated every corner of the country. With the arrival of the consumer economy, members of Japanese society gained greater access to information and mass-produced goods. The growth of consumerism had a leveling effect in postwar society: new products found homes even among residents of the countryside and blue-collar workers, who had traditionally lagged behind in economic development. Images disseminated through the fast-expanding media, especially television, in turn generated desires for new commercial goods. Television also ensured a greater degree of homogeneity in the information that the nation consumed. The immediacy, the expediency, and the visuality of information shortened the perceived distance between disseminators and consumers. Through this new circuit of consumption, the nation attained a greater sense of cohesion and commonality within the everyday lives of its members.

Television's role in this development was not limited to transmitting audiovisual information. Placed at the heart of the domestic space, television opened the innermost realm of private life to the larger society. Viewers actively participated in the circular flow of information, transforming themselves into inhabitants of the enlarged, national televisual space. In this space, viewers acquired a new level of reflectivity on their relations with the larger society by beginning to see themselves as if they were inside their own visual field. I use the term *metavision* to describe this new way of seeing: thanks largely to television, individuals gained an outside perspective from which to view themselves critically. Exposed to the outside—television's—gaze, they crawled out of the security of their private selves and assembled new, collage-like selves from media images and commercial products.

While highlighting the transformational power of television, *Japan, 1972* insists that television was not the only catalyst for change. Popular weekly magazines that developed contemporaneously with television also played a key role in reorganizing social space. Carrying behind-the-scenes stories and celebrity gossip, the weeklies augmented television's ability to blur the boundaries between private and public. In youth culture more specifically, weekly manga magazines developed in tandem with television, forcefully extending the reach of the new visual culture. This volume offers not a history of particular media but rather a study of the new multimedia visual environment and its effects as seen in popular cultural expressions.

These developments generated rebuff and resistance. Whether they took action inspired by their frustration with the national drama or not, detractors yearned for narratives that would better realize their free and independent agency. However, besides the traditional left's perennial search for an untainted outside position in a segment of society left behind by the general progress, ready-made models for alternative narratives were hard to find. It was becoming increasingly apparent that the traditional left's oppositional framework failed to address the socioeconomic conditions emerging in the high-growth economy. If the "outsiders"—blue-collar workers and peasants whose marginalized status was essential to oppositional politics—were eager to share the spoils of growth with the insiders, there seemed little point in discussing critical outside stances. In other words, there was hardly any "outside" left at the end of Japan's high-growth period. The outside as a category lost its singular status, being reduced to abstract, consumable signs. A geographical outside appeared as an exotic, temporally lagged site, while a temporal outside—the future—became a mere extension of the present. It was impossible to imagine a radical difference within the consumer society, saturated by visual media. The sociologist Miyadai Shinji describes this state of sameness, from which an escape is unimaginable, as the "never-ending everyday" (*owarinaki nichijō*).[7] Yet the inside/outside binary continued to drive the search for alternative political narratives as the detractors desperately hoped to make a clean break from the regime of high growth.

Many critical searches for an outside position occurred in the realm of visual culture, a fact that highlights the degree to which Japan had embraced visuality as a basic condition of living in this period. The new and old visual media had been so ingrained in postwar Japanese life by the early 1970s that even oppositional discourses were constructed within the newly emerged visual field, which was constitutive of the mass consumer society. A number of artists endeavored to visualize the ramifications of the paradigmatic shift in contemporary society, while some political activists sought to exit the visual (and national) field completely, as in the case of the United Red Army (URA), whose members tried to establish mountain bases—an imagined outside—from which to attack the regime responsible for the conditions of contemporary Japan. They failed spectacularly in their attempt, subsumed along the way by the very visual field they tried to escape from: their battle against the police force in February 1972 was nationally televised and widely consumed as a thrilling media event in viewers' living rooms. Many saw their defeat as a clear end to Japanese radical politics. What their failure also announced was the impossibility of escaping the media's vision, which had become intertwined with Japanese society under the high-growth economy. *Japan, 1972* foregrounds the visual experiences of the 1960s and early 1970s—from the introduction of television to the spectacle of the URA's armed struggle—as it critically explores contemporary Japanese artists' and political activists' critiques of Japan's mass consumer society.

The following chapters underscore the male dominance at the scenes of cultural production and the extent to which the defense of male identity was a central concern of the critical imagination. The production/consumption split, inscribed by the male/female binary, produced the distinct categories of masculine production and feminine consumption, which stood in hierarchical relation. The production-masculine axis was privileged as a foundational value, while the consumption-feminine one was denigrated as derivative. The male-dominated cultural industry of the late 1960s and early 1970s strove to reconstitute Japanese manhood through imaginary heroes' struggles against the purportedly deleterious, feminizing effects of mass consumption. The success of these counternarratives ironically owed much to the consumer capitalism that they ostensibly loathed. Forced to serve simultaneously as detractors and epitomes of mass consumer culture, their heroes appear both valorous and vulnerable. It is that admixture of conflicting qualities that this volume explores.

Lest we begin to valorize the works discussed here, I want to add a cautionary note about the structural gender imbalance. Men dominated and controlled most of the production process for popular culture, with a handful of notable exceptions.[8] Women were systematically excluded from film and television production crews because of these industries' deep-seated prejudice against women's creativity. The only way for a woman to participate in film production was to be a script supervisor or hairstylist. When Hamano Sachi, best known for her directorial work on more than three hundred soft-porn films, began to work as an assistant director in 1968, she experienced "all kinds of sexual harassment and bullying" but remained silent, fearing that raising a voice against the wrongdoers would dash her dreams of someday becoming a director.[9] At most of its production sites, Japan's cultural industry was a bastion of the masculinist myth that men alone are inherently capable of creative work.

This volume does not attempt to critique this male-dominated cultural sphere by seeking an alternative perspective in the form of critical female voices: these kinds of critiques can be found elsewhere.[10] I have chosen male artists and writers and their works—the dominant voice of the industry—as the subjects of analysis here, primarily focusing on the internal criticisms that emerged in popular culture. I am interested in the question of how men responded when they realized that the traditional masculinist narratives no longer worked in Japan's new society. Japanese masculinity was cracking under the weight of what it had helped produce—mass consumer society. This vulnerability actually became a rallying point in Japan's cultural industry. The fear that masculinity might be collapsing in front of their eyes motivated creators' critical examinations as well as their desperate efforts to reimagine manhood. The cases discussed in this volume are some of the most visible and imaginative examples of the results.

The cultural reimagining of masculinity, however, did not translate into real-life changes in postwar Japan's gender relations. Men were forced to accept a new—and supposedly feminine—consumer identity but were comforted by the gender roles that they reinforced at home, school, and work.[11] Male consumers had few reasons to challenge the gender gap as they embraced their newly assigned role as providers for the middle-class family (they should not forget to bring home a bottle of wine). In the fantasy space of popular culture, they could engage in hopeless yet heroic battles while comfortably ensconced in the new life that consumer society afforded. Japanese men seem to have clung to what they believed were their vested interests in heteronormative relations precisely because they experienced the crisis of masculinity as such an imminent threat.

## The Field

The 1960s has been the topic of lively conversations—both popular and scholarly—in Japan. While a number of works have explored in depth the connection between the art and politics of the period, few comparable studies exist on the topic of popular culture. Politics, particularly in the form of protest movements, has been the privileged topic with regard to this period; popular culture has often been relegated to a secondary category because of its seemingly apolitical nature.

The sociologist Oguma Eiji's *1968*, a voluminous work on the student movements from the mid-1960s to the early 1970s, exemplifies this hierarchical view of political activism and popular culture.[12] At the beginning of his project, Oguma unabashedly declares that he excludes popular culture from his historical inquiry, portraying it as a stockpile of throwback values that the youths desperately and nostalgically clung to. It served only escapist fantasies: the yakuza films that many youth activists frequented, for example, merely demonstrated that the young audience's thinking and behavior were still rooted in traditional mores. Oguma rhetorically suggests that avant-garde culture might deserve his attention, if only it had been relevant to contemporary youths. The corollary of this rule is that the relevance of cultural expressions must be measured by their proximity to political activism: the more political, the more relevant.[13]

Recent English-language scholarship about this period of Japan's history has been primarily concerned with avant-garde art. Among the works exploring the political resonances of artistic expression is Miryam Sas's critical study of theater, dance, film, and photography from the 1960s to the early 1980s. Sas focuses on experimental artists' struggle to decenter their agency and destabilize the institution of art, closely examining works by such luminaries as Betsuyaku Minoru, Terayama Shūji, Hijikata Tatsumi, and Moriyama Daidō, and revealing divergent forms of critical practice as well as intermedia resonances.[14] Sas is particularly interested in reading artistic practices against twentieth-century intellectual traditions, both Japanese and European. Bruce Baird offers formal and philosophical analyses of Hijikata Tatsumi's *butoh* dances, positing them as critical responses to the production regime of the high-growth era. Baird treats Hijikata (and his body) as a nodal point at which contemporary theories and social forces intersected.[15] William Marotti examines the works of Akasegawa Genpei in the context of his compatriots' activities, with particular focus on Akasegawa's court battle in 1967 against charges of currency counterfeiting. For Akasegawa and his associates, the practice of art served as a means to problematize and challenge the state's will to dominate the everyday life of 1960s Japan, where the high-growth economy seemed to have completely displaced earlier political energy. Their art playfully mocked state authority, while dislocating the traditional concept of direct action (*chokusetsu kōdō*), a popular tactic of oppositional movements.[16] Yuriko Furuhata's book on experimental filmmaking and political activism similarly finds correspondences and echoes in contemporary art and oppositional politics. She explores artistic expressions of the late 1960s as an extension of political discourse, reading them against contemporary socioeconomic conditions.[17] Reiko Tomii instantiates the contemporaneity of the 1960s through a close look at the works of regionally based artists (i.e., those outside Tokyo artistic centers) like Matsuzawa Yutaka and two artist collectives, The Play and GUN. Tomii's study unpacks their creative endeavors to demonstrate the connections and resonances among artists and critics in the 1960s global art scene.[18]

These works, amid a growing body of scholarship, offer a sophisticated look into this exciting decade of avant-garde production in Japan.[19] Popular culture from this period, however, has received scant scholarly attention. Isolde Standish's book is exceptional in treating Japanese porn film as a topic of scholarly inquiry, but it discusses the works largely within the framework of political protest.[20] The most popular form of pornography—the soft-porn films that major studios produced and distributed—is largely excluded from analysis. Most discussion of the period's popular culture has happened outside academic circles. Alexander Zahlten's work is exceptional in that it gives serious attention to independently produced, low-budget, sex-themed films, many of which have been denigrated as frivolous (read apolitical) and inconsequential. Rather than focusing on individual works, however, he devises the category of industrial genre, through which to examine the interactions of creative efforts, industrial practices, and larger socioeconomic forces.[21]

Although the intersection of art and radicalism has been a fertile area for critical inquiry, I submit that this link has also served as an exclusionary device, blocking inquiry into popular culture itself. Because they lack easily discernible subversive meaning, the works of mass-produced culture have been deemed less significant, unworthy of academic attention. There is probably a common, albeit unarticulated, perception that discussing popular (read: low-brow) culture would bring one down to the lower level of the masses—whereas the defiant stance inherent in radicalism serves as a vertical structure allowing scholars to pull themselves up to a respectable height. This is precisely the means by which artists and critics in this period tried to distance themselves from the deleterious effects of mass consumer culture. Tightly adhering to the connection between art and politics would mean uncritically replicating their critical strategies in analyzing late 1960s and early 1970s Japan and its culture.

In so doing we would be reproducing the myth of cultural heroes: individuals who challenged and transcended the existing political and cultural system with the power of their imaginations. (Perhaps the unspoken assumption is that we could vicariously assume their critical position by studying them.) Scholars, constantly on the lookout for a subset of heroic artists, have celebrated a group of male creators for their individualistic and iconoclastic stance. Perhaps this predilection is most visible in the disproportionate attention paid to such auteurs as Ōshima Nagisa, Yoshida Yoshishige (Kijū), and Wakamatsu Kōji. Artists like Terayama Shūji, Kara Jūrō, and Hijikata Tatsumi have similarly been lauded as men who embodied the defiant spirit of a tumultuous period. The manga artist Shirato Sanpei, because of his Marxist stance, has been a darling of Japanese critics. The concept of cultural heroes implies that some people powerfully resist, by the force of their creative genius, the constraints of contemporary society (and artists often acted out such self-images). It is difficult, however, to sustain such a fantastic vision in the face of commercial culture, which easily converts images deemed cutting edge or avant-garde into appealing commodities. Depicting sexual intercourse on the screen, even discreetly, was a defiant act in the 1960s, but it became an integral part of the Nikkatsu Studios' survival strategy by the early 1970s. A number of experimental artists were commissioned to exhibit their works at Expo '70, an event that many believed epitomized Japan's economic success. Commercial culture metamorphosed at a monstrous pace, tapping into the creative energy of the counterculture. To continue buttressing the image of cultural heroes is to replicate the comforting masculinist myth that exceptional men can defy the deleterious effects of historical forces.

The valorization of defiant hero figures also diverts our attention from the not-so-heroic fact that nobody could escape the long reach of consumer capitalism. Some of the artists discussed in the following chapters have been less visible in critical discussions of this tumultuous period, both inside and outside Japan, because of their less-than-recalcitrant attitude toward contemporary political conditions. For example, Yamada Yōji joined Shōchiku Studios in 1954, a year later than Shinoda Masahiro and a year earlier than Ōshima Nagisa and Yoshida Yoshishige, but had a radically different career as a filmmaker. Shinoda, Ōshima, and Yoshida won accolades as iconoclastic filmmakers (the popular media tagged them as the leaders of Shōchiku's new-wave cinema) and subsequently left Shōchiku to establish their own independent production companies. By contrast, Yamada has stayed on with the company and continued to produce films for the mass market. Although Yamada critically explored what it meant to live in contemporary Japanese society in the early 1970s, he is largely known as a maker of comforting, comedic films (such as the enduring *It's Tough Being a Man* series), and his critical vision has received little sustained attention.

The situation for the manga artist Tsuge Yoshiharu is slightly different, but it has nonetheless affected the ways in which his work has been discussed among critics. A pioneer of experimental manga, he has earned his credentials as a countercultural icon. However, the absence of an explicit political message in his work has kept him away from the art-radicalism dyad. Discussions about Tsuge have tended to divorce his work from contemporary socioeconomic conditions, while highlighting the nostalgia and existential angst that his readers find in abundance in his manga world. Yamada's and Tsuge's noncombative styles should not deter us from examining their critical and creative look into life in a radically transforming society.

*Japan, 1972* expands critical inquiry into Japan's popular culture in the late 1960s and early 1970s by bracketing oppositional politics. The subjects of this study are selected not on the basis of their creator's explicit commitment to cultural or political resistance, but according to the works' power to critically engage with the conditions of contemporary society.

Rather than simply denouncing the effects of consumer culture, they grappled with present conditions in Japan and strove to work through the complex emotions arising from radical socioeconomic changes. I have chosen them also because they were popular and commercially available. The fan bases of the cartoonist Tsuge Yoshiharu and the writer Kaikō Takeshi were not as expansive as those of yakuza film and the enormously popular manga serials in *Shōnen magajin*. Yet the circulation figures for the experimental manga magazine *Garo*—a main outlet for Tsuge's work—reached as high as eighty thousand in 1967 and 1968,[22] and Kaikō's novels went through multiple printings in a short period.[23] Tsuge's and Kaikō's texts, furthermore, continued to circulate in subsequent years. The works discussed in this volume are iconic for this period and have remained relevant in Japanese society. *Japan, 1972* is not only a historical analysis of Japan's mass consumer culture but also a critical appreciation of what it produced.

## Memories of War and the United States

Japan's economic recovery and subsequent high-growth were essential to the process that transformed the memories of the Asia Pacific War into benign and abstract images. Those memories were discursively cleansed as Japanese society regained its order and peace. Popular culture and media played key roles in this containment of traumatic memories, making them palatable to consumers: they revised the images of the United States in order to dissociate the former enemy from the destructive role it had played in the war, while touting it for its material and scientific power.[24] The two nations have maintained close relations thanks in no small part to the conciliatory popular representations of the United States in Japan.

The United States thus gave an impetus to the development of Japan's mass consumer society in the early postwar years, but I would hesitate to call this process of socioeconomic transformation "Americanization." In the early years of the postwar period, residents in Japan were introduced to American middle-class life through various media. For example, the comic strip *Blondie*, which began to appear in the *Asahi shinbun* in 1949, impressed its readers with the affluence, namely, appliances and abundant food, that seemingly characterized American homes. Sociologist Yamamoto Akira (1932–1999) recalls that reading *Blondie* made him wonder when he would have that kind of "luxurious life."[25] Japanese television stations relied heavily on American programs in the early years of their operation, when they were still learning how to produce content. The Japanese audience thus learned about American life—albeit highly stylized and idealized versions of it—through popular television shows like *Father Knows Best*, *The Donna Reed Show*, *The Adventures of Rin Tin Tin*, *Laramie*, and *Ben Casey*.[26] A female viewer, Kōno Hiromi, years later recalled that she had watched *Father Knows Best* thinking that "freedom, dreams, and civilization were over there."[27] It should also be noted that in order to create a powerful anticommunist propaganda platform in Japan, U.S. agencies assisted the president of the Yomiuri Shinbun group, Shōriki Matsutarō (1885–1969), in his effort to establish the first commercial network, Nippon Television.[28]

While media images helped foster pro-American sentiments among Japanese audiences, their responses to American television shows were not all positive, and they changed over the years. The media scholar Kunihiro Yōko interviewed Japanese "boomers" (the Japanese boom generation is generally defined as people born between 1947 and 1949) who expressed reservations about what they saw on television in the late 1950s and 1960s. Of the interviewees, one felt ambivalent about the United States as a model, while another rarely registered the Americanness of the American images. The Vietnam War negatively affected their generation's perceptions of the United States.[29] By the second half of the 1960s, U.S. programs were no longer central to Japanese broadcasting in general, and Japanese programs saturated prime time.

The Japanese reception of American television images was also complicated by the process of domestication. Jayson Makoto Chun carefully documents the process through which images of *Laramie*'s lead actor Robert Fuller were Japanized: Japanese media circulated the image of Fuller as a man with "'Japanese' values, mentality, and even a Japanese physique." Chun contends that "television pulled Japan into the U.S. cultural orbit by making the United States one of the main sources of Japanese values."[30]

While inspired by the U.S. example, Japan's consumer society was a product of the country's unique historical development. Japanese merchandise—both software and hardware—replaced its American counterpart in the process of economic development, creating a national space of consumption.[31] This was a contradictory process through which the defeated nation distanced itself from the former enemy by domesticating its overwhelming presence. The aforementioned Yamamoto Akira, when he visited the United States for the second time in 1973, found that the country offered nothing that piqued his curiosity: instead, he experienced the deeply nationalistic sentiment that Japan had caught up and possibly surpassed the United States.[32] This volume's underlying message is that the post–World War II consumption of U.S. culture in Japan not only was anchored in the national experience but also helped reinforce the national identity.

*Japan, 1972* consists of three parts. Part 1 documents the larger historical changes in Japan under the high-growth economy and the ways in which television influenced those changes, helping to realize a new national space. Chapter 1 emphasizes that Japan's economic expansion resulted in a more even distribution of income among its people, allowing millions more people to participate in the emerging consumer society. Amid the national excitement, however, the gender divide deepened. Women were allowed to take advantage of Japan's growing economy as dependents, while their husbands put in long hours in the workplace. Men may have been transformed into cogs in the corporate machine, but they could find solace and a new masculine pride as providers for their families. Television was an integral part of postwar Japan's economic growth: economic expansion made television sets affordable, while television enhanced the desire for consumption. Chapter 2 demonstrates that viewers responded not just to the visual and audio content delivered to the private spaces of their homes but also to the complex affective experience of watching television. Weeklies augmented that experience by blurring the boundaries between the private and public spheres. By creating circular flows of desire—for television itself and for the products it popularized—television helped to transform those who used to stand outside the reach of urban modern life into consuming subjects.

The three chapters in part 2 focus on three artists' efforts to conceive of a masculine identity that could counter the stifling effects of mass consumer society. Traveling to different locations, they try to find a symbolic "outside"—an alternative to Japan under the high-growth economy. The escape attempts, however, all end in ways that reconfirmed the new paradigm's long reach. Chapter 3 discusses two films from the early 1970s in which the director Yamada Yōji casts a sympathetic gaze on a family man's efforts to maintain his male pride and independence in the face of the gargantuan shift in Japan's industrial structure. While deeply concerned about the state of Japanese society, Yamada is able to offer a hopeful message in the conclusion of *Where Spring Comes Late* (1970), but somber realism prevails in *Home from the Sea* (1972). Chapter 4 focuses on Tsuge Yoshiharu's three travel manga from the period between 1968 and 1973, in which he tries to locate pockets of Japan left behind by the progress of time, keenly aware that he will never be able to depart the world of consumerism and escape into his fantasy space. The chapter also explores the resonance between Tsuge's creative work and the 1970 multimedia advertising campaign for Japan National Railways. Kaikō Takeshi's literary work, which takes its theme from his experiences in the Vietnam War, is the main topic of chapter 5. Kaikō tries to encounter the naked reality of war as a way to escape a Japan that has been anesthetized by peace and prosperity. He gets what he wishes for: he witnesses prevalent violence and gets caught in an ambush by a unit of the National Liberation Front. His naïve idea about the heroic masculine witness is thoroughly imploded by this almost fatal experience. But as soon as he returns to safety, Kaikō hits on a dreadful realization: the war that he witnessed is no more extraordinary than television images.

The chapters in part 3 are organized around cultural expressions of violence and a political movement that ended in extreme violence. Here I explore the connections between popular culture and politics to demonstrate how they both strongly responded to the radical changes in the socioeconomic conditions in Japan in the late 1960s and early 1970s. Chapter 6 analyzes yakuza films, a genre that student radicals enthusiastically supported. Yakuza films called on the past to critique contemporary conditions in postwar Japanese society, as the protagonists' violent acts in the films' final scenes effectively negate the restrictive forces of tradition as well as the deleterious effects of the modern world. After the yakuza genre's first wave subsided around 1972, the second wave temporarily revived the genre with a new type of hero appropriate for the television age: the protagonist who serves as a seer or witness rather than a doer inside the complex interfactional yakuza conflicts. Chapter 7 discusses the two best-known manga serials from the late 1960s and early 1970s: *Star of the Giants* (*Kyojin no hoshi*) and *Tomorrow's Jō* (*Ashita no Jō*), both of which featured scriptwriter Kajiwara Ikki. With their relentless pursuit of a masculine identity that transcends postwar Japan's historical condition, Kajiwara's teenage heroes grabbed young readers' imaginations. The protagonists use their athletic bodies as a means to distance themselves from the historical conditions that brought material prosperity to Japanese society. While *Star of the Giants* largely retains the optimism of Japan in the high-growth era, the plot of *Tomorrow's Jō* turns deeply philosophical as its protagonist becomes mired in the world of boxing, losing his original position as an outsider. In the final chapter we turn to oppositional politics, focusing on the struggle of the United Red Army. URA members burned with revolutionary fervor, aspiring to establish outside positions from which to attack the regime of high growth. Yet their desperate efforts ended in a way none of them could have imagined: as a spectacular event that millions eagerly watched on television. The popular sympathy for Japan's new left politics effectively died as the Japanese media subsequently reported on the group's internal killings. The URA grossly underestimated their powerful adversary—mass consumer society—and paid dearly for their arrogance.

The epilogue briefly discusses Tanaka Kakuei's (1918–1993) controversial tenure as prime minister from 1972 to 1974, effectively the end of Japan's high-growth period, and looks at how men involved in visual and print culture responded to the sudden shift in the economic landscape. Despite the drastic adjustments in the Japanese economy since that time, mass consumerism and metavision remain as basic conditions of Japanese society. The masculine dramas of 1972, constitutive of and constituted by these conditions, still demand our critical attention.

# PART ONE
# Television

CHAPTER 1

## Reflections on the Consuming Subject

*The High-Growth Economy and the Emergence of
a New National Community*

Television is a once-in-a-life-time purchase. Please choose the one carefully.
—PANASONIC ADVERTISEMENT, 1955

On June 17, 1972, after serving as prime minister for seven years and eight months, the second longest continuous tenure in Japan's modern history, Satō Eisaku (1901–1975) was slated to announce his resignation at a lunchtime press conference.[1] When Chief Cabinet Secretary Takeshita Noboru, acting as spokesperson for the occasion, began to speak, Satō suddenly interrupted the proceedings. "I want to talk to the people directly. Where is the NHK's TV?" he grunted, referring to Nihon Hōsō Kyōkai (Japan Broadcasting Corporation). He continued: "Television shows things as they are, but once printed, they are distorted. I hate partisan newspapers. Where is TV? TV, come forward."[2] Confronted with a collective outcry from newspaper reporters, Satō stormed out of the room with a stern expression. Ten minutes later he returned and, despite even stronger protests from the gathered reporters, banged on the table and demanded that they leave the room. He eventually got what he asked for: in a room vacated by the newspaper reporters, he talked uninterrupted to a television camera for about twenty minutes (figure 1.1).[3]

The Satō administration presided over an extended period of high economic growth and enjoyed steady approval ratings.[4] Satō's retirement announcement came on the heels of a major diplomatic success—the reversion of Okinawa in May 1972. (In 1965, nine months after assuming power, he had declared that Japan's postwar period could not end until the

*Figure 1.1* Prime Minister Satō Eisaku announces his resignation before a television camera, June 17, 1972. Courtesy of Mainichi Newspapers.

United States returned Okinawa to Japan.)[5] At the end of his long tenure, however, Satō's relationship with the newspapers was contentious. Particularly in the last years of his premiership, his administration was plagued by a number of formidable issues, from environmental destruction to high inflation. It also faced a turbulent international situation after the United States shook the world in July 1971 by declaring its intent to establish diplomatic relations with the People's Republic of China. Before the aftershocks from that decision had worn off, President Richard Nixon announced a unilateral cancellation of the convertibility of dollars to gold, further disrupting the previous international equilibrium. Prime Minister Satō's blunt personality undermined his relations with the Japanese media, which were growing critical of his seeming inability to navigate in the new political environment. At the moment of his resignation, he decided to forge a fantasy connection with "the people" by bypassing the print media altogether and emulating Nixon, who televised his speeches from the Oval Office.[6] Satō had wanted to announce his retirement without the presence of reporters, as if he were talking directly to the Japanese people in a private space, but the press corps requested time for a round of follow-up questions due to the public nature of the event. The prime minister's office had made a small compromise to minimally accommodate this request: reporters would be allowed to sit in and take notes while Satō spoke to a television camera, but no questions were to be asked during or after his announcement. The retiring prime minister's behavior, however, suggested that he was unaware of this prearrangement.[7]

Satō was cognizant of earlier political contests over television programming. Since the late 1950s the leaders of the ruling Liberal Democratic Party (LDP) were concerned about the power of television to "politicize" the masses.[8] Satō complained bitterly, for example, about television's partisan (*henkō*) coverage of the 1968 street protests against the arrival of the nuclear-powered USS *Enterprise* at the Sasebo Port.[9] The prime minister was convinced that the television coverage of police brutality against the student protestors turned citizens' sympathies toward the protests.[10] To capture this power for themselves, leaders of the conservative LDP used their political clout to keep liberal programs off the air. During Sato's tenure as prime minister, the LDP-led government successfully pressured television stations to cancel a number of scheduled programs. Television journalists and labor unions not only fought back against the government interventions but also succeeded in canceling programs with a conservative bent. As the opposition movements in Japan gained momentum in the late 1960s, the tension between liberal television media and the government intensified.[11] By 1972, however, Satō was perhaps confident that the LDP leaders were gaining the upper hand and that NHK's close ties with the government would ensure a faithful transmission of his message to the people. Apparently absent from his thinking was any suspicion that "the people" whom he tried to reach directly had been greatly affected by their television viewing experiences and the economic growth that made television sets household items. Media commentators summarily dismissed Satō's emotional behavior as a cheap parting shot at the print media, without questioning his presumption of television's transparency.[12] This minor drama of 1972 illuminates how thoroughly television had been naturalized in Japanese society—so thoroughly that hardly anybody took notice of its ubiquitous presence.

Television was not the only presence hiding in plain sight. Equally invisible were the extraordinary economic conditions that brought a television set to almost every household in Japan. When Japanese television broadcasting began in 1953, television receivers were prohibitively expensive, beyond the reach of most households. People instead gathered in the thousands for public viewings of television programs on units that Nippon Television Broadcast Corporation installed at urban transportation hubs in the Kantō area.[13] The domestic production of television sets gained momentum as the Japanese economy began to take off in the late 1950s. Prices dropped precipitously (table 1.1), and televisions quickly became common household items, along with refrigerators and washing machines. By the mid-1960s more than 90 percent of households in Japan owned one or more black-and-white television receivers. In 1972 more than 60 percent of households owned one or more color sets. The ubiquitous presence of television was but one marker for the Japanese economy's amazing rate of growth since the mid-1950s, and the radical changes that Japanese society experienced in those years.

The effects of economic success were both personal and social. The growing economic pie fostered a stronger sense of national belonging among members of society by providing tangible benefits. The new national community that emerged under the regime of high growth in turn supported the economic system through its participants' dedication to

TABLE 1.1

Price ranges for a 14-inch television and average monthly income of urban working households (cities in Tokyo area)

| Date | Price Range | Average Monthly Household Income (¥)* |
| --- | --- | --- |
| February 1953 | 175,000–180,000 | 26,025 |
| May 1954 | 127,000–156,000 | 28,283 |
| May 1955 | 108,000–129,000 | 29,169 |
| May 1956 | 78,000–82,000 | 30,776 |
| May 1957 | 72,000–77,500 | 32,664 |
| May 1958 | 60,000–69,000 | 34,663 |
| May 1959 | 59,600–61,000 | 36,873 |
| May 1960 | 56,500–62,000 | 40,895 |
| May 1961 | 48,000–60,000 | 45,134 |
| May 1962 | 45,000–60,000 | 50,817 |

*Yearly average.

Sources: Ishikawa Hiroyoshi, *Yokubō no sengoshi* (Tokyo: Taihei shuppansha, 1981), 55–56; Bureau of Statistics, Office of Prime Minister, *Japan Statistical Yearbook 1958* (Tokyo: Japan Statistical Association, 1958), 368; *Japan Statistical Yearbook 1962*, 384; *Japan Statistical Yearbook 1965*, 442.

production and consumption. The two chapters in part 1 highlight the extraordinary nature of Japan's transformation under the high-growth economy and the importance of television in those changes. The goal is to visualize what appeared transparent and to historicize what appeared natural. The present chapter focuses on the historical changes that produced a nation of mass consumers, while chapter 2 explores the ways in which television served as a catalyst for this socioeconomic transformation, powerfully interacting with members of Japanese society.

## Japan Under the High-Growth Regime

I illustrate the new national community that formed under Japan's high-growth economy by juxtaposing two images. The first image represents Japan circa 1950 (figure 1.2). Here I mimic the pattern of the national flag to emphasize that the national political and economic structure was in place at the beginning of postwar Japan's economic expansion. The second image represents Japan under the high-growth economy, circa 1972 (figure 1.3).

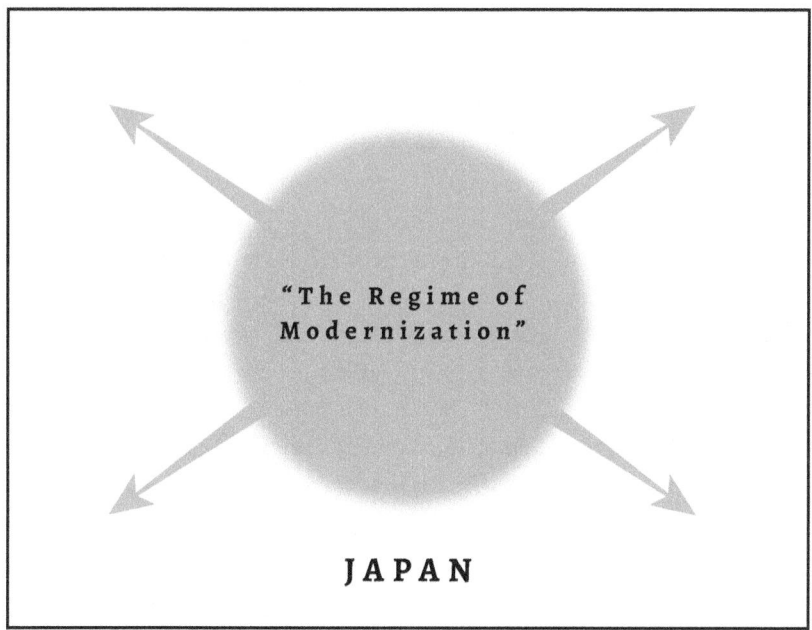

*Figure 1.2* Japan before the high-growth economy, circa 1950. Illustration by author.

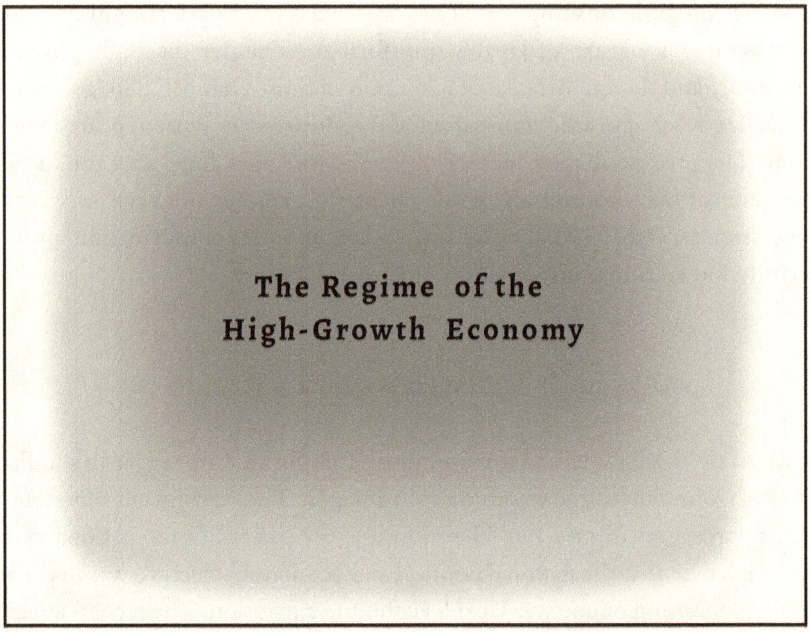

## The Regime of the High-Growth Economy

*Figure 1.3* Japan under the high-growth economy, circa 1972. Illustration by author.

In it, I figure mass consumerism's almost total absorption of Japanese society as a television screen to underscore television's centrality to that process.

Figure 1.2 represents Japan in the early 1950s at the cusp between the recovery-oriented postwar economy and the high-growth period. The area within the rectangular frame represents Japan's legal territories and the people who resided within them. Since the Meiji period (1868–1912), Japan's political leaders had used various political means and institutions to make loyal national subjects out of its residents. The international wars that Japan engaged in were particularly effective in channeling citizens' energy toward national goals. By the early twentieth century Japan had attained a high degree of political unity and cohesion—a far cry from the inchoate state of the nation when it first remerged from its self-imposed seclusion in the mid-nineteenth century. Although all citizens—at least in the metropole—purportedly enjoyed equal stature in the eyes of the law, some, mostly males with Japanese citizenship, were endowed with more privileges than others and stood closer to the center of power: the nexus of government, industry, and education.

The circle represents the "regime of modernization," or the sections of society that saw direct benefits from Japan's industrial success in the first half of the twentieth century (and from its colonial enterprises before 1945). Throughout the period of industrialization, the circle gradually expanded to include more "outsiders"—those who had been marginalized in society—within the regime of modernization. The lighter-shade border around the circle illustrates that the regime had begun to permeate to the outside. Urban and rural elites initially constituted the primary membership of a tight circle. In the 1920s and the 1930s the burgeoning class of urban white-collar workers gained admission as the circle's newest members. However, the largest segments of society—tenant farmers in remote regions and blue-collar workers in urban areas—remained outside the circle. Japan's industrial structure rewarded these populations meagerly, while the central regime placed heavy taxes on them to finance its national projects.[14] Despite some mobility, clear distinctions remained between the lives of people inside and outside the circle. The clarity of these differences simplified the traditional left's task of critiquing the existing economic and political system at this stage. They expended their critical energy on establishing an oppositional position and taking a stand against the regime of modernization.

The circle rapidly expanded in the years of the high-growth economy, from the mid-1950s to the early 1970s, drawing tens of millions of the economically marginalized into the cycle of production and consumption. Despite radical socioeconomic changes during the high-growth era, the economy generally realized a more even distribution of income, which in turn benefited the underclass. Many who had been disadvantaged in the hierarchical system found a place within Japan's newly emerging economic regime. Because of the expansion of the economy and education, the changing employment pattern, and the rise of new media, the "outside"—the unshaded area in figure 1.2—was fast incorporated into the regime of the high-growth economy.

Figure 1.3 illustrates the conditions that resulted from this transformation. The boundaries between inside and outside grew more porous, blurring the distinctions between the two spheres. Even residents of the most remote regions and the most economically disadvantaged populations benefited from the growth of national wealth and gained access to a new national space of consumption. (Women were offered a different path to the inside: initially as young workers and then as dependent housewives.)

Those who made it inside the shaded area could easily see that they were no longer excluded from the economic benefits of the high-growth regime. Life inside the circle (the television screen–shaped area, which also signifies the reach of television) was constantly improving and was deeply valued by the many who finally gained admission to it through their hard work. It is important to recognize that Japan's high growth was made possible by incorporating the vast majority of its citizens into the system of production and consumption, and television was essential to this process. Through their participation in this system, a new sense of belonging emerged in Japan.[15]

In the remainder of this chapter, I will analyze the causes and effects of Japan's high-growth economy, preparing for the next chapter's discussion about how Japan came to love television.

## High Growth and Its Leveling Effects

Japan's economic success in the postwar era was greatly assisted by external conditions, particularly U.S. Cold War policies. To develop Japan into a bulwark against communism, the United States provided the country various forms of economic assistance, including relatively unhampered access to the U.S. market, a favorable yen–dollar exchange ratio, and generous technology transfers.[16] Additionally, U.S. wars in Korea and Vietnam infused large amounts of cash at key points in Japan's development. The economist Noguchi Yukio also submits that the absence of Chinese competition was a key to Japan's success. If the People's Republic of China, with its cheap labor, had been competing with Japan in the 1960s, Japan's high growth would have been utterly inconceivable.[17]

Japan's high-growth economy did not, of course, depend solely on help from external forces. Japanese businesses, working closely with government agencies, created a more inclusive system while effectively stimulating domestic consumption. A series of reforms in the immediate postwar period helped prepare a more level field for economic competition in subsequent years. The agricultural land redistribution carried out from 1947 to 1950 thoroughly undermined rural landowners' economic basis by transferring ownership of a large portion of their land to tenant farmers. Although the tenants paid the landowners cash for the land, hyperinflation made the payments almost worthless.[18] In the cities, wartime laws still on the books strictly protected tenants' rights while making it extremely difficult to raise rents.[19] Urban landowners' rental income also suffered from inflation. Furthermore, 1946 saw the wealthy saddled with new property taxes, totaling up to 90 percent of their possessions.[20] The early postwar reforms and policies achieved a more even distribution of wealth, extending economic stability to millions more people.

Japanese society experienced drastic changes during the period of the high-growth economy, which lasted from the late 1950s to the early 1970s. Recovering from the lost years of the Asia Pacific War, Japan focused on economic growth under LDP rule. In the fifteen years from 1958 to 1973, the national income per capita grew eightfold (more than tenfold in U.S. dollars), from ¥104,827 ($291) to ¥844,534 ($3,108).[21] Adjusted by the consumer price index, the 1973 level was about three and a half times as high as the 1958 level.[22] Table 1.2 reflects studies of Gini coefficients in Japan.

TABLE 1.2
Changes in Gini coefficient in Japan

| Year | Gini Coefficient | |
|---|---|---|
| | I | |
| 1923 | 0.505 | |
| 1930 | 0.512 | |
| 1937 | 0.547 | |
| | II | III |
| 1956 | 0.313 | |
| 1959 | 0.357 | |
| 1962 | 0.382 | 0.376 |
| 1968 | 0.380 | 0.346 |
| 1974 | | 0.344 |
| 1980 | | 0.337 |
| 1985 | | 0.359 |
| 1990 | | 0.372 |

*Note*: Series I, II, and III are from three separate studies.
*Source*: Minami Ryōshin, *Nihon no keizaihatten to shotokubunpu* (Tokyo: Iwanami shoten, 1996), 108.

The Gini coefficient is a measure of how evenly income is distributed within a given society; it ranges from 0 (the lowest level of inequality) to 1 (the highest). The figures in the table suggest that income disparity grew in the early years of the high-growth economy but slightly decreased after the early 1960s for about two decades. Labor shortages stemming from the economic boom raised the level of wages overall, which resulted in a more equitable income distribution. This postwar trend also shows a stark contrast to the growing income disparity of the 1920s and 1930s.[23] By the early 1970s the economic pie had grown large enough for a majority of working people to enjoy a bigger slice. Correspondingly, the number of people who lived under the poverty line steadily declined. As much as 20.8 percent of the population lived below the poverty line in 1955. The ratio dropped to 12.1 percent in 1965 and to 9 percent in 1970.[24]

The LDP-led government devised economic policies that, alongside business and labor practices, also helped to reduce wage gaps.[25] In particular, those who worked in agriculture and workers in small to medium-sized businesses gained, while workers in large-scale corporations continued to receive substantially better compensation. As a result, what had once been the privilege of urban white-collar workers in 1920s Japan—a modern lifestyle characterized by access to mass media and culture—diffused to every corner of Japanese society in less than half a century.[26]

## The Transformation of Rural Japan

The transformation in the countryside was notable in both quality and scale. Gaps between urban and rural populations in the area of consumption, once of great contrast, quickly disappeared under the high-growth economy. Because the LDP's subsidiary-driven agricultural policies protected those who remained in the countryside, household incomes within agrarian communities reached a level comparable to those of urban workers by the 1970s.[27] With their growing disposable income, rural residents, much like their urban counterparts, prioritized the purchase of household appliances. Owning televisions and other latest-model devices assured them of their membership in the emerging consumer society. All were equal as consumers of information and material goods, regardless of where they resided.

The countryside had experienced a brief advantage over cities during the dire food shortages of the immediate postwar period. The land reform implemented under pressure from the occupation authorities redistributed most of the tenant-worked land to the actual cultivators. The tenant farms' share of Japan's farmland dropped from 45.9 percent in November 1945 to 10.1 percent in August 1950. New owner-farmers, however, faced a different kind of financial burden: the national government, seeking funds to redevelop key industries, immediately levied heavy taxes on them. Living standards for the rural population thus continued to lag behind those in urban areas. The agricultural sector greatly benefited from its strong support for the LDP, which sought to protect and enhance the economic bases of rural constituents through a system of agricultural subsidies. The government guaranteed the purchase of rice—the staple grain in the Japanese diet—at artificially high prices and sold it at lower prices.[28] Yet despite the rise in agricultural income, employment in nonagricultural sectors provided the largest increase in rural household income. Mechanization and the increasing use of chemical products (i.e., fertilizer and herbicides) reduced labor needs on the land.[29] With the LDP's seeming guarantee of ever-rising rice prices, agricultural cooperatives made loans readily available to individual farmers for the purchase of farming equipment.[30] Members of rural households typically held temporary employment at construction sites to augment their income, and pro-rural LDP politicians ensured the availability of numerous construction projects in the countryside.[31]

Many men also left their families during the winter season for construction work in cities and remote sites (*dekasegi*). Generous official unemployment benefits incentivized this practice. Anyone who worked for six months was eligible for unemployment benefits: for 180 days in the early postwar years (1947–1954) and later (1955–1974) for 90 days. Men from agrarian communities would work away from the farm for six months, from summer to winter, and then return home to work on their land while receiving unemployment benefits. (In the case of seasonal workers like the men from rural communities, they could receive a full-month credit if they worked at least eleven days in a month. Therefore they could be eligible for official unemployment benefits with as few as sixty-six workdays in six months.)[32] In 1955 agricultural income accounted for 71.4 percent of an agrarian household's total income. The proportion shrank to 50.1 percent in 1960 and continued to decline in subsequent years, reaching 13.8 percent in 1990.[33]

One of the goals of the Agriculture Foundation Law (Nōgyō kihon hō) of 1961 was to streamline agricultural practices in order to free up enough labor to fulfill the needs of other industries. Although the number of people engaged in agriculture steadily declined in the 1960s, an unexpectedly high number of residents remained in the rural areas. Individuals seeking employment opportunities relocated to cities, but an entire household rarely abandoned its land altogether.[34] For many families, complete relocation was too big a risk to take.[35] Millions of young people nevertheless left the countryside for employment in cities, as education and the media (particularly television) made urban life and culture more attractive to rural residents. Though rural households did well economically during the high-growth era, they were steadily hollowed out as young, productive members left for the cities.

The waves of the high-growth economy that reached the countryside radically transformed the rural way of life. As subsisting on a small plot of land in a remote community ceased to be an attractive option for young people, depopulation became a serious issue in many rural communities. In 1955, for example, 100 percent of agrarian households knew who was going to inherit the family agriculture operation; that figure had dropped to 57 percent by 1967.[36] The philosopher Uchiyama Takashi points to a different kind of change in the countryside as well. In Japanese folk belief, foxes and raccoon dogs (*tanuki*) are mischievous animals that play pranks on people. Uchiyama claims, on the basis of his conversations with numerous rural residents, that foxes stopped fooling the Japanese around 1965. In exchange for modern conveniences, Japanese rural residents lost the rich world of folk symbolism.[37] Television was not the only reason for these changes, but foxes and raccoon dogs could not compete with the new media's chimerical power.[38]

### New Patterns of Employment and Reinforced Gender Roles

Japanese corporations became less hierarchical in their organizational structure in the postwar years. An imperial ordinance in 1946 purged the incumbent managers of major businesses and ushered in a new group of executives from the ranks of middle managers. Having worked closely with the other employees through wartime challenges, the newly promoted executives were more sympathetic to workers' needs and demands.[39] The change in corporate structure was indicated by the shrinking wage differentials between senior executives and rank-and-file employees. In 1927 company presidents on average made 110 times as much as new hires with a college degree. That differential declined to 23.6 to 1 in 1963 and 19.0 to 1 in 1973.[40] The rigid distinction between white-collar and blue-collar workers began to dissolve in corporate culture, though the wage differential persisted between employees of large-scale businesses and those of small or midsize companies. Meanwhile, female workers were often placed in a separate employment track regardless of the scale of their employer. Women were expected to work until marriage and then retreat into the household to offer domestic support to a husband who worked long hours. Gender inequality, reinforced through the employment pattern and government policies, including education policy, was an integral part of the concerted effort to produce dedicated corporate men.

In the 1920s white-collar workers in large-scale corporations benefited from a wage and promotion system based on seniority and merit. Blue-collar workers were excluded from the new system at its inception and were generally less valued within the corporate culture.[41] But as more Japanese labor unions began to organize both white- and blue-collar workers in the early postwar years, those unions increasingly championed blue-collar workers' demands for equal treatment and protection.[42] The psychological rift between the two groups of workers grew less salient as they shared the extreme hardships of the war and the immediate postwar years.[43] Thanks to union pressure as well as the corporate need to retain skilled workers, blue-collar workers began to work under the same wage and promotion scale as white-collar workers, thus removing an arbitrary ceiling for their promotions in many corporations. Their starting salaries, however, remained depressed compared to those of their white-collar counterparts.[44] Japan's postwar labor unions also fought to eliminate hierarchical distinctions by adopting a more inclusive nomenclature for white- and blue-collar workers.[45] In prewar and wartime Japan, for example, the terms *shokuin* and *kōin* were widely used to designate white- and blue-collar workers, respectively. In the postwar period, Japanese corporations replaced them with new names, such as *jimushoku* (office worker), *gijutsushoku* (technical worker), and *sagyōin* (workers).[46] The term *shain* once applied only to workers in managerial positions, but it came to be used in the postwar period for all employees, including production workers.[47] It also became customary for them to wear the same uniform (at worksites which required uniforms) and to eat the same food at a common cafeteria.[48] With these changes, blue-collar workers who had been outsiders within a business entity began to be assimilated into the body of regular workers, accepting the increasing demands for stronger corporate loyalty. The system's wider application produced stronger identification with corporate interests among the workers and also served as a powerful disincentive to postwar labor movements. Workers focused their energies on improving their standing within corporations rather than taking oppositional stances outside the corporate framework.[49]

Wage hikes in small and medium-sized businesses, however, were not as impressive as the gains achieved by rural residents. A "dual structure" for wages—with small and medium-sized businesses on one level and large corporations on a higher one—persisted. Although concerned about this gap, the LDP did not pour subsidies directly into smaller businesses. By taking advantage of cheap domestic labor, the postwar Japanese economy secured the workforce it needed for rapid economic growth, and the gap slowly narrowed amid the increasing labor demand. (The economy reached full employment in the early 1960s.)[50] Many manufacturing businesses could afford higher wages thanks to updated production technologies and stable business relations with the buyers of their products.[51] Government assistance to those who worked for small businesses came in the form of universal health care and national pension systems, instituted in 1961.[52] Japan's social security system provided thin but wide coverage to the millions who lacked corporate-subsidized safety nets.[53]

Not only were workers in large-scale corporations better compensated, but some people were categorically excluded from their labor force. Major businesses and government offices set arbitrary discriminatory standards for applicants—for example, excluding ethnically Korean residents on the basis that they were not Japanese citizens.[54] Burakumin—a group who have long faced discrimination for historical (and geographical) reasons—were similarly turned away at the door.[55] Children hailing from single-parent households (and orphans, regardless of what kind of home took them in) were often rejected because of their purportedly deficient upbringing.[56] Japan's company-based unions were unwilling to champion the cause of workers outside their membership, so they did not intervene.[57] Those who did not boast what the large corporations considered to be a proper social background were forced to accept less, regardless of their qualifications. They too may have benefited from Japan's fast-growing economy (some of them sought business opportunities outside Japan's corporate system), but they were socially marked as the other within a society where prewar class distinctions were fading away.[58]

By contrast, while female workers gained admission to the ranks of large-scale corporations, they were treated as outsiders within the corporate labor system, which maintained strict gender barriers. As Simon Partner demonstrates, readily available low-wage female workers gave Japan's electronics industry a competitive edge in the 1950s and 1960s.[59] Unlike their prewar counterparts, who sought employment in the textile industry, the postwar generation of young women found jobs on assembly lines in electronics factories. These workers gained considerable purchasing power through their employment, but businesses kept their wage levels arbitrarily lower than those of their male counterparts by forcibly terminating women's work contracts at a relatively early age. In the 1950s some corporations even made it mandatory for married women to retire, assuming that their husbands would bring wages and benefits home for the entire family. For example, on joining Mitsui Shipbuilding's Osaka office in 1963, Suenami Kazumi was forced to sign a pledge affirming that she would quit when she got married. Her company's labor contracts were partially revised that year, allowing women to continue to work on a temporary basis even after marriage (married women were required to renew their contract each year). But many women remained subject to the stipulation that they must quit their jobs once they had a child. According to a 1970 study conducted by the Labor Ministry's Women and Juvenile Bureau, 22.7 percent of the surveyed businesses officially maintained the early-retirement system for female employees. Yet even when there were no explicit rules about early retirement, businesses used various tactics to force female employees to quit, such as transfers to distant branch offices.[60] These corporate practices were implicitly structured to produce particular gender roles at the expense of female workers.

In the 1950s scores of major Japanese businesses launched the programs collectively known as the New Life Movement (Shin seikatsu undō) to promote "rationalization" (*gōrika*) at workplaces and home. The movement traced its roots to prewar and wartime modernization campaigns, especially the ones focused on the countryside. According to Andrew Gordon, this movement is also notable for its interest in gender roles. It viewed the larger society as an extension of the corporate world, in which women were expected to become rational and efficient household workers.[61] In 1961 the government officially sanctioned corporate-based gender models by instituting tax exemptions for spouses who contributed below a certain level to their family finances, thus limiting women to ancillary roles.[62] In the education system, changes to the curriculum reinforced society's prescribed gender roles. Vocational and homemaking courses in middle schools were reorganized along the gender divide: in 1958 the technology course was pushed on male students and the homemaking course on female students. Two years later the Education Council recommended making high school education sensitive to gender characteristics. In 1963 curricular changes were made for the high schools: only female students were required to study home economics, while male students spent extra hours in physical education classes.[63] Amano Masako argues that gender expectations were reinforced within the stable triangular network of education, family, and corporation in postwar Japanese society.[64]

Within this institutional triangle, women were invited to share in the postwar economic growth, not as full-fledged members of corporations, but as temporary workers during their youth. Later they were restricted to roles as dependent housewives or part-time workers.[65] In the 1960s the proportion of temporary and daily employees among male workers declined significantly (from 9.3 to 5.8 percent), while the ratio for females held steady at around 14 percent (table 3.1).[66] Gender inequity was reinforced at workplaces in order to maintain the vision of patriarchy at home. In exchange for accepting their dependency on corporations, male workers were granted control over the domestic sphere as the family providers.

The appliances that young female workers assembled were integral to the efforts to naturalize new gender roles for Japanese women. The sociologist Yoshimi Shunya argues, for example, that in the advertisements for household appliances after the mid-1950s, "housewives were portrayed not as passive recipients, but as subjects who managed and promoted home life with electronics. . . . Such an image of the housewife was widely disseminated through newspapers, popular periodicals, and television to every corner of the nation."[67] Women were redefined as efficient and productive workers in their own homes. For many women, embracing their reinvented gender role was a prerequisite for participating in the consumer regime of the high-growth economy.

Two print advertisements for vacuum cleaners from the late 1950s portray the alleged need for modern intervention in the area of female

TABLE 1.3
Ratio of male and female temporary and daily employees in 1960 and 1970 (in ten thousands)

|      | Male | | | Female | | |
|------|---|---|---|---|---|---|
|      | Regular Employees | Temporary Employees | Daily Employees | Regular Employees | Temporary Employees | Daily Employees |
| 1960 | 1,426 | 75 | 77 | 596 | 56 | 45 |
| 1970 | 2,082 | 62 | 66 | 941 | 103 | 52 |

*Source*: Statistics Bureau of Japan, "Historical Data 4-1: Employed Persons by Status in Employment—Whole Japan," http://www.stat.go.jp/english/data/roudou/lngindex.htm (accessed April 2, 2020).

domestic labor. Both use the words "efficient" (*nōritsuteki*) and "hygienic" (*eiseiteki*) to illustrate the power of modern technology while emphasizing the archaic state in which housewives had been working. In the background of the Panasonic ad (figure 1.4), a woman goes to backbreaking lengths to manually clean her house, while in the foreground she tilts her head and contemplates what she could do to make her work more effective. The ad presents the vacuum cleaner as the answer to her desperate search: "Madam . . . There is a way to make cleaning—dusting, wiping, and sweeping—more efficient and hygienic." The advertisement by Toshiba (figure 1.5) suggests, with its product, "efficient and hygienic" cleaning is as easy as lifting a finger. The fine print sends an alarmist message that every household is bombarded with invisible dust: "It is said 41 tons of dust falls from the sky on each square kilometer [247.1 acres] in Tokyo every

*Figure 1.4* Panasonic product catalog, circa 1959, advertisement for vacuum cleaners. Reproduced from Masuda Ken'ichi, *Zoku natsukashikute atarashi shōwa retoro kaden* (Tokyo: Yamakawa shuppansha, 2014), 104.

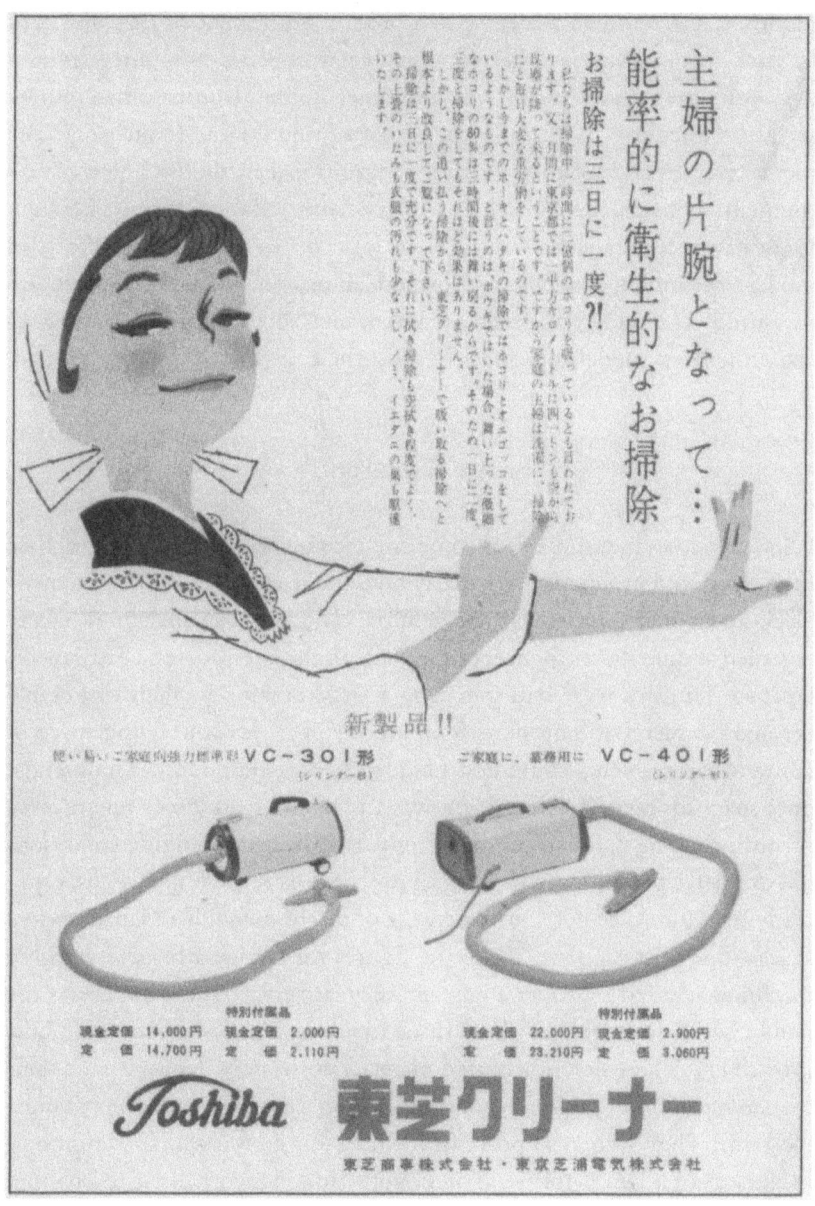

*Figure 1.5* Toshiba flier, 1959, advertisement for vacuum cleaners. Reproduced from Masuda Ken'ichi, *Zoku natsukashikute atarashi shōwa retoro kaden*, 104.

month. . . . When you sweep with a broom, 80 percent of tiny dust will be back in three hours. Therefore, even if you clean two, three times a day, you don't really make any difference." The Toshiba ad mobilizes scientific discourse to quantify the threat of fine dust and underscore the ineffectiveness and ultimate futility of traditional methods. These advertisements convert the households into scientific laboratories, in which housewives simultaneously serve as technicians to measure the effects of modern technology and also as glorified lab rats on which these effects are measured. The underlying message is that men should work hard and purchase the latest model appliances to assist their wives' scientific enterprise.

## You Are What You Buy

Rapid increases in disposable income enhanced workers' ability to purchase mass-produced products, particularly household appliances. Three items—black-and-white televisions, refrigerators, and washing machines—were regarded as must-haves for every household in the late 1950s and early 1960s. Japanese families were still spending a large portion of their disposable income on such basic needs as food and drink,[68] and the living space of many urban residents could best be described as cramped.[69] The average floor space for each Tokyo resident was 3.37 tatami mats (60.48 square feet), according to the national census of 1960. But these challenging conditions did not deter people from rushing to purchase expensive appliances, especially televisions. In 1965, 90.3 percent of the households in Japan owned at least one television set, while the figures for refrigerators and washing machines were 62.4 and 72.4 percent, respectively.[70] Figure 1.6 charts the rapid rise in ownership of these three major appliances during the high-growth era. These newly acquired material possessions demonstrated their owners' steadily improving economic and social status in the most tangible form. They were also proof of membership in a national community in pursuit of a better future. The countryside, which had lagged behind cities in receiving modern amenities, caught up in the 1960s, erasing the signs of a temporal lag that native ethnographers had traditionally valorized as an antidote to urban modernity. For example, in 1960 a mere 11 percent of rural households owned a television set, in contrast to 55 percent of their urban counterparts. By 1964, the year of the Tokyo Olympics, 82 percent and 94 percent of households in the respective areas had

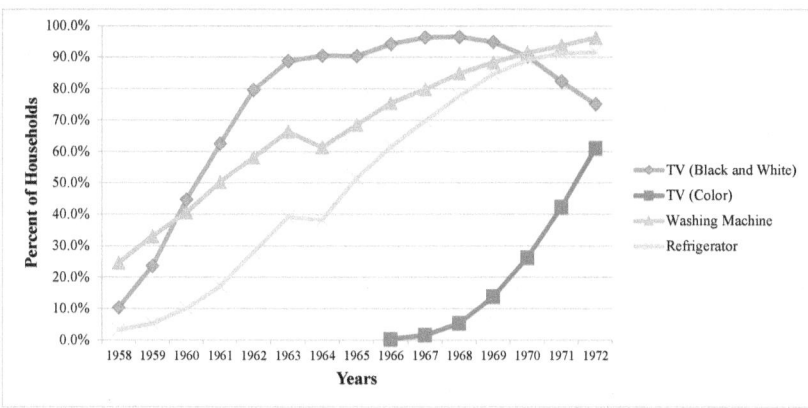

*Figure 1.6* Percentage of households owning major appliances. The dips between 1963 and 1964 for refrigerators and washing machines were due to changes in data collection. Prior to 1963 only nonagrarian urban households were surveyed. Statistically, too, the countryside was being integrated into the nation. Nihon nōritsu kyōkai sōgō kenkyūsho, ed., *Kurashito keizaino deita sōran 2005* (Tokyo: Seikatsu jōhō sentaa, 2005), 176–77 (for refrigerators, washing machines, and televisions [color]); Kokumin seikatsu kenkyūsho, *Showa 42 nendo ban Kokumin seikatsu tōkei nenpō*, 135; and Kokumin seikatsu sentaa, ed., *Kokumin seikatsu tōkei nenpō '77* (Tokyo: Shiseidō, 1977), 90 (for televisions [black-and-white]).

purchased at least one television set.[71] In 1964 Japan trailed behind only the United States in the total number of television sets in use.[72]

Japan's distribution system for commercial goods evolved to accommodate this change. In 1972 the supermarket chain Daiei became the largest retailer in Japan, surpassing the department store group Mitsukoshi. Originating as a family-owned drugstore in Osaka in 1957, Daiei had become a ninety-three-store chain that claimed annual sales of more than ¥300 billion.[73] By developing its own distribution network, Daiei aggressively expanded its supermarket-style operation under the slogan "Quality Goods at Affordable Price" (*yoimono o yasuku*). The Daiei chain offered discounts on its merchandise, which included household appliances. Retail prices were less than those dictated by manufacturers' strict pricing "guidelines." Daiei's combative approach, which often resulted in disputes with manufacturers, derived from the founder, Nakauchi Isao, and his populist conviction that consumers, rather than producers, should ultimately control the prices of goods.[74] Priced at 40 percent below other companies' comparable products, the 13-inch color television that Daiei introduced to the market in 1970 best symbolized the company's populist stance and was another daring move in the retailer's thirty-year battle with the giant appliance maker Panasonic, which insisted on producers' right to set prices.[75]

Under the high-growth regime, Nakauchi's supermarket chains helped to expand mass consumer society by offering modern lifestyles at more affordable prices. Daiei's retail strategies posed a challenge to those of department stores. Daiei valorized consumers' needs rather than upward social mobility. Inspired by Mao Zedong's writing, Nakauchi promoted the revolutionary nature of his enterprise—the liberation of consumers from the oppressive power of manufacturers to fix prices.[76] Nakauchi's success in empowering consumers was limited: giving deep discounts continued to be difficult in the face of major manufacturers' control over distribution networks and retailers. Yet by relentlessly pursuing economies of scale and smaller margins, Nakauchi's chain achieved price advantages over competitors. Offering mass-produced items at lower prices, supermarkets such as Daiei helped transform consumerism into a genuine mass phenomenon.

Daiei's dethroning of Mitsukoshi was symbolic of the changes that Japanese society experienced under the high-growth economy.[77] Since their emergence in the early 1900s, Japanese department stores had offered a radically new retail space that displayed merchandise for the masses.[78] They served as an institution of enlightenment and cultural taste, which both defined and distributed the trappings and accessories of urban middle- and upper-middle-class life, but for a significant price.[79] The shoppers in turn affirmed, through their purchases, their social standing. By capturing the desire for upward social mobility of the emergent urban middle class in prewar Japan, department stores established themselves as leading retailers. Their glittering interior spaces showcased life inside the new consumer society. All were welcome to explore, though actual membership remained beyond the financial means of many.

Nakauchi aspired to make consumer society truly accessible to all. Discussing his retail philosophy, he contrasts Daiei with department stores: "I have claimed that 'Daiei is striptease shows, while department stores are Kabuki theaters.' Department stores sell reputations and images that they have built over a long period of time. Daiei sells the goods themselves. Daiei's sales style is like displaying naked girls without paying much attention to the theater's interior or signboards."[80]

Nakauchi was using provocative images to highlight the fundamental difference between the two modes of sales: rather than the aura of cultural taste, Daiei sells the merchandise itself. Yet consumers' desire is rendered naked within his striptease analogy. His underlying message is that consumers should embrace their desire to consume—no need to cover it with a veil of cultural refinement.

New transportation networks served as an impetus for a new mode of distribution. Daiei and other supermarket chains took advantage of the transformation in Japan's distribution infrastructure in the 1960s. Road and highway systems connecting major consumption centers were constructed at a brisk pace; most notably, the highway between Kobe and Nagoya and the one between Nagoya and Tokyo were completed in 1965 and 1969, respectively. In January 1965 the Resources Council of the Science and Technology Agency adopted a recommendation on modernizing Japan's food distribution system to improve the Japanese diet. The resultant document, commonly known as the "Cold Chain Recommendation," provided rationales for and detailed descriptions of cold chains: low-temperature distribution systems for perishable goods.[81] The Science and Technology Agency tested the application of cold chains throughout fifteen Tokyo stores in 1966.[82] The frozen-food market in Japan grew rapidly in the 1960s and the first half of the 1970s (table 1.4). Daiei began building its own cold chains in 1971.[83] The Tokyo Central Wholesale Market began to trade more frozen fish than fresh ones in the same year.[84] As more households became equipped with a freezer, processed frozen foods such as fried shrimp and cream croquettes quickly became familiar items in the Japanese diet.[85]

The new distribution infrastructure was a sine qua non for the expansion of the mass market. Through the act of mass consumption, citizens attained a greater sense of social inclusion and integration within their everyday lives. The boundaries that separated rural and urban Japan gradually blurred. Members of agrarian communities and the economic underclass gained admission to the regime of the high-growth economy and enjoyed access to commercial products. By taking advantage of the relatively cheap labor of "outsiders" within Japan, the Japanese economy produced affordable goods. In turn, these goods found eager consumers, including the outsiders who gained a measure of purchasing power through their employment beyond the countryside. This rapidly expanding cycle of production and consumption sustained an egalitarian image of the

TABLE 1.4
Annual growth rate of the frozen-food market in Japan, 1965–1974

| Year | Growth in Volume (%) | Growth in Monetary Value (%) |
|---|---|---|
| 1964–1965 | 30.0 | 35.3 |
| 1965–1966 | 43.4 | 73.3 |
| 1966–1967 | 42.6 | 66.8 |
| 1967–1968 | 42.4 | 60.9 |
| 1968–1969 | 60.2 | 27.8 |
| 1969–1970 | 14.4 | 35.1 |
| 1970–1971 | 30.2 | 39.5 |
| 1971–1972 | 33.1 | 55.0 |
| 1972–1973 | 29.7 | 43.3 |
| 1973–1974 | 6.6 | 29.4 |

*Source*: Umeno Kenjirō, ed., *Kōrudo chein nenkan 1976* (Tokyo: Sankei maaketengu, 1976), 939.

national community, where each member was purportedly entitled to the fruits of his or her (or her spouse's) hard labor.

## Education for the Masses

Japanese businesses sought workers with better educational credentials as part of their strategy to increase productivity through technological innovation. The government devised new education policies accordingly, and hundreds of thousands more youths gained access to higher education, which had traditionally been reserved for members of the elite. The gains in higher education during the high-growth economy were impressive. In 1955, for example, only 51.5 percent of the high-school-age cohort attended high school, while 10.1 percent enrolled in college or junior college. By 1972 the rate of enrollment in high school had increased to 87.2 percent, and the rate of postsecondary enrollment had grown to 17.9 percent. Only five years later (1977) these numbers were 93.1 percent and 37.7 percent, respectively.[86] Higher education—once limited to the middle and upper-middle classes—opened to the masses. Yet the experiences of the new college students, especially those who matriculated at a large private university, were often negative, and many blamed the economic motives that deeply penetrated Japan's higher education.

The new education policy placed heavy emphasis on science and engineering, but it also allowed the student population to expand in the humanities and social sciences.[87] The government accomplished the task of rapidly expanding postsecondary education in a cost-effective way by largely entrusting it to private colleges and universities. While the number of students at national and public institutions increased by 61 percent (from 222,796 to 359,698) in the decade after 1960, the number of students at their private counterparts increased by 159 percent in that period (from 403,625 to 1,046,823).[88] The majority of private schools lacked adequate facilities and resources to deal with their fast-growing student bodies. Private schools could offer a higher education at a relatively low cost, and more parents and students could afford the tuition thanks to their rapidly increasing disposable incomes, but classroom instruction fell by the wayside. There was little incentive for colleges and universities to revise their existing curricula or train their instructors better when students flocked to schools regardless of their educational quality. Classes in huge lecture halls without teaching assistants were the norm on crowded private campuses. Often the assigned classrooms could not accommodate the students registered for classes, and one of the instructors' major tasks was to discourage them from showing up. This was not an environment that encouraged dialogue either inside or outside the classroom.

Takano Etsuko (1949–1969), who entered Ritsumeikan University in 1967, describes her very first class there on April 17: "The class was in a large lecture hall. It was like taking a class in Utsunomiya Women's High School's auditorium [her alma mater]. From where I was, in the back of the room, I saw the rows of heads lining up toward the far end. Professor Kimura was talking to the crowd, not to the individuals. I was listening to the lecture in the crowd. *Somehow I felt lonely*" (emphasis in original). She quickly realized that the lecture was mostly based on the assigned textbook, so there was no need to attend future meetings. Her first class concerned sports science, a required course that hardly anybody took seriously. Almost all classes were conducted in a similar fashion, with the exception of smaller language classes and a handful of seminars. Takano immediately began to skip classes, like so many of her classmates. Although she admonishes herself for this on April 28, she confides to her diary two weeks later that she has missed even more classes.[89] Takano was not alone in finding her university courses tedious and irrelevant. Throughout Japan, first-year students who entered college with high hopes quickly became disillusioned. The dullness Takano found in many lecture courses was a symptom of larger structural issues.

The teaching conditions at Ritsumeikan University were typical of large-scale private institutions, who admitted far more students than the campus facilities could reasonably accommodate in the second half of the 1960s. A study produced by a faculty committee reported that 9.9 percent of the classes at Ritsumeikan had more than five hundred students. An unspecified department in the social science division had more than five hundred students packed into 55 percent of its courses, while only 2.5 percent of classes in the same department had fewer than one hundred students in 1967; even the smallest class had eighty-seven students (excluding seminars, which were capped at thirty-five students). In the same year the ratio of students to full-time faculty members at Ritsumeikan was as high as 69.2 to 1, far exceeding the national averages (the average ratios for private and public institutions were 29.5 and 8.3 to 1, respectively). The numbers were even higher in social science departments. In the Economics Department, the ratio was as high as 118 students to 1 full-time faculty member. The Literature Department, to which Takano belonged, was slightly better, with 66 students for each full-time faculty member. The physical facilities were equally wanting. Ritsumeikan's library space was extremely limited, with 2.76 square feet per student. The annual book purchase budget in 1967 was a mere 500 yen ($1.39) per student.[90] Takano was not exaggerating when she wrote in her February 22, 1969, entry: "The library does not have the kind of books that I want to read"—books on recent history, music, and contemporary writers like Takahashi Kazumi.[91]

The nature of Japan's higher education system changed radically as it opened the doors to the masses. Colleges and universities were once not so much intellectual training grounds as elite incubators, where individual students accumulated cultural capital while forming fraternal communities that would help their later careers via alumni connections. Although the postwar incarnations of Japanese academic institutions never completely abandoned that mission, students clearly sensed that the emphasis had shifted to the production of technocrats to promote economic expansion. The competition to enter prestigious schools served as a screening mechanism for identifying individuals who were intelligent and motivated enough to later join the corporate world. A growing number of youths were invited into the new and expansive education system as beneficiaries of and future boosters of Japan's economic success. Once the initial excitement of matriculation was over, however, they realized that they were being treated as products moving along a mass production line. The fierce campus activism of the late 1960s, aimed at school administrations and government authorities, was in no small part driven by the students' desire to regain a sense of agency against the collusion between higher education and corporate needs.

## The Monstrous Middle

Reflecting the new economic conditions, a large majority of people came to identify themselves as belonging to the middle stratum of society (*chūryū*) by the early 1970s. According to "Kokumin seikatsu ni kansuru yoron chōsa," opinion surveys conducted by the prime minister's office, 72 percent of people claimed in 1958 to belong to the middle stratum of Japanese society, with 37 percent choosing the middle of the middle stratum. In 1975 the figure was 89.9 percent (59.4 percent for the middle of the middle). Over the same twenty years, the portion of people who identified themselves as occupying the bottom stratum or the bottom of the middle stratum decreased from 49.0 percent to 28.7 percent.[92] This trend was confirmed in the National Survey of Social Stratification and Social Mobility (SSM), a sociological survey conducted every ten years since 1955.

In the postwar years Japanese academics grappled with the nature of this expansion of the middle stratum. The economist Murakami Yasusuke (1931–1993) memorably described it in 1977 as a "monster." This new and homogeneous social group is monstrous, he argued, because it defies the existing conceptual frameworks of left and right. "The binary oppositions of the exploiting and exploited, or the ruler and ruled, completely fail to address the emergence of this new middle stratum."[93] His essay was an attempt to construct a framework to capture and tame this enormous and elusive social entity—*shin chūkankaisō*, or "the new middle mass." His strategy was to produce a conceptual grid by listing conditions that contributed to the growth of this segment, including the erosion of the divide between white-collar and blue-collar workers and the recent urbanization of the countryside. Murakami also emphasized the homogenization in information and social consciousness:

> The development of mass communication and mass higher education leveled the contents of information and consciousness. Almost all households [in Japan] subscribe to one of the major newspapers, the contents of which are virtually homogeneous, and watch the same television programs. The ratio of students who enter colleges and universities is about to reach 40 percent. Absolutely nobody would be surprised to see sons and daughters of blue-collar workers and farmers go to colleges. The high-growth economy was a gigantic blender that has produced homogeneous middle stratum that includes at least 60 percent of the population.[94]

Murakami's figurative "gigantic blender" conjures up the image of the helpless masses being agitated with violent force, and yet many must have welcomed these changes. His essay describes the agitation from a safe distance while glossing over the fact that people eagerly embraced the new educational opportunities as well as the information flow that postwar media facilitated.

The blender is an apt appliance through which to discuss the state of Japan's consumer society. As the cultural critic Tada Michitarō observed through architect Kawazoe Nobuo, it was a source of hope and a site of greater aspirations: "Enshrining a glittering blender in the center of their nearly bare dining table, people found it easier to dream about an affluent and tranquil family home in the future. The blender was both a symbol of that future and the first concrete step toward realization of the dream."[95] In the early phase of the high-growth era, an electric blender was valued more for its symbolic status than its utility. As families filled their small living space with other appliances, the once idolized object lost its luster and was stored away in a closet (because its application was limited and cleaning it took much effort).[96] Soon families no longer adored the blender as a symbol of consumerism, for they now lived inside the insatiable world of consumerism, Murakami's "giant blender."

Murakami's perspective is external and stable, betraying no hint that he himself might have been consuming new products and tumbling inside the blender along with the rest of the society. Murakami ultimately diagnosed these middle strata as status quo–oriented because they sought to protect their vested interests in contemporary society, while he props up their passivity as the last defense against autocratic rule: if the government's economic policies fail and these middle strata disappear, there might be no historical subjects left to resist the rise of a powerful and centralized political authority.

Murakami's argument gained traction at the time because it meshed well with the discourse of Japanese uniqueness: a belief that Japanese culture and society were exceptional. According to him, traditional class structures in England and France, the presence of immigrant workers in Europe, and racial tensions in the United States hampered the growth of the middle strata in these nations, while there were no such conditions in Japan. Japan leapfrogged England, France, and the United States and came to the forefront of history precisely because it did not carry the baggage of historical legacies. Murakami's version of historical determinism (in which, ironically, the absence of history determined present-day culture and social relations in Japan) inhibited inquiries into the historical process through which this monster was created: if there was no history, historical inquiries were inconceivable. For Murakami, the important question was not what went on in the gigantic blender; it was how to keep the monster well fed, since it held the "last historical agency that strives for a post-industrial [read "classless"] society."[97] The monster was the last and best hope for Japan to win the race to the end of history.

The sweeping tone of Murakami's essay irritated some Japanese academics. The Marxist scholar Kishimoto Shigenobu refused to recognize that the new middle stratum was real, insisting that Murakami's proposed concept would merely serve to conceal the fundamental inequality between employers and employees, or capitalists and wage workers.[98] Kishimoto's rebuttal seemed to confirm one of Murakami's points: the inability of the "old progressivism" to think beyond the binaries of oppressor and oppressed. Kishimoto was justified in claiming that social and economic disparities remained in Japanese society, as other sociologists later demonstrated empirically. But he was not able to offer any conceptual tools with which to examine the widely shared *chūryū ishiki*: that is, the consciousness of belonging to the middle social stratum.

Meanwhile, the sociologist Tominaga Ken'ichi grudgingly accepted that it was possible to recognize the large middle stratum on a macro level while still insisting that the individuals that constituted the "monster" were not as homogeneous as they were made out to be. Citing the relatively low correlation among professional prestige, education level, and income, Tominaga insisted on the existence of a "diverse middle."[99] He also pointed out that Murakami's terminology might cause confusion because there was already a well-established sociological term, "new middle class," that generally designated white-collar workers.

None of these academics showed much appetite for historical analysis because Murakami's ideological bent had set the terms of the debate. While he merits credit for identifying the conceptual challenges posed by the newly emerging social group, his discussion mostly served to mystify contemporary Japan. In the end, he appealed to a commonsense understanding (you know a monster when you see one); Kishimoto offered a formulaic Marxist denunciation of Murakami's vision and the false consciousness of the masses (the monster is just an illusion); and Tominaga, without questioning Murakami's framework, insisted on the superiority of quantitative analysis (let's study the monster). Kishimoto's and Tominaga's earnest rebuttals had the unintentional effect of complementing Murakami's argument. The exchanges that took place within the bounds of Murakami's well-prepared ideological terrain all conspicuously carried the assumption that Japan had finally reached the point where it could debate about an issue primarily associated with advanced nations. The dire poverty and inequality of the immediate postwar period seemed to belong to bygone days. The debate participants collectively allowed Murakami's monster to distract themselves and their contemporaries from the historical evidence that might have been useful in analyzing this phenomenon.

Following the debate, a number of sociologists in Japan tried to give the monster a more concrete form but, in the end, failed to make the middle stratum any more concrete than the 1977 exchanges had. Analyzing the data from the fourth (1985) SSM survey, Mamada Takao concluded that the sense of belonging to the "middle stratum" could not be based on such objective criteria as ownership of durable goods or living standard.[100] More recently, Sudo Naoki candidly admitted that "it has been extremely difficult for researchers to discern the common characteristics among people who thought they belonged to the middle." Regardless of the academic and media hype about middle-stratum consciousness in the 1970s, Japanese society remained stratified in all but its own mind. Sudo relegates the sociological conundrum of the middle stratum to Japanese people's consciousness: insofar as they were fixated on their middle-stratum status, the evidence against it became invisible to them. As social stratification gained more attention in recent years, people have become more aware of examples of social and economic disparities.[101] While taking consciousness seriously as a sociological issue, Sudo's conclusion resembles that of the Marxist scholar Kishimoto Shigenobu. The debate and the sociologists' subsequent efforts to clarify the issue ultimately appear to have reached a dead end, merely confirming that *chūryū ishiki* was neither rigorous nor useful as a scholarly concept.

The experts have so far largely failed to describe life inside Japan's high-growth regime: to borrow Murakami's expression, we have not carefully examined what was happening in the giant blender. By recognizing the middle-stratum status as a set of processes rather than static conditions, or by focusing on what it *did* rather than what it *was*, I believe it is possible to give *chūryū ishiki* a new analytical life. In other words, we are not done with it just yet. I propose that we see the people who found themselves in the middle stratum not merely as products of their environment but also as agents who helped to transform it. This approach encourages us to examine social dynamics like consumption, gender relations, and media effects—particularly those of television and weeklies—that have been largely omitted from the sociological discussion of Japan's middle stratum.

This chapter has focused on external forces: how the blender agitated the contents. In the following chapter we turn to the process through which the subjects of consumer society were produced: what happened inside the metaphorical blender. Through this process, people in Japan developed radically different relations with their social environment. The way in which television and the weeklies affected society under the high-growth economy was far more complicated than the simple mechanical agitation of Murakami's metaphor may suggest. Both media served as powerful catalysts for internal changes within individual consumers. Chapter 2 explores the deeply emotional interactions between the new media and their viewers and readers.

## CHAPTER II

# Circular Vision

## *The Metavisuality of Television*

Speaking of television, even when the programs are rather vulgar, that is, when one does not think one's whole self is absorbed, usually one's whole being as a human is absorbed.
—SHIMIZU IKUTARŌ, "TEREBIJON JIDAI" (TELEVISION AGE), 1958

Television was just like love.
—WATANABE TOKIKO, DOROBU ELEMENTARY SCHOOL STUDENT, 1960

The Medium is the message.
—MARSHALL McLUHAN, *UNDERSTANDING MEDIA*, 1964

Television's affective impact on Japanese society is often underestimated, yet the dramatic transformation that Japan experienced under the high-growth economy was not only socioeconomic but also intensely visual. That is, the ways in which individuals saw themselves in society radically changed amid the whirlwind of high growth. Japanese people became embedded in the emerging national space, and they were keenly aware of it. While television viewers acquired a social vision as expansive as the cameras' reach, they also internalized television's gaze, turning themselves into the objects of that same gaze. Their lives were thus visually linked to a national drama called "Japan under the high-growth economy" as it dynamically unfolded on their televisions. They began to see their own everyday lives as if they were on the television screen.

In this chapter we revisit the early years when television was still a novelty. It was exciting to take part in the rags-to-riches story of the high-growth economy at any level of society. Japan not only recovered from the devastation of the Asia Pacific War but became an economic giant in a little over two decades. Millions of actors in this national drama saw handsome rewards. The nation's GDP grew at a remarkable rate, while both inflation and unemployment remained low. Japanese citizens saw economic growth in tangible forms: workers could expect a substantial raise every year, and new appliances filled households. Millions of families moved into modern, efficient—albeit small—units in new housing complexes known as *danchi*. People counted on rewards for their long hours of work. Society appeared to be filled with energy and optimism. Yet, as we saw in the introduction, jubilance was not the only emotion that people experienced under the high-growth economy.

In the previous chapter we observed that under the regime of high growth, a new national space of production and consumption emerged. This chapter contends that new media, particularly television, played an instrumental role in forming this space, even as the space itself provided the conditions under which television became pervasive. With regard to the relationship between the print media and emergent national consciousness, Benedict Anderson's argument has become a baseline of academic discussion. The rise of periodicals and especially newspapers enabled readers to imagine millions of unconnected people as fellow citizens in an embryonic national space. The print media "made it possible for rapidly growing numbers of people to think about themselves, and to relate themselves to others, in profoundly new ways."[1] Anderson's exclusive focus on the print media, however, confines his discussion mostly to the nineteenth- and early twentieth-century context. Television not only extended the imagining of communities but also brought that imagining to a new level through its profound power to engage viewers. The social impact of new Japanese weeklies was based not on their position as offshoots of the traditional print media but on their status as responses to, and operations within, the new media space opened by television. The weeklies' focus on the personal and quotidian complemented television's far-reaching gaze: together, they destabilized boundaries between the public and the private.

## Television's Gaze

Early encounters with television in Japanese society confirm that television sets were far more than a cool electronic gadget. Viewers liberally identified with and transferred their affections to the new appliance. Although it was often seen as a frivolous medium in the early years after its introduction, it quickly became an integral part of most people's everyday lives, greatly affecting their rhythm and even family relations.[2]

Its development facilitated and was simultaneously supported by the high-growth economy, helping to produce a new national community where the images that circulated in the media became the links among its members. Television facilitated a new field of vision in which individual viewers acquired a new capacity for self-reflectivity—metavisuality—about their relationship with the larger society. Television's effects were most dramatically demonstrated in remote and economically disadvantaged rural areas.

The ethnographer Miyamoto Tsuneichi (1907–1981) provides fascinating accounts of television's impact on the lives of Japanese people in the countryside. Many, including Miyamoto, argue that images rendered on television have contributed to a leveling of lifestyles in areas that would otherwise have experienced an information-deprived temporal lag. In an essay published in January 1966, Miyamoto discusses the two contrasting responses to the protests against the Treaty of Mutual Corporation and Security between the United States and Japan (1960; commonly referred as the U.S.-Japan Security Treaty). Many were morally outraged by reports about police brutality against protestors and the death of a female university student in a clash between police and demonstrators at the National Diet compound.[3] Both radio and television covered the anti-U.S.-Japan Security Treaty protests extensively, each resorting to its respective strengths as a medium.

Carrying a microphone connected to a relay car by cable, radio journalists reported from the site of violent confrontation. On June 15, when seven thousand students clashed with the police in the National Diet compound, Radio Kantō's reporter provided a live, blow-by-blow account from the scene:

> In front of my eyes, policemen are swinging their batons. They are yelling, "Konoyarō, bakayarō" [you bastard, son of bitch]. They are now beating [students]. Let's get closer with the microphone. The police squad is extremely violent. They are dragging the microphone away.... The police grabbed me by the neck. This is a live broadcast, but the police hit me in the face.[4]

The radio reporter also repeatedly announced that a female student had died, although the details were still unknown at that time.[5] The developing story on the radio added to the chaotic and tense atmosphere.

On the same night, TV reporting teams brought 16-mm film cameras to the protest site, where student protesters were beaten and dragged away by the police. Even in black-and-white, the images vividly attested to the police's forceful tactics and the physical toll that they took on the protesters. While bird's-eye views established the enormous scale of the protest, close-up shots conveyed the sense of urgency and the desperation of the protesters.

Although both radio listeners and television viewers gained sufficient information as to what transpired in the Diet compound that night, their responses to the protests greatly diverged, at least in the countryside. According to Miyamoto, radio listeners were more sympathetic to the cause of the student demonstrators, while farmers who watched events on television screens tended to be more critical of them. One possible explanation for this perception gap is socioeconomic: given that television sets were still exorbitantly expensive relative to average household income, the early purchasers of television sets were wealthier and likely more progovernment.[6] Miyamoto insists, however, that there was more to the process through which country residents formed their opinions about the student protesters. They listened to or saw the event through the cultural framework they were accustomed to. The farmers who listened only to the radio coverage constructed, in their minds' eye, their own images of the student demonstrators. The students they envisioned were rallying in straw coats with banners of straw mats, the "traditional" attire of peasant uprisings in premodern times.[7] It was not difficult to empathize with protestors draped in folk symbolism. But if the sounds of radio could blend into the life of agrarian communities without disturbing their worldview, television highlighted the difference between the scenes on and in front of the screen. For the farmers who watched the conflict on television, the students were simply making a ruckus in their nicest clothes at the busiest time of the year. (The demonstrations peaked in May and June, when many farmers were busy transplanting rice seedlings.) One woman told Miyamoto that she could not stand watching the demonstrators get their clothes dirty struggling with the riot police because it was so wasteful.[8] Miyamoto's anecdote suggests that the new visual media forced the country viewers to abandon their long-held worldview by exposing them to the stark reality of the outside world.

A second episode from the 1960s illustrates television's transformative effects on the countryside as a more interactive process. When he was teaching at Kanagawa University, Miyamoto told his students to write about what they learned during summer break. Of the ten who wrote about housing conditions, three—from three separate regions—observed that many farmers had been renovating their houses because of television. These farmers had internalized the gaze of modernization and become ashamed of their living conditions. In contrast to its depiction of modern life as replete with clean living spaces and tidy clothes, television always made the lives of farmers and fishermen appear "dark, irrational, and feudal." Consequently, the farmers began to think of their own lives as wretched, and every time they cast their eyes on the television screen, they felt that city people were somehow peeping into those lives.[9] In the farmers' imaginations, television sets could return their gaze. They increasingly internalized the outsiders' gaze as their own to the degree that they were moved to transform their living spaces into the images of what they saw on the television screen. At its most basic level, Miyamoto's second anecdote insists that private space and the countryside no longer existed beyond the reach of mass society.

A television screen at the heart of family life, commonly regarded as a window to the world, helped to define and also exposed the inner sanctum of the private sphere.[10] Television receivers provided a universal gaze into an individual household: the private experience of seeing was externalized and returned as the social gaze through the television.

### "Television Was Just Like Love": *Dawn Over the Mountains* (1959–1960)

From April 1959 to March 1960 a fascinating social experiment using a 17-inch television set took place in the remote mountain hamlet of Dorobu, located 3,000 feet above sea level in the northern Tochigi Prefecture (map 2.1). Dorobu consisted of twenty-seven households totaling a mere 170 residents, whose livelihood came mainly from logging and charcoal production. There was not a single doctor or shop in the area, and access to the outside world was limited to a logging road, part of which merged with the riverbed in a place where many bridges had been washed away. In this remote community, which had been largely left behind despite Japan's burgeoning postwar economy, a television set arrived as part of an educational research project conducted in 1959 and 1960. Responding to the

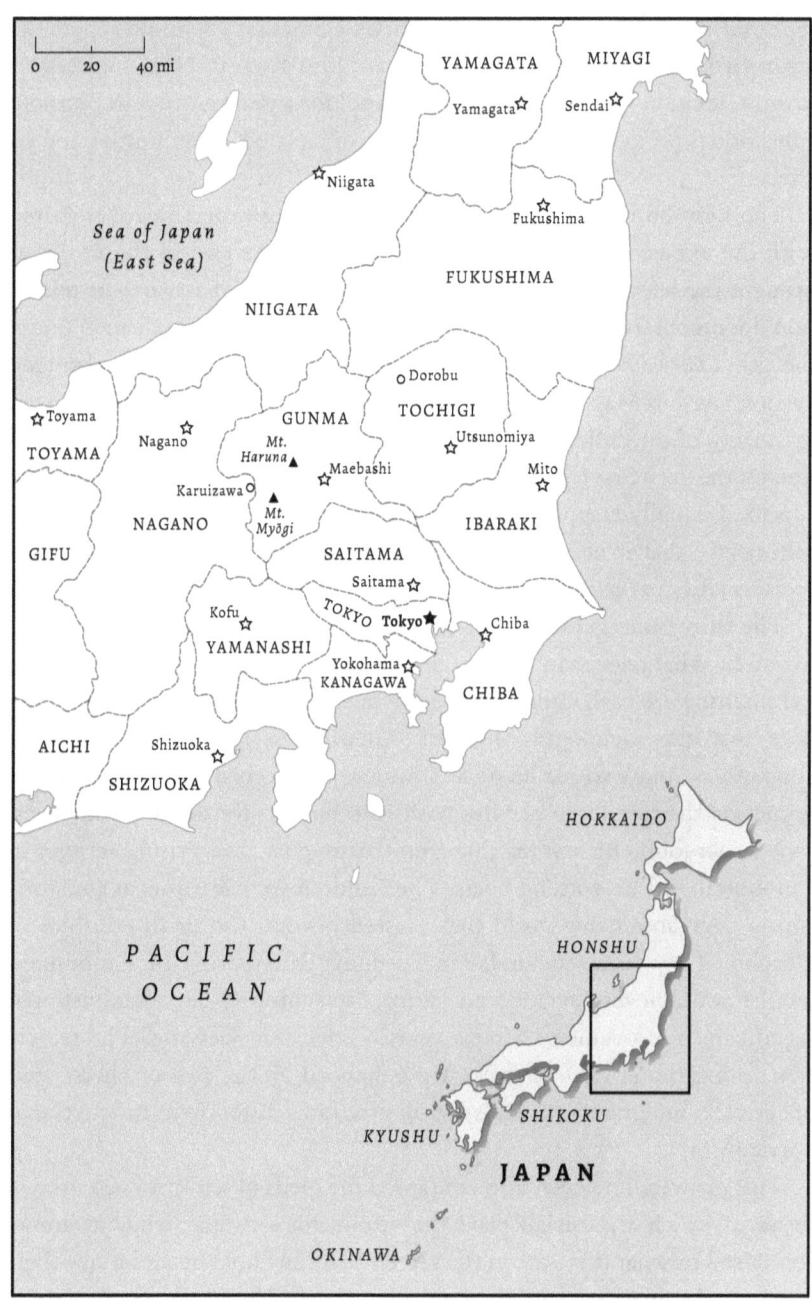

Map 2.1 Map of central Japan.

repeated requests from the community's elementary schoolteacher, the Japan Broadcasting Corporation (Nihon Hōsō Kyōkai, NHK) agreed to loan a television set to Dorobu's lone school for a year in order to promote educational programming in the schools of isolated communities and its effects.[11]

The Dorobu children's first television-viewing experience was paired with the experience of being seen by outsiders. As part of the deal that brought the television to their school, NHK produced a two-part television documentary, which aired in November 1959 and March 1960 under the title *Dawn Over the Mountains* (*Yamano bunkō no kiroku*). An abridged version aired in May 1960.[12] The circular flow of the gaze was epitomized by images of the children watching their own encounters with the television on the very first television screen that they had ever laid eyes on. They appeared happily trapped in television's scopic field and the intense self-reflectivity that it demanded. The Dorobu experiment thus showcased metavisuality par excellence.

The thirty-one grade-school-aged children were voraciously absorbed in and by what television had to offer. In many scenes the camera captures the intense gaze each child casts on the television screen, instantiating the state that the sociologist Shimizu Ikutarō describes in this chapter's epigraph as "one's whole being as a human is absorbed." One day parents witnessed their children playing with soap bubbles for the first time ever. One father found his son making a miniature boat, a surprising activity in a mountain village with no boats. The children were learning at an astonishing pace about the world that existed beyond the small confines of Dorobu. They received intellectual stimuli that the life of a mountain hamlet could never have offered. Before-and-after IQ tests demonstrated significant improvements after a year of television viewing. The television's educational value was greatly enhanced by the two teachers, who effectively integrated the television programs into their instructional curriculum.[13]

This growth, however, also contained the seeds of self-criticism. In one scene in which a musician plays the violin, for example, students are so immersed in what they see on the screen that they hold up and move their hands to play imaginary instruments (figure 2.1). This heartwarming scene must be read against the documentary's framing scene, which focuses on the backward living conditions of the Dorobu community. When teaching about string instruments without the help of television, the teacher

*Figure 2.1* Playing imaginary violins. *Dawn Over the Mountains (Yama no bunkō no kiroku)* NHK, May 5, 1960.

brings out a stage prop violin made for the previous year's stage play (figure 2.2). The crudely shaped, solid piece of wood impresses on the audience a deprivation that the children are not even aware of. It is only when they see the professional violinist on TV, experience the absence of their own instrument, or watch their crude imitation in the documentary that they begin to register their lack.

Television not only fills the informational void in their lives but also teaches them about the hazards of living in such a simple state. Through comparisons with the world outside their village, the Dorobu children develop critical attitudes about themselves and their community. As Miyamoto's anecdote about home improvements illustrates, the power of television was not limited to its ability to disseminate information. After watching programs that promoted modern and hygienic living arrangements, one student insisted that her family's kitchen be made into a cleaner, more functional space.[14] Having internalized the didactic perspective of earlier educational programs that were critical of whatever was deemed backward and unhygienic, the student saw her domestic

*Figure 2.2* A stage prop violin. *Dawn Over the Mountains.*

space as inadequate.[15] Accepting her appraisal, her father renovated their kitchen.

The children also cast their critical and reflective gaze on life in Dorobu in general. After a student's father was injured on the wooden track built for transporting charcoal down a mountain, a team of students investigated the cause of the accident. Their findings were presented to the parents during a gathering for the school's annual day of stage performances, one segment of which was entitled "Our Television Journey: Dorobu," which mimicked the format of television travel programs. On stage was a large television frame through which a student "newscaster" introduced the segment (figure 2.3). Kamiyama Tsutou then described from the stage the circumstances in which his father fell off the precipice, concluding with a gentle appeal that the users of the wooden track better monitor its condition. After Tsutou's presentation, "Our Television Journey: Dorobu" turned to a discussion of economic conditions in the community. After noting that, apart from its dangers, there is not much money in charcoal production, the students recommended that the villagers diversify their local economy by marketing Dorobu's scenic locale to tourists.[16] With their newly

*Figure 2.3* A student reporter inside a model of a television set. *Dawn Over the Mountains.*

acquired knowledge of outside communities, the children turned their eyes onto their own lives, recognizing the hardships of living in a remote mountain hamlet. They slipped in and out of the television, splitting themselves into the subjects of the investigative gaze and the objects under investigation.

Encounters with television similar to the one documented by the NHK's camera crew were repeated in remote communities throughout Japan in the early 1960s, awakening residents to the need to modernize their living conditions.[17] City residents also welcomed television with a sense of wonder and fascination.[18] Yet television's impact was most apparent in the countryside because the medium easily transcended the geographical distance that had traditionally maintained the urban/rural cultural divide. Amenities such as movie theaters and large-scale retail outlets had literally been beyond the reach of most country residents. Rural residents could now appreciate urban cultural life and consumerism at a safe distance, without the burden of long-distance travel. It is noteworthy that the Dorobu children's desire for the television initially was sparked by a rare experience in the city of Utsunomiya (map 2.1): Dorobu's graduating students were given the opportunity to study for a day at a city school, where they saw educational television programs for the first time. The scenes of the children walking down the narrow mountain paths and then walking through streets filled with cars and people in Utsunomiya illustrate the astounding contrast between the two environments. The flow of information is demonstrated by the gifts the students exchange with their counterparts in the city: they brought the bracken (*warabi*) they gathered in the mountains as a gift and in turn received used magazines from the city children. The students symbolically traded their way of life for the information that television offered.

The self-reflective gaze that television facilitated, a central attribute of metavisuality, was not entirely new to postwar Japanese society. As Fatimah Tobing Rony argues, long before the advent of television, film had already offered its audience a similar sensibility: a double consciousness of seeing and being seen.[19] This double consciousness resonates with the self-reflective attitudes that the children of Dorobu acquired by watching educational programs. Through partially identifying with an outside gaze, the viewers learned to view themselves and their environment from an outside perspective.[20]

Yet film's ability to interpolate self-reflective subjectivity was not nearly as far-reaching as television's for three reasons: most theaters were in major cities, fewer hours were spent viewing films, and film watching was a public event. In the early years of the postwar period, 90 percent of towns and villages had no movie theater. During the occupation period, the Civil Information and Education Section of the General Headquarters decided to use 16-mm documentary shorts as a means to propagate democratic ideas, directing the Ministry of Education to create the system of distributing and showing them throughout Japan. According to film scholar Tsuchiya Yuka, "those films were enthusiastically embraced, given the lack of other forms of entertainment." On average, by July 1951 each Japanese person had watched slightly more than ten films over several years. Total viewing hours, however, were still minuscule in comparison to later television-viewing figures.[21]

Even commercial films at their pinnacle of success did not approach television in terms of viewing hours. The total number of paid cinema admissions in Japan peaked at more than 1.1 billion in 1958.[22] This statistic is impressive compared with today's dwindling figures, but it means that, on average, a Japanese person visited a movie theater eleven times a year, with an individual's total annual viewing hours likely amounting to no more than thirty or forty.[23] That number would be substantially larger for adult residents in cities, but it was still far lower than the average television-viewing time in 1965, which exceeded three hours a day, or more than a thousand hours a year.[24] Television viewing came to dominate the non-working hours of everyday life in Japan; sleep and work were the only activities that the Japanese engaged in for longer hours. Television viewing had become a national pastime.

Besides the long hours of viewing at home, television's affinity to everyday life distinguished it from cinematic experiences. Drawing on the binary concepts of *hare* (extraordinary/singular) and *ke* (quotidian/everyday) first discussed by Yanagita Kunio, the television director/scenario writer Konno Tsutomu emphasized the everydayness of television viewing in an essay in 1967.[25] In Dorobu, the students greeted the television with "Good morning" when they arrived at the school and bade it "goodbye" when they left for the day.[26] At the end of the academic year in March, the school was obliged to return the television set to NHK (it was later donated to the school once the study was completed). The children were understandably sad to see it go. A sixth grader, Watanabe Tokiko (the student who had her father renovate their kitchen), wrote a poem to express her feelings about the imminent departure:

> The third quarter is coming to an end
> We have to return the television
> Since the television set came
> I brightened up and studied [hard]
> When the television is gone
> It is the same as no sun shining
> Like the time the horse that our family raised was being sold
> When television is gone
> I will pretend to turn its switch on
> I will probably think that was a wonderful time
> Television was just like love.[27]

Although Tokiko's television viewing was confined to her school, it had become an object of her affection like the domestic animals that her family raised. She compared the flow of information that the small television set afforded to the sun's rays, which were the foundation of everyday life. Once it was gone, she feared that her world would once again be insipid and colorless. She would repeat familiar gestures and delve into fond memories, as if she had lost a loved one. Love is perhaps the most powerful impetus for internalizing the other's gaze, a gaze that mercilessly exposes one's inner self. Tokiko had learned to love the benevolent apparatus of television in her everyday life.

## Television Worth Fighting Over: Ozu Yasujirō's *Good Morning* (1959)

It is often claimed that children were most susceptible to the effects of television. Miyamoto Tsuneichi recalls a conversation he had with a town administrator from Amarume-machi, in Yamagata Prefecture, who insisted that television was ultimately responsible for the practice of *dekasegi* (male farmers leaving their hometowns during the winter to work at construction sites) that was prevalent in the Tōhoku region.[28] According to the administrator, the families in the region once lived within their means. Their income level defined their lifestyle. But once families caved in to their children's pleas to buy a television set, they were caught up in the fever of consumption. The children wanted everything that they saw on the television screen, regardless of their families' economic standing. To support their newly formed habit of consumption, the families had to seek new sources of income.[29] The children should not, in fact, be blamed for the birth of this widespread labor practice (as already discussed, unemployment benefits served as powerful incentives). The adults may have been less willing to own up to the desire for consumption, but they were just as driven by it.

Ozu Yazujirō's (1903–1963) film *Good Morning* (*Ohayō*, 1959) poignantly portrays children acting out their desire for television and the problematic behavior that prompts adults to face their own fascination with it. Set in Tokyo's outskirts, the story, as in many other Ozu films, revolves around the everyday lives of suburban middle-class families. To demonstrate television's effects on a community, however, the director situates the drama in a newly developed housing complex. Each home is a detached wooden, single-story building, reminiscent of the highly standardized space of a danchi complex, which typically consists of low-rise concrete buildings.[30] In one scene a drunk neighbor comes home to the wrong unit and does not notice his mistake right away.[31] This homogenized space is also fertile ground for rumors and gossip. Some residents are fixated on finding even slight differences among their neighbors. As a source of jealousy and envy, still-expensive television sets (and, to a lesser degree, a washing machine) seem to have enormous importance in this imaginary community.

Unlike NHK's documentary, which highlights television's positive attributes, Ozu teases out the deleterious effects of the new technology. Yet his view of it is ultimately benign in that he portrays television as a harmless social lubricant and uses humor to endorse the desire for it. The two plot lines of the film, which revolve around whether one family should buy a television and how another family afforded a washing machine, foreground the promises and perils of consumerism. Mimicking the format of a television family comedy, the film gently satirizes consumer culture even as it works to mitigate its anxiety-producing changes.

The movie's central conflict is a generational one between a father and his two boys over whether to buy a television for the Hayashi family. Once again, children serve as vanguards of an emerging consumer society: the boys are consumed by their desire for a television. The father, who is a company man nearing retirement, views the question purely through a utilitarian and pragmatic lens: What is the use value of the television, and can they justify its expense? While the father regards the television with suspicion and resistance, the children embrace it, regularly going to a neighbor's house to watch sumo wrestling on their television. They throw a fit when their parents refuse to buy a set. In the ensuing argument, Minoru, the older of the two children, defies parental authority, insisting that his father cannot control his desire to watch television. The boys' uncontrolled desire threatens the family's patriarchal order. The father, Keitarō, tries to restore his authority by silencing their complaints: he tells them not to say "superfluous things" (*yokeina koto*). To this, Minoru retorts that the adults always say superfluous things: greetings and pleasantries. The two boys prove the importance of "superfluous things" by refusing to talk for the next few days. With their silence, the Hayashis' communications with the neighbors break down, breeding suspicions about the mother's character in the neighbors' minds.

Throughout the film, the television disrupts communal norms. The neighbors who own a television work at a cabaret in Ikebukuro, Tokyo's bustling entertainment district. They are marked as "that kind of people" by the gossiping neighbors. Here television owners are pictured as operating outside of middle-class mores: wearing "Western nightgowns, even during the daytime" they bring the Western values of consumption and the promiscuity of Ikebukuro's nightlife into the everyday lives of the suburban middle-class community. By contrast, the homemaker characters are all dressed in kimono. By luring the boys outside of the home and into the streets—the boys go to the neighbor's house despite their parents' stern prohibitions and are later found watching television by the train station late at night—television is also represented as a corrupting force on family life. Television, the movie insists, is a dangerous force that defies family values and threatens the boundaries and security of the home.[32]

Meanwhile, at a nearby bar, Keitarō talks with a neighbor about his reluctance to embrace television. He says it is excess with no practical use, and it may even be harmful, making reference to the social critic Ōya Sōichi's famous warning that the television will turn Japan into a nation of idiots (*ichioku sō hakuchika*).[33] Keitarō has the means to purchase an exorbitantly expensive television set, but he cannot rationalize such a big purchase.[34] The real fear is perhaps not about turning into an idiot per se; it is more about undermining his patriarchal authority by desiring frivolous entertainments or superfluous things.

His authority is already threatened. The fact that his neighbor Tomizawa has retired from his office job and now sells appliances reminds Keitarō that he is close to his own retirement. With this realization, Keitarō is left alone in a room, brooding over the inevitable. The scene is reminiscent of the closing of *Tokyo Story* (*Tokyo monogatari*, 1953), in which the aging father sits alone in an empty house after his wife's death, facing his waning years. While both scenes portray the deep pathos of the declining patriarchy (Ryū Chishū plays both fathers), Keitarō manages to salvage his paternal authority through his ability to purchase a television.

When the two Hayashi boys return home at night (they have left home to avoid trouble), they find a television in a box. The children immediately regain their cheerful dispositions. The father is obviously just as excited, though he tries to hide his emotions. Unable to admit to his own desire, Keitarō needs his children's help. The television resolves his personal crisis and the Hayashis' communication breakdown. Furthermore, the family's neighborly gesture (the Hayashis purchase a set through Tomizawa) helps to restore their reputation, at least in the eyes of the direct beneficiaries, the Tomizawas.

Another neighbor, Mr. Haraguchi, who appears much younger than Keitarō, is more open about his own material desires. He candidly admits that he wants a set but cannot afford one. The two families—the Hayashis and the Haraguchis—are contrasted in interesting ways. The peace and order of the financially better-off Hayashis, as well as Keitarō's patriarchal authority, are all restored through the purchase of the "unnecessary thing." For the Haraguchis, however, the purchase of an appliance seems to cause more trouble than it can fix. The Haraguchis take a different approach to their first major appliance purchase: they make the mistake of buying one, a washing machine, on the basis of practical need. The film offers subtle signs that point to the differences between the two families. Mr. Haraguchi is able to articulate his own desire, probably because he has a lower stake in male authority as a *mukoyōshi*, a man who married into the Haraguchi family and took his wife's family name. Marginalized in his own family, he constantly tries to quell the bickering between his mother-in-law and his wife. The decision to purchase a washer rather than a television appears to have come from his disgruntled wife, Kikue. From a male perspective, it is a selfish purchase from which she alone benefits. Manufacturers initially had to battle against the idea that washing machines were only for lazy homemakers.[35] A symptom of her pragmatic and selfish motives, the washing machine will never relieve her of the familial duties from which she tries to escape.

The film offers self-reflective commentaries on the director's penchant to pay attention to seemingly superfluous quotidian objects. The circulation of insignificant things, a process into which television fits readily, sustains the rhythm of everyday living. Ozu's tongue-in-cheek perspective is obvious when the Hayashis unintentionally enact the popular television game show *Charades* (*Jesuchaa* [gesture]) as the boys try to communicate what they need with gestures alone (NHK ran the show weekly from 1953 to 1968).[36] Televisual space has already been realized in the Hayashi household even before the set's arrival. Perhaps *Good Morning* was the director's magnanimous gesture to the new medium, whose growth had steadily eroded the financial basis of the film industry: although it might appear menacing at first, television would soon blend into quotidian life, while enhancing neighborly communication.[37] (Ozu's untimely death in 1963 at the age of sixty spared him from witnessing television's decimation of the Japanese film industry.)[38]

Unlike other appliances, television opens the domestic space of the family to the outside world. It is entirely conceivable that the neighbors will be invited to watch television shows at the Hayashis, and that neighborhood boys will hang out at their house to watch sumo wrestling on the television. But this temporary openness will no doubt soon end, as the neighbors rush to purchase their own sets, with the excuse that they want to stop their children from constantly bothering the Hayashis.

Real-life testimonies reveal that even families with limited financial resources were pressured to buy a set in order to avoid awkward social situations with their neighbors.[39] In the book *Terebi: Jinsei dokuhon* (Television: Life stories), for instance, a man recounts his bittersweet experience of 1960 and 1961 from the vantage point of the economically comfortable 1980s.[40] Because of an injury suffered in the Asia Pacific War, his father was unable to adequately provide for the family. Exasperated by the fact that his two youngest sons (the writer's younger brothers) kept going to wealthy neighbors' houses to watch television despite his scolding, he took his frustration out on his wife by beating her. The young children's strong desire for television undermined the traditional boundaries that used to contain the poor and the wealthy in separate life spheres, exposing their family's poverty to outsiders. Their father's embarrassment and agony over their poverty would have been much less prominent if not for the children's defiant pursuit of television viewing.[41] A tiny second-hand television that the father subsequently brought home was a relief to everybody in the family. Through the purchase, the father reestablished his parental authority, and the poor family stood equal to wealthier ones in this respect. Television ownership signaled that a whole family (not just their curious children) had made it into the newly emerging socioeconomic space.

The economist Yoshikawa Hiroshi discusses fascinating statistics on rates of television ownership from February 1966. Ownership rates for durable goods—with the exception of black-and-white televisions—roughly corresponded with household income levels (figure 2.4). In the lowest annual income bracket of less than ¥300,000 ($833.33), only 14.8 percent of households owned a vacuum cleaner. In the highest income bracket of ¥1,500,000 and beyond, 84.2 percent owned one. The ratios for refrigerator ownership were 27.0 and 94.9 percent for the respective brackets. Regardless of income level, however, the television ownership rate was extremely high. Even in the lowest income bracket, almost 80 percent of households owned a set.[42]

*Good Morning* carefully lays out the socioeconomic tensions that underlie middle-class life in suburban Tokyo. These tensions are in turn accentuated

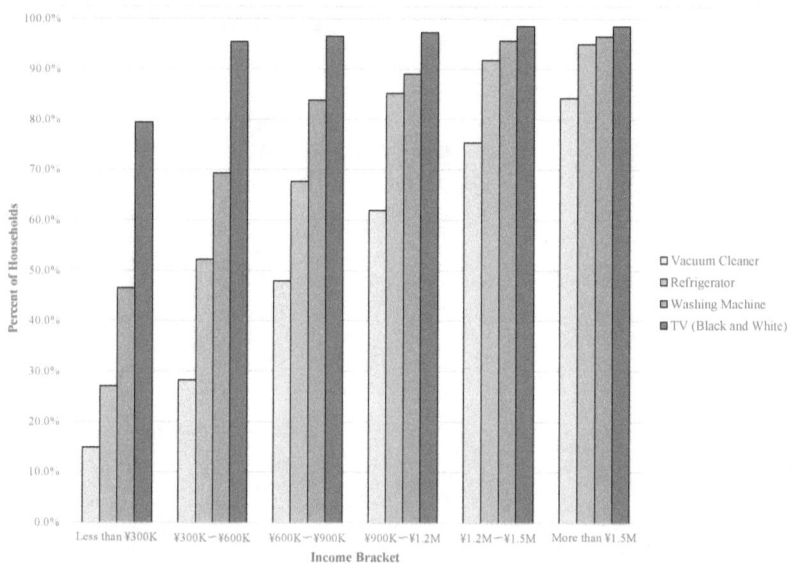

*Figure 2.4* Ownership rates for durable goods by income level (February 1966). Keizai kikakuchō, *Shōhi to chochiku no dōkō, Shōwa 41 nendo ban* (Tokyo: Ōkurashō insatsukyoku, 1966), 75–77.

by the introduction of new commodities. After experiencing short-term turmoil, the families regain equilibrium as the new commodities find their places in the respective households. Through the film's seemingly happy ending, the television is shown to have social benefits rather than simply feeding individual desire. The film's final image of the television, however, suggests Ozu's continued uneasiness with television's power: sitting in the hallway still in its shipping box, it is not yet fully invited into the family's living space or its potential unveiled (figure 2.5). In 1959 when the movie was made, television was still a Pandora's box of sorts. Its meaning was hidden: Would it release chaos and disruption or access to a better future? By 1972 that meaning would become clear: it would be the foundation of family life. The underlying message of *Good Morning* directly contradicts the sociologist Yoshimi Shunya's claim that television was never seen as an "alien object invading the enclosed space of the family." The film's ending, however, supports Yoshimi's ancillary observation that television viewing created and maintained intimate family time.[43] Television dramas and comedies not only brought families

*Figure 2.5* Minoru smiles at the television. *Good Morning* (*Ohayō*), dir. Ozu Yasujirō, 1959.

together but offered models to emulate in real life. Internalizing the gaze of television, viewers remade their private sphere into its public image.

### "The TV Boy" (1965)

Mizuki Shigeru's (1922–2015) award-winning short manga piece "The TV Boy" (Terebi-kun) illustrates television's instrumental role in propagating consumer society and its homogenizing effects. While Ozu's *Good Morning* ventriloquizes the Japanese film industry's suspicion toward television, Mizuki's work offers mostly a kinder view on the new medium's effects on its viewers.

A fantastic tale told once again from a child's perspective, the story revolves around a TV boy who can move in and out of the television screen (figure 2.6). Inside the television, TV Boy inhabits commercials where he eats the food they advertise: chocolate, cake, shaved ice, even sake (*MS* 58:6–12). He is the sign of voracious consumption. Having found a clue as

*Figure 2.6* "The TV Boy," title page. *MS* 58:5.

to how to slip into the television, while staring at it intensely, he is also a sign of television's role in absorbing viewers into consumer society. Only visible to child viewers, TV Boy serves as a model for the younger generation, visualizing the ways in which television will absorb and literally consume them. (TV Boy is also visible to television insiders—a television executive, production crews, and sponsors—and they are happy when he appears on the screen because the advertised products sell better.)

TV Boy also shows the leveling effects of this new medium. Wandering through Japan with his TV set in hand, he helps disadvantaged children who lack economic means. Santa, one such child, lacks not only economic stability—his father is dead and his mother is sick—but also a television (*MS* 58:15, 22). TV Boy appears as a real-life figure and gifts advertised merchandise to Santa, giving him the means to support himself (a bicycle for his paper route, clothing items for himself, and medicine for his mother), as well as a small transistor television (*MS* 58:22–23). TV Boy's benevolent largesse transforms Santa from an outsider of consumer culture to an insider—Santa not only possesses consumer goods including the television set but is also made to feel special because he now shares TV Boy's secret. Television is the agent that brings Santa into the circle of the high-growth economy. His intimate relationship with this new medium signals television's hold over even the most marginalized in society. Like the rural girl in the Dorobu documentary, who imagines television as a life-giving sun and all-consuming love, Santa learns to find his place in society through television's interactive lens.

Mizuki himself was perhaps the biggest beneficiary of TV Boy's benevolence. This publication in a major manga magazine—the quarterly version of *Shōnen magajin*—was a huge break for the starving manga artist, who was still clinging to the dying rental book market in the early 1960s.[44] To cater to the juvenile audience, he modified his artistic style, replacing his signature dark, grisly, and uncanny images with clean, genial, and humorous drawings.[45] Yet Mizuki effectively uncovered the fantastic quality of the television medium, capturing his young readers' imagination. For that, he received the sixth Kōdansha Jidō Manga-shō (Kodansha children's manga award) and subsequently became a regular contributor to weekly manga magazines, which paid more than ten times as much as rental book publishers (MS 102: 557). In 1966 *Akuma-kun* (The Devil Boy) was aired as a live-action television drama. Two years later, *Gegege no Kitarō* (Kitaro) was made into a successful television animation series.[46] As his characters began inhabiting both weekly magazines and television screens, Mizuki permanently escaped the dire poverty he had endured in the first twenty years of his career.

"The TV Boy" ends in an unexpectedly somber mood. In the final frame, Santa still wears his patched shirt and shorts and continues to cover his newspaper route on foot (MS 58:36). While the secret knowledge about TV Boy's true identity buoys Santa's spirit, TV Boy's gifts have not transformed his everyday life. The wonderful world of television remains unreachable to Santa, while the print media literally continues to support his marginal life. The boy's physical labor contrasts to TV Boy's easy way of life. Santa delivers evening papers with his back turned to the reader, running toward the darkness. "The TV Boy" expresses his desire to remain a while longer in the poverty-stricken yet familiar life that he has led at the margins of print culture. With the success of "The TV Boy," however, Mizuki was thrust into the new media space, in which the print media co-evolved with early television.

# Voyeurs Are Us: Television, Weeklies, and the Community of Gossip

Regardless of economic class or place of residence, people from all walks of life could easily access an identical set of information through television. Visual information had great leveling effects on postwar Japanese society. Yet as the aforementioned examples of early encounters demonstrate, television did more than merely convey information. The visual as well as affective experiences that the new media brought to the private space of households demanded a radical redefinition of each individual's relations with society. Rather than passively accept what was offered through television, viewers actively projected their personal feelings and emotions onto the screen.

In a 1968 essay, the literary scholar Muramatsu Takeshi (1929–1994) expresses his anxieties about television's ability to rip individuals from the private sphere:

> It is now common to talk about the dignity of individuals. The hideouts that protected the dignity of individuals used to be homes, the space for private life. There used to be an invisible curtain between private life and the public. The picture tube burst open the borders, so to speak. The viewers believe they are just receiving information and knowledge from outside. But this convenient apparatus will eventually suck individuals into the public.[47]

For Muramatsu, watching television was not an innocuous activity. Traditional Japanese homes were not known as the "space for private life" as Muramatsu suggests (such an association was probably new, emerging contemporaneously with Japan's new middle class). The more central claim is that the relationship between "private life and the public" completely changed with the arrival of television. The new media relentlessly exposed an inner sanctum, and individuals, in response, anxiously searched for a stable identity in the face of the medium's powerful gaze.

Addressing Muramatsu's anxiety-ridden response to television, I would like to add another layer of inquiry: the weekly magazines, whose proliferation in the 1950s and early 1960s directly resulted from the development of television. The weeklies fed on television's voyeuristic characteristics, which boosted viewers' desire to share others' secrets. By converting personal information into a social commodity, the nexus of television and the weeklies mercilessly destabilized the traditional boundaries between the private and public realms.

Television dominated in the task of delivering information, but as television sets became gradually more affordable, weekly magazines also gained mass circulation.[48] The first two weeklies catering to a mass readership, *Shūkan asahi* (Weekly Asahi) and *Sandei mainichi* (Sunday Mainichi), were inaugurated in 1922, at the dawn of urban consumer society in Japan. Monthly magazines, however, continued to dominate the periodicals market until the 1950s, when *Weekly Asahi* and *Sunday Mainichi* dramatically increased their circulations, paralleling the drastic increase in television viewers. *Weekly Asahi*'s circulation peaked at 1.5 million in 1958, the largest ever for a newsweekly.[49] New weeklies were introduced to capture the growing market.[50] In the decade after 1956, more than fifty weeklies were introduced to the market.[51] In 1959 alone, twenty new weeklies were launched, including the two manga weeklies, *Shūkan shōnen sandei* (Weekly Shonen Sunday) and *Shūkan shōnen magajin* (*Weekly Shonen Magazine*), both of which would later boast circulations in the multimillions.[52] That year the weeklies' total circulation surpassed the monthlies' for the first time.[53]

Curating news stories with a defined editorial focus and, often, strong narratives delivered in a user-friendly format, weeklies helped their readers to navigate an ever-expanding flow of information, to which television massively contributed.[54] A symbiotic relationship between television and the weekly magazines propelled their contemporaneous rises in postwar Japan. The two media facilitated the production of the new national space by fashioning a sense of familiarity—particularly through exposing the lives of celebrities to the public gaze. As demonstrated in Dorobu, television reduced the distance between the scenes on and in front of the screen, making whatever appeared on television common elements of viewers' everyday lives. The sociologist Katō Hidetoshi explains the difference between television and cinema: "In a movie theater, the audience is forced to identify with the images on the screen. There, it is acceptable to have images that have little to do with the audience's everyday life. However, in watching television, the audience assimilates the images on the screen. There, materials that have little to do with everyday life are avoided."[55] Television viewers were interested in learning about the actual personal lives of television stars, whereas film audiences showed more fascination with the characters that the stars played.

A parallel change occurred in Japanese print media with the rise of the weeklies. The monthly *Heibon*, which ruled celebrity reporting in the earlier postwar years, always offered larger-than-life images of the stars. They were all beautiful, wearing impeccable smiles.[56] By contrast, the new weeklies catered to readers' desire to learn about celebrities' private lives, just as they enjoyed gossiping about neighbors.[57] *Shūkan heibon* (Weekly Heibon), first issued in 1959 by the publisher of the monthly *Heibon*, exemplifies this approach. The weekly was "a gossip magazine," according to Amakasu Akira (1929–2013), a member of its editorial staff in the early years. In an interview, Amakasu recollects that the weekly's chief editor made a clear distinction between the two publications: "The difference is that monthly *Heibon* establishes extremely close relationships with the stars. By establishing close and individual relationships, we will be allowed to take unique photos. On the other hand, *Weekly Heibon* also needs to write things that the celebrities would dislike." Some celebrities did indeed reject photo shoots with the monthly *Heibon* because *Weekly Heibon* printed gossip about them.[58] Similarly, the first chief editor of *Josei jishin* (Women's self), Kurosaki Isao, confirmed his weekly's focus on celebrities' private lives with his instruction to his staff not to take beautiful pictures of actresses. He directed them instead to cater to the readers' desire to see them "without make-up, in their everyday activities." Kurosaki went so far as to instruct a cameraman leaving for a photo shoot with Yamamoto Fujiko, a former Miss Japan turned actress, "not to take ordinary pictures, but capture the moments when she is unconscious of the camera, like when she is peeing."[59] To appeal to the new audience, Kurosaki's crass advice insists, weeklies must embody the ubiquitous voyeuristic gaze.

Television brought celebrities into viewers' living rooms, and simultaneously consuming the weeklies' candid images of celebrities in the private domestic space helped to foster a sense of familiarity toward them.[60] The weekly magazines complemented television by telling stories about the stars' lives off the screen. It is noteworthy that *Weekly Heibon* was introduced into the market with the catchphrase "An entertainment magazine for a living room furnished with a television set."[61] Those in charge of marketing the new weekly were keenly aware of the supplemental role it would play in relation to television. By packaging the private lives of celebrities in consumable and often familiar narrative forms, the weeklies augmented television's ability to market its stars. Celebrities were turned into safe objects of gossip, whose circulation was largely regulated by the media of television and weeklies.[62] To be in the know meant, in this case, to be part of the virtual community that consumed this prepackaged information. To maintain this community, these media constantly needed new celebrities who could provide fresh gossip to their audiences.

## The Royal Wedding of 1959

Arguably the biggest celebrity in the early years of Japanese television and weeklies was Shōda Michiko (b. 1934), who married Crown Prince Akihito (b. 1933) in April 1959. Television and weeklies reported extensively on the couple's courtship and engagement, which they billed the "romance of the century," while more established monthly magazines accorded the relationship hardly any coverage.[63] Although she came from a wealthy family, Michiko was still the first "commoner" to marry into the imperial family in its centuries-long history. Weeklies immediately published personal information about her, including her bust, waist, and hip measurements.[64] The political theorist Matsushita Kei'ichi compared the aggressive media exposure to a striptease: while it helped turn Akihito's fiancée into a celebrity, it "violated her human rights."[65] Many were eager to consume images of the "commoner" princess, whom they saw as one of their own. Michiko also became a fashion icon for young women and retailers. In a nation where economic conditions were visibly improving each year, the private life of Princess Michiko became a symbol of national optimism.

Three television networks competed with one another to cover the royal wedding parade on April 10, 1959, mobilizing four helicopters, 108 television cameras, and more than 1,500 staff members.[66] At key points along the five-and-a-half-mile-long parade route, tracks for television cameras were laid to follow the horse-drawn royal carriage. Their combined distance was nearly a mile. It is estimated that about fifteen million people watched the parade on television, while a half million people lined the streets.[67] According to an interview survey conducted by the Newspaper Research Center at the University of Tokyo, only 17.1 percent of the interviewees answered that at least one household member went to see the parade in person, though they all lived close to the parade route.[68] Many actually preferred to watch the event on television, not only to avoid the crowd but also to access television's extensive coverage—as opposed to hours of waiting for a few seconds of viewing the carriage. The average viewing time for the surveyed households was as many as ten hours and thirty-five minutes.[69]

It has been widely claimed that many families purchased a television set for the royal wedding, and that the weeklies simultaneously expanded their circulations by aggressively covering the royal couple.[70] One weekly paid a high price for underestimating the national obsession. Although the first issue of *Women's Self* was published shortly after the announcement of the royal engagement, editor Kurosaki Isao did not dare to cover the royal couple. As a result, fewer than half of the inaugural issue's copies were sold, despite the newly minted weekly's novelty factor.[71] From the second issue on, *Women's Self* zealously covered the royal couple—so zealously that other weekly journalists teasingly called it *kōshitsu jishin* (the imperial household's self).[72] Another magazine, *Shūkan bunshun* (Weekly Bunshun), made its investment in the royal wedding clear at its inception by running a full-page advertisement in newspapers: "The day after tomorrow is the crown prince's wedding. Today *Weekly Bunshun* goes on sale."[73] The weekly appeared to have completely merged with the object of its coverage.

If television was a source of light—"like love"—to the wide-eyed Dorobu child, weeklies illuminated the underside of love, where envy and jealousy emerge from the shadows. Not all coverage of the royal courtship and wedding was glowing with compliments: some weeklies amplified voices that expressed doubts and even complaints about the glorified images of the royal marriage.[74] Michiko was not uniformly welcomed into the inner circle of the present and former royal or aristocratic families. Matsushita Kei'ichi argues, however, that exposés and gossip about the imperial family would have been detrimental to the divine image of the traditional imperial institution but actually helped to popularize the postwar concept of the people's emperor (*taishū tennōsei*).[75] Thanks in no small part to the weeklies' coverage, Akihito and Michiko became celebrities of the television age, familiar figures that the masses could easily relate to.

# The Emperors' New Clothes

Sexuality is also an essential ingredient of gossip, but that subject was screened out of early television coverage and left for weeklies to explore liberally in their behind-the-scenes stories.[76] From the beginning, television and weekly magazines complemented each other, offering the most intimate and personal aspects of life as a form of entertainment. The disturbing effects of this interaction were not fully revealed until the 1970s.

Their symbiotic relationship deepened as their coverage grew more aggressive. We can see the culmination of this trend in a one-hour program called *Television Scandal News: Weekender* (*Terebi sanmenkiji: Wiikuendaa*) that Nippon Television introduced in 1975. This low-budget program translated gossip weeklies into a television format, with the reporters offering sensationalized accounts of sexual crimes and scandals.[77] Despite public outcry over its crude and sexualized content, the program consistently scored high ratings in its nine years of existence.

The media scholar Fujitake Akira's analysis of exposé weeklies and television, made from the vantage point of the mid-1980s, offers insight into the effects of this new media environment on Japanese society. The introduction of new photo exposé weeklies in the 1980s seemed to take voyeuristic coverage to new extremes.[78] Fujitake laments the vulnerability of people exposed to the media gaze. Expanding on Marshall McLuhan's characterization of photographs as "the brothel-without-walls," Fujitake compares these media to a peep show with a one-way mirror, where the voyeur enjoys his view in privacy without being seen himself.[79] In McLuhan's words, the camera fixes "people in a superior stare, as if they were objects." He discusses the photograph in sexualized terms: "The photograph extends and multiplies the human image to the proportions of mass-produced merchandise. The movie stars and matinee idols are put in the public domain by photography. They become dreams that money can buy. They can be bought and hugged and thumbed more easily than public prostitutes."[80] Claiming that "mass-produced merchandise has always made some people uneasy in its prostituted aspect," McLuhan explains their discomfort as anxiety over the sexualized object of "mass-produced merchandise," whose promiscuity threatens to transgress proper social boundaries, as seen in the middle-class anxieties Ozu revealed in *Good Morning*.[81]

The most sexually appealing product is the secrets of others, especially those hidden in their bedrooms. Television and the weeklies allow the masses to consume extraordinary events as bystanders while staying within the safe boundaries of their everyday lives. This sense of security lets them assume a superior position in relation to events. Being free to comment however they want on whatever events they choose, they can even express empathy toward those who were actually affected by the events.[82] The virtual community of gossip is maintained at the expense of those others, whose private lives are relentlessly exposed to the ubiquitous gaze of the camera. Fujitake finds the media's invasive gaze deeply disturbing to the social and political order of postwar Japan. The voyeuristic gaze mercilessly pursues its targets to quench the insatiable desire to consume the secrets of others. Fujitake insists that a society that feasts on its members' secrets paradoxically allows nobody to have secrets. The tension that used to exist between the two opposing desires of keeping and exposing secrets dissolves in the face of aggressive media coverage, leaving individuals' interior selves unprotected. Insofar as the voyeur focuses his gaze on celebrities' private lives, he can maintain the fiction that he would not be subjected to a similar gaze. The voyeuristic gaze of the new media (internalized by each person) refuses to honor such a fiction and constantly threatens to uncover people's inner lives. Completely exposed in the middle of the visual field, each individual feels deep anxiety over the loss of his or her inner realm.[83]

Theorizing the voyeuristic gaze of television and exposé weeklies leads Fujitake Akira to a gloomy conclusion about Japanese society in the 1980s, whose members, he claims, suffered from a sense of powerlessness in the face of media's ubiquitous presence. It is possible to see democratic potential in this development: the masses expanded their egos in proportion to the growth in media coverage. In exchange, however, they internalized the media's gaze, which does not recognize the boundaries of individuals. In an often-cited episode of Jean-Paul Sartre's *Being and Nothingness*, a solipsistic voyeur is caught in a tangled web of social relations the moment he discovers that somebody is watching him. Similarly, television viewers lose their transcendence as omnipotent seers once they sense that their gaze is reciprocated.[84] Sartre's episode insists that the gaze always contains a countergaze, which necessarily complicates the seeing agent's relation to the world. While the French philosopher comments on the general state of subjectivity in the visual field and ultimately in the

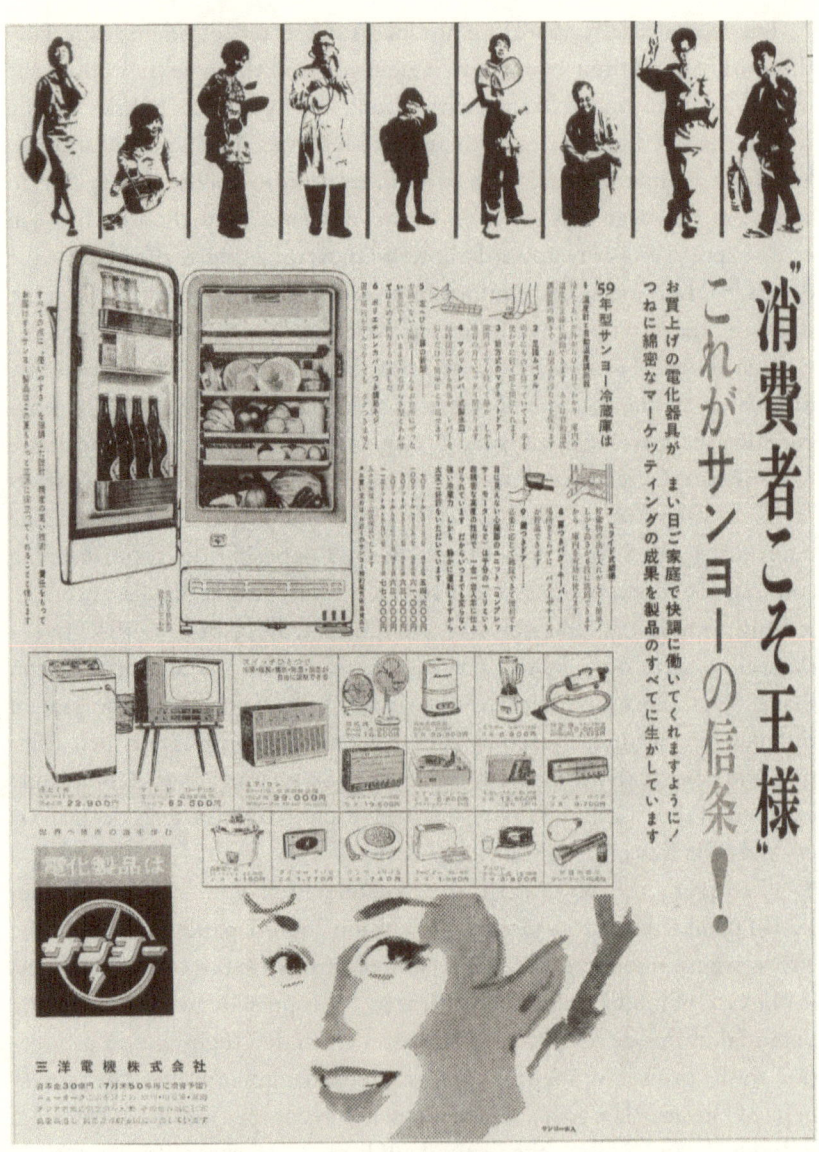

*Figure 2.7* Sanyō advertisement: "Consumers are the King. That's Sanyo's motto." The woman at the bottom of the image, called "Mrs. Sanyo," was intended to feminize the company's image. *Asahi shinbun*, June 7, 1959.

field of bodily senses, Fujitake is primarily concerned about the degree to which individual beings have come to be mediated through the modern technology of seeing.

The disturbing developments of the 1980s that Fujitake analyzes were already underway in Japan in the high-growth era, albeit ensconced in a more optimistic outlook. It was genuinely exciting then to acquire a new way of seeing and to be part of a visual field as expansive as the nation. The optimism was replaced with anxiety as the initial exhilaration quickly wore off and the whole experience grew mundane. At first in Dorobu, the television was the source of light that illuminated the dark countryside. To the farmers that Miyamoto Tsuneichi's students interviewed, however, the television exposed the darkness in their inner living sphere to the outside world. The gaze returned by television (complemented by the weeklies) transformed the inner sanctum of home into the "brothel-without-walls" where consumers were treated like sovereigns—who were nonetheless in a constant search for a new fig leaf, commodities, behind which to hide their naked selves. A Sanyō advertisement in 1959 lionized consumers as kings but insisted that their kingdoms had to be filled with modern appliances (figure 2.7).

## The Happiness Race

The excitement and anxiety associated with modern living were perhaps most visible in the concrete structure of danchi (defined as "a cluster of living units constructed according to a planned layout"), where families enjoyed the amenities afforded by the high-growth economy.[85] Those who were caught up in the frenzy of mass consumerism were not necessarily unhappy to perform for the ubiquitous gaze, according to the literary critic Akiyama Shun (1930–2013). In 1959 he moved to Hibarigaoka danchi in a Tokyo suburb, where he witnessed the ways in which material possessions became the signs of suburban happiness. The modern, highly standardized units of danchi were coveted living spaces for many during the high-growth era: The danchi residents were, in Tada Michitarō's (1924–2007) words, the "vanguard" of the nation's aspiring middle-class.[86] In September of that year, Crown Prince Akihito and Princess Michiko came to visit Akiyama's housing complex before they left for a U.S. tour, adding to the allure of danchi living (figure 2.8). The political scientist Hara Takeshi (b. 1962),

*Figure 2.8* Crown Prince Akihito and Princess Michiko visit Hibarigaoka danchi, September 6, 1960. Courtesy of Mainichi Newspapers.

who grew up in two different danchi complexes in Tokyo (he spent the first three years of his life in Hibarigaoka danchi), recalls the pride he took in his residence as a child: "Living in a danchi apartment was the most advanced lifestyle of the time." His pride was also anchored in a sense of security: the reinforced concrete structure would withstand fires and earthquakes.[87]

Akiyama saw different and less pleasant aspects of danchi living. He was most struck by the lack of privacy. He was guilty of trying to peep into the neighbors' apartments with a telescope, he confides, but he soon realized that everything was so predictably similar that there was no need to pry:

> I never thought human life could take such an undifferentiated form. One living pattern visible through the windows would probably apply to the other 23 units in the exact same way. First I hear the sound of water, and then see somebody move and open windows. The noises that the children make come next, and then a meal starts. These daily rituals continue with cleaning, grocery shopping, and family time in the evening. Even the locations of a table and a washing machine

in the apartments do not deviate the slightest bit. There would be no more boring show than 24 sets of very similar humans displaying very similar life scenes.[88]

What to many was a desirable environment proved to be a dystopic space to Akiyama. There were no interstices where one could hide secrets. Fujitake's alarmist vision of Japanese society in the 1980s seems to have been realized years earlier in the danchi.

Amid the suffocating uniformity of the danchi, residents found materialistic ways to one-up each other in order to differentiate themselves. Akiyama was a bystander to the "happiness race" (*shiawase kyōsō*) in which his neighbors engaged. The eight families on his floor competed by constantly purchasing the latest model of consumer goods. Children scouted each apartment unit to see which neighbors had bought new appliances. These little informers were probably redundant: television and other media already provided a plethora of information about what one must acquire next in order to stay ahead of one's real or imagined neighbors.[89] Akiyama and his wife did not own a television and had no desire to participate in the competition, but he had to feed some plausible excuses to the meddlesome neighborhood children, who could not fathom why anybody would not want to watch television.

Just as they showed off their new cars, which were always of slightly better quality than their neighbors', the adult family members even competed over how often they copulated.[90] What Akiyama witnessed was not all that different from what was taking place throughout the nation in the early phase of the high-growth economy.[91] Male workers' masculine identity was recuperated through their efforts in building happy family lives. Their absence from family life, stemming from long hours of work and commuting, was compensated for with the objects that tangibly demonstrated their worth. Sexual acts were perhaps just further proof of virility, a reminder that their labor was essential in starting the nuclear family. A more pessimistic observer would claim that even sex—the most private human act—had come to be regimented like work. As Akiyama's anecdote intimates, millions more male householders eagerly performed family happiness (besides consuming the images of happy families showcased in television dramas and the royal wedding) before the eyes of their immediate neighbors as well as the imagined audience in the newly emerging national space of consumption.[92]

As Hara Takeshi's comparative studies demonstrate, there were characteristics that distinguished danchi from the rest of Japan. Danchi residents, for example, tended to be more politically progressive than people in more traditional dwelling types.[93] Political activism also differed in degree and nature among the new housing complexes, reflecting the issues the residents faced.[94] Furthermore, danchi evolved to cater to different needs as the nation finally caught up with its housing shortage in the early 1970s.[95] Yet throughout the high-growth era, everyday living in danchi most vividly displayed what was actually going on inside the giant blender, to return to Murakami's simile (see chapter 1). In the early years of the high-growth era, danchi life embodied the cutting edge of modern living in Japan. Japan's new media and physical environments were like catalysts that accelerated the reaction motivated by the participants' desires and anxiety.

The shiny image of the happy family, however, was already beginning to tarnish in the 1960s. According to the narrative disseminated through the popular media, adult male residents of danchi were not terribly successful in proving their masculine identity. Overworked and sleep-deprived, they could not sexually satisfy their wives. Meanwhile, cooped up in small concrete boxes with little money at their disposal, housewives were fantasizing, engaging in extramarital affairs, or even participating in prostitution rings. The life created by the high-growth economy affected both men and women, but their deep-seated anxieties about the new environment were sexualized and articulated through the deviant sexuality of danchi wives.[96] Tapping into this popular narrative, Nikkatsu released *Danchi Wife: Affairs in the Early Afternoon* (*Danchi zuma: Hirusagai no jōji*) in 1971, as its first "roman poruno," a low-budget softcore pornographic film. In it, a housewife living in a danchi apartment invites her demise when she engages in an illicit affair and then prostitution. The film expresses male fears of something subversive beneath the beautiful façade of everyday life—represented by insatiable female desire. Yet male viewers may also have desired a disastrous outcome that could effectively implode the rigidity of modern living. Even though a woman was cast as a main character in *Danchi Wife*, threatened masculinity looms large as the real subject of the drama.

This chapter has traced the development of Japan's mass consumer society, with the focus on changes in everyday life. It was an exciting and also an anxiety-ridden process to be part of the national drama of the high-growth economy. Over the course of the postwar period, television came to infiltrate everyday life and change the way people saw themselves in relation to society. No one escaped its gaze. Rural and urban, working and middle classes all formed themselves through its images. Its screen became a site of self-reflection that enabled Japanese people to assimilate themselves into a newly emerging mass social space.

In the following chapters we will turn our attention to the popular media's strong concerns about masculinity during the high-growth era. This excessive focus on male identity is partly a function of the fact that the men who dominated the Japanese media dictated what was to be represented in the media space. But another attendant factor was that the changes during the high-growth era strengthened gender roles in Japanese society. A rigidly gendered paradigm dictated the terms: men were burdened not only with the responsibility to provide for their families but also with a critical responsibility in society. The rest of the book will examine products of the popular imagination that revolved around men and their anxieties—not to reinscribe the gender divide but to demonstrate the enormous efforts that went into buttressing their masculine images in the face of the society's radical transformation.

In the next chapter the focus turns from television to movies, as we explore Yamada Yōji's efforts to imagine an alternative to the regime of the high-growth economy. Yamada, best known for the long-running series *It's Tough Being a Man*, directed two critical films in the early 1970s that highlight the precarious ground on which ordinary men and their families stood. Chapter 3 analyzes this precarity in detail, demonstrating that in this era of high growth, it could indeed be tough to be a man.

## PART TWO
## Travel

CHAPTER III

## Japan on the Move, a Family on the Run

*Yamada Yōji's Countervision of Contemporary Japan*

> What is this big thing? Everybody tells you that you can't beat the flow of the age or the big thing. What is this big thing? Why can't I beat the big thing? Why can't I continue this job of rock ferrying with you on the sea I love?
> —SEI'ICHI IN *HOME FROM THE SEA (KOKYŌ)*, 1972

> This past November [1972], I was attending a symposium about video.... While all the attendees were talking about the usefulness of video, I suddenly recalled that a family in Hokkaido abandoned the land that they had reclaimed and cultivated for some ten years and moved elsewhere just because they could not watch television there.
> —KONNO TSUTOMU, "THE DAWN OF MEDIA ECOLOGY"
> (MEDIA SEITAIGAKU KOTOHAJIME), 1972

In two films from the early 1970s, *Where Spring Comes Late* (*Kazoku*, 1970) and *Home from the Sea* (*Kokyō*, 1972), the director Yamada Yōji (b. 1931) both criticized a society that pursued economic development at all costs and paid homage to ways of life that were fast disappearing at the margins of that society. Read against the decline of the Japanese film industry, the films also reveal Yamada's own anxiety as a filmmaker facing a paradigmatic shift. *Where Spring Comes Late* deploys audiovisual techniques associated with documentary filmmaking to defamiliarize everyday life under the high-growth regime while striving to make audiences see Japanese society from the perspective of a marginalized family. At this point Yamada was still able to envisage a happy end to the drama: the family gains the chance of a new life in Hokkaido, in Japan's geographic periphery.

Two short years later, however, Yamada seems to have abandoned optimism in the face of Japanese society's fundamental transformation. One of his characters in *Home from the Sea*, Sei'ichi, ponders "the big thing" that has forced him and his family to abandon their way of life. He speaks to the sense of injustice in contemporary society that Yamada himself feels.

While the populace's optimism for Japan's economic future was still running high, Yamada delivered a somber assessment of what economic changes would actually entail. By paying detailed documentary attention to a family's way of life, the film acknowledges its inevitable loss. The camera focuses on the family's everyday life, which is about to change irrevocably. The alluring images on the screen, however, resemble those of contemporary tourism campaigns that aestheticized everyday lives at Japan's geographic margins. With his career as a filmmaker secure thanks to the continuing success of the series *It's Tough Being a Man*, Yamada was able to afford to mourn the dissolution of the traditional lifestyle.

*Where Spring Comes Late* is the primary subject of this chapter. In it, Yamada is bitter but still buoyant. The film is a testimony to his personal struggle to maintain a critical and creative stance as he faced radical changes in the film industry and Japanese society more broadly. *Home from the Sea*, discussed in the chapter's final section, shows a less hopeful Yamada settling for more realistic visions of contemporary Japan.

### Iōjima: Paradise Lost

In *Where Spring Comes Late*, the patriarch of a family experiences an identity crisis when faced with the bleak prospect of abandoning his job in a coal mine and seeking employment outside his small island near Nagasaki. The protagonist, Kazami Sei'ichi (thirty-five years old, as revealed by a synopsis that Yamada submitted to Shōchiku Studios), decides to maintain his autonomy by relocating his family to a dairy farm that his friend runs in Hokkaido.[1] The family's exodus is a symbolic declaration of war against the regime of the high-growth economy, which already has broken the independent spirits of many others. The film chronicles their five-day railway journey to Hokkaido and their initial reaction to life at the farm (map 3.1 and table 3.1). Despite its happy ending—Sei'ichi grows confident that he has made the right decision after all—the film largely portrays the challenges that the family faces in the new economy. To reach their dream destination, the family must first traverse hostile territories that celebrate unprecedented economic prosperity.[2]

The opening scene establishes the Kazamis' marginal identity in Japanese society: they are Catholic, part of a religious minority who endured severe persecutions in early modern Japan.[3] The film opens with the sound

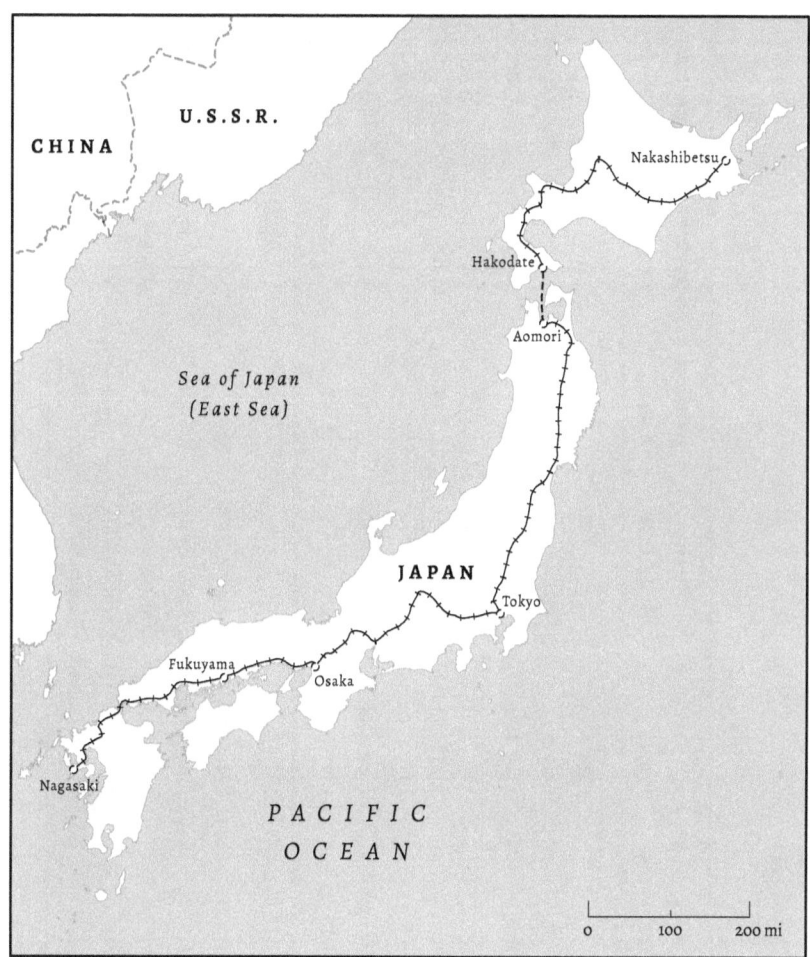

*Map 3.1* The Kazamis' 3,000-km journey.

of a church bell and the image of a small seaside church. Sei'ichi's wife, Tamiko, walks through a rice paddy adjacent to the church toward their house. The camera captures Sei'ichi's father, Genzō, paying his final visit to a hilltop graveyard, filled with upright grave markers with small crosses on top. These symbols of Catholicism signal the historical connections of the Kazamis to their land and community as well as the devastating power of economic changes: even the strong communal bonds cannot withstand the forces of economic development. Yet the film also intimates that Sei'ichi's religious identity is connected to his independent streak.

TABLE 3.1
The Kazamis' six-day itinerary

| Originating Point | Destination | | Train Name | Date | Train Schedule | Duration (hours) | Distance (km) | Cumulative Distance (km) |
|---|---|---|---|---|---|---|---|---|
| Iōjima | Nagasaki Port | Ferry | | Day 1 (4/6) | | | 12.6 | 12.6 |
| Ōsugami | Nagasaki Station | Tram | | Day 1 (4/6) | | 0:03 | 0.7 | 13.3 |
| Nagasaki | Kokura | Train | Inasa 2 | Day 1 (4/6) | 10:14–14:26 | 1:50 | 228.9 | 242.2 |
| Kokura | Fukuyama | Train | Hana | Day 1 (4/6) | 14:50–19:38 | 3:57 | 317.1 | 559.3 |
| Fukuyama | Osaka | Train | Tomo 2 | Day 1 (4/6) | 08:01–11:16 | 3:15 | 234.8 | 794.1 |
| Osaka | Shin-Osaka | Train | Loop line | Day 2 (4/7) | | 0:05 | 3.8 | 797.9 |
| Shin-Osaka | Tokyo | Train | Hikari 62 | Day 2 (4/7) | 16:05–19:16 | 3:11 | 552.6 | 1350.5 |
| Tokyo | Ueno | Train | Yamanote line | Day 2 (4/7) | | 0:07 | 3.6 | 1354.1 |
| Ueno | Aomori | Train | Towada | Day 4 (4/9) | 12:10–23:45 | 11:35 | 753.9 | 2108 |
| Aomori | Hakodate | Ferry | Seikan-renraku | Day 5 (4/10) | 00:05–03:55 | 3:50 | 113 | 2221 |
| Hakodate | Iwamizawa | Train | Local | Day 5 (4/10) | 08:10–18:20 | 10:10 | 321.6 | 2542.6 |
| Iwamizawa | Takigawa | Train | Local | Day 5 (4/10) | 18:52–19:41 | 0:49 | 54 | 2596.6 |
| Takigawa | Kushiro | Train | Local | Day 6 (4/11) | 00:30–09:31 | 9:01 | 311.4 | 2908 |
| Kushiro | Shibeccha | Train | Local | Day 6 (4/11) | 10:06–11:20 | 1:04 | 48.1 | 2956.1 |
| Shibeccha | Nakashibetsu | Train | Local | Day 6 (4/11) | 11:24–12:30 | 1:06 | 47.1 | 3003.2 |

The farewell scenes also establish that Iōjima's main source of employment is coal mining, an industry on the brink of extinction in the late 1960s under the high-growth economy.[4] Although domestic coal production supported modern Japan's heavy industry through the early postwar years, it faced competition from cheap imported oil in the years following the Korean War. As the coal industry tried to bolster overall productivity through mechanization, layoffs, and closure of unproductive mines, the unions strongly opposed these rationalization measures.[5] After the prolonged labor dispute at the Mitsui Coalmines in Kyushu ended with the union's defeat in 1960, coal mining came to be regarded as the epitome of industrial decline.[6] Left behind in a sector failing to adapt to the new economic environment, Sei'ichi has no part in the high-growth regime. (The mine on Iōjima was in fact closed in March 1972, seventeen months after the film's release.)[7]

Once the Kazamis are aboard the train, Yamada reveals through flashbacks the situation that forced them to move to Hokkaido. What is at stake in the drama is preserving Sei'ichi's male pride and independence from the encroaching corporate world. He is keenly aware that there is no future in the coal industry, but he is unwilling to seek employment in the nearby city of Nagasaki, as so many of his coworkers have done. His solution is to move to Hokaiddo, where he can own his own land, plan his own life, and work for himself. Bypassing the Japan that lives under the high-growth economy allows Sei'ichi to maintain his autonomy while providing for his family. Understandably, his rather fantastic plan creates tension with his wife, despite his assurances that they can count on assistance from a trailblazing friend who had left the island eight years before and established himself as a successful dairy farmer. Sei'ichi explodes in reaction to Tamiko's rational observation that there are plenty of jobs in Nagasaki, so there is no need to go all the way to Hokkaido: "A woman should not meddle with a man's business!" His male pride as a provider has been threatened by the rapidly changing industrial structure. In the end, Tamiko accepts her husband's plan as her own and agrees to relocate the entire family.

Sei'ichi's plan is actually less extreme than the decisions made by some actual coalminers and their families as they confronted the demise of the industry. In the 1950s and 1960s, thousands of families, including some from Iōjima, migrated to Latin America. The writer Ueno Eishin (1923–1987), who laboriously documented the lives of former coalminers and their families, reports a conversation with a young man who worked at the Iōjima coal mine until 1961. The youth, who was about to complete his agricultural training and leave for his destination abroad, confided to Ueno: "I had no other choices.... Japan, I never really had real connections with this country."[8] The Ministry of Foreign Affairs eagerly promoted emigration but neglected to provide long-term support to the emigrant communities in Latin America.[9] Many migrants were forced to clear thick vegetation without heavy machinery on land that was often too poor to grow crops, sometimes without easy access to water. Their agricultural endeavor devolved into a fight for survival. Some were also caught up in local political turmoil and were even subjected to looting by locals.[10] The explosive growth of Japan's economy in the 1960s, however, extended economic benefits even to the most disadvantaged in Japanese society, making migration to developing countries a less attractive proposition. (The government-subsidized emigration program ended in 1972.) Sei'ichi seeks independence from the high-growth regime, but his project is more a journey of self-discovery—albeit a challenging one—than a desperate effort to secure the family's survival.[11]

*Where Spring Comes Late* is best characterized as a "railroad" movie with a documentary aesthetic. The film takes place in the early stage of Japan's motorization, when car ownership was still a sign of privilege. In February 1970 only 22.1 percent of Japanese households owned a car.[12] Air travel, not yet widely available, remained prohibitively expensive. Although the Japan National Railways began to experience a yearly loss in the mid-1960s (it would raise fares in the mid-1970s to address, belatedly, its financial woes), its extensive national network was still the most cost-effective way to travel long distances. The Kazamis' class affiliation is thus visually underscored by their presence in train cars. Yet in exchange for the affordable fares, the family loses the freedom and flexibility that an automobile would have allowed. Sei'ichi and his family must work with rigid train schedules—the epitome of industrial rationalization—for several days before they reach their destination. To anchor the narrative in the social reality of Japan in 1970, the nearly forty members of the film's crew and cast actually traveled a total distance of more than 11,000 km (6,875 miles) for about three months, far beyond the distance that the fictional family travels onscreen.[13]

To enhance the film's documentary aesthetic, cinematographer Takaha Tetsuo filmed with a lightweight Arriflex while simultaneously recording dialogue with an ultra-cardioid microphone.[14] Both telephoto lenses and a hiding device were used to make the camera's presence less obtrusive at the shooting sites. Takaha explains that he "shot the opening sequence in Iōjima and the last scenes in Hokkaido using standard processing (ASA 80), while resorting to push processing to double the film's sensitivity (to the equivalent of ASA 160) for shooting elsewhere."[15] Push processing allowed Takaha to compensate for inadequate lighting. The resulting images, grainier and less colorful, create a sense of being present at the scene and make the action seem less staged. Ordinary people were recruited at different shooting locations to perform their own professions—nurse, doctor, store clerk, dairy farmers, etc.—onscreen.[16] The director sought to create a microcosm of the larger outside world by populating the diegetic space with real-life people.

While the film's content is critical of what television represents—the regime of high growth—Yamada's approach to filming deeply resonates with the world of television, which had become the main arena for documentary expression.[17] Television's circular vision, collapsing the distance between viewers and the object of the gaze, was conducive to documentary inquiries that sought to close in on social reality. Contemporary film directors such as Ōshima Nagisa and Imamura Shōhei produced documentary programs for television and in turn incorporated documentary techniques into their filmmaking.[18] Yamada's own experiments were also a means to cast a critical gaze at contemporary Japanese society under the high-growth economy. Yoshida Naoya, a pioneering television documentarian, characterizes television documentary in a way that helps us understand what Yamada was trying to accomplish through his experiments. "TV documentary began with reportage on the mysteries of the unknown worlds," Yoshida explains. "That is to transform the 'unknown' into the 'known.' However, that 'unknown' is actually what everybody used to think of as the 'familiar world.' The actual process was to transform the familiar world into the 'unknown.'"[19] Echoing the Brechtian concept of the alienation effect, Yoshida claims that the conversion of the known into the unknown is the key to engaging viewers in documentary inquiry.[20] Similarly, Yamada's goal was to defamiliarize what was a "familiar world" to many—life under the high-growth economy—while familiarizing the little-known livelihoods at the margins of Japanese society.

Train windows dramatically illustrate the Kazamis' troubled relationship with the industrialized world of contemporary Japan. While their trains move at high speed, the landscape flying by outside the windows is reduced to panoramic images—a flat surface—while the sense of distance is collapsed. This is the experience that Wolfgang Schivelbusch describes in *Railway Journey*, although 1960s Japan was vastly different from nineteenth-century Europe, where railway networks were first developed.[21] The economic power of 1960s Japan transformed not only train systems but also the landscape that passengers saw outside the windows. High-speed trains cut through land radically altered by the infrastructure that massive economic activities required. The Kazamis, sitting inside the train cars and looking out through glass windows, are cut off both economically and symbolically from the world outside. They have few economic ties with it, and their railway journey only confirms that fact.

The film uses images of glass to visually mark the family's marginality. This transparent yet rigid boundary is the key to Yamada's critique of contemporary Japan. Transparent doors and windows serve as invisible barriers separating the family from the rest of society. While they are allowed to peep into the world on the other side, their admission is strictly prohibited. The Japan that the Kazamis encounter on their journey is reduced to flattened images on glassy surfaces, as if they were on a television screen. It is impossible to establish meaningful relations with a world that lacks depth. In contrast, by using documentary techniques and casting ordinary people, Yamada presents the diegetic space of *Where Spring Comes Late* as an extension of the real world, where genuine human interactions occur.

As figure 3.1 illustrates, the Kazamis stand at the rural margins of Japanese society, which is now rapidly collapsing under the pressure of the high-growth economy. In his efforts to find a new place comparable to his old one, Sei'ichi moves his family to another far corner of Japan. Hokkaido's geographic distance from political and economic power makes it comparable to Iōjima off the coast of Nagasaki in Yamada's film. Yamada made his cinematographic decision to visually mark this dual structure: standard exposure and processing give the scenes shot in Iōjima and Hokkaido full color, while the push process technique emphasizes the gloomy quality of life under the high-growth economy. The Kazamis must travel almost the entire length of Japan (3,000 km/1,875 miles) in order to reach one of the few remaining spaces in Japanese society beyond the reach of the high-growth economy. Given their lack of interest in the "inside," the trip must be completed as expeditiously as possible, with minimal contact with the Japan to which they do not belong and at the lowest possible expense. As if traveling in an enclosed glass bottle, the Kazamis remain separated from

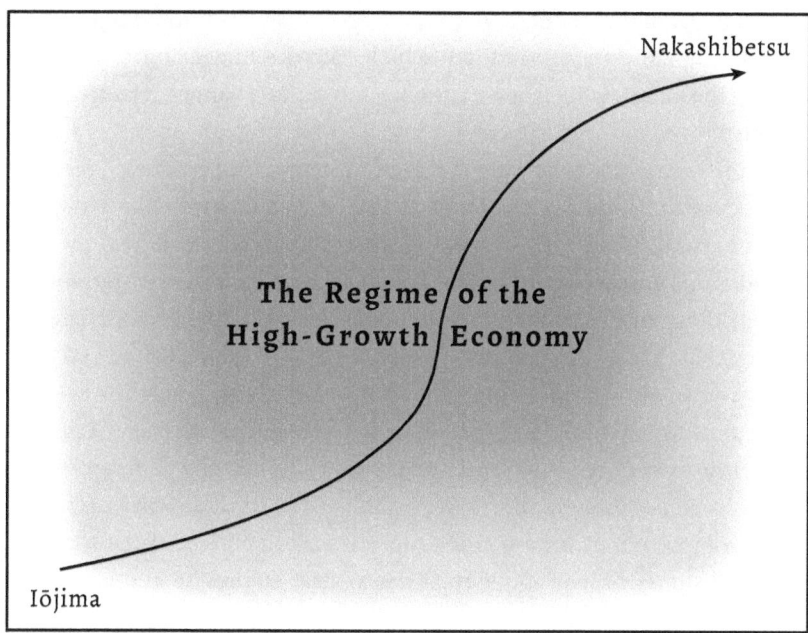

*Figure 3.1* The Kazamis' journey through the high-growth regime. Diagram by author.

the other world, except when they inadvertently come into contact with its deleterious effects at a few key locations.

Yamada expended his creative and critical energy on reversing the conventional hierarchy of center and periphery. By locating genuine human connections and feelings at the margins of Japanese society, he establishes an outsider's perspective from which to criticize the regime of modernization. Seen from the outside, Japanese society under the euphoric influence of the high-growth economy is inhumane and materialistic. The Kazamis represent hope precisely because of their marginal status in Japanese society—they have not yet been completely co-opted.

## Fukuyama: The Price of Success

To reach the promised land of freedom and independence, the family has to cross the country—hostile territory controlled by the high-growth regime. They take trains because rail fares are more affordable than airfare. Most of their contact with the larger society is limited to the vista seen through the train windows. Much like the images on a television screen, the scenery in front of them constantly changes, reducing the various sites of Japan to ephemeral visual stimuli. Japan appears as a landscape through which the family travels. The moving images in front of them show the audience two contrasting aspects of Japan: the industrial and the rural. While they travel through the industrial regions that extend from northern Kyushu to Tokyo, gigantic industrial compounds and buildings of overwhelming scale in Osaka and Tokyo punctuate the scenery that flies by. By contrast, once the family escapes Tokyo and continues north, rural scenes come to dominate the vista, which is eventually reduced to twilight and then distant lights in the darkness. The scenic contrast serves to underscore the urban/rural binary in contemporary Japan, corresponding to the changing mood of the adult characters as it shifts from extreme anxiety and a hint of excitement about their relocation to disillusionment about their unrealistic enterprise and a sense of defeat.

The Japan that appears through the train windows does not remain a passive visual image. As the Kazami clan makes stops at Fukuyama, Osaka, and Tokyo, family members interact with the world on the other side of the glass. Sei'ichi's father, Genzō, originally plans to move to Fukuyama and live with Sei'ichi's younger brother, Tsutomu, and his family. Everything that Genzō tells other family members about Tsutomu suggests that he has made a good life in the city: he works for a large corporation (he appears to be employed at Nippon Kokan's Fukuyama plant, which began operations in the 1960s), earns a good salary, and owns a car and a house. While Genzō's descriptions are accurate in general, the life inside the high-growth economy that Tsutomu and his family have embraced proves to be far less impressive. The minuscule car that Tsutomu drives to the station to pick up his brother's family—a Suzuki Fronte SS nudged along by a 0.356-liter engine—is underpowered and barely large enough for four adults, two small children, and their luggage (figure 3.2). Although Tsutomu was planning to take them home in a taxi, the guests insist on riding home in his car. With the luggage tied on top and Tsutomu and the Kazamis packed inside, this is no easy feat. In the middle of busy city traffic, trucks harass the slow-moving car and drive it out of its lane. Once they reach Tsutomu's modest, cookie-cutter house in a suburb, it immediately

*Figure 3.2* Tsutomu's minuscule car on the road. *Where Spring Comes Late (Kazoku)*, dir. Yamada Yōji, 1970.

becomes clear that there is not enough room for the father to move in. According to the final script, Tsutomu's house is a typical "2DK" danchi, consisting of a kitchen-dining area and two small rooms, about 500 square feet in total.[22] With his pregnant wife, three children, and monthly loan payments for the house and the car,[23] Tsutomu is barely in a position to extend hospitality to his family, much less house his father.

The film carefully places Tsutomu's household commodities onscreen to make a critical commentary on what he and millions of others achieved in this period. The two brothers drink far into the night, arguing over Sei'ichi's impractical plan, while the two women keep them company; Genzō ostensibly has retired to the adjacent room to put the children to sleep, but he stays awake listening to his sons' conversation. As the night goes on, their choice of drink switches from sake to cheap whisky. The bottle of Torys whisky on the table—one of the cheapest domestic brands—stands in contrast to the bottles of more expensive domestic whisky behind the glass doors of a cupboard in the background.[24] They are visible through the glass but out of reach for the two men. Tsutomu may have created the façade of prosperous middle-class life, but he does not get to fully enjoy the fruits of his labor. The rewards for submitting one's independence to corporate demands seem dismally small.

Tsutomu's insignificance and powerlessness as a mere cog in the economic system are visually marked. After bidding farewell to his brother's family through an open train window at the Fukuyama Station, Tsutomu

*Figure 3.3* Tsutomu inside his car. *Where Spring Comes Late.*

*Figure 3.4* Tsutomu's car reduced to a dot in the screen's bottom left corner. *Where Spring Comes Late.*

drives his car alone to work, crying. After capturing his gesture of wiping away his tears in a closeup shot from the rear seat of the car (figure 3.3), the scene cuts to an aerial shot that follows his car as it heads toward the gigantic steel mill.[25] The camera then leaves the car behind and pans to the right, showing the entire expanse of the compound (figure 3.4). While the scene inside the car visualizes the driver's internal agony at being unable to help his brother's family, the aerial view explains why he cannot. Tsutomu's ego is literally as big as his car—what little he can afford—and it appears as a mere dot on the screen in the bird's-eye view. Against the overwhelming scale of the industrial complex, Tsutomu's car embodies the smallness of his emotional being.

## Osaka: Progress and Harmony for Humankind

Sei'ichi and his family make their second stop at Osaka, overflowing with the festivities of Expo '70. In this extremely crowded urban center, everything they do—even having a quiet lunch—proves an ordeal. A hidden hand-held camera follows them into underground passageways filled with shops and people.[26] Background noise and the camera's unsteady motion accentuate the sensory overload they experience, exhausted and lost amid the swirling flows of people. Ultimately, they retreat from the underground passages and find a restaurant above street level, where they look down through glass windows at throngs of people (figure 3.5).[27] The family's peace and composure are momentarily restored as their interactions with the hostile world are reduced to visual contact. Once comforted by food and beer in this trainlike space, Sei'ichi proposes to check out Expo '70 while they wait for their bullet train.

Expo '70 was an international exposition held in Osaka from March 15 through September 13. Total attendance surpassed sixty-four million. (The actual number of attendees was a little over twenty-three million: almost one-fourth of Japanese people attended, many of them multiple times.)[28] With the Japanese government's strong financial support, ninety-two international bodies, including seventy-six national governments, and thirty-one domestic organizations participated in this event, whose main theme was "Progress and Harmony for Humankind." The sociologist Yoshimi Shunya characterizes it as "a magnificent monument through which one

*Figure 3.5* The Kazamis in a restaurant. *Where Spring Comes Late.*

hundred million Japanese reconfirmed their achievements—postwar Japan's economic recovery and high growth."[29] The Japanese actor Lily Franky (b. 1963) recalls in economic terms the hype about Expo he witnessed as a child living in Kyushu: "If you could not go to Expo, you were not even a human. You were just dirt poor."[30] Yoshimi's statement suggests that Lily's "human" should actually be read as "Japanese."

This national event was also an opportunity for Japanese citizens to experience temporal and geographic "outsides"—the future world and foreign countries—while in Japan. In its 820-acre lot, visitors were transformed into tourists of a future city where national boundaries were momentarily transcended. In other words, Expo '70 offered in more lively forms what television had provided for its viewers. Many shared the same space with foreigners and experienced cutting-edge technology for the first time. It was like jumping into the world depicted on their television screens. As Sadakane Hiroyuki and Kitada Akihiro have suggested, the outside lost its outside status in Expo '70: the outside was displayed as a set of signs to be consumed, but not as the space against which to reconfirm Japan's symbolic boundaries.[31]

Filled with visual images displayed through multiscreen projection systems and sounds generated by multitrack audio systems, the self-enclosed space of Expo '70 also functioned much like a television. According to the magazine *Small Gauge Film*, thirty-two 70mm film projectors were operating at forty-one exhibits at the exposition site.[32] The number is impressive, given that only two such projectors were in operation in Tokyo at the time.[33] The Astrorama of the Midori Pavilion wrapped audiences in images projected on a dome by five synchronized 70mm film projectors,[34] and sounds amplified by an eleven-channel system with 515 speakers.[35] The Mitsubishi Pavilion offered perhaps the most sophisticated spectacle of sound and image. Its "horizontal mirror screen" system deployed 70mm film projectors, multiple screens, and two-way mirrors to re-create storms and volcanic explosions. Visitors traveled through moving images of sharks projected onto a large smoke screen, the first of its kind.[36] At the end of the 1,500-foot-long moving walkway, they encountered the Silhouettoron, which captured and transformed their images into large mosaic patterns on an electronic display wall.[37] This was metavisuality in its most elementary form, as the device turned visitors into part of the very attraction that they were attending.

The Kazamis look into this space of national celebration with weary expressions on their faces, but they do not step inside. The Expo '70 sequence begins with a shot of a gigantic face on the Tower of the Sun—the central structure designed by the artist Okamoto Tarō, who served as "theme producer" for the entire event—accompanied by the fanfare composed for the Expo's opening ceremony. (The fact that Satō Masaru composed both the Expo fanfare and the score for *Where Spring Comes Late* suggests that the director's vision of outsider identity was already compromised.)[38] The camera then tilts down to capture Sei'ichi, Tamiko, and the children (Genzō has apparently decided to stay behind) on a train platform, trying to find a way to the Expo venue. Background traffic noise replaces the music by the time the camera spots the Kazamis. The shot thus bifurcates the space into high and low: the realm of festivity exists above the bottom world to which the family belongs. Outside the station, a hidden camera follows the family as they negotiate the overwhelming flow of people. Upon reaching the central gate area, however, the Kazamis realize that they do not have enough time to enjoy the national event. Expo '70 is a mere afterthought to them; they cannot spare the time or money amid their odyssey. Their position as bystanders echoes their relation to the high-growth economy. They are excluded from the regime that has embraced the future and global connections as consumable signs. The director, who was thinking about John Ford's film *The Grapes of Wrath* (1940) while shooting *Where Spring Comes Late*, saw Expo '70 as just the setting with which to underscore the family's exclusion from the postwar prosperity.[39]

Although Sei'ichi and Tamiko may be resigned to their marginal status, the high-growth regime will not let them off easily. At the gate, there is a humorous encounter with a sleazy moneylender who personifies the shady side of capitalism. Before leaving Iōjima, Tamiko "borrowed" ¥30,000 ($83.33) from the man, implying that Sei'ichi is leaving for Hokkaido alone. Hoping to use the loan to pressure her into accepting his sexual advances, the moneylender offered her the money with no interest and no definite term for repayment. Attending Expo '70 with a young mistress, however, he spots Tamiko and accuses her of deceiving him. Although Tamiko tells off the sleazy moneylender, money seems to mediate all aspects of the family's forced interactions with society under the high-growth regime. As soon as their train leaves Nagasaki, Sei'ichi and Tamiko begin to count and record the money that their neighbors have given them as parting gifts. The money that they have received (a few thousand yen each) becomes a powerful symbol of neighborly love. After parting with Tsutomu in Fukuyama, Sei'ichi and Tamiko open the envelope that Tsutomu handed them. Finding ¥10,000 ($27.78) in it—the same amount as the monthly payment for his car, or a piece of his middle-class life—Tamiko asks: "Tsutomu overextended himself, didn't he?" Even family affection and guilt are expressed through currency, or the language of capital. While battling the high-growth regime, the Kazamis must speak the same language, no matter how foreign it may sound. In their next stopover, Tokyo, they experience its cold, alienating effects.

### Tokyo: The World Inside Television

*Where Spring Comes Late* addresses a newsworthy issue from the late 1960s—the public outcry about the challenges of finding emergency care in a timely manner in Tokyo—in order to underscore the uncaring environment of the metropolis.[40] When the Kazamis force their way into the vortex of city seeking medical care for their baby girl, Sanae, the help comes too late. She dies. The infant is a casualty of the family's battle to reach a safe haven. To the Kazamis, Tokyo is as much a television-like space as Expo '70 is: they are allowed to look into it but cannot enter.

As the exhausted family arrives in Tokyo at dusk, the silhouettes of the buildings loom ominously large on the bullet train windows. At Ueno Station in Tokyo, Sei'ichi, Tamiko, and Genzō debate what to do with Sanae, who has not been eating much. Sei'ichi is eager to make a connection and head north immediately in order to minimize expenses, even though Sanae has fallen ill. He lists the reasons: doctors in Tokyo are expensive; if they stay overnight, they will waste their tickets for a limited express train; they have no money to spend on overnight accommodations. Even after the family settles at an inn, Sei'ichi and Tamiko continue to argue. Sei'ichi opens the little notebook where he has kept track of the trip-related expenses. According to the notebook, they spent ¥2,300 in Osaka alone. Money seems to have displaced familial considerations in his thinking. Tamiko and Genzō insist that Sanae should see a doctor, but her condition suddenly becomes worse.

Visual clues mark the inhospitable environment of the metropolis, where the images streaming through the television screen appear to command more attention than the real world in front of the television. At the inn near Ueno Station, the Kazamis' fatigued figures are contrasted to the owner in the foreground, reclining and completely absorbed in watching television. Even when the inn maid asks about the room rate for the night, he barely raises his eyes from the screen. Yet as the family head toward a room, he casts a brief inquiring look toward their backs. A few shots later, he is still watching television in the sitting area. The camera looks down from the top of the dark stairwell, toward the bottom, where the lit sitting room appears as a self-enclosed space. The owner does not hide his reluctance to stop watching television even when the maid relays the family's urgent inquiry about the locations of doctors' offices. Before disappearing from the screen to look up the information, he cheerfully comments on the characters on the screen, as if to erase the nuisance that he has to deal with: "These guys are really funny." The glow of television is at the heart of the hostile environment that blithely desensitizes its members to the pain of others.

The Kazamis desperately seek help in Tokyo, but the metropolis is just as unaccommodating as the two-dimensional world of television. Sei'ichi desperately bangs on a door and a window of the first clinic they visit until a passerby tells them that nobody is on duty there at nighttime. Even when they finally reach a hospital with emergency facilities, they have trouble entering the premises. Again Sei'ichi pounds on a glass door asking for help. A nurse eventually appears from inside the hospital to open the glass door (figure 3.6). Before realizing the seriousness of Sanae's condition, she

*Figure 3.6* The nurse gesturing that the other doors are unlocked. *Where Spring Comes Late.*

irritably informs them that the other door is unlocked. Sei'ichi and Tamiko are almost there, but the glass doors prevent them from entering the alien space beyond the transparent threshold. Like the visual streaks seen through the train windows earlier in the film, the metropolis exists merely as a kind of flattened image that the family see but cannot reach on their own. When the protagonists overstep the invisible boundaries, their act leads straight to a tragic outcome—Sanae's death.

The following day, the couple has been thrown outside the transparent threshold. A medium shot from the inside of the hospital cashier's office shows a distressed Sei'ichi. Through the small opening of the office's glass window, the cashier says: "This time, we are deeply sorry for your loss. Here are two copies of the death certificate." Literally in the same breath, she adds, "The hospital fee is ¥4,500." There are also cash registers in the foreground, lest the audience miss the irony (figure 3.7). Through a transaction mediated by a glass window, the family's devastating loss is translated into the cold language of capitalism. Sei'ichi can do nothing but speak the same language, dutifully completing the transaction.

Genzō, a retired coal miner, appears more confident than Sei'ichi when facing the challenges of this alien world. When his son returns to the inn in distress, Genzō admonishes him: "In a time like this, the father must be strong." Amid crisis, Genzō behaves like a true patriarch. Perhaps as a result of being relieved from the day-to-day burden of supporting the family, he can afford to preserve the ideal image of the paterfamilias. Claiming that he still has some money for himself, he hands ¥30,000 to Sei'ichi. Although Sei'ichi pushes it away, his meek, perfunctory gesture (in contrast to Genzō's

*Figure 3.7* Sei'ichi paying the hospital bill. *Where Spring Comes Late.*

newfound dignity) suggests that he will eventually accept his father's money. The money offered for Sanae's cremation and funeral arrangements in Tokyo is also for settling accounts with the world on the other side of the glass threshold. The family will owe nothing to the hostile world when it leaves it behind. By offering ¥30,000—the exact amount that Tamiko "borrowed" from the moneylender—Genzō maintains the symbolic equilibrium of transactions.

While Sei'ichi arranges Sanae's funeral and obtains permission for her cremation, Genzō takes his grandson, Tsuyoshi, to the Ueno Zoo. The scenes there make it poignantly apparent that they do not belong to the everyday life of the metropolis. Yamada contrasts the image of the boy and his grandfather resting on a bench with the scores of preschoolers and their parents sitting in the background. Tsuyoshi, in the foreground with a blue striped cap, stands out in a shot filled with preschoolers wearing caps of bright red or yellow. Detached from the rhythm of everyday life, the pair is there just to kill time. Nonetheless, Genzō takes pride in their autonomous, outsider status: he tells Tsuyoshi to pay for a bun that a store clerk has given him out of kindness. No debt—whether emotional or monetary—should be accumulated while in enemy territory.

The family is yet to complete its difficult journey, but at least the hardest part, their battle in Tokyo, is over. As the family heads north with Sanae's ashes, the scenery seen on the train windows becomes dominated by farmland under the gray, dreary sky. The landscape externalizes the family's mental state after enduring a tragedy, while also signaling what awaits them in the future. Enthusiasm has long dissipated, and anxiety looms large in each adult's mind.

## Heading North

The tensions that have been building between Sei'ichi and Tamiko blow up once they are on a ferry bound for Hokkaido. In this emotional scene, the actor Atsumi Kiyoshi plays a minor yet pivotal role in their safe passage to the unknown world.

While waiting in Aomori for a ferry to Hokkaido, Sei'ichi and Tamiko have a brief conversation with a stranger, played by Atsumi. As a man excessively afraid of seasickness, his brief appearance not only provides comedic relief but also ventriloquizes the family's anxiety about crossing the channel that separates Honshu and Hokkaido. In fact, Atsumi has already appeared in the film—playing a comedian in one of the programs on the owner's television in the Tokyo inn where the Kazamis stayed overnight. Stepping out of the television screen and interacting with the Kazamis, he serves as a guardian who facilitates their exodus from the drab and affectionless world under the high-growth economy to the blissful land of promise where they will recover their human feelings.

It is noteworthy that another character played by Atsumi made an exodus from the television world almost contemporaneously. Atsumi first played the protagonist Kuruma Torajirō—an itinerant huckster (*tekiya*)—in the television serial *It's Tough Being a Man* (*Otoko wa tsuraiyo*: October 1968– March 1969), for which Yamada wrote the scripts. Torajirō is a comedic incarnation of the yakuza heroes who populated the screen in the late 1960s and early 1970s. While he embodies one form of the male ideal—untethered by social conventions and in charge of his own fate—his imprudent behavior creates friction in a society where everybody appears to pursue middle-class happiness. The serial, which consisted of twenty-six episodes, gradually gained popularity. Yamada prepared a rather unusual conclusion for a television comedy, however, believing that "there is no way a man like Torajirō can survive an age like today."[41] Torajirō dies from a snake bite. Fans complained bitterly, outraged by what seemed like the station's callous treatment of him (though the decision to kill him on the screen was Yamada's). Encouraged by their emotional responses, Yamada persuaded reluctant Shōchiku executives to make a film version of *It's Tough Being a Man*.[42] Torajirō—an outsider to the high-growth regime— was expelled from the world of television and resurrected in cinematic space. Film offered a refuge to the man who was irreverent toward the middle-class values that the world of television wholeheartedly embraced.[43]

When audiences embraced the film, Shōchiku executives encouraged Yamada to work on a sequel immediately. The sequel was followed by forty-six more in the next twenty-six years.[44] Yamada directed the first three films of what became the *It's Tough Being a Man* series in just one year before releasing *Where Spring Comes Late* in 1970. The box-office success of the series secured Yamada's position as a Shōchiku director, allowing him to shoot more socially minded films periodically.[45] The story inspired by Atsumi's real-life experiences and enacted by Atsumi himself buoyed Yamada's film career and the Shōchiku Studios in a society where film was fast losing its former glamour.[46]

Atsumi appears at a crucial juncture in the Kazamis' journey to serve a similar function: he shows them a safe way out of a world dominated by television. At night on the ferry en route to Hokkaido, Atsumi's character wakes up struggling to suppress his nausea. (He appears to be a working-class man, but the scene does not provide any clues as to his identity.) Once he realizes that he is not going to throw up, he goes back to sleep.[47] The camera then tilts up to show Sei'ichi in another open compartment, drinking while intently examining his black notebook. Awoken by a baby's cry, Tamiko breaks down, sobs, and tells Sei'ichi that she wants to go back to their island. Filled with his own anxiety, Sei'ichi is unable to comfort her and ends up projecting his own guilty feelings onto her, blaming her for Sanae's death. But just as Atsumi manages to avoid the worst physical reaction on the ferry, Sei'ichi and his family survive their biggest crisis. After being admonished by Genzō, Sei'ichi walks up to the deck and gazes into the dark sea, bearing the weight of his own decision. Atsumi makes one last appearance after the family reaches Hokkaido. His smile affirms that everything is going to be fine for them now that they are in Hokkaido, and Tamiko smiles for the first time since Sanae's death.

The Kazamis complete their long journey, finally arriving at their friends' house in Nakashibetsu, a town in eastern Hokkaido. As if to announce that his task is complete, Genzō dies in his sleep shortly after their arrival. His body is buried next to Sanae's ashes on the expansive land of Hokkaido. His Catholic-style funeral suggests that the Kazamis have found their community of faith, albeit much smaller than the one they left. The image of a wooden cross bearing Genzō's Christian name resonates with the early scene of his bidding farewell to Iōjima's graveyard. Genzō himself has become the founding ancestor of a new family in the land of promise. His body is the spiritual root through which Sei'ichi and Tamiko establish a connection to the land. In the film, their Catholic faith signals their outsider status in a society where the pursuit of economic efficiency seems to have destroyed the importance of human bonds (as seen in Tokyo). Their religious identity enables their rejuvenation at the end of the film. When Sei'ichi breaks the news of Tamiko's pregnancy to their friend Ryōta, he describes the blessing as his religious burden: "In a case like this, it is hard to be Catholic."

Even at a time of crisis, Tamiko accepts their new home in Nakashibetsu far more readily than her husband does. After losing his father less than two days after their arrival, Sei'ichi questions his decision to relocate the entire family to Hokkaido. Equally saddened by this second death, Tamiko talks about her newfound optimism. Embracing Sei'ichi, she urges him to look forward to an intense spring that will revive the land, animals, and people in two short months. From a close-up shot of the couple, the camera cuts to their figures reflected on a windowpane. Their blurry image, reflected on the glass against the dark wintry night, eloquently expresses their anxiety about the unseen future. No longer threatened by what is behind glass, they are finally able to embrace the reflection of their inner feelings. Glass ceases to be the transparent barrier now that they have escaped the hostile world.

While portraying Tamiko as the true mainstay of the Kazami family,[48] Yamada in the end appears to suggest that "traditional" gender relations may remedy deep social confusion.[49] Tamiko is cast in a purely supportive role: devoid of her own ambition, she embraces Sei'ichi's as hers. It is her decision to keep the family together when Sei'ichi announces his plan to work in Hokkaido. She is the mother figure who comforts him in a moment of deep self-doubt. The film concludes with scenes of spring, the season of renewal. Aerial shots capture the deep green of the forest and pastoral land, where cows are grazing. Sei'ichi and Tamiko become firmly rooted in the land and the community by living new lives. They not only receive a newborn calf from Ryōta but also inform him of Tamiko's pregnancy. Sei'ichi's patriarchal agency is recovered fully by impregnating his wife, whose body is portrayed much like the farmland waiting to be sown.

Such a fantastic yet conventional conclusion was still conceivable to Yamada in 1970, though he was keenly aware of the grim realities of Japanese dairy farming.[50] Although the Kazamis are excluded from the festivities of Expo '70, the filmmaker was still able to offer them an idyllic vision, a way out of the economic system that was about to change their lives drastically.[51] Viewed in hindsight after several decades, the optimistic ending seems rather incongruous in relation to the serious tone of the rest of *Where Spring Comes Late*. In Hokkaido and elsewhere in Japan, the actual economic conditions of dairy farming were not encouraging in the decades after 1970. Like rice, milk had been heavily protected by the Japanese government, which set purchase prices for producers. Overproduction from the early 1970s on depressed purchase prices. The situation eventually led to the government's imposition of strict production quotas on dairy farms in 1979.[52] Furthermore, as Yamada Yōji acknowledges, a sizable fund is needed to start and maintain a dairy farm.[53] As a new operation with insufficient capital, the Kazamis would certainly have struggled just to stay afloat in a business sector that depended on economy of scale. They would most likely incur deep debt to buy large machinery in order to engage in the "American-style" dairy farming that Sei'ichi desired. As soon as their enterprise began to see some returns in the 1970s, the Kazamis would surely be hit by the effects of overproduction and the subsequent production quotas.[54] While many abandoned dairy farming altogether, the surviving farmers struggled to raise productivity by enlarging and modernizing their enterprises.[55] In the end, Sei'ichi would realize with bitterness that even dairy farming in Hokkaido is vulnerable to the forces that ruled the rest of Japan: there would be no way to maintain his autonomy, wherever he set down roots.

Yamada offers what may be a postscript to his 1970 film in *A Distant Cry from Spring* (*Harukanaru yama no yobigoe*, 1980)—the third and last film in which actress Baishō Chieko plays the lead role of Tamiko—though the details are slightly altered. After her husband's death in 1977, Tamiko raises their son, Takeshi, on their small dairy farm in Nakashibetsu. Tajima (played by Takakura Ken) is a fugitive who one day shows up at the farm and starts working for, and eventually falls in love with, Tamiko. He is on the run for accidentally killing the loan shark who publicly insulted his wife for committing suicide rather than paying back the large amount of money she owed him. Tajima must be normalized before he enters into conjugal relations with Tamiko. Through demanding physical labor on the farm, he works through his past and becomes ready to embrace the future. At the conclusion of the film he is sent to a penitentiary, while the mother and son decide to give up farming and move into an apartment in a nearby town. Although the film ends by strongly intimating that they will eventually be united, it evades the question of whether he will be happy working in town. Would he ever be satisfied in circumstances where he is alienated from the source of his joy? Yamada had already grappled with and offered a melancholic answer to essentially the same question in an earlier film, which we will discuss next.

### *Home from the Sea*: Battling the "Big Thing"

In 1972, two years after the release of *Where Spring Comes Late*, Yamada completed the film *Home from the Sea*, which portrays a family facing difficult choices. With the same set of actors as the main characters, *Home from the Sea* revisits a family's struggle to survive the new socioeconomic reality of the high-growth economy. Yet unlike the 1970 film, *Home from the Sea* spends a considerable amount of time depicting the family's everyday life in its own community on a small island near Kure, Hiroshima. Sei'ichi and Tamiko, the operators of a tugboat-sized wooden ship, must decide between continuing their small-time operation transporting rocks for land reclamation and finding employment in a nearby town. Their way of life is contrasted with the mechanized operations of the large-scale transporters.

Sei'ichi and Tamiko are denizens of a disappearing world. Leaving their house early in the morning, often with their youngest daughter, the pair spends many hours on a small ship, partaking equally in the demanding work. Their final journey is the highlight of the film. Crosscut with flashbacks, the long sequence captures the couple's routine in its entirety. After they arrive at the quarry, the couple load the boat with rocks, pushing and shoving with a small winch to distribute them evenly on the deck. They continue until the boat's flat top is almost underwater. While there is no music to dramatize their dirty, dangerous, and demanding job, a melancholic theme song accompanies their final run on the sea. At the delivery point, they cause the boat to list and slide the load off by swinging out a small net-full of rocks hanging on the movable arm attached to the mast.[56] The moment when the rocks are dumped is dramatized in slow motion, and the boat then regains its balance. There is little need for Sei'ichi and Tamiko to exchange words on the boat because they are thoroughly familiar with each other's movements. As if they are the last practitioners of a traditional ritual, the couple try to continue their operation on the sea as long as possible. The slow, painstaking nature of their activity, however, explains why it must end.

The idyllic scenery of the inland sea is contrasted with the difficult decision that Sei'ichi and Tamiko must make. On the way back from the final delivery job, they spot an acquaintance's old wooden ship set alight on the shore. Envisioning a similar end for their boat, Sei'ichi expresses his sorrow in the form of a question: "What is the big thing? Everybody tells you that you can't beat the flow of the age or the big thing. What is this big thing? Why can't I beat the big thing? Why can't I continue this job of rock ferrying with you on the sea I love?" Sei'ichi probably knows the answer to his own question, but he does not wish to name it, fearing that doing so would finalize his defeat. The "big thing" that he succumbs to is nothing but the regime of high growth, which has transformed everyday life into a site of constant struggle. Unlike their counterparts in *Where Spring Comes Late*, Sei'ichi and Tamiko come to accept the reality of early 1970s Japan without putting up much of a fight.

Lacking the capital to build a bigger ship to compete in the rock-ferrying business, Sei'ichi decides, after a frustrated outburst, to seek employment at a large shipyard in Onomichi. The new job forces the couple to relocate with their two children and leave his aged father alone in their house on the island. The traditional patriarch, a man of the Meiji era (1868–1912), no longer serves as the family foundation—a far cry from Genzō's proud status in *Where Spring Comes Late*. Sei'ichi and Tamiko's equal participation in their work on the sea will be replaced by gendered labor practices on the land. Sei'ichi will become the family breadwinner; Tamiko will likely make a minimal financial contribution to their household even if she finds employment. The intense and intimate time that they spent on the sea as working partners will be forever lost.

*Home from the Sea* should also be read as an homage to the declining film industry. The total attendance figure for movies in Japan peaked at 1.127 billion in 1958 and precipitously declined to 187 million in 1972—about one-sixth of what it was fourteen years earlier. In the same period, overall film-distribution income shrank from ¥39.4 billion to ¥28.7 billion. In this ever-shrinking film market, the five major production companies—Daiei, Nikkatsu, Tōei, Tōhō, and Shōchiku—fell from their dominant positions. Between 1958 and 1972 the number of feature films released by the five dropped from 503 to 186, while the overall number of feature films released increased slightly (from 673 to 683) as foreign films and works from independent or smaller production companies filled the gap without reversing the general downward trend in attendance.[57] The five companies all dealt with the crisis differently. Daiei and Nikkatsu stayed operational in the late 1960s and early 1970s by selling their studios, head-office buildings, and other real estate assets. The former filed for bankruptcy in 1971, and the latter resorted to churning out low-budget soft-porn films. Tōei survived as a business entity by radically reducing its film production sections while diversifying its operations into foreign film distribution, hotel management, and real estate.[58] Tōei also shifted much of its remaining resources to producing television programs and yakuza films in the second half of the 1960s.[59] Nikkatsu's and Tōei's film productions targeted young male audiences, providing what television could not: more sexual and violent content. In the midst of this crisis, Tōhō and Shōchiku struggled to maintain their corporate identities as makers of family-friendly films. Despite each film company's efforts, however, the downward spiral continued, albeit at a slower rate, until the 1990s, when numerous employees were laid off or departed by choice—to work in the world of television.

Yamada Yōji was one of the exceptional individuals who thrived within a studio production system that appeared to be on the brink of extinction. He joined Shōchiku in 1954, starting out as an assistant director, and worked his way up to directing his own feature films. His early career was overshadowed by filmmakers like Ōshima Nagisa (1932–2013), Shinoda Masahiro (b. 1931), and Yoshida Yoshishige (Kijyū, b. 1933), leaders of the New Wave movement in Japan, who would leave Shōchiku in the 1960s after denouncing the company's indifference toward their creative endeavors.[60] Yamada remained a Shōchiku director. The president of Shōchiku, Shiroto Shirō, repeatedly offered him opportunities to direct films, seeing him as the next bearer of the so-called Shōchiku Ōfuna style, known for its sympathetic attention to the quotidian lives of ordinary people.[61] Yet his early comedic films, while highly regarded by film critics, were hardly commercial successes. Only with the popularity of the *It's Tough Being a Man* series did he gain enough latitude within the Shōchiku studio system to make *Where Spring Comes Late* and *Home from the Sea*.

When the scriptwriter Katsura Chiho heard Sei'ichi's line about "the big thing," she immediately recalled the Shōchiku Ōfuna Studio and "a number of Shōchiku directors, whose films [she] was familiar with but who disappeared from the film world without even a trace."[62] Like Sei'ichi and Tamiko, filmmakers just wanted to keep doing what they loved—making films—but socioeconomic shifts in contemporary society rendered their craft obsolete. Yamada was angry at the state of the industry, where talented colleagues were forced to give up filmmaking because they simply could not make a living.[63] But the film's melancholic end—Tamiko and Sei'ichi, with their daughter, leave their island for a city—perhaps reflects the director's anxiety rather than his anger. So far he has managed to stay in business, but there is no assurance for the future. Yamada might be the next man to be forced out of the cinema world.[64]

In 1972 it was no longer possible to imagine a fight against or an escape from the forces that dictated "the flow of the age." At the tail end of the high-growth economy, the expansive web of the media and the economy swallowed up what little was left of the outside in Japanese society. Torajirō in the series *It's Tough Being a Man*—a questionable outside figure—metamorphosed into an unthreatening character. Horikiri Naoto observes: "Torajirō was originally a pushy, brazen, and even violent character. But these traits gradually faded away in the series."[65] The writer Kobayashi Nobuhiko claims that the change was more sudden than gradual: after the first five films, he argues, Torajirō's antisocial huckster identity is deemphasized, and "he becomes an angel-like character."[66] With Torajirō mainstreamed, the series turned into a repository of the beautiful human sentiments that, the audience wanted to believe, once existed in Japan.

The sea that signals outside-ness in *Home from the Sea* was slowly reclaimed through Sei'ichi's and Tamiko's own labor: the film even suggests that Sei'ichi and his little brother had, years before, helped the project of land reclamation at Mukōjima, the site of Sei'ichi's future employment. They all have been more or less complicit in the process of economic development. Sei'ichi and Tamiko finally confront and accept their own complicity in 1972. Moreover, despite the idyllic scenes on the sea, the waters were suffering from heavy industrial pollution. Japan's seas had served as the "outside" for the industrial structure, the place where corporations and local municipal governments released their effluents to *externalize* social costs. As in Minamata, whose residents suffered severe consequences, including death, from mercury poisoning, environmental pollution was affecting the quality of life throughout Japan.[67] The idea of the seas as "outside" was disappearing fast. The ailing seas were demanding, as it were, admission to and recognition in Japan's national space.[68]

Unfortunately, accepting their places within the regime of the high-growth economy would not, in the long term, ease Sei'ichi and Tamiko's struggle with the flow of the age. In the following years, when the brisk stride of Japan's economy suddenly slowed down, the "big thing" in which Sei'ichi sought refuge would not be so secure. The shipbuilding industry, where he finds employment in the film, was hit particularly hard by the oil shock in 1973 and experienced a serious decline in that decade. The total number of employees in the industry declined from a peak of 360,000 in 1974 to 230,000 in 1979.[69] As a lowly temporary worker at a subsidiary company, Sei'ichi would be in a most vulnerable position: he almost certainly would be one of the first workers to be laid off.[70] Japanese industry would withstand the two oil shocks of the 1970s while adjusting to the new international economic environment, so Sei'ichi would still be able to land a new job. Yet it is easy to imagine that this job would be even farther removed from the sea that he loved.

Both *Where Spring Comes Late* and *Home from the Sea* cast a sympathetic gaze on families facing difficult situations, yet Yamada portrays the families from two divergent perspectives. The 1970 film tries to defamiliarize socioeconomic conditions that the audience takes for granted. The gloomier and more realistic ending of *Home from the Sea* does not disguise the camera's focus on the exotic quality of the modern-day seafarers' life. The director expends his creative energy capturing on film a way of life that is about to disappear. In 1972 Yamada perhaps saw no point in continuing to fight against the big thing: the best he could do was to bear witness to a disappearing world. Yet in so doing he idealized what Japan had supposedly lost in the high-growth era—familial and communal bonds fostered in a beautiful countryside. His critical vision thus became merged with nostalgia for a beloved, lost Japan, a sentiment that Japan's tourist industry tapped into in the early 1970s.

In the following chapter, we turn our attention to the Japan National Railways' advertising campaign, which thoroughly aestheticized the countryside, and the manga artist Tsuge Yoshiharu, who cast a self-reflective gaze on his own nostalgic desire for the lost Japan in the early 1970s.

CHAPTER IV

## Lost in Transition

*Travel, Memory, and Nostalgia in Tsuge Yoshiharu's Travel Manga*

What do you think is the [biggest] rival of travel? Television.
—FUJIOKA WAKAO, 1970

Travel to stare at, travel to be stared at.
—DISCOVER JAPAN CAMPAIGN COPY, 1970

In 1968 the manga monthly *Garo* published a highly successful special issue featuring the work of Tsuge Yoshiharu (b. 1937). The following year, impressed by Tsuge's artistic talent, the poet Amasawa Taijirō boldly declared: "For our arts, the year of 1968 must be remembered for the emergence of a strange manga artist, Tsuge Yoshiharu."[1] Far from reveling in his growing popularity, however, the artist literally tried to run away from it. Faced with his own commercial success, this painfully shy man decided in September of that year to drop everything and flee to Kyushu. There he intended to lead a new, anonymous life with a female fan whom he knew only through the letters they had exchanged.[2] Predictably, perhaps, this plan fell apart after two weeks, and Tsuge returned to Tokyo, where he spent much of 1969 on hiatus, working as an assistant to Mizuki Shigeru.[3] Nonetheless, his escape attempt reveals the degree to which this artist struggled—in both his life and his work—to secure a place for himself in a radically transforming society.

The early death of his biological father and his mother's remarriage to an abusive man exacerbated the extreme poverty Tsuge experienced while growing up during the Asia Pacific War and the immediate postwar era.[4] To support his family, he worked odd jobs in his early teens, missing his entire middle school education. By his late teens, Tsuge had found his calling: drawing manga allowed him to use his artistic talent and work in solitude, a boon for a man who found contact with others painful (*TYZ*

[ 115 ]

suppl.: 146). In 1955 he made his debut as a freelance author for the then-thriving rental manga market.[5] Although he published numerous works over the following decade, he continued to struggle financially, occasionally even selling his blood at a blood bank to survive.[6] For Tsuge, in his early career, the primary purpose of drawing manga—like drawing blood—was his and his family's survival.

Meanwhile, the medium of manga was undergoing a massive transition.[7] In the early 1960s the market for rental manga books began to collapse as weekly publications rapidly expanded their readership. Consequently, the manga art form, once deemed marginal and insignificant by the mainstream media and publishers, gained new legitimacy. Some authors adapted to the changing market and achieved considerable commercial success. Tsuge took a different path. In 1966, after giving up his own career as a rental manga author, he began working as an assistant to Mizuki Shigeru, producing his own short pieces in his spare time.[8] Rejecting the larger (and hence more lucrative) market of the weeklies, he chose *Garo*, a monthly magazine more open to experimental works, as the main outlet for his art. There he found a temporary niche and, with a score of highly acclaimed short pieces that appeared between 1965 and 1968, attained financial stability even as his work pushed the boundaries of manga expression.

Tsuge felt uncomfortable with his own success because it forced him out of the social class to which he was accustomed. Although benefiting from a sizable royalty income, he rejected the fiction, as he saw it, of his newly minted elite status and struggled to maintain his working-class identity. In the second half of the 1960s his search for his lost identity in the midst of financial success led him to various rural locations in Japan. He sought space where he could capture the shadows of a disappearing past. Deliberately staying at shabby inns, he indulged in the fantasy that he was a castaway in postwar society. These experiences, he later claimed, satisfied his desire for self-negation.[9] Tsuge's creative works based on his journeys strongly suggest that he sought in his travels a piece of a past that he and his country were losing to commercial modernity. The shabby inns were attractive precisely because they offered him a life—albeit in an imaginary form—for which he felt a strong affinity. Echoing this experience, his stories from the second half of the 1960s are often set in rustic locales left behind by the economic growth of contemporary Japan, as if to reconfirm the protagonists' affinity with the disappearing world of rural Japan. Yet, just as Tsuge realized the impossibility of sustaining his fantasy, his protagonists are invariably aware of the distance that separates them from the object of their nostalgia. Tsuge's angst-filled travelers remain in a constant state of unease, never successfully blending into the fictional world.

Tsuge's fast-growing fame was a paradoxical outcome of his desire to remain unaffected by economic progress. The more earnestly his work expressed his tenuous relationship with the idealized past, the harder he was thrust into the commercial world by his success. The imagined past also served as a shield against traumatic memories of his early life: Tsuge concealed his shy, battered self in the comforting space that he created in his fictional world. But growing more contemplative and self-aware about his own imaginary operation as financial security freed him from material concerns, he was forced to grapple with his uneasy relationship with contemporary society. Tsuge reached a breaking point in his ontological struggle and tried to run away from it in 1968, but the several years leading up to that point were the most intense and productive period in his creative career.

"Gensenkan Master" (Gensenkan shujin), one of Tsuge's best-known works, first appeared in 1968. In contrast to his later travel manga, "Gensenkan Master" operates in a space where the forces of commercialism threaten but have not yet overcome the author's fictional world. While suggesting that an encounter with mass consumer society is inescapable, the work only intimates the tragic consequences that will result. By the time Tsuge published "Yanagiya Master" (Yanagiya shujin, 1970) and "A Rustic Inn" (Riarizumu no yado, 1973), he had lost his tenuous ties to his fantasy world and was keenly aware of this loss. In these two later works, loss appears as an inescapable condition under which Tsuge's characters travel. The success of his work brought more than financial reward to this artist of humble origin: awareness of his complicity in the commercial world drove him out of the comfort of his fantasy world. Although the fictional characters, who resemble the author, keep returning to the same imaginary pre–economic boom realm, they experience greater discomfort with each return. Society rediscovered and commercialized the rustic settings, and the artist's indictment of this commercial regime was complicated by the fact that he also benefited from the domestic travel boom of the late 1960s and early 1970s. A close look at the Discover Japan campaign, launched in 1970 by the Japan National Railway—arguably the best-known domestic tourism campaign of the time, to which Tsuge contributed—offers insights into his creative struggle and the new aesthetic appreciation of the nation that the high-growth regime promoted.

The drastic changes in Tsuge's work in the late 1960s and early 1970s attest not only to the artist's continuing struggle with contemporary society but also to the speed at which his imaginary space was collapsing. Reflecting on his own creative process and sensing that collapse was inevitable, his attention turned inward, toward himself and his past. Three of his travel manga from this period, "Gensenkan Master," "Yanagiya Master," and "A Rustic Inn," demonstrate how Tsuge struggled with this crisis in his artistic life and his angst over the drastic transformation of Japanese society. Juxtaposing these works with a consideration of the Discover Japan campaign situates his personal struggle, more specifically, inside the newly emerging media and cultural environment and reveals the imaginary state of masculinity that precariously balanced on an admixture of nostalgia and commercialism at the tail end of the high-growth era.

## "Gensenkan Shujin": The Premonition of Loss

Although Tsuge felt threatened by the waves of commercialization that swept Japan in the late 1960s, in 1968 it was still possible for him to imagine a fantastical realm independent of contemporary society. The opening pages of "Gensenkan Master" suggest that just as the shadow of the past is disappearing, the author has managed to catch it in a desolate hamlet left behind by economic progress.[10] Despite the protagonist's apparent comfort in this location, he experiences profound fear and anxiety about revealing his alien status there. "Gensenkan Master" insinuates that the protagonist arrives at the scene only to destroy his own fantasy world. His belated arrival exposes his belief that he belongs to the long-gone past as delusional.

"Gensenkan Master" opens with the protagonist's arrival in a small, dreary hot-spring hamlet, for which he instantly feels a strong affinity.[11] The arrival scene serves as a frame for the master's tale, which occupies a substantial portion of the piece (seventeen out of twenty-eight pages). Black and gray tones dominate the scene, with the darkness rendering an impression of the hamlet as completely enclosed within itself. The man appears to dissolve into this darkness (figure 4.1). Everything there appears to have been the same for a long time, quietly decaying all the while. The only people that he encounters are older women sitting in the darkness or

*Figure 4.1* Entry scene, "Gensenkan Master." *TYZ* 6:30.

playing children's games (*TYZ* 6:33). At a cheap confectionery store that caters to these childlike elders, the proprietor remarks on the protagonist's resemblance to the master of the nearby inn, Gensenkan, and volunteers the story of how he came to settle there (*TYZ* 6:34–36). According to her, the man who is now called the master (*shujin*) of Gensenkan arrived at the rundown inn some time before and became sexually involved with the inn's deaf and mute mistress. Since then he has lived there as her husband. The protagonist declares that he, too, must go to Gensenkan. He disregards the people who gather around him and warn that if he goes there, something catastrophic will happen. In the end he arrives at the entryway of Gensenkan, facing the inn's master and mistress (*TYZ* 6:55). He steps toward the couple, whose faces seem stricken with fear. The story ends with a frame in which the protagonist wears a long-nosed goblin (*tengu*) mask on his face (*TYZ* 6:57).

Several key visual codes in the story provide insight into this rather opaque narrative. The features of the man later known as the master of

Gensenkan are portrayed clearly throughout most of the story. In the single instance of him appearing in silhouette, he is talking to the elderly maid at the inn about former lives. Here the conversation starts with his questions about the deaf woman who manages the inn:

MAN: Was she born like that?
MAID: It must be destiny from her former life.
MAN: Former life? What do you mean by former life?
MAID: It is a mirror.
MAN: Do you believe so?
MAID: Yes, because we could not live without a former life.

The maid goes on to insist that were it not for former lives, all humans would be ghosts (*TYZ* 6:42). At this point in the exchange, the man's face suddenly turns into a featureless silhouette. Sensing his ghostly existence, the maid becomes fearful. Reflected in the mirror of his former life, the man appears merely as a dark void. His featureless face reveals that he has lost all ties with the past, whereas such ties remain vital in the hamlet.

Although the story establishes a striking resemblance between the two characters through the store proprietor's words, the protagonist—the master's double—appears only in dark silhouette. The one exception occurs when he confronts the master at the very end of the story and his face disappears behind a goblin mask purchased earlier at the confectionery store. The newcomer presents himself as a ghostly shadow on the surface of a world that belongs to a former time. The master is revealed as a ghostly figure seeking the past, a search that has anchored his existence in this hot-spring hamlet. While he may have found his "former life" within this forgotten community at the margins of society, he still faces an imminent end to his dream of embracing the past. His dark double arrives from the commercial realm to remind the Gensenkan master that he is an imposter in the timeless world of the hamlet.

The master indulges in a nostalgic fantasy as he sexually engages with the middle-aged mistress, who is dressed in a kimono and wears her hair in a traditional Japanese style. Through the sexual relations that the master initiates (he forcefully demands sex and the mistress consents), he inserts himself into a scene of nostalgia. The corpulent sexual figure dressed in traditional attire—the feminine embodiment of his nostalgic desire—is almost completely deprived of speech as she makes herself available to the masculine outsider. (The only word that she communicates is *heyade* [in the room], which she writes with her finger on a steamed-up bathroom wall, acquiescing to the man's demand.) By sexually consuming her, the man becomes the "master." During this episode the master is shown wearing a goblin mask, just as his double does at the conclusion of the story (figure 4.2). The goblin's nose in the shape of an erect phallus announces his determination to recover his masculine identity by possessing the home and the body of the feminine object of his nostalgia. The absence of any other males in this community suggests that unrivaled sexual conquest is part of the nostalgic fantasy, even as it marks the Gensenkan master as an intruder. In narratives of mass culture, the object of nostalgia is almost invariably coded as feminine. Yet this happy state of union with the nostalgic world is about to be disrupted by the encounter with his double.[12]

The protagonist belatedly arrives at the scene as a shadowy double of the Gensenkan master, mocking the master's pretense that he is the sole master of nostalgic memories. The goblin mask that the protagonist buys at the store reminds the reader that the masculine identity the master gained at Gensenkan lacks originality and is commercially available. The double arrives as an emissary from the world where even objects of nostalgia are commodified in the marketplace. The couple is afraid to face the double, sensing that their union is about to be exposed to outside forces. His arrival, a repetition of the original encounter, intimates that the event will repeat itself endlessly in the marketplace. That is, the market will make the feminine object of nostalgic desire available to anybody with the means to purchase it. Tsuge's nostalgic dream ends in nightmarish fashion, with his protagonist rendered immobile, as if the slightest move would annihilate his imaginary world. The nostalgic union is an ephemeral dream that lasts only until the arrival of postwar Japan's economic development.

## "Yanagiya Master": Prefiguring Loss

It was still possible for Tsuge to situate his protagonist within the space of nostalgia in "Gensenkan Master," although the story ultimately predicts his inevitable eviction. By the time Tsuge resumed publishing his work in 1970, the situation surrounding his angst-filled fictional travelers had changed drastically. In "Yanagiya Master," one of the first works he published after his ill-fated attempt to escape success, there is little pretense

*Figure 4.2* Consummation scene, "Gesenkan Master." *TYZ* 6:52.

that one can recover a relationship with the lost past. The sexual act through which the protagonist recovers his male identity in the 1970 work is safely contained in the protagonist's fantasies, and the author is far more self-reflective about his own fantasies. In 1968 he had described the inevitable and painful separation from his fantasy world only in premonitory fashion; two years later he seems to have accepted this inevitable severance. The high degree of introspection distinguishes "Yanagiya Master" from Tsuge's earlier work. The author returns to his fantasies to confirm that there is no place for him within them. The protagonist—Tsuge's alter ego—is constantly aware of the distance that separates him from the object of his nostalgia. He becomes a farcical figure, caught in repetitive returns to the past.

"Yanagiya Master" repeats many of the themes found in "Gensenkan Master." Visiting a rustic hamlet, the protagonist stays in a rundown eatery, where he finds an object of sexual interest. The darkness that dominates the work and the protagonist's representation as a black silhouette in many frames are reminiscent of scenes from "Gensenkan Master." Yet the author adds a framing device to the story and anchors it in a first-person perspective through opening and closing scenes set in the time of the narrator's recollection—a time that resembles Tsuge's contemporary world. By portraying the movement between the everyday realm and the artist's imaginary world, the story underscores the unreality of the nostalgic space. The fantasies are contained as fantasies and never admitted into everyday life.

The story opens with a scene in which the protagonist visits a "nude studio" on a back street in Tokyo. There, a naked woman exposes her private parts to him, listlessly giving each part the name of a Tokyo landmark: "This is Shiba Park. This is Tokyo Tower and the Waterworks Bureau. Hama Detached Palace. Tokyo Gas" (*TYZ* 5:148–50). The man sitting in front of her, who physically resembles the author, shows little interest in her bodily display (figure 4.3). While the landscape of Tokyo is sexualized through the juxtaposition with the woman's body parts, the representation is devoid of sexual allure. This opening scene establishes the impossibility of the protagonist recovering his masculinity by embracing the corrupt and commercially available object of nostalgia. He finds no connection with the metropolis in the woman's figure, apathetically gazing at it in close proximity. He eventually turns his back to her, noticing the theme song of a popular yakuza movie series, *A Man from Abashiri Prison*

*Figure 4.3* The woman displays her "Hama Detached Palace," "Yanagiya Master" (1970). *TYZ* 5:149.

(*Abashiri bangaichi*, 1965–1972) playing downstairs (*TYZ* 5:151). The series romanticizes the marginal identities of the inmates of the penitentiary in Abashiri, Hokkaido.[13] Inspired by the song, Tsuge's protagonist suddenly flees the scene and jumps on a train heading east (*TYZ* 5:153–55).

The protagonist eventually finds himself in "N-ura," a desolate community across Tokyo Bay.[14] A few frames later, a flashback returns the story to the nude studio. The crosscutting of the two scenes emphasizes the protagonist's depressed state as he arrives at his destination on a rainy night. The flashback reveals that he has visited the woman at the studio many times. Although she shows concern for him, she cannot provide the comfort he seeks. The dimly lit space of the studio projects his dark mental state. The woman asks if he is addicted to sleeping pills, commenting: "It makes you no good." When he asks, "No good at what?" she describes his general decline in energy, but her comments insinuate his impotence. The conversation with the model spirals downward, ending with her self-denunciation: "I am hopeless" (*TYZ* 5:158–59). Even in the nude studio, the protagonist is not allowed to indulge in the sexual fantasy mapped onto the urban landscape. He must escape Tokyo in order to recover what he has lost in the metropolis.

Cutting back to the hamlet where the protagonist has arrived, the story traces his footsteps for the next twenty-four hours. Alone at the train station late on a rainy night, he asks the station employee how to reach the beach. Though the protagonist has arrived there with no clear plan, he goes along with the other man's presumption that he is going to stay in the hamlet overnight and go shell gathering the following morning (*TYZ* 5:161–62). After finding overnight accommodations at the local eatery, Yanagiya, he exchanges words with its female proprietor and her daughter, the latter in her late twenties, while speculating to himself about the daughter's sexual encounters with local youths (*TYZ* 5:164–65). As in "Gensenkan Master," the sexual fantasy serves as a medium for approaching the scene of nostalgia. After a flirtatious conversation between the protagonist and the young woman, the story abruptly cuts to a frame portraying the dark exterior of the decrepit wooden building in the rain (*TYZ* 5:167).

That night, the man lies on his futon unable to fall asleep, hyper-aware of his own presence in the room. His heightened sense of self in the unfamiliar environment manifests itself through the contrasting visual styles used to depict his image and that of the interior. While the protagonist is portrayed in simple line drawings, the inside of the room is depicted in thick detail with numerous lines. The nature of the contrast becomes clearer a few pages later when Tsuge portrays the man's encounter with a local woman who peddles clams on the street (figure 4.4). In contrast to the woman, who appears in rich three-dimensional detail, the protagonist is a flat figure, lacking depth.[15] In other frames he appears as a dark void—a silhouette—making it clear that he does not belong in the world he desires to inhabit. Except for the peddler dressed in traditional work attire, nobody in the story possesses a visual affinity to Tsuge's nostalgic and yet lugubrious-looking land, whose landscape is intricately depicted in a preceding frame.

Away from Tokyo, the protagonist allows himself to indulge in a sexual fantasy involving the young woman at the eatery. Triggered by her

*Figure 4.4* Contrasting drawing styles between the peddler and the protagonist, "Yanagiya Master." *TYZ* 5:179.

suggestive behavior in the middle of the night—she looks into his room with her nightwear almost exposing her breasts—he plots a fantastical narrative for them that begins with a sexual encounter and ends with him settling there as master of the eatery (*TYZ* 5:172–73). Yet his exploit is safely contained as a fantasy. Before the sexual encounter scene, the man retrospectively admits as the narrator that he had been indulging in a fantasy.[16] In "Yanagiya Master," the never-to-be-satisfied sexual desire epitomizes the distance between the protagonist and the object of his fantasy. He is alienated from the site of nostalgia even before he arrives there. In "Gensenkan Master," though the double ultimately shakes him out of the

*Figure 4.5* The fantasy master of Yanagiya, "Yanagiya Master." The caption reads: "I cannot help but remember the scene in which I and she, both aged, stand in front of the eatery, as if I was looking at an old, faded commemorative photograph (*kinen shashin*)." *TYZ* 5:175.

dreamlike space, it was still possible for the protagonist to play out his fantasy. Two years later Tsuge could not find even the tiniest space in his personal fantasy for such a drama. At the culmination of the protagonist's fantasy is an image of himself and the innkeeper's daughter as a middle-aged couple standing in front of Yanagiya. He imagines himself as a figure in a snapshot with faded colors (figure 4.5). He is buried in the chores of everyday life, and their relationship appears devoid of sexual chemistry, thus severing his nostalgic connection to this particular location (*TYZ* 5:175).

In the image, his traumatic childhood memories momentarily rise close to the surface, despite his general reluctance to include them in his early fictional works.[17] From 1937 to 1941 his father worked as a cook and his mother as a maid at a Japanese inn on Ōshima. "During those [first] four years [of his life]," Tsuge writes, "our family had a peaceful time" (*TYZ* suppl.: 221). In 1941, however, his family moved to a fishing village in Chiba, while his father began working at an inn in Tokyo. Tsuge does not specify the reasons for the relocation; he simply states that his own psychological issues—difficulties in interacting with others—began to manifest in that same year as he started kindergarten. In 1942 Tsuge's father passed away at the age of forty-two. He had been confined to a futon storage room because of his psychotic derangement and ultimately died there (*TYZ* suppl.: 221–22). The tragedy shattered the family's peaceful life: they suffered dire poverty for years, and Tsuge later lived in fear of his violent stepfather. The fact that the imaginary scene is denoted as a "commemorative photograph" (*kinen shashin*) suggests that it represents the upbringing he desired but never had. In the photo are a cook and his wife who have worked long years and now run their own eatery. A patch on the woman's trousers and a crack on the lower left wall imply that they are struggling financially, though the overall tidiness of the couple's appearance and the storefront suggest the stability of their life.

Tsuge slips into the image in order to reenact the alternative reality and protect it from the misfortune that awaits his family. In his right hand, the man grasps a kitchen knife, turned slightly upward. The object represents a cook's pride and could be used as a weapon if needed. His left hand is folded into a fist, hiding the thumb. Since the early twentieth century Japanese people have often been told to hide their thumbs when encountering a funeral procession or motor hearse in order to protect their parents.[18] According to folk belief, if the thumbs are exposed, the parents may die young or one might not be able to be with them at the moment of their death. In premodern times the thumbs were believed to be the most vulnerable parts of the body, through which the soul of the deceased can enter.[19] The fact that the Japanese word for "thumb," *oya-yubi*, literally means "parent finger" probably shifted the focus of protection from oneself to one's parents.[20] In this commemorative picture Tsuge therefore simultaneously stands in for his father and attempts to protect him from the menacing world. The woman stands next to him as both mother and wife, hiding her hands under her apron. The young woman at the eatery has no memories of her own father, who left for the war in 1944 when she was four months old and never returned.[21] Into this fatherless woman's life, the man insinuates himself as both a husband and a father.

The location of "N-ura," which Tsuge identifies elsewhere as Nagaura in Chiba, is perhaps too close to home.[22] Tokyo's industrial complexes are visible across Tokyo Bay, while his mother's hometown, where the family moved in 1941 and where he began experiencing psychological issues, is also in Chiba, twenty-some miles away. In contrast to the remote hamlet of "Gensenkan Master," the story that revolves around Yanagiya seems to reveal far more autobiographical material than the author is willing to share with his readers. To reestablish a symbolic distance between himself and his imaginary refuge, Tsuge casts his narrative into a liminal space—the beach—at its conclusion.

A year after the original visit, the protagonist returns to Yanagiya, hoping that the daughter will remember him. Nothing has changed at Yanagiya, and the woman has no recollection of him (*TYZ* 5:177). Unable to establish even a fantastical connection to the place, he again appears as a deep void against the scenery. Disappointed, he purchases a bag of clams from the aforementioned peddler and heads toward the beach. Here, in the darkness of night, his shadowy existence no longer conspicuous, the protagonist finally finds provisional comfort. As in some of Tsuge's well-known works from the late 1960s and early 1970s, the sea sets the stage for the narrative's resolution.[23] When he was a teenager, sensing that the sea was the only source of salvation (*sukui*), Tsuge actually tried to stow away on a foreign cargo ship (*TYZ* suppl.:145).[24] In the liminal space of the beach (the threshold between land and sea), the man suspends his anxious search for belonging. He seems to find brief solace in being on the deserted beach with a stray cat. Lying on the sand, he sings the theme song of *A Man from Abashiri Prison*, signaling that he has found his own *bangaichi* (the land without street numbers and thus outside the government administrative system), a space where he can temporarily sever ties with contemporary society as well as his personal history (*TYZ* 5:184–86). He will soon leave this location and return to everyday life in Tokyo, from which he will periodically try to flee. Yet his escape is destined to fail because the chasm that separates him and his dream destination is too large even for his fantasy to fill.

In two short years Tsuge had come a long way from the drama of "Gensenkan Master." In that story, after being rudely awakened from a half-sleep state by his double, the antihero is still allowed to return to the fantastical world; although he may physically reach the longed-for locale, however, he can never blend into its scenery. The focus of Tsuge's early works was on the process through which a character comes to this realization. By contrast, the narrative of "Yanagiya Master" revolves around the self-conscious state of the angst-filled traveler. It appears that as he became more self-reflective about his own desire and its frustration, Tsuge struggled to produce his work. After publishing "Gensenkan Master" in July 1968 and another work in the following month, Tsuge did not publish manga for fifteen months, spending much of his time traveling.[25] Between 1969 and 1970 he visited various rural sites around Japan with the photographer Kitai Kazuo (b. 1944) for a travel series in *Asahi Graph*, a weekly photography magazine. Although he eventually returned to publishing manga, he never reestablished intimate relations with his own precommercialized fantasy world. As his fantasy lost its historical grounding, Tsuge began to examine himself as a fantasy object. By introducing autobiographical elements into his stories, he both intentionally and unintentionally confused the boundaries between his fiction and his life, as if intending to dissolve his everyday existence into fantasy. Thus, in these later stories, travel merely provides the stage for Tsuge's deep contemplation of his own inner world.

## Discover Japan, Discover Myself

In the two years that Tsuge spent on the road, a major multimedia campaign helped reshape Japan's domestic tourism. Dentsū, Japan's biggest advertising agency, launched the Discover Japan campaign in October 1970 on behalf of Japan National Railway (JNR).[26] This campaign departed radically from past marketing practices, signaling a new phase of Japan's capitalism, at least in the estimation of Fujioka Wakao (1927–2015), who led the Dentsū team's efforts. Although uncorroborated by other sources, a fascinating account claims that the whole campaign was inspired by the *Asahi Graph*'s travel series to which Tsuge contributed illustrations. The writer Ōsaki Norio, who accompanied Tsuge and the photographer, Kitai Kazuo, on the *Asahi Graph*–sponsored trips in 1969 and 1970, learned from the magazine's editorial staff about their travelogue's impact on Dentsū's work.[27] If this is correct, the campaign's true origins were well-concealed by the heroic narrative that Fujioka tirelessly promoted for media consumption.

Although Tsuge and Fujioka had diametrically opposed stances vis-à-vis tourism, their creative efforts deeply resonated with one another in the early 1970s. Tsuge cast a self-critical gaze on his ill-fated attempts to escape consumer society, while Fujioka reasserted his masculine identity with the claim that he almost singlehandedly redefined the tourism industry and market in 1970s Japan.[28] If the manga artist believed that fantasy space was all but gone in Japan, the Dentsū man took it upon himself to transfigure it into consumable images for the masses. Despite their seeming disagreement, their respective works engaged with the question of what it meant to travel in a society permeated by mass consumer culture. For Tsuge and Fujioka, nostalgia seemed to be an operative concept, but their operations went far beyond simple recovery of nostalgia's objects.

Tsuge took advantage of the so-called travel boom, which the Discover Japan campaign boosted. He produced a number of works on the theme of travel, appealing to a wider audience, and the royalties that he received allowed him to remain on the road for extended periods. His illustrations twice adorned the covers of the JNR promotional magazine *Discover Japan* (*Deisukabaa Japan*). The one on the cover of the winter 1972 issue portrays life in a small fishing village in a style familiar to Tsuge's fans (figure 4.6). It is a composite of images from prior and future works. The man sitting inside the small shack, for example, is from "Chōhachi's Inn" (Chōhachi no yado, 1968), and the boy who is receiving a buzz cut would soon appear in "A Rustic Inn" (Riarizumu no yado, 1973). The dark figure leaning on the pole, like the silhouetted figure in "Yanagiya Master," seems to represent the artist's self-image as a ghostly intruder. Thus, even while riding the high tide of tourism, Tsuge strove to maintain his critical perspective.

The Discover Japan campaign promoted travelers' self-awareness, but in a much more positive way than Tsuge did: rather than see themselves as a dark void, they are encouraged to be their real selves—as defined by campaign strategists—against the beautiful scenery. The Dentsū team redefined travel as a performative act that would restore a sense of personhood in a consumer society where individual identity was a constellation of fragmentary desires and marketed images. What they sold was not a ticket to an aesthetically pleasing destination per se but entry to a stage where one could become the master of oneself. Dentsū's promotion complemented Tsuge's artistic vision in that it offered a dark void—like a cutout hole—to be filled by travelers. Furthermore, the traveler does not need an authentic theater in order to seek an authentic self: the most generic setups suffice to signal the break with everyday routine that facilitates that search. When initially developing ideas for "Gensenkan Master," Tsuge contemplated portraying the hamlet as nothing but a set of façades propped up from behind, like a movie set.[29] The artist's imagination plainly articulated the artificial nature

*Figure 4.6* One of the two *Discover Japan* cover images by Tsuge Yoshiharu (1972).

of travel in mass consumer society, a condition that the Discover Japan campaign actively promoted as a stage for self-discovery.

The specifics of the Discover Japan campaign reveal the Dentsū team's strategy for reviving domestic tourism in the wake of Expo '70. JNR spent a substantial amount of money (¥40 billion), mostly on augmenting the bullet train system, to meet heightened demand during the expo.[30] Although JNR recovered three-quarters of its investment before the national event closed, its executives began exploring ways to permanently raise demand for railway travel. Rather than focusing on practical tactics, the Dentsū team, led by Fujioka Wakao, espoused a larger vision that would appeal to contemporary Japanese society, positing travel as something beyond mere physical transportation. The team ultimately embraced a spiritual message that equated travel with discovering oneself. From its earliest incarnation, the Discover Japan campaign was dubbed the "Discover Myself" campaign in the Dentsū strategists' internal discussions.[31]

In the sales presentation to JNR representatives, Fujioka explained what JNR was up against: "What do you think is the [biggest] rival of travel? Television." Fujioka later explained what he meant by this provocative statement:

> If the pleasure of television is in sharing information, the pleasure of travel is in "discovering oneself." Thus, in order to beat television, we must promote "Discover Myself" as the [basic] concept of travel. What I refer to here as television, of course, is television as a metaphor for [modern] civilization. Television vividly displayed the ray of 1960s high growth and prosperity, but it also deprived people's minds of the capacity to sense others' pain.[32]

In Fujioka's thinking, travel must become an antithesis to the material prosperity that Japanese society sought in the high-growth era. "The ability to sense others' pain" that he mentions registers not so much a physical sensation as empathy toward what each Japanese person has lost in an affluent society.

His postcampaign comments suggest that Fujioka anchored his critical thinking in the simple binary of spiritual versus material, calling for the former's restoration. Indeed, he saw the Discover Japan campaign as an extension of his previous project, From Gung-ho to Beautiful (Mōretsu kara byūtifuru e), which he coordinated for the Fuji Xerox Corporation earlier in 1970. Without focusing on Fuji products, the campaign delivered social messages criticizing the obsessive state of Japan's economic life—the state that the word *mōretsu* came to represent—and offering beauty as the antidote to the ill effects of the high-growth economy. The first television commercial was a thirty-second spot that showed the musician Katō Kazuhiko (1947–2009) walking down a Ginza street holding a banner bearing the handwritten word "beautiful."[33]

The inward turn that Fujioka orchestrated, however, derived not from his quest for spiritual meaning but rather from his efforts to liberate commercial advertisement from the narrow confines of agent-client relations. As high-quality merchandise saturated the market, he argued, it was increasingly difficult to differentiate products. Consequently, advertisements had split off from their original referential function—promoting particular goods—and evolved into a distinctive cultural medium. Rather than follow the current trend of Japan's ad industry and produce advertisement for the sake of advertisement, Fujioka was determined to anchor his work in the expression of larger social values. This new approach, which he called "de-advertisement" (*datsu-kōkoku*), implied that no direct return was expected from the promotional efforts: by tailoring ads to address mass society and social issues (as opposed to individual corporations), the ad agencies could liberate themselves from subservience to business clients and gain more latitude for their creative maneuvers. Fujioka emphasized that the message "From Gung-ho to Beautiful" stemmed from his personal desire to sound an alarm about the adverse effects of economic growth on the environment and humanity.[34] The contents of the message, however, ultimately mattered little to his de-advertisement project, whose primary goal was to instill creative agency in advertising firms. Philosophical messages served as pigments with which to brush beautiful corporate images onto a social canvas.

What did it mean, then, to discover Japan or oneself in the brave new world of 1970s Japanese corporate advertising? Fujioka's accounts suggest that the JNR campaign replicated de-advertisement by refusing to identify exactly what it was advertising. What individual travelers would actually discover could not have mattered less. The all-male Dentsū team had a clearly defined target, single women from nineteen to twenty-four, breaking from the dominant perception of travel as a male activity.[35] Fujioka harbored moral suspicions about young female travelers because of the popular association between travel and male sexual desire (which Tsuge explores in his travel manga).³⁶ Fujioka's intention, however, was not to guide these young women in moral conduct but to let them lead the whole society to the frontier of consumption, where images were among the hottest of commodities.

Fujioka conceived of travel as an imaginary stage where young women would present themselves as heroines—or, rather, present their completely different traveling selves as heroines:

> Travel is a stage set or a stage indispensable to realizing such selves. A stage needs proper actors, and actors need a proper stage. They [young women] seek the right stage, on which they can be "traveling selves." . . . When someone transforms herself from an ordinary woman to a traveling woman, the change should not be obvious to others, but should at the same time be recognized by others. There is nothing harder for a woman than not being looked at!³⁷

Fujioka did not explain what the "traveling self" actually meant, but it required a stage from which women could be seen. Discover Japan thus strove to produce the visual space where each traveler was supposed to find her unique self by transforming herself into the object of an imagined gaze.

Discover Japan was not alone in targeting young female consumers. Two new women's monthlies, *an·an* and *nonno*, inaugurated in March 1970 and May 1971, respectively, delivered similar messages to their readers, powerfully connecting fashion and travel. Filling the gap left by Discover Japan, *an·an* and *nonno* provided readers with specific instructions on how they should tailor their appearances to stage their unique selves.³⁸ Fujioka acknowledges that his team owed much of the campaign's success to the two magazines.³⁹ Meanwhile, Kinameri Yoshihisa, the inaugural coeditor of *an·an*, felt more confident about the magazine's unconventional editorial decisions when he saw the Discover Japan posters for the first time.⁴⁰

Both magazines regularly featured articles on domestic tourist sites, accompanied by color photos of female models clad in the latest fashion. Young women were literally expected to fashion their new selves out of the images they found in fashion magazines. The women who dressed like *an·an* and *nonno* models and traveled to popular tourist sites with copies of those magazines were popularly labeled the "an-non tribe" (*an non zoku*). Discussing the magazines' far-reaching impact, the sociologist Nanba Kōji cites two women's recollections of earnestly embracing the trend. The first voice of a de facto an-non tribe member belongs to the writer Nakano Midori, who was born in 1946:

> I have some photos from the time I traveled to Kyoto and Kobe with my little sister. The *an·an* style sought an interesting contrast by placing young girls in edgy fashion against an old town that exuded the weight of history. . . . Both I and my sister were totally into it. We were feeling as if we were acting out a page of *an·an*. . . . It is not an overstatement to say that back then we traveled to take *an·an*-style photos.[41]

The writer of the second account, Nakazawa Yuriko, was born in 1954 but had similar experiences:

> I was fascinated by the articles with beautiful photos that introduced readers to paths associated with literary works and shops. I went to Kyoto by myself. I felt a kind of freedom, being caught in late spring snow on the Togetsukyō Bridge [in Kyoto]. I went to Nagasaki, Takayama, [and other places], taking streetcars with an illustrated magazine in hand or walking back streets. *an·an* and *nonno* were the textbooks for "my travel through which to search for another me." One year, when I was walking down Sannenzaka in Kyoto, I saw a woman dressed similarly and looking around the same age, walking toward me with the same magazine. Then I noticed that girls around me, looking very similar, were walking into the same shop. I discreetly put away my magazine.[42]

The encounter with her doubles in Kyoto echoes the final scene of "Gensenkan Master" in that it mercilessly revealed the unoriginality of her performative act. Although she shares the episode to convey the strong sense of embarrassment, she candidly admits its initial powerful grip on her.

Some unconventional photographs used in campaign posters attest to the campaign's emphasis on visuality—the marked presence of a camera—rather than specific information about the travel destinations. The very first poster distributed to JNR stations throughout Japan, for example, featured an extremely blurry image of a young woman holding a rake in a grassy field (figure 4.7). This photograph is reminiscent of the experimental style—often characterized as "rough, blurry, out of focus" (*are, bure, boke*), with a

*Figure 4.7* The first Discover Japan poster distributed to JNR stations nationwide (November 1970). Photo by Iizuka Takenori.

hint of irreverence—associated with the short-lived magazine *provoke* (1968–1969).[43] The magazine had a tremendous impact on the contemporary Japanese photography scene, and its provocative style was immediately "accepted"—that is, copied and consumed.[44] One of its founding members, Nakahira Takuma, strongly reacted to JNR's alleged appropriation, denouncing its corrosive effects on the *provoke* collective's experimental spirit.[45] But was Nakahira entitled to his moral indignation if, in the media scholar Yasumi Akihito's words, he indeed insisted that "both the world and the self are fragmented and thrown into fluid relations"?[46] Although they critiqued the assumed transparency of the photographic medium by calling attention to the camera's motion and presence, did the sensational works of *provoke* not also offer a view from inside the giant blender of contemporary culture, reconfirming the social conditions in which they were produced? The first Discover Japan poster seems to communicate exactly that: it offers no stable concept of self as such, but only a process through which to find one's self as a conglomeration of fragmentary images. As the poster promises, the imaginary camera will be there to capture each traveler's performative act, through which that traveler can produce a collage-like self.

This visual field that the Dentsū team offered to travelers was ultimately anchored in an equally imaginary Japan, devoid of historical and geographic associations, as exemplified by the campaign's subtitle "Beautiful Japan and Myself" (Utsukushii Nihon to watashi). Fujioka readily admits that it was inspired by the title of Kawabata Yasunori's Nobel lecture, "Utsukushii Nihon no watashi," in 1968.[47] The official English title of the lecture is "Japan, the Beautiful, and Myself."[48] In Kawabata's original title, however, the possessive particle *no* signifies the nested state of "myself" within Japan, whereas the particle *to* in the Dentsū version does not suggest any hierarchical order between the two nouns: "Myself" is as expansive as Japan, which is also reduced to a generic symbol. Fujioka sensed an affinity between his campaign and Kawabata's literary imagination, as both transformed Japan into an "ambiguous" and aesthetic space.[49]

To Tsuge, performing a unique self was more complicated than Discover Japan made it out to be. His fundamental discomfort with Japan's fast-changing society imbued him with a desire to recover pieces of the past, yet he was keenly aware of the impossibility of such a project. While visits to rustic sites allowed him to indulge in the fantasy world of yesteryear, travel was quickly becoming an extension of mass consumerism, as attested by Discover Japan. The harder he pursued his fantasy, therefore, the deeper he plunged himself into the commercial world, where the past was transformed into another nostalgic image for consumption. The changes from "Gensenkan Master" to "Yanagiya Master" discussed earlier demonstrate his growing distance from his imaginary world, which he eventually evacuated completely.

"A Rustic Inn" (1973) takes a straightforward look at the increasingly dismal condition of travel in contemporary Japanese society, indicting the author for his complicity. The story ends with a protest—albeit a rather lackadaisical one—against the narcissistic vision of travel that Discover Japan promoted.

## "A Rustic Inn": The Realism of Poverty

In "A Rustic Inn," there is not even a pretense that the male protagonist is in search of emotional ties with the site he visits. The motive for his travel is purely commercial: he is hunting for themes for his work. In Ajigasawa, a desolate fishing community in Aomori, the northernmost part of Honshu, the protagonist stumbles on the brilliant idea of setting his stories in the cheap inns that cater to itinerant traveling salesmen, a formula that will allow him to spend less on accommodations while cashing in on the recent travel boom (*TYZ* 5:192). If his counterparts in the previous two works are seeking refuge in a rundown inn and an eatery, the man in "A Rustic Inn" sees the inns as cheap, exotic objects waiting to be exploited commercially.

As a complete outsider, the protagonist of "A Rustic Inn" casts a cold and calculating gaze on the hamlet and its people. The work's title frame is explicit about the symbolic distance between the traveler and the lives of the residents (figure 4.8). On a small, unpaved road leading to a sea hung with clouds, the protagonist stands holding a camera and looking down on a local man who is stooped under the weight of the seaweed on his back. The man appears to notice and feel annoyed by the gaze of the camera, but he is unable to return it. The belabored man has become part of the photogenic scenery. A thatched shack and fishing paraphernalia conspicuously fill the background immediately behind the traveler. A life that lags behind the rest of Japan's economic progress and is burdened by poverty appears alien and exotic to the protagonist, who stands there as a curious

# リアリズムの宿

*Figure 4.8* The ethnographic gaze, "A Rustic Inn" (1973). *TYZ* 5:187.

outsider. The camera's lens physically and symbolically mediates his invasive gaze.

The author is keenly aware of his complicity in the commercial boom that has lured visitors to Japan's countryside, as the Discover Japan campaign has done. His protagonist hunts for nostalgic worlds purely for commercial gain. This frame, however, is portrayed through a third eye, detached from the protagonist's perspective, which attests to the author/protagonist's awareness of his own intrusive ethnographic gaze (the local man's eyes are not visible).[50] Tsuge's split gaze also expresses his mixed revulsion and identification with respect to the impoverished country scene. As a former "native" of the "other Japan," he recognizes the problematic nature of his gaze.

Unlike the other two works discussed in this chapter, "A Rustic Inn" includes the name of the hamlet along with information on the surrounding region. This geographic specificity reduces the fantastical quality of the work.[51] The protagonist finds himself staying in a family-run inn that is in the most wretched of conditions: cold, rundown, and unsanitary. His room is in the midst of the family's living quarters, has a warped floor, and offers no views. He tries to run away from the premises, but the family has placed his shoes in a hard-to-reach place. The dinner they serve is most unsatisfactory (*TYZ* 5:207). Later, in the bath, he realizes that he is the last one to bathe and that the water in the tub is filthy from all the family members' use (*TYZ* 5:208).

Infuriated by the conditions and with himself for choosing the place, the protagonist decides to go to bed early. Lying on the futon, he hears the family's fifth-grade son reading from his school textbook an excerpt from Akutagawa Ryūnosuke's "The Spider Thread": "Buddha stood on the edge of Lotus Pond, quietly watching the whole hubbub.... Kandata received a punishment proportionate to his merciless mind, which was bent on letting nobody else escape Hell" (*TYZ* 5:209–10). In Akutagawa's fable, Buddha looks into the Lotus Pond and finds the notorious criminal Kandata suffering in Hell. Buddha remembers the man's one good deed—sparing a spider's life—and for that, Kandata receives a chance for redemption. Buddha casts a thread from a spider's web toward him. Kandata finds the thread and climbs up, hoping to escape from Hell. Realizing, however, that thousands of others are also clinging to the string beneath him, he yells at them to get off, afraid that the string will break from their weight. The story ends with Buddha, disappointed by Kandata's selfishness, cutting the string just above him and letting all the hopefuls fall back into Hell.[52] After hearing the passage, the artist lies quietly on the futon, enveloped by darkness (*TYZ* 5:210).[53] Although far from prosperous, he is not condemned to stay in the dire poverty that he finds at the inn. The selfish motives of Kandata, who tries to save just himself, mirror the protagonist's self-righteous anger.

In the final frame of "A Rustic Inn," the author comments on the boy's hesitant reading. This detail is particularly poignant in view of Tsuge's own youth, when he missed many days of elementary school and his entire middle school education while he worked to supplement his family's meager income (*TYZ* suppl.:144–45). Lying silently in the darkness of the room, the traveler acknowledges his own arrogance. As a stand-in for Tsuge himself, the character's recognition gestures toward the author's self-reflection. Like the selfish criminal, he has cursed fellow human beings who happen to live in wretched conditions for their self-centered behavior. He recalls that the objects of nostalgia are beautiful only through one's sanitized reminiscences. This work from 1973 highlights the distance between the author and the *riarizumu* (realism) of the poverty that he has escaped. "A Rustic Inn" mocks his goal of simultaneously rejecting and benefiting from his fortune. Fully ensconced in a new class, the author is no longer able to find his place in the corners of Japan left behind by economic progress.

The use of voice saves this story from becoming an overly didactic moral tale. In thinking about voice, it is worth contrasting this manga to Fujioka's advertising copy on a Discover Japan poster: "Closing my eyes . . . what should I see?" The accompanying photograph shows a young woman meditating in a large room that appears to be part of a Buddhist monastery.[54] The poster eloquently articulates the centrality of the traveler in relation to the visual field: she gets to choose what she wants to see, regardless of the scenery surrounding her. The traveler as visual observer is expected to act as a consumer par excellence. By contrast, it is much harder for Tsuge's protagonist to shut out the sound that comes from an adjacent room. The voice is like a ghost that anchors the man in the past and exposes the hidden layers of the here and now. Yet hearing has a secondary place in relation to the dominant perceptual mode: vision. The boy's reading voice reaches the protagonist in the darkness, where he is momentarily liberated from the tight hold of vision. He pulls the comforter over his eyes and just listens to the boy's faltering reading. The voice insists on its presence only tentatively, because it speaks for a world that remains invisible to Japan's larger society.

In the five years from 1968 to 1973, Tsuge covered a great distance in his fantastical travel. At the end of the 1960s he was still just able to imagine himself in the fantasy world of Japan's preindustrial past. A few years later he was no longer able to indulge in his own nostalgia. The shift in Tsuge's position with respect to his nostalgic objects corresponded with a change in the larger Japanese society and its relationship to the past. Under the regime of the high-growth economy, the remote countryside was incorporated into the modern space of postwar Japan as an exotic tourist attraction. This symbolic transformation of the countryside startles Tsuge's angst-ridden travelers from their dreams. In his travel manga we find the figure of the author himself, condemned to live as a ghost in a capitalist society, where even the past is manufactured and merchandized.[55] He was deeply implicated in this transformation, however: he had taken advantage of it for his artistic expression as well as his career. Tsuge's entanglement with Discover Japan—whether intentional or not—evidences the affinities that existed between his artistic imagination and the campaign's commercial vision. However, Tsuge's poignant portrayals of elusive masculinity counter the all-male Discover Japan campaign team's exclusive focus on young women, and their unspoken premise that men retained their autonomous agency in consumer society.

Finding no more comfort in nostalgia, Tsuge can only hope to sustain his being in a self-reflective gaze. He eventually finds refuge in the self-enclosed space of semiautobiographical works set in the everyday life of the recent past. Since the publication of "A Rustic Inn," Tsuge has never replicated the emotional intensity demonstrated in his works of the late 1960s and early 1970s, an intensity engendered by his own desperate efforts to work through the trauma of Japan's radical transformation.[56]

The next chapter takes the discussion of travel in a different direction by focusing on the writer Kaikō Takeshi, who tried to burst out of the bubble of Japan's mass consumer society by witnessing firsthand the war in Vietnam. Much like Tsuge, Kaikō struggles to reestablish his autonomous identity through his travel but seems to succeed only in dismantling this masculine project.

CHAPTER V

## The Ethics of Witnessing

*Kaikō Takeshi's Vietnam War*

In November 1964 the prize-winning writer Kaikō Takeshi (1930–1989) left Tokyo for Saigon to work as a special correspondent for *Weekly Asahi* (*Shūkan asahi*). Accompanied by the photographer Akimoto Kei'ichi (1930–1979), he spent the next hundred days in South Vietnam, reporting on the nation's precarious situation under the growing tension of the civil war.[1] Upon returning to Japan, Kaikō revised and published his weekly reports as a book, *Vietnam War Report* (*Betonamu senki*, 1965).[2] The reading public welcomed the book, which offered a timely firsthand account of a nation that was fast sliding into large-scale military conflict. The publication's timing helped to make it a national bestseller, just as the publisher anticipated. Shortly after Kaikō's return to Japan, the United States escalated its involvement in Vietnam by bombing North Vietnam and committing ground forces. Japan did not participate in direct military operations in subsequent years, but it rendered substantial and substantive support for the U.S. war effort. The U.S. bases in Japan became an integral part of America's Vietnam strategy, and Japanese industries provided materials needed for the war, reaping enormous economic benefits. U.S. cash infusions into the Japanese economy played an important role in Japan's astounding economic growth in the late 1960s and early 1970s.[3] The Vietnam War in turn provided exciting content for Japanese television and other forms of media. While oppositional political groups, such as labor unions and student organizations, fiercely criticized Japan's complicity in the Vietnam War, Japanese society watched the war unfold at a safe distance, insulated from its physical effects.[4] In the Japan that celebrated its own economic success, there was intense sympathy toward the people of Vietnam, but the war that tore the region apart was consumed largely in the form of media images with little bearing on everyday life.

When he arrived in Saigon in 1964—before intensive media coverage of the conflict began—Kaikō's primary goal was to close in on the reality of war. Having grown up during the Asia Pacific War, he was no stranger to war, yet that familiarity had faded as Japanese society rebounded from wartime devastation. Kaikō initially (and naively) hoped that he could somehow recover what he had lost in postwar Japan at "a place where real things are happening" (*genjitsu no genba*) (*KTZ* 22:89–90). The writer may have succeeded in temporarily stepping out of the peace and prosperity of postwar Japanese society, but he would grapple with the death and destruction that he witnessed in Vietnam for the rest of his life. In the end he tried to be more than the opportunistic observer that he had initially appeared to be.

Critics agree that Kaikō's fictional work acquired a new dimension when he began to work through his experiences in Vietnam.[5] Two texts in particular, *Into a Black Sun* (*Kagayakeru yami*, 1968) and *Darkness in Summer* (*Natsuno yami*, 1971), the products of his introspection about those experiences, are often celebrated as the best works of his career and among the greatest in postwar Japanese literature.[6] In this chapter, by focusing on the narrative of *Into a Black Sun*, I explore how Kaikō grappled with his Vietnam experiences. In many ways the book reads as an antithesis to a popular cultural discourse that idealizes a masculine autonomous subjectivity as the protagonist's vision proves powerless in creating a critical distance from the chaotic conditions that surround him. Although the story begins as a quest for a heroic counteridentity that transcends the deleterious effects of mass consumer society, the narrative twist in the final scene mocks the protagonist's masculinist project by denying him clear vision—a sine qua non for his unfettered subjectivity—while allowing him to imagine a utopian space where he achieves a primordial bond with what he observes. We begin by tracing the creative trajectory that led Kaikō to Vietnam.

## Copywriting

Kaikō Takeshi's early career was tightly intertwined with the development of postwar Japan's consumer culture. In the second half of the 1950s the aspiring writer worked in the marketing department of the whisky distiller Kotobukiya (present-day Suntory), and his exceptional talent for both literary work and advertising won almost immediate public recognition.[7] In 1958 he received the coveted Akutagawa literary prize; the following year his marketing team was awarded a Mainichi Industrial Design Award primarily for a series of television commercials.[8] Even as he faced growing pressure to dedicate more time to his literary career, he continued to work on the whisky maker's successful multimedia ad campaigns.

In the early postwar period Kotobukiya's executives made a bold adjustment in their marketing strategies. They abandoned the conventional approach of selling whisky as a luxury commodity and instead began merchandising it as an affordable alcoholic beverage for the masses. Saji Keizō, who later became Kotobukiya's second president, called this move "revolutionary."[9] Under this plan, Kotobukiya promoted the Torys label. This simulacrum of whisky was heavily marketed through multimedia ads. Malt whiskey made up less than 3 percent of its actual content, and was mixed with ethanol derived from molasses and water colored with caramel.[10] When Torys was conceived, the advertising team's charge was to surround the product with sophisticated images and thereby elevate its consumption as part of an urban lifestyle. (As discussed in the introduction, Suntory used the same marketing strategies for Delica products.) After joining Kotobukiya in 1954, Kaikō initially served as the editor of its public relations magazine and then wrote copy for newspaper ads. Starting in 1956, ads featuring designer Yanagihara Ryōhei's illustrations and Kaikō's copy appeared regularly in the major newspapers. The very first newspaper ad that Kaikō created with Yanagihara unabashedly linked Torys to an urban middle-class lifestyle that was at that point aspirational in Japanese society: "You want to live a bright, fun life. That feeling means 'Buy Torys.' You want to set flowers casually for the dinner table. That feeling means 'Buy Torys.'"[11] (Recall that Sei'ichi and Tsutomu drink Torys rather than more expensive whisky in *Where Spring Comes Late*.)

In 1958 Sakai Mutsuo and Yamaguchi Hitomi joined the duo to work on producing television commercials.[12] From 1956 to 1958 Kaikō was also the editor of Suntory's legendary in-house magazine, *Liquor Heaven* (*Yōshu tengoku*), which was distributed to bars and bar patrons.[13] Kaikō humorously recalls the days when he worked on ads for Torys:

> Day in and day out, I kept writing Torys ads. Kakubin and Old [Kotobukiya's higher-grade whisky brands] would have sold even without any advertisement. Ads for them actually would have encouraged the customers to search through liquor stores for something that they couldn't find. The malt whisky that we used in Old needed to mature over years. If we had shipped as much [Old] as there was a demand for, our cellar would have been emptied out right way. Since we limited the shipment of Old, it was Torys that we needed to sell through [heavy doses of] advertising. (*KTZ* 22:53–42)

Kaikō enjoyed working as a member of the Kotobukiya PR team.[14] As soon as he established himself as a literary figure, however, he experienced a bout of depression, caused by years of overwork and post–Akutagawa prize letdown.[15] He had exhausted possible topics for his fictional work and failed to meet publishers' demands and deadlines.[16] As if to compensate for churning out empty signifiers for subpar Suntory products, Kaikō yearned to write about socially relevant matters, trolling for topics in Japan and eventually overseas.[17] In the 1960s, during a time he later called his "Age of Exploration," he made frequent overseas trips, seeking to step outside Japanese society, and particularly postwar Japan's consumer society. His extensive itineraries included visits to China and Auschwitz in 1960; the following year he attended Adolf Eichmann's trial in Jerusalem. He subsequently wrote two books, *Nations of Past and Present* (*Kako to mirai no kuniguni*, 1961) and *A Voice Hunter* (*Koe no Karyūdo*, 1962), as well as numerous articles about his overseas visits in those years.[18]

## The Passage to Vietnam

Reporting on Vietnam was a particularly attractive project for Kaikō precisely because of the prospect of a full-scale war there. A close encounter with wartime conditions would, he hoped, help him recuperate his creative energy. The journalist and writer Hino Keizō (1929–2002), a fellow mid-1960s Vietnam correspondent, spoke about Kaikō's attraction to the city of Saigon in a conversation with Mukai Satoshi, Kaikō's long-time friend:

> The situation was that the social order had broken down at its foundation, and the kind of chaos that existed before the social formation reappeared. That resonated with the situation that we experienced [in Japan] immediately after the defeat [in the Asia Pacific War] at the ages of 15 or 16. Everything was falling apart. With anxiety and dizziness, chaos began to appear. You know the Chinatown, called "Cholon," that he often wrote about. People swarmed the place, streets and back alleys, even on a regular day. The place was filled with energy, the kind of energy emanating from the people's determination to survive at whatever cost. It was absolutely hopeless, but it was a hopeless situation filled with absolute energy.[19]

According to Hino, Kaikō kept returning to Saigon searching for "a hopeless situation filled with absolute energy" that had once existed in the chaos of postwar Japan. While the manga artist Tsuge Yoshiharu looked for his spiritual home in the pockets of Japan left behind by economic progress, Kaikō found his in Saigon.

But it was not mere nostalgia, insists Hino, that compelled Kaikō to return to the city. In a eulogy for Kaikō, Hino elaborates on this point, stating that his friend visited Vietnam "to recuperate powers of spirit, which have been growing soft in the increasingly benign days under the high-growth economy." But the price for his visits was high. Hino intertwines their experiences, addressing Kaikō: "You and I, ourselves endowed with postwar Japanese humanism, crumbled, corroded by 'Mars's' ferocious atmosphere."[20] The comparison between the Southeast Asian nation and the planet is borrowed from a conversation in one of Kaikō's short stories (*KTZ* 8:65–67). Although Hino does not define the term "postwar Japanese humanism," elsewhere in the same text he lists it with "liberation, freedom, and progress," calling them all collectively a "glow on history's surface." The phrase suggests an optimistic belief in human agency and the ability to produce a better future.[21]

Kaikō explained his attraction to Vietnam in different terms. In an interview that he gave right before leaving Japan, he despaired of what he saw as the vapid state of contemporary Japanese literature, filled with "words,

words, and words. A reader could feel neither resistance nor the reality of [living]." Vietnam offered a chance to break out of this occlusion: "In it, I will be ground down, and tested. I might lose my words, get lost, or find some hope. In any case I would like to throw myself into that chaos and try it out, hoping to start with what is left and write a work."[22] The writer was aware of the difficult situation he was getting into, although he was perhaps too optimistic about its transformative effects.

Kaikō's transition from Tokyo to Vietnam was also strategic. Prior to his departure, he serialized a thirteen-month-long report in *Shūkan Asahi* on various aspects of Tokyo life when the city frantically prepared for the 1964 Olympics (Kaikō discusses their opening and closing ceremonies in the final installments).[23] The weekly reports under the headline "Right on, Tokyo" (Zubari Tokyo) presented an opportunity to capture the chaotic state of a city where "night and day, rich and poor, and modern and premodern" were indistinguishable. He later admitted the ulterior motive of finding materials for his literary production as well (*KTZ* 22:80). Kaikō the urban explorer found colorful subjects in the interstices of the metropolis—from urban farming to the Ueno Zoo—and provided entertaining weekly reports on them. As diverse as his topics were, the overall selection was grounded in his and the editorial staff's desire to locate something exotic in the middle of Tokyo. Even when the subject was not especially unusual, the writing carried heavy doses of humor and irony, as well as a patronizing tone.[24] Impersonating a cynical observer gave Kaikō a solid position from which to tackle and tame a megalopolis that was metamorphosing fast under the high-growth economy. Impressed by Kaikō's reports, the weekly's editor, Ashida Terukazu, wanted him to continue to write for the magazine, but even though staff members searched far and wide, they were quickly running out of noteworthy topics in Tokyo (*KTZ* 22:82). Ashida then suggested that the writer go to Vietnam. He initially pictured the whole endeavor as a "somewhat serious overseas research trip," expecting Kaikō to report on Vietnam in the same manner that he reported on Japan's capital.[25] Indeed, most installments of the new series carried the subtitle "Right On, Overseas Edition" (Zubari kaigai-ban), genealogically linking them to the Tokyo reports. When he accepted the assignment, Kaikō (and the editor) envisioned a seamless transition from Tokyo to Vietnam, casually choosing a site where the writer would continue to behave as a curious seeker of adventure.

## An Anxious Observer

Kaikō was not entirely naïve about visiting a country where large-scale military conflict was obviously just over the horizon. He had been deeply concerned about Japan's role in Cold War geopolitics and was interested in Vietnam on an emotional and intellectual level. The country offered an opportunity to witness how the abstract forces of politics manifested themselves as concrete historical changes. It was also a site where he could contemplate the extreme conditions of war, just as he had reflected on the legacies of World War II through his previous overseas travels. His familiarity with English, working knowledge of French, extensive journeys abroad, and experience writing for a journalistic outlet made him more than a casual visitor.[26] He was frustrated, however, with the dearth of information about Vietnam available in Japan and subsequently found himself ill-prepared to write about what he witnessed there, either in the reports he filed under the "Right On" heading or in the book he subsequently compiled from them: *Vietnam War Report* (*Betonamu senki*, 1965). Although he tried to reflect on his own relationship with the objects of his observation, the results satisfied neither him nor some of his contemporary critics, who evidently expected him to offer more fully developed analyses.

An example of the underdeveloped quality of Kaikō's insight is his often-discussed account of the public execution of a student. Although he tried to register his own stance, his insight was buried in the verbose text, as will become clear in the following summary of his experience. In the early morning of January 29, 1965, according to *Vietnam War Report*, Kaikō stood with his photographer Akimoto in the square in front of a central market in Saigon. They were there to witness the execution of a twenty-year-old high school student who had been arrested and sentenced to death in a military court for carrying explosives. The execution was carried out methodically. Ten MPs shot the youth with their rifles. An officer finished him off by shooting him in the temple with a handgun. As his body was carried off, American, French, British, and Vietnamese photographers swarmed to the site. After they left, soldiers removed the sandbags, while a fire truck washed the student's blood off (*KTZ* 11:100–102). Akimoto had readied his camera to capture the reactions of local bystanders at the moment of shooting but was shocked to find "no change in the people's expressions."[27] It must have been just another display of state-sponsored violence for people desensitized by the ever-escalating violence in their everyday lives.

*Vietnam War Report* describes how the author felt at that moment: "When I heard the sound of the shooting, something inside me was shattered. My knees shook, hot sweat covered all of my body, and nausea rose inside me" (*KTZ* 11:100). These visceral reactions are followed by his self-analysis, which discloses the real source of the shock:

> In the square, I was forced to just "watch." I was a safe third party standing behind a military truck. The MPs lined up like machines, knelt down, pulled the triggers, and left. The child was killed in the way he was supposed to have been. I was a mere witness and a privileged one. Something inexplicable, something that overwhelmed me, emerged from this position in which I could do nothing but "watch" the ritualized barbaric act. The sense of relief shattered me. If I experienced a crisis, it was born from the sense of relief. In the square, everything was still. In the dusk, everything was still and concentrated. The only movement was to keep the eyes open and "watch." Not being able to stand this simplicity, I was shattered. (*KTZ* 11:101)

The passage unequivocally declares that it was not the execution itself but his disconnection from the scene that shattered him. His whole being was reduced to a gaze; nothing could touch him. The security from which he witnessed the scene—being "a safe third party"—shook him to the core.

Quoting the same passage, the social and literary critic Yoshimoto Taka'aki hurled a scathing critique at the author of *Vietnam War Report* in 1965. Its journalistic origins perhaps colored Yoshimoto's judgment of the text. He begins by questioning Kaikō's motives for being in Vietnam:

> Why, for what purpose, did this writer go to Vietnam? Even after reading this book, it is not clear. My only guess is that he went there because, one day, he received an invitation from the media to report on the Vietnam issue. . . . The way in which this "report" is written suggests that he accepted the invitation thinking there must be a

different situation in Vietnam, something that cannot be found in peaceful Japan, where death and life are indistinguishable; there is a civil war there; the international powers are also, openly and covertly, present there; let's go there and observe everything.[28]

Yoshimoto rebuked Kaikō for his "journalistic" curiosity, intimating that he went to Vietnam looking for a kind of newsworthy drama that he was no longer able to find in "peaceful Japan." In his mind, Kaikō's work replicated the worst kind of journalism—the kind that sought tragedies elsewhere while remaining blind to the everyday life of Japan.[29]

Yoshimoto also posits Kaikō as a member of the class of Japanese progressives who righteously impose their intellectual framework on their objects of study. Although Kaikō tries to be conscious of his own position as an observer, his text is in fact vulnerable to Yoshimoto's categorical accusation, for it uncritically uses conventional images in its effort to find a resolution to the writer's ontological crisis. As if to avoid his own dreadful insights, Kaikō falls back on a generic description of war: the executed student "could be a 'hero' or a 'murderer' depending on how one sees his belief. That's 'war'" (*KTZ* 11:101). At one point he blames everything on human nature: "Human beings are two-legged animals with a degenerate cerebrum that emerged on the earth by 'nature's' accident. This is the thought that was moving through my body. I was depressed and despaired of myself and humans" (*KTZ* 11:102). These comments are indeed so vacuous that they probably deserve to be called "smart-alecky (*sharakusai*) conclusions" by Yoshimoto.

Yoshimoto was not alone in criticizing Kaikō's *Vietnam War Report*. In a conversation with Abe Kōbō, Mishima Yukio insists on the need to integrate action and seeing and brings up Kaikō's writing as a counterexample:

MISHIMA: We must restore the action [*kōdōsei*] of seeing. I have been thinking lately that seeing also constitutes an act and, in a writer's life, the action can be found in something extremely static. This is a familiar example, but Kaikō Takeshi writes about an execution scene in Vietnam. He saw nothing. I was surprised. It is better to be in my office in Tokyo and write about it through imagination. If one stops believing in seeing to that degree, one is in a state of extreme infirmity. Certainly, a writer must see, seeing is . . .
ABE: I agree with that.

MISHIMA: Not to mention Kobayashi Hideo, but seeing itself must be equated with action . . .
ABE: I completely agree with you. To contrast seeing with action is a very romantic way of thinking. In the first half of the twentieth century, it was not uncommon. But the question is how to overcome it.[30]

From Mishima's and Abe's perspectives, seeing should not be relegated to a secondary status in relation to action. The corollary is that writers can and should act—engage with reality—through the act of seeing. In their estimation, Kaikō is guilty of failing to see properly and thus failing to act as a writer. Mishima's and Abe's unqualified belief in the act of seeing seems to belittle Kaikō's ontological crisis of being reduced to a gaze (ironically, they both later created fictional characters whose being is pure gaze).[31] Like Yoshimoto, these writers in effect demanded that Kaikō elevate seeing to a form of action without prescribing a proper way of seeing.

Yoshimoto, Mishima, and Abe all seem to hold an idealized and masculine notion about seeing: the idea that there is a genuine gaze through which one encounters, comprehends, and engages with reality.[32] Kaikō, however, is exposed to their criticisms precisely because he shares that notion and is striving hard to engage with the reality of Vietnam through vision. He did not need their prompting to continue working through the ontological crisis that he experienced in Vietnam. He was struggling to become an ethically responsible agent of seeing when he recast his experiences in the fictional work *Into a Black Sun*.[33] By actively affirming his role as a seer, the story's protagonist strives to overcome the inertia to which he has grown accustomed in postwar Japan and to engage with the situation unfolding in front of his eyes. Nevertheless, at the end of his exploration he learns that the eyes are powerless to reveal the reality of war to the beholder. Kaikō instead tries to grope his way out of the realm where his vision fails; he knows all too well that other bodily senses are just as powerless in a world saturated with media images.

The following reading of *Into a Black Sun* highlights Kaikō's inner struggle to maintain intellectual honesty while "consuming" Vietnam for the sake of his literary production. In this fictional work, he initially offers a narrative of transformative encounters—only to critique and dismantle it at the very end. A heroic figure develops in order to be debunked at the critical moment. The reality of war, presented as a threat to his life, will undermine the protagonist's powerful status as an observer.

## Into the Black Sun (1968): The Act of Seeing

In the narrative of *Into a Black Sun*, the public execution acquires a different meaning. "I," the unnamed protagonist, refuses to moralize his own experience but instead mechanically describes the changes that happen to him following the execution. Gone is the sense of guilt about standing on safe ground that Kaikō expresses in *Vietnam War Report*. The protagonist instead seems to acquire a new level of confidence as an observer. He now refuses to let his emotions get in the way of his observation. Although deeply shocked by the scene, in a few hours he recovers psychological equilibrium, calmly contemplating the state of his mind:

> Exhaustion and a sullied feeling, as though semen had been smeared on my face, had taken hold, and a dull but menacing fear still crouched somewhere, sneering. But something had already changed. I could sit cross-legged and puff calmly on a cigarette, letting my mind drift in a haze of association and reflection, indolent. (*KTZ* 6:163/135)[34]

The protagonist's metamorphosis into a confident observer is expressed in sexualized terms. His masculinity is at stake. The display of naked violence figuratively makes the protagonist a recipient of semen in the face. He was violated by what he saw. Yet he is already beginning to recover from this state of subjugation; in a postevent contemplation, he gets ready to reassert his masculinity.

To prove his toughness and machismo, the protagonist makes a repugnant choice for his lunch, the first meal he eats after watching the execution: red wine and a Chateaubriand, cooked rare.

> When I first drew my knife across the rare meat, fragrant with garlic, a puddle of pale red blood oozed out. I put my fork down and stared at the red liquid spreading over the white plate. The pink cross-section with its blackish crust was exactly like a wound—a wound where flies would swarm, sucking, feasting, fucking on some peasant's body found abandoned in high grass. I speared a piece of meat and chewed it slowly. It was succulent, delicious. There was no physical revulsion. No resistance on the way down. (*KTZ* 6:164/136)

The recovery was fast and complete. The protagonist could no longer be touched by what he has seen: he now feels "completely protected" (*KTZ* 6:164/136). His abhorrence toward violence and his sense of guilt about observing from a safe place—the security that he has grown accustomed to in peaceful postwar Japan—are no more; the protagonist consumes the bloody meat and the red wine in defiance of the noncommittal, pacifist position that keeps its distance from violence at all costs. The existence of the photographer is erased from the narrative to underscore the completeness of the narrator's transformation into a seer par excellence.

The book conveys a sense of progression toward the scene of the execution, which occurs two-thirds of the way into the narrative. Earlier in the text, the protagonist repeatedly expresses his frustration about his frivolous status as an observer in a violence-filled land. He is immune to the "shutter reflex"—the despondent state into which Vietnamese soldiers supposedly fall when facing an unpleasant situation (*KTZ* 6:83/61). At one point, he compares himself to a hyena:

> I had seen dozens of mutilated corpses on the dikes between rice fields, in army hospitals, and in the grasslands after a battle, but never experienced that shutter reflex. I always seemed able to bounce back and squeeze out enough words for a story and send it off to Tokyo. I was paid, had the money credited to my account in a Saigon bank, ate Cantonese food, and inexorably gained weight. The more havoc I saw, the keener my reports became—a hyena feasting on carrion. (*KTZ* 6:83/61)

There is a significant difference between seeing corpses and seeing an execution. At this point in the narrative, he is still a "hyena feasting on carrion," the one who arrives at the scene of violence only after the act is completed. He is twice removed from the act of killing. By witnessing the execution there and then, the protagonist takes one step closer to participating in war.

This narrative progression is marked by the subtle distinction that the author makes between two uses of the term *shikan*, which consists of two characters: *shi*, "seeing," and *kan*, "raping."[35] The term thereby compares the act of seeing to the violent act of raping. The protagonist uses the term for the first time when he calls himself a *shikansha*, one who commits the act of *shikan*:[36]

I had eyes only for atrocities. Corpses I found atrocious because I wasn't involved. Were I in any way involved, I would have been able to go beyond them. But the fact is, I didn't kill, so nobody killed me. I knew it was possible I might be bombed someday at a restaurant or a bar, but it wouldn't be because I was a revolutionary or an antirevolutionary or even a nonrevolutionary. I was only a *shikansha*, lurking in the narrow ribbon of a twilight zone. (*KTZ* 6:92/71)

The noun *shikansha* describes the state of inaction in which the protagonist has grown utterly frustrated. He yearns to act to define his own destiny, to regain agency in a violent place. Yet he only lurks "in the narrow ribbon of a twilight zone," waiting for something to happen while expecting that nothing will actually happen before his eyes.

The term appears for the second time in verb form, suggesting the observer's active involvement in a violent scene. There is even a hint of satisfaction about his newfound agency. After witnessing a second public execution at the same location on the following morning, the protagonist describes his tranquil mental state: "My eyes could see, my ears could hear. No fluster, no panic. I was as serene as a thicket of waterweed in an old pond. I committed *shikan* (*watashi wa shikan shitanoda*)" (*KTZ* 6:167/139). While the protagonist may still be a voyeur, he has actively sought out the opportunity to witness the act of execution. It elevates him from passive bystander to active, complicit witness in the violent process. It is a far cry from the guilty feelings that Kaikō nurses in *Vietnam War Report*. The protagonist calmly embraces the act of *shikan* as the only way to come closer to the essence of war.

In *Into a Black Sun*, the protagonist's status as a seer is challenged by the eerie sensation that he is being watched by others. His existential angst about his hyena-like existence manifests in a feeling that someone or something is casting a sharp gaze at him. Right before the first execution, he senses that numerous sets of eyes "twisted with hatred stabbed at me from somewhere behind objects; [I felt] the persistent gaze on the back of my ears, my shoulders, and the back of my head; eyes glazed with fury, boring into me from somewhere in the crowd or behind some yellow plaster wall nearby" (*KTZ* 6:160/132). The gaze from "somewhere in the crowd" is less an actual expression of the local people's feelings toward the foreign correspondents than a projection of his own anxiety onto the crowd. He is uncomfortable with the privileged position from which he watched the execution (the reporters were allowed to witness it up close, while the crowds were roped off at a distance). Twenty-four hours later, when he witnesses the second execution, he no longer senses the same gaze on him or feels the same angst about his role as an observer. The public executions are part of the everyday life of local residents; they gather for "a free show." The protagonist has learned to see them as the locals do.

The gruesomeness of the public execution awakens him to his complicity in the scene as well as to his own agency as an observer. This dramatic shift in attitude is also a response to an earlier scene where the narrator-protagonist feels that he is no more than a bystander in Vietnam. Particularly through interactions with Captain Wain, an ideologically committed American military officer, he grows more reflective about his inaction. The officer is there to act, while the protagonist sneers at himself for clinging to the idea of neutrality (*KTZ* 6:50/35). In a friendly conversation with the American officer, the narrator dishes out the information that the majority of Japanese do not support the U.S. effort in Vietnam and see it as an "unjust war." Pained by this candid assessment, the captain sinks into a deep reflection. The sight seems to awaken in the protagonist a desire for action: "Watching his broad back recede, I suddenly felt a kind of strength, as well as envy. How long was it since I'd last suffered for a cause of any kind? I had focused my energy on avoiding suffering, armed myself with frigidity, and now was drifting slowly into a coma" (*KTZ* 6:100–101/78). The protagonist does not yearn for a cause of his own —a clear political vision— because that would require emotional investment. But he begins to imagine himself out of the state of spiritual coma: the peace and comfort of postwar Japanese society that he has grown so accustomed to. Through fully embracing his role as a seer, he eventually tries to rise from the state of nonengagement.

## In the Realm of the Senses

If *Into a Black Sun* ended at this point of the narrative, it would be the genuinely heroic tale that some critics claim it is, though it would be a far less appealing story. The philosopher Washida Koyata, for example, sees the essence of the Hegelian Spirit in the protagonist's newfound resolution to be an ethical witness.[37] According to Hegel's description: "Spirit is this power only by looking the negative in the face, and tarrying with it. This tarrying with the negative is the magical power that converts it into being."[38] Kaikō's protagonist is ready to look into the death and destruction in Vietnam and tarry with it. But he is more than a philosophical abstraction: he is flesh and blood, and he acts out his bodily desires. His project of engaging with the reality in Vietnam includes sexual relations with a local prostitute. Detailed descriptions of his bodily pleasure highlight the masculine identity that is at stake within the heroic narrative, while his unthinking behavior and speech resemble those of an arrogant colonial master. But Kaikō props up this arrogant self only to implode it in the final scene of the story.

While the American officer's idealism invigorates the protagonist's vision, the locals with whom he comes in close contact provide an immediate association with Vietnamese society. In particular, his affair with To-nga, a Vietnamese woman, constitutes a symbolic link with the nation, much as sex is the way for Tsuge Yoshiharu's characters to establish relations with their fantasylands (chapter 4). In 1966 Kaikō serialized *That Which Arrives from the Shores* (*Nagisa kara kurumono*, hereafter referred to as *From the Shores*); he would later rework many of its themes in *Into a Black Sun*.[39] In the earlier work the meaning of sexual intercourse is explicit. The protagonist, a newspaper reporter, describes a fictitious country called "Agonesia": "In the core of the soft and warm flesh in the darkness is Agonesia. When I sleep with [an Agonesian] woman, I sleep with Agonesia."[40] The man recovers his masculinity through copulating in and with the fantasyland of Agonesia.

The protagonist of *Into a Black Sun* feels far less guilt about sleeping with To-nga than about watching a public execution.[41] While vision relentlessly reveals the chasm between him and Vietnam, sex with his Vietnamese mistress allows him to crawl into an imaginary relationship with the nation. The relationship with To-nga is described primarily in corporeal terms. The man buys a 100-watt bulb for the dimly lit garage where she lives (*KTZ* 6:111–12/87–88). Although she is initially excited about its bright light, she replaces it with the original dingy, dim bulb as soon as the New Year's festivities are over. Light only underscores the darkness that fills her everyday life: "She stinted on light the way peasants stinted on salt. Light was a special treat here, used freely only twice a year: at New Year's and the Festival of the Dead in summer" (*KTZ* 6:132/105). Lacking a common language, they have rudimentary conversations in a mixture of English, French, Japanese, and Vietnamese—the multiple layers of the colonial past. In the darkness, they explore each other's bodies, their only means of substantive communication.

For the protagonist, it is not enough to have physical and emotional connections with a society torn by violence. He must see the war with his own eyes. He was at the front before, but it was quiet then. He decides to return to the front to experience the real war as his own. He will not fight, but he still desires to "stand up and face something absolutely real, authentic" (*KTZ* 6:224/188). The only remaining choice of action is to reconstitute himself as an active subject of seeing in Vietnam. "I don't fight, don't kill, don't help or plow or carry; I don't instigate or plan or take anybody's side. And I can only expect to die like a dog, quivering, eyes glazed. By seeing something one becomes that thing" (*KTZ* 6:224/188). By giving up a safe vantage point and risking his life for the sake of seeing, the protagonist tries to recover his agency in the act of seeing. Seeing is thereby compared to the battles that Vietcong youths engage in in the jungle:

> They acted out their dreams. And fulfillment might be flawed, they might feel doubt as soon as they began to act, but pride would cover up the cracks. And they might even lose their faith and, disillusioned, turn back toward the jungle they had started from, and find that they had lost their freedom to resist; and some would crouch down on the ground, feeling helpless, and some might rise again with only clubs to fight with and be killed. And as for me . . . I couldn't lift a finger. I watched. Yes, watching was all I'd ever do. (*KTZ* 6:224–25/189)

The protagonist makes it clear that he is not trying to reclaim his youthful hope and possibility in the war fought in the jungle. He has no false hope: he is there just as a witness. Yet by describing the two kinds of acts—their fighting and his watching—continuously within the passage, he strongly suggests their equivalency. He rationalizes his presence on the battlefield on the dubious ground that he too engages in action through his vision. The next morning, just as leaving for the front, the man assuages his anxiety about his problematic status as an observer, by declaring to himself: "This war is mine" (*KTZ* 6:226/190).

As soon as he decides to go to the front, the piercing countergaze returns.[42] It now penetrates into his inner sanctum, the moment of rendezvous with To-nga. He spends the night before his departure for the battlefield with her, feeling the "powerful, vacant, and immobile, tireless, undiscriminating gaze" (*KTZ* 6:221/186). As if to answer the silent gaze, he insists to himself that his relations with To-nga attest to his benign intent:

> The hours I spent with To-nga had an animal innocence, had depth and subtlety, with none of the staleness of custom. She was an island with fine forests and secluded shores, and I had landed there and strolled along the forest verge, but not effected any change or even wanted to.... What could be more secure and peaceful than sitting in the dark distilling simple sounds like "bat," "owl," "basket," word by word? She'd clapped her hands like a child, and cocked her head, absorbed. I was a pilgrim who'd smiled at her, and picked up shells in the sand, and would move on. (*KTZ* 6:223–24/188)

Not mentioned here is the fact that the protagonist must pay an exorbitant amount of money to the bar at which To-nga works every time he wishes to be with her (*KTZ* 6:70/52).[43] He has enough money to purchase the "island with fine forests and secluded shores" for temporary pleasure. In his mind, he is an innocent pilgrim who leaves things as he finds them. Even the fact that they have so few words to share is offered as proof that he changed nothing about her. To-nga's childlike innocence absolves him of his guilt and anxiety about being in her country.[44] When he leaves her place, possibly for the last time, he places "an envelope stuffed with money on the windowsill" (*KTZ* 6:225/189): the final payment for his purchase of innocence. He seeks to complete his colonial enterprise by sexually mastering the natives and then looking for war as a way to embellish his masculinist quest.

### The Naked Reality of the War

According to *Vietnam War Report,* Kaikō and Akimoto relocated to the Ben Cat base, some thirty miles north of Saigon, in January 1965. From there, they joined a South Vietnamese battalion planning to penetrate a Vietcong stronghold farther north (*KTZ* 11:104–5). The operation, originally scheduled to last three nights and four days, ended on the first day after the 200-men battalion sustained heavy damage under a Vietcong attack: 8 died, 33 suffered serious injury, and 4 were missing (*KTZ* 11:154). At the end of the action, Kaikō and Akimoto counted only 17 of the original 200 (*KTZ*

11:150).⁴⁵ *Vietnam War Report* suggests that Kaikō, Akimoto, and the 17 fighters were pinned down in one location, while the rest—138 of them—were likely scattered in small groups waiting for their opportunity to retreat to safety. The combat scene describes only what Kaikō and Akimoto saw in the moment of crisis (rather than the out-of-sight 138 men).⁴⁶

This encounter with the Vietcong force sets the stage for an anticlimactic ending to *Into a Black Sun*. Kaikō's alter ego joins the Vietnamese battalion with a heroic determination to be a cool witness. He is proud of his own action: leaving To-nga's place for the front, he "grasped [his] own self in hand, feeling the intense and solitary joy of the stoic" (*KTZ* 6:229/194). What he encounters on the battlefield overwhelms all his senses, however, forcing him to abandon his self-assigned post. The self-portrait of his innocent and invincible self—the image carefully built up through the narrative to this point—is mercilessly destroyed at the end of the episode.

The operation that he participates in is utterly ill-conceived. Although the battalion can expect the support of an artillery unit, it does not have nearly enough combined force to subdue the "at least five hundred members of the crack 'Autumn' unit of the VC's 300th Battalion" (*KTZ* 6:228/193). The operation is at best a "demonstration" (*KTZ* 6:230/195) and could turn into something far worse. The grim prospect does not deter the protagonist from joining the action. But he returns to the base before the operation to "put on two pairs of new underpants," in case he loses control over his bowels (*KTZ* 6:232–33/196).

A crisis that the seer experiences in the visual field foreshadows his eventual disintegration on the battlefield. As soon as the combat begins, he dives to the ground, where he sees ants minding their own business: "I kept blinking, nose buried in the dark fertile smell of rotting vegetation. And in separate, fleeting frames, I saw numerous ants fidgeting around my eyes, one reeling along with a dead leaf clamped in its jaws, the leaf much larger than itself" (*KTZ* 6:239/201). Like the ants on the ground, he can see only his immediate surroundings, and he reels along dragging a pride much bigger than himself. In the chaos of the battle, his sovereign position as a seer proves untenable and is literally brought to the ground. Early in the story, the protagonist laments: "Everywhere, I looked down on the dead; my eyes never peered up from the ground, from the eye level of the dead" (*KTZ* 6:91/69). He finally comes close to seeing from their eye level when he falls from the erect position of the seer, though the act of seeing is still central to his sense of self.

The literary critic Yoshida Haruo points out how a subtle difference in the treatment of the same battlefield scene in *From the Shores* and *Into a Black Sun* illuminates a radical shift in perspective.[47] *From the Shores* describes a scene in which the protagonist "witnesses" Vietnamese soldiers' strange behavior:

> *I saw two strange scenes.* . . . The little soldier the size of a junior high school student was eating banana with his carbine on the ground. His young eyes were empty, and his jaws moved with slow deliberation, finishing one mouthful at a time, enjoying the taste of it. A bit later, when the firing shifted to the left, I rolled back to the tree and squirmed over to the left, then I rolled back to the tree and squirmed over to the other side. And when I rolled back to the left again, the soldier was still peeling another banana leisurely and eating it one mouthful at a time. I believe it was at this point that *I saw another strange scene out of the corner of my eye. Another* soldier was sitting near him, but flat on the ground, eating a bowlful of rice that he'd scooped from a washbasin.[48] (Emphasis added)

The protagonist casts his gaze on the Vietnamese soldiers, gauging the peculiarity of their behavior. Although this Japanese journalist is thoroughly shaken by the commotion around him, he never loses his sovereign position as an observer. He remains in control of the scene, distancing himself from their strange conduct.

A virtually identical scene in *Into a Black Sun* contains one crucial difference: the soldiers return the protagonist's gaze. The first soldier calmly watches him while eating the banana; the second gives him "a perfunctory glance showing no interest in him," demoting "I" from the superior position of singular seer (*KTZ* 6:241/202). In the soldier's vision, the protagonist is relegated to the status of an inconsequential object. With his clear vision gone, the protagonist is no longer a master who defines and rules the visual field. As if a powerful source of light has been switched off, he is finally able to sense the shadows that surround him. Vietnamese soldiers are more than two-dimensional props in his war drama, and the war itself is more than moving images projected onto a screen.

The narrator discovers the Vietnamese soldiers are fellow humans, but they are all on the cusp of death. Only as they face imminent danger can their unique existence be acknowledged: "I seemed to have made a terrible mistake. For some time, I'd thought these people sometimes lovable, sometimes cruel, but dummies, men of straw" (*KTZ* 6:249/208). Liberated from his own arrogance, he is now capable of comprehending what is about to be lost—soldiers' lives:

> The dead had been robbed blind, though they themselves had robbed. Their meager earnings had been siphoned off by officers to pay, allegedly, for coffins and gambling debts they didn't owe. But they had stolen chickens, cabbages, and sugarcane themselves when they were on maneuvers—and earned the peasants' hatred and contempt. They'd scraped and schemed and sometimes put enough together to buy a cigarette, and smoked it down in little puffs, savoring it, peering at the dwindling butt. . . . The dead had loved eating and sleeping more than anything else—there wasn't much to choose from. They'd laughed a lot, pursing their mouths, and they'd been good at keeping dogs and parrots and making crickets fight. (*KTZ* 6:249–50/208–9)

The soldiers remain anonymous but are no longer faceless. The loss of clear vision allows the protagonist to discover them as fellow humans, but it does not bring him closer to them. It takes a bodily crisis to be able to join the nameless soldiers, and the narrative builds toward this climax.

A scene of chaos follows. In a fierce exchange of fire between two choppers and Vietcong youths, he sees "the war's ghastly beauty, if only for a moment" (*KTZ* 6:253/212). As soon as he is awed by the beauty, he is on the run, desperately trying to escape enemy fire. Tangled with another Vietnamese soldier in muddy water, the protagonist barely controls his bodily functions. The moment he turns to survey the swamp that he has just crawled out of, a "rattling thunderclap of guns" is so overwhelming that he involuntarily closes his eyes (*KTZ* 6:255/213). Gone is his firm determination to keep his eyes open in the face of physical danger. The cool seer is easily taken over by his reflexes. He abandons the bag that he has been carrying, which proves to have born great symbolic meaning.[49] Although it contains only a towel and a paperback book, it has kept him from disintegrating: "For, holding it, I still retained some fragment of myself. But when that residue of strength had fled, my pride—most subtle of all factors controlling human behavior, instinctive guardian of the human soul—had vanished with it" (*KTZ* 6:255/214).

At the conclusion of *Into a Black Sun*, neither determination, self-respect, nor a bag could protect the protagonist. Driven by a primordial instinct for survival in the battlefield, he runs for his life:

> On down the gantlet we ran and, on each side, that brutal invisible force still shrieked and moaned among the sounding trees. And I was rigid, sealed shut, and heard my heart pounding in my ears, rumbling like surf in the dark; and I was pulverized, and began to cry. Tears ran down my cheeks and off my chin. Small salty bodies bucked and shoved, a silent tide, and in it, without disgust or shame, I numbly shoved them back as we fled on into the forest. The dismal odor of moss brushed my wet cheeks. And tumbling from the hot, black belly of the whale into its bowels, I ran on, panting, gasping, through the vast, hairy primeval night. And the forest was quiet. (*KTZ* 6:255–56/214)

The protagonist's sight is powerless to guide him out of peril, while "the brutal invisible force" has crushed the pride that held him together. The final images of narrator and soldiers tumbling down "the hot, black belly of the whale" suggest their descent into the netherworld. At the threshold of life and death, he joins the South Vietnamese soldiers as an equal, shoving their "small salty bodies" back "without disgust or shame." He is left on the "vast, hairy, primeval night" of the battlefield, running for safety in perpetuity.

*Into a Black Sun* closes with this dreadful scene, with the protagonist's ego disintegrating as he glimpses the ultimate darkness of death.[50] The extreme experience in the battlefield strips him of the ability to signify what he is experiencing. Literally deprived of clear vision in the jungle and made dependent on his basest bodily senses, he is incapable of looking into the negative. He may have succeeded in bursting out of the comfort and complacency of postwar Japan, but the "outside" that he finally steps into is ruled by a darkness that defies symbolic representation. Yet this dark space is also utopian in that it accepts both the protagonist and the soldiers unconditionally. While his masculine, colonial project of becoming an ethical witness is shattered, he is effectively saved from the naïveté and arrogance that he earlier displayed toward the locals.

## War on Television

Twice Kaikō witnessed television's astounding reach. Safely returned from the battlefield with his photographer, Akimoto Kei'ichi, he witnessed a scene that, in his words, attested to the "perversion of the modern world." In a conversation with the literary critic Yamazaki Masakazu, Kaikō describes the scene that he encountered when he returned to the Majestic Hotel in Saigon: "In the hotel lobby, American Special Forces veterans of numerous battles, desk-duty officers, and all kinds of guys were hanging out and watching television. They were watching the show *Combat!*, in which Vic Morrow played [Sgt. Chip Saunders]."[51] A mere 70 kilometers (43.5 miles) away from the chaotic front, members of the American forces gathered to watch a popular television war drama about a U.S. infantry squad on the frontlines in Europe during World War II. The world in front of the screen seemed to coalesce with the images flowing from it. What the eyes of Kaikō's protagonist failed to give a meaning to, the television did.

One may argue that the television provided more palatable images to substitute for the war's hard reality: the Americans in front of the television set were merely trying to escape from that reality. Yet Kaikō found himself in a similarly perverse situation three months after he returned to Japan, and this was not about substitution. On the evening of May 9, 1965, Nippon Television aired the first installment of a three-part documentary on the war in Vietnam, *War Chronicle of a South Vietnam Marine Battalion* (*Betonamu kaihei daitai senki*). The camera follows a South Vietnamese Marine unit as it engages in a search-and-destroy mission in central Vietnam. In one sequence, several unit members drag a middle-aged farmer out of hiding and interrogate him about the whereabouts of Vietcong soldiers. He is beaten and kicked until he divulges the location of a buried Vietcong weapons cache. The information turns out to be false, and the marines exact a hefty price. They lead the farmer into an empty hut, and when he emerges, he has two fewer fingers on his right hand. The camera also captures, albeit from a distance, a seventeen-year-old Vietnamese boy who has been beaten, killed, and decapitated.[52] A soldier lifts the boy's head by the hair, the neck still dripping blood.

Nippon Television had prescreened the documentary for a committee of twenty public figures, including Kaikō Takeshi; none of them had objected to airing it.[53] Yet showing such cruelty on primetime television aroused controversy, and Nippon Television executives canceled the airing of the second and third parts.[54]

Viewers of part 1 watched the execution of the boy in their living rooms at a safe distance. What was the difference between that act and Kaikō's witnessing executions in Saigon? Were his accounts of it in *Vietnam War Report* consumed just like the television images of the war? Was Kaikō's experience more genuine because he was there at the site? Kaikō never discussed the television documentary or the questions that it might have posed. Yet his connections with the work, no matter how tenuous they may have been, illuminate the media environment in which the writer contemplated his experiences in Vietnam. Writing in a postwar Japan saturated with media images, Kaikō could not pretend to be a neutral observer with altruistic motives who happened to encounter catastrophic events. In *Into a Black Sun*, he takes his own vision to task while exploring his complicity in transforming Vietnam into consumable images. Mimicking a camera's cold gaze is a sine qua non for a protagonist seeking to establish a masculine and transparent agency, and Kaikō does indeed try to embody a camera's mechanical and disinterested gaze. Other bodily senses are called into service to establish the narrator's sovereign self as a new colonial master, the one who sees. In the struggle for life, however, the body finally rebels, bringing the eyes down to the level of the other, baser senses. Sight in the end proves powerless in facing the naked reality of war, which envelops the senses in destructive darkness. A corollary is that television could never transmit this darkness to its viewers precisely because it offers clear and bright vision with images that lack the depth that Kaikō explored with his bodily senses.

## The Cycle of Life and Death

In the final scene of *Into a Black Sun*, the protagonist gropes toward the underbelly of war, where clear vision cannot reach. The body stands as a dreamy passage leading to the other side of the mundane reality that he has so loathed. Several scenes explore the protagonist's and other characters' bodily senses, leading up to the climax. Kaikō extends his exploration into his later stories. The novel *Darkness in Summer* (1971), the second volume of Kaikō's "darkness trilogy," which derived its theme from his

Vietnam experiences, delves into the sensual, sexual pleasures that his alter ego experiences with his lover.[55] These works departed from Kaikō's self-inhibition about giving autobiographical materials center stage in his fictional works. Abhorring the Japanese literary tradition of the I-novel, which endlessly describes trivial matters from the author's everyday life, Kaikō aspired to write stories with social relevance. Yet his brush with death in Vietnam perhaps served as an impetus to reconcile two things that he used to think were incompatible—the author's internal world and external events—by demarking the body as a unique interface between life and death.

Critics and his fans welcomed *Darkness in Summer* as a work of high aesthetic quality.[56] Rather than focus on its literary appeal, however, I would like to explore the meaning of the inward turn that Kaikō took in this novel. The entire narrative of *Darkness in Summer* is dedicated to portraying the protagonist's love affair with his Japanese lover in Germany. For him, the affair is an escape from his tiresome quotidian life as well as an extension of his travels over a decade. The narrator makes connections between travel and the search for self: "For the past ten years I have done nothing but travel. . . . Regardless of my motivation, traveling is, ultimately, a journey through myself, using the foreign land as a catalyst; but a journey having myself as the goal will sooner or later arrive at a terrible void" (*KTZ* 7:411–12/103). He continues to reach for a dreamlike state as he tries to delve deeper into his inner self. As the excitement of the love affair eventually becomes routine, however, he falls into a deep ennui and begins to look for a way out again. The protagonist's Vietnam experiences cast a long, dark shadow on his life: he was an observer and one of the survivors of an ill-fated operation in Vietnam three years earlier (*KTZ* 7:491/181). When he hears about an imminent large-scale campaign by the National Liberation Front, the protagonist decides to return to Vietnam.

Kaikō's narrative acquires a fantastical quality at the end of *Darkness in Summer*, whose closing scene graphically portrays the dissolving distinction between life and death. In the unnamed city (the description suggests that it is Berlin), the protagonist and his lover ride a train on the elevated loop line. Kaikō seats his characters in an almost empty train that endlessly circles the city, crossing the boundaries of its two sections: from the East to the West, then back again. "The train stopped or continued obstinately, diligently, accurately, but everything stayed the same. It crossed over and cried 'Life!' and passed back and shouted 'Death!'" (*KTZ* 7:519/210).

The East was dark and echoing; and the West was bright and expansive. But as I looked out of the window of the train that stopped, and then ran, stopped, and then ran, without seeing the backs of any passengers getting off or any faces boarding—as I watched, leaning against the hard board of the seat—the darkness gradually brightened, then the glow gradually dimmed. East and West ceased to be distinguishable. I could not tell "Over there" from "Over here." I no longer knew whether the train was running or standing still. (*KTZ* 7:520/210)

East and West initially appear as distinctively different zones, but their contrast loses meaning as the protagonist loses the sense of motion in the end. The story abruptly ends with the protagonist's monologue: "Ten o'clock . . . tomorrow morning . . ." (*KTZ* 7:520/210). (The English translation ends the novel more explicitly.) Vietnam is an absolute outside where death looms large, but the closing scene suggests that it will soon merge with life under the high-growth regime. While *Into a Black Sun* posited the body as a possibility through which to escape the quotidian life, *Darkness in Summer* explores and ultimately forecloses that possibility. The man loses the ability to process the physical stimuli flowing through his body; a return to Vietnam is unlikely to shake him out of this state of inertia.

Although Kaikō struggled to step outside of the stifling conditions of 1960s Japan, his creative arc ironically followed the contour of the postwar media evolution. The private realm of everyday life was forcefully opened to the outsider's gaze in Japan's new media environment. As we saw in chapter 2, the postwar Japanese media transformed even the most private human activity—sexual intercourse—into marketable information. Kaikō's uninhibited description of sexual intimacy therefore fits the cultural scene of postwar Japan.[57] (The Nikkatsu Studios began to churn out softcore porn films in the same year in which *Darkness in Summer* was published.)[58] Furthermore, he paired his literary exploration of bodily senses with the decision, in 1972, to begin appearing in television commercials for Suntory products, happily acting out the message that whisky is what every man needs to fulfill his inner life. Suntory appropriated Kaikō's literary stature, due in no small part to the success of *Into a Black Sun* and *Darkness in Summer*, to endow its products with a classier image. His efforts to reach outside in the 1960s firmly planted him deep inside the hyperconsumerism of 1970s and 1980s Japan.[59]

Although Kaikō continued to enjoy a successful career as a writer in subsequent years, he never completed the final work of what he had originally conceived as the Vietnam trilogy, *Darkness in Ending Flowers* (*Hana owaru yami*).[60] His project was perhaps outpaced by the changes in Japanese society. The radical contrast between light and darkness that Kaikō struggled to capture ceased to be his literary inspiration as postwar commercial culture made it as mundane as the flickering of a television screen.[61]

# PART THREE
# Violence

CHAPTER VI

## Heroes in Crisis

### The Transformation of Yakuza Film

> Yakuza film was for men. It was structured around a long period of repression and a momentary ejaculation [of violence]. This structure also framed optimism about the future of the national liberation struggle in Vietnam and the campus activism at various colleges. At the very end, the violence that has built up inside you while enduring hardship is released, and a victory is achieved. The momentary release resembled the moment of ejaculation.
> —TATEMATSU WAHEI, *CINEMA SUPREMACIST, FUKASAKU KINJI*
> (*EIGA SHUGISHA, FUKASAKU KINJI*)

While relishing the postwar society's economic achievements, Japanese consumers also felt deep anxiety about drastic socioeconomic changes and envisaged alternatives to mass consumer society. Some attempts to imagine a way out of contemporary society and its symptoms took extreme—even violent—forms, as in the case of radical student politics. The cathartic explosion of violence—the "ejaculation," to use the writer Tatematsu Wahei's term—that audiences found in yakuza film was a cultural response to the drastic changes of the late 1960s and early 1970s.

Yakuza heroes break away from the traditional community's constraints and resort to violence in order to challenge evil capitalists. Such lone heroes were the expression of a cultural desire to find independent agency within complex socioeconomic conditions. In yakuza film, the effects of mass consumer society were reduced to the greed of capitalist antagonists, while its heroes offered the possibility of action against encroaching social change. By the 1970s, however, these fantastic catharses no longer appealed to audiences. To put it schematically, once individuals recognized themselves as beneficiaries of the material wealth of mass society, it grew increasingly difficult for them to imagine an outside position from which to criticize capitalist development. Even the countryside, traditionally posited as city culture's counterterrain, embraced the fruits of the postwar Japanese economic miracle (as explored in chapter 1). The outlaw protagonists of yakuza film stood among the last marginal figures in postwar society, and even this position became foreclosed as mass consumer society strengthened its hold on Japan in the early 1970s. Champions of society's underbelly, yakuza heroes were also redeemers of the declining Japanese film industry. Toei and other film companies released hundreds of yakuza films between 1961 and 1972. The genre that embraced anticapitalist heroes saved the market, at least for that short span of time. Yet even with the success of yakuza film, the film industry failed to reverse the tide of film's diminishing popularity in postwar Japan.

This chapter's primary focus is on the two waves within the yakuza genre: the first wave in the 1960s and early 1970s features yakuza heroes that transcend the historical conditions of diegetic time (roughly from the 1860s to the 1930s), while the second in the following years imagines antiheroes weighed down by the ugly reality of the yakuza world. Yakuza film's popularity peaked with the first wave in the late 1960s and quickly waned as contemporary audiences rejected its fantastic narratives as unrealistic. First-wave yakuza began, critics maintain, with the success of Daiei's *Tough Guy* (*Akumyō*, dir. Tanaka Tokuzō, 1961) and Toei's *Theater of Life: Hishakaku* (*Jinsei gekijō: Hishakaku*, dir. Uchida Tomu, 1963).[1] Popular series included *Tough Guy* (1961–1974), *A Man from Abashiri Prison* (*Abashiri bangaichi*, 1965–1972), *Brutal Tale of Chivalry* (*Shōwa zankyōden*, 1965–1972), *Nippon Chivalry* (*Nihon kyōkakuden*, 1964–1971), and *Red Peony Gambler* (*Hibotan bakuto*, 1968–1972). Other major studios also produced scores of yakuza films, though Toei dominated at the box office. Yet the boom was short-lived. By the early 1970s, yakuza film fans showed less enthusiasm for new releases.

Yakuza film enjoyed a brief resurgence in 1973 and 1974 with the success of the series entitled *Battles Without Honor and Humanity* (*Jinginaki tatakai*; hereafter referred to as *Battles*).[2] This series was popular not only because it departed from the banal and formulaic conventions of the genre but also because it was sensitive to the social and political shifts of the early 1970s. The yakuza hero ready to sacrifice himself for social justice in the late 1960s—the darling of oppositional politics—was replaced in the early 1970s with the antihero who is aware that his actions will make little difference in the yakuza world he inhabits and is therefore incapable of acting.

In reading key films from the two waves, I emphasize the affinities as well as the tensions between the two. I also want to challenge the popular belief that the *Battles* series broke away from the aesthetics of the first wave.³ The *Battles* films were as deeply embedded in the cinematic conventions of yakuza film as their predecessors, despite their shift toward the anguished antihero. Their success stemmed ultimately from the filmmakers' ability to negotiate those conventions and channel the realities of the early 1970s into their creative process.

## The Conventions of Yakuza Film

Yakuza—members of traditional criminal gangs—were not new to Japanese society, or to the movie screen, in the 1960s. The premodern folk imagination often romanticized them as heroes who challenged corrupt officials (e.g., Kunisada Chūji and Shimizu Jirochō). The Japanese film industry, too, frequently portrayed them as heroic figures, starting in the 1920s.⁴ When yakuza figures began to appear en masse in 1960s films, they were transplanted from a premodern rural setting to a post-Restoration urban environment and thrust into the middle of a battle between the traditional and the modern.⁵ Partially because of its continuity with earlier traditions, first-wave yakuza film soared in popularity as a response to popular anxieties triggered by Japan's radical economic and social transformations.

Yakuza film also served as one of the last strongholds of the struggling Japanese film industry, which was losing its market share to the newer mass medium of television. The genre appealed largely to young adult males as it portrayed the underworld and violence in a way that family-oriented television programs could not. The yakuza film audience identified with what had been left behind in the progress of society. For example, in writing about *Big Gambling Ceremony* (*Bakuchiuchi: Sōchō tobaku*, 1968), Mishima Yukio carefully describes the *mise-en-scène* of his viewing experience:

> The small alley that I took, following a stranger's directions, was dark and wet from rain. Deep in that alley was a small, old movie theater. A tacky picture on the sign looked bleak.... The door on the right side of the screen constantly squeaked: whenever somebody opened it, it made a banging sound, and the draft that came through it carried abundant toilet aroma.... In this ideal environment, I saw *Big Gambling Ceremony*.⁶

Mishima found it appropriate to watch a yakuza film in a dingy space tucked away from the ordinary life of Japan and the everyday comfort that the high-growth economy offered.[7] The sensory conditions—smell, noise, and feel—of the viewing environment enhanced the audience's identification with the underdogs on the screen.[8]

Yakuza film in its 1960s incarnation criticized capitalism as the prime cause of social disintegration and often used a greedy capitalist figure to represent the complex mechanism of commercial development. (Neither politicians nor government officials were a target of criticism in the first wave yakuza film.) The audience found catharsis when yakuza heroes violently struck down an easily identifiable capitalist villain. Viewers appreciated the patently predictable and often schematic plots. One of the best-known works of the genre, *Brutal Tale of Chivalry 7: Hell Is a Man's Destiny* (*Shōwa zankyōden 7: Shinde moraimasu*, dir. Makino Masahiro, 1970), exploits the form's main characteristics by locating the struggle of capitalism within a feud between two gang families.

Typical plots of yakuza film revolve around a rivalry between a "traditional" gang group and an upstart one. In general, Toei yakuza films set their stories mostly in the periods associated with Japan's modernization: the Meiji (1868–1912), Taishō (1912–1926), and early Shōwa periods (1926–1930s). The traditional gang has its financial base in legitimate businesses such as construction, lumber distribution, and wholesale commerce (although members still engage in illegal activities such as gambling). *Hell Is a Man's Destiny* is set in the late 1920s, a time of extreme financial volatility in the early Shōwa period. A feud between the long-established Terada family and the parvenu Komai family over a high-class restaurant drives the narrative. Both families are based in Fukagawa—a bastion of Edo culture in the low-lying area of eastern Tokyo—and participate in the shipping business. While the Teradas stand for the traditional code long honored by the Fukagawa bosses, the Komai family behave like ruthless modern capitalists. The Terada boss backs the restaurant, Kiraku, because its owner has been an integral part of the Fukagawa community, while the Komai gang try to take it over in order to symbolically undermine the rival family's control over the area. When the Terada family's don is murdered in a struggle over Kiraku's title deed, the two cooks indebted to him—Hanada Hidejirō, played by Takakura Ken (1931–2014), and Kazama Jūkichi, played by Ikebe Ryō (1918–2010)—attack the Komais' headquarters. Hanada avenges himself by killing the Komai family's evil don, though Kazama dies in the fight.

Despite some minor variations, the binary struggle between the traditional and the modern is the foundation of the first-wave yakuza film (table 6.1). The division is visually marked. The traditional yakuza bosses appear in kimono, while the modern capitalist bosses often wear Western attire. (The Komai family's leader wears a kimono, but his office contains Western furniture and decor.) In *Hell Is a Man's Destiny*, the Kiraku owner's adopted son represents capitalist greed. He is an enemy within. He repeatedly loses money on commodity speculations and asks the Komai family for loans in order to speculate more. As a consequence, he loses the restaurant's title deed to the Komais. The man who pours money into the volatile commodity market of the late 1920s threatens traditional mores and appears in Western suits. The traditional/modern binary is reinforced in the film's final scene, where the protagonist fights with a Japanese sword against adversaries with guns.[9] His sidekicks may carry guns as well, but guns are never the hero's chosen weapon.

The dramatic narrative within yakuza film—endurance of extreme hardship, ending in a final resolution of tension through violence—is predictable. As is often noted, a similar motif is present in such popular Tokugawa kabuki plays as *The Treasury of Loyal Retainers* (*Kanadehon Chūshingura*, 1748) and reproduced in numerous period dramas (*jidaigeki*) that feature sword fights.[10] In *Chūshingura*, the loyal vassals of Lord Asano attack the mansion of Lord Kira despite the Tokugawa shogunate's prohibition against unauthorized vendettas. The tension in *Chūshingura* arises from the conflict between feudal social mores based on human bondage

TABLE 6.1

Binary structure of first-wave yakuza films (*Brutal Tale of Chivalry: Hell Is a Man's Destiny*)

| Terada Family | Komai Family |
|---|---|
| Good | Evil |
| Traditional | Modern/capitalistic |
| Benevolent | Greedy |
| Peaceful/bringing order | Violent/bringing disorder |

(lord and vassals) and the institutional mandate to maintain peace in Tokugawa society. By portraying Lord Kira as an evil villain who is concerned merely with his own personal gain, the play offers an emotional justification for the loyal vassals to challenge the bakufu's mandate. The use of violence suspends, albeit temporarily, institutional dictates and allows the protagonists to fulfill their feudal obligations to their master. Yakuza film faithfully replicates this pattern in its production of catharsis, and many filmmakers have acknowledged their indebtedness to *Chūshingura*.[11] The heroes silently endure difficult situations, including taunts and violent provocations from the rival gangs, in order to honor the deceased patriarch's command to maintain peace at all costs. When the hero's forbearance reaches its limit, often after the death of his right-hand man or a man to whom he feels morally indebted (for example, the death of the Terada family's don in *Hell Is a Man's Destiny*), he takes up arms and attacks the enemies' headquarters.[12]

Yet there are some key differences in the historical settings of *Chūshingura* and yakuza film. For example, good and evil clash within a coeval space in *Chūshingura,* whereas they belong to separate temporal spaces in yakuza film. In the latter, the traditional is equated with peace and stability and the modern with merciless change and boundless greed. To highlight this conflict of values, yakuza film foregrounds the disruptive effects of modernization: modern capitalist greed for selfish gain is identified as the prime evil. Yakuza are squeezed out of their traditional habitats and desperately resist the pressure of the evil modern forces in society. Only corrupt yakuza embrace capitalist avarice and logic, though the films offer a schematic explanation for their drive. Often villains seek material and monetary gains simply to fulfill their evil personas. When motives are offered, the villains' humble origins as yakuza members are foregrounded. These individuals hold grudges against a traditional system that marginalized them, while capitalism offers them a powerful means to challenge the cause of their suffering. For example, in *Brutal Tale of Chivalry 2: The Chinese Lion and Peony Tattoo* (dir. Saeki Kiyoshi, 1966), Toramatsu of the Sōda family reveals his humble past as a rock cutter who worked for the Sakaki family. Toramatsu is determined to destroy his old employer and his organization in retaliation for the hardship he suffered under them. Kakurai in *Red Peony Gambler* (dir. Yamashita Kōsaku, 1968), who experienced hardship as a déclassé samurai in the early years of the Meiji era, is determined to climb the social ladder at any cost. For his personal gain, he is willing to destroy a rival group and pit them against a person who had saved his life.

Yakuza film thus reduces the complex capitalist system to the source of an individual grudge. The socioeconomic changes that capitalism promotes provide the villains with the means to act out their ill resentment. Their extremely personal motivation is often thinly disguised with the language of capitalism: they do it for the sake of development. When the two principal characters finally let their anger lead them in the final sequence of *Hell Is a Man's Destiny*, they are morally victorious, not only over the evil characters but over capitalism itself. Yakuza film's fantastical endings hence offer a moralistic critique of contemporary society with few real-life ramifications. The audience can denounce the deleterious effects of capitalist transformation safely while embracing materialistic progress in their everyday life. First-wave yakuza film encouraged viewers to cast a nostalgic gaze on Japan's recent past, purportedly still hanging on at the margins of modern Japanese society.

## Tensions Between the Traditional and the Modern

What yakuza film presents as the traditional is just as problematic as its construction of the modern. It is an Orientalist project, one that aspires to locate authentic Japanese tradition in an ahistorical cultural space. Traditional mores are on the cusp of disappearance in the larger society, but they remain intact within the secret realm of yakuza society, hidden away from law-abiding ordinary citizens.[13]

To highlight their authenticity, yakuza films pay particular attention to details. The "traditional" is constructed out of a matrix of cultural practices where the protagonist's every gesture is given meaning. Hence scenes portraying ritualistic greetings among yakuza members and elaborate protocol at a gambling house constitute crucial parts of each film.[14] Every aspect of a yakuza hero's carriage signals that he is firmly anchored in his community.

The hero's body itself is often burdened with cultural significance through his tattoos. The *Brutal Tale of Chivalry* series exploits the popular association between yakuza and tattoos in order to dramatize the hero's final attack. *Hell Is a Man's Destiny*, for example, effectively uses the tattoos inscribed on the protagonist's back to emphasize his deep, hidden connections with the yakuza world. Although Hanada Hidejirō has severed ties with his former yakuza associates and is trying to live the life of an ordinary man, his tattoos constantly remind him of his past. The physical pain associated with tattooing is also underscored (tattoo is called *gaman*, "forbearance," in the film) to suggest the protagonist's self-restraint.[15] In the final fight scene, his enemy's sword cuts open the back of Hanada's kimono and dramatically reveals the tattooed images of a mythological creature, *karajishi*, and peonies (figure 6.1). Together these images symbolize bravery: in the Kamakura period (1185–1333), samurai warriors depicted them on their weapons and armor. The revelation of bodily inscriptions intimates that Hanada strikes from the depth of tradition—he is physically anchored in it—but he must abandon the security of tradition in order to fulfill moral mandates. Peony provides a safe resting place for *karajishi*, according to conventional understanding.[16] In *Hell Is a Man's Destiny*, Hanada's lover, Ikutarō, serves as a peony figure, who offers a temporal refuge from the violent yakuza world in the form of heteronormative love. Her association with the flower is strengthened through intertextual referencing: the actress Fuji Junko plays both Ikutarō and the heroine gambler, who identifies herself as Oryū the Red Peony (Hibotan no Oryū) in *Red Peony Gambler*. Hanada leaves Ikutarō, anticipating his own violent death. The peony on his back is covered with his own blood—a sign of forceful separation—by the end of the battle.

Yakuza film features a curious inversion. Men characterized as outlaws or associated with illicit activities appear as staunch defenders of the social order. They do not live in the lawless, anarchic space where violence rules:

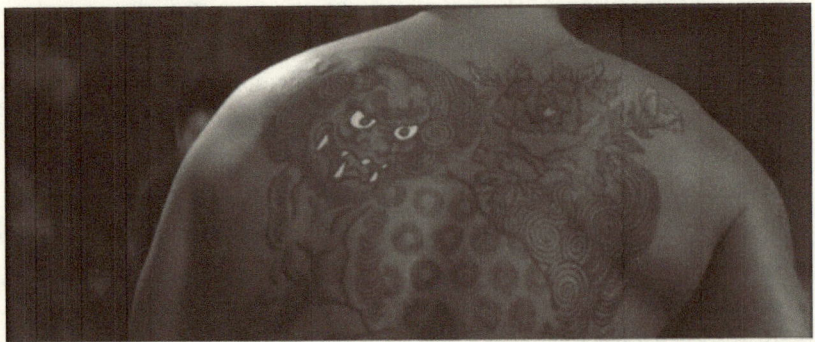

*Figure 6.1* Hanada Hidejirō's tattoos revealed, in *Hell Is a Man's Destiny*.

their behavior is regulated through a network of fictive familial relations and a sense of indebtedness to patriarchy. In a bifurcation of modern and traditional life, the virtuous yakuza gang—left at the margins of society—serves as a stand-in for the larger traditional society that existed prior to Japan's modernization. The yakuza world is presented as a sanctuary imbued with honor and honesty.

The protagonist's final act of violence, however, does not stem from traditional attitudes alone. Through his violent acts, a yakuza hero transcends the conflicts between the traditional and the modern. He is a liminal figure, maintaining a distance from the tight-knit society ruled by traditional values. The protagonist may be portrayed as an itinerant gambler or a man returning to his own community after a long absence, as Hanada Hidejirō in *Hell Is a Man's Destiny* returns to Kiraku after a prison term. This symbolic distance allows him to act as an independent agent even as he is burdened with ritual codes of behavior. His liminal status as a yakuza is crucial, permitting him to stand outside the tumultuous transition from the traditional to the modern. While adhering to traditional social mores, a yakuza hero achieves his agency through violence and hence remains independent from social bonds. Honoring the traditional patriarchy's command to maintain peace and order—often the boss's final words before his death—the protagonist endures the rival gang's taunts and harassment until, in the end, he reaches his limit and resorts to violence. In *Hell Is a Man's Destiny*, Hanada Hidejirō works hard as a chef at the restaurant while putting up with the Komai family's bullying. When the Komais kill the Terada family's boss, Hanada's rejection of the modern is clear: he cloaks himself in traditional attire as he expresses his moral indignation toward the evil capitalist yakuza. Yet the final explosion of violence also announces the hero's departure from the traditional values that have confined him in the state of inaction. The outburst of moral indignation finally grants him agency to fight social injustice, overcoming both the traditional and the modern.[17]

To be a man of action, a hero must be anchored in the community of manhood. As Saitō Ayako cogently argues, via Eve Sedgwick, this onscreen community was filled with tensions between homoerotic and homosocial sentiments.[18] Erotic feelings—whether heterosexual or homosexual—are sacrificed for the sake of maintaining homosocial bonds. In *Hell Is a Man's Destiny*, for example, the protagonist bids farewell to his geisha lover, Ikutarō, before the fight. Ikutarō is actually a male name. Starting around the 1780s, Fukagawa geisha began taking male names and dressing like male prostitutes in order to compete with their male rivals for customers.[19] This piece of history adds another layer to Saitō's reading. Although Ikutarō does not dress like a male prostitute, her name exposes the homoerotic undertone—a gender trouble—in her relationship with Hanada. Heterosexual love is already shaped in the mold of homoeroticism. The sequence in which Hanada and Kazama run into each other, exchange intense gazes, and proceed to their deathly revenge can best be compared to a kabuki convention of *michiyuki*, in which two lovers proceed toward their certain deaths (often in the form of double suicides).

Their homoerotically charged bond ends with Kazama's death—he dies in Hanada's arms—in order to keep their homosocial brotherhood intact (figure 6.2). Even when the protagonist is a woman, as in the case of Hibotan O-ryū in the *Red Peony Gambler* series, she is a stoic figure who never enters into a romantic relationship and demands that she be treated like a man. The protagonists' acts transcend mere capitalist self-interest, and their homosocial bonds are ultimately tested and reinforced by the self-sacrifice that they are willing to make. However, the violent expression of the hero's subjectivity in opposition to modernity also deprives him of his ideal community. In the final scenes of the *Brutal Tale of Chivalry* series, the hero survives the final battle, but his partner falls to the enemy's attack. The hero, now alone, must embrace the consequence of his own ethical choice.

The freedom to act is short-lived. The hero's violent act at the end of the film often leads to his arrest by the police. Although the Film Classification and Rating Committee (Eiga rinri kanri iinkai, the industry's voluntary screening board) preferred such anticlimactic conclusions, these

*Figure 6.2* Hanada Hidejirō holds Kazama Jūkichi as he dies, in *Hell Is a Man's Destiny*.

resolutions problematically affirm law enforcement's ultimate authority, despite their continual impotence until this moment. When the conflict of good and evil ends with a violent resolution, the agent of violence is neutralized and rendered safe. The hero's arrest physically removes him from the everyday life of ordinary citizens. (As the police takes Hanada away in handcuffs, Ikutarō offers a workman's coat to cover his tattoos.) Yet by portraying prisons as liminal space, yakuza films preserve their heroes' marginal identity, which cannot be completely subjugated to the regime outside the yakuza subculture. The series *A Man from Abashiri Prison* (*Abashiri bangaichi*, 1965–1972), for example, offered an extradiegetic reference point for other yakuza films by portraying life within the Abashiri penitentiary as an extension of yakuza society, quarantined from the modern world. Although there are numerous penitentiaries in Japan, many fictional yakuza find themselves in Abashiri Prison, including those in *Gangster VIP* (*Burai yori daikanbu*, 1968) and *Battles Without Honor and Humanity*. In the first half of the twentieth century, Abashiri Prison housed serious criminals at its facilities in an eastern coastal province of Hokkaido.[20] In the films, it stands as the last piece of the "outside" in the postwar regime of high growth:[21] the "bangaichi" in the Japanese title designates the land with no street address—the liminal space beyond administrative recognition.[22]

## The Fan Base

In late 1960s Japan, yakuza films found an enthusiastic following—not because they managed to smuggle traditional values back into a society threatened by radical transformations (as suggested by Oguma Eiji and others), but because they rejected the modern as well as the traditional while urging viewers to maintain their critical position even within deplorable situations.[23]

The yakuza hero offered an answer to the existential quest that many youths embraced at that historical moment. It was a quest for a means of political commitment and action in the ever-more-complicated socioeconomic conditions of postwar Japan. In yakuza film, many moviegoers found conditions that mirrored their own. There was no longer a clearly defined ground of moral authority. The traditional was steadily diminishing and functioned only as an inflexible patriarchy unable to respond to the radical transformations of contemporary society. Youths were increasingly critical of the modern—the capitalist economy—for its deleterious effects, including environmental destruction and the involvement of Japanese corporations in the Vietnam War. In yakuza film, as the protagonist struggles to maintain his integrity within a radically changing society, he eventually breaks away from the traditional and strikes out at the modern. His act is heroic in that he rejects the historical trajectory from the traditional to the modern. Caught within the political issues of their own time, the audience identified with the hero who courageously claims his own agency. His independence allowed the young audience to dream, momentarily, about a third way by which to transcend both traditional and modern.

For many youths in the audience, watching a yakuza film was an intense and personal experience. The television writer Takada Fumio—one of the numerous college students who enthusiastically embraced onscreen yakuza heroes—recalls how his generation identified with them:

> At the end, with the masterpiece song "Karajishi botan" [the theme song for the *Brutal Tale of Chivalry* series] playing, we saw Takakura Ken and Ikebe Ryō walking in the snow toward their final battle. How we juxtaposed ourselves, college students who were not able to accomplish anything in real life, with them and cheered for them. For our generation, that movie *Brutal Tale of Chivalry* was our youth.[24]

Sometimes the cheering was literal. In the late 1960s some of Tokyo's downtown theaters began hosting all-night film showings, often featuring several yakuza films. Young viewers—many veterans of student political movements—transformed the dark space into a political and convivial participatory space, responding emotionally to key scenes.[25] They shouted "nonsense" at the screen when the don of the evil gang spoke; when the hero, Takakura Ken, told the evil don, "Shinde morauze" (you shall die), they cheered "Iginashi" (no objections).[26] The young audience treated yakuza film like a kabuki-style performative art, where audience response is an essential part of the enjoyment. The filmmakers were self-conscious about shooting overwrought kabuki-esque drama. According to the writer Yamadaira Shigeki, when Saeki Kiyoshi was directing *Brutal Tale of Chivalry*, he refused to shoot the scene where Takakura Ken and Ikebe Ryō walk toward their final showdown. The assistant director Furuhata Yasuo and the cinematographer Hoshijima Ichirō shot it instead. Other staff members were embarrassed by the overdramatized direction, while the producer Shundō Kōji pronounced: "All right, we've gotta go with the theater world."[27] But interaction allowed the young audience, albeit momentarily, to experience the hero's moral action as its own. Ōshima Nagisa relates an episode from an all-night showing in downtown (Ikebukuro) Tokyo of Ōshima's *Night and Fog in Japan* (1960). As the audience grew disgusted by the long-winded speech given toward the end by one of the characters—an autocratic party leader—one man shouted: "Ken-san [i.e., Takakura Ken], please cut this guy in two!" The whole theater, "though momentarily stunned by the comments, soon cheered and erupted into huge laughter."[28]

Yamadaira Shigeki's personal recollection illustrates the emotional ties between yakuza film and the student movements through the voice of a participant: "At the leftist meetings, I was singing 'The Internationale.' But I had the posters of Takakura Ken and Fuji Junko up on walls of my tiny apartment room. There I sang . . . .'Karajishi botan.' [Yakuza film] powerfully appealed to our feelings back then."[29] Both yakuza film and the student left shared a will for radical change—a will that emerged within the historical conditions of postwar Japanese society.[30]

The appeal of yakuza film waned in the early 1970s.[31] Overproduction—a symptom of capitalism—certainly (and ironically) contributed to its decline: hundreds of yakuza films had appeared in the span of about ten years.[32] Screenwriters exhausted their plots, and actors grew tired of playing hackneyed roles in film after film.[33] Toei's female star, Fuji Junko, best known for her lead role in the *Red Peony Gambler* series, got married and retired. On March 4, 1972, amid intense media hype, Toei released a film with an all-star cast to commemorate her career. In the words of Toei producer Kusakabe Gorō, "So many fans came to see the film, which is far from being a masterpiece, to say a goodbye to Fuji Junko as well as to yakuza film in general."[34] Kobayashi Nobuhiko recalls the audience's response to the film: "*Kantō Hizakura Ikka* is an all-star film that filled theaters. The audience, however, came to their senses and felt apathetic when they saw yakuza film's first happy ending ever—Takakura Ken and Fuji Junko hit the road as a couple. I was there in the theater. I understand that for the majority of fans, this film spelled an end to yakuza film."[35] In the final scene of the film, Fuji looks straight into the camera and thanks the audience for their years of support. As she leaves the fictional yakuza world on the screen, she recovers her heteronormative identity: Fuji was a bride to be sent off by the Toei family.[36]

There were also external reasons for yakuza film's precipitous decline. The conventions of the genre lost their resonance in a larger society where searches for an alternative socioeconomic order were ending in disillusionment. In the late 1960s radical political movements gained the support of college students who were not affiliated with established leftist political groups (so-called nonsect radicals). Students shut down more than one hundred college campuses, and political rallies often ended in violent conflicts with the riot police.[37] A considerable number embraced the prospect that a revolution could take place in Japan. Despite their willingness to resort to violent means, however, the movements failed to achieve any tangible gains. By the early 1970s, campus political movements were virtually defunct. Many student participants and sympathizers turned their attention to their studies and job hunts, while nursing a sense of defeat.

The biologist Saishu Satoru (b. 1936), one of the leaders of the student protest movements at the University of Tokyo in the late 1960s, experienced frustration when it became clear that the student movements had failed spectacularly. He struggled to remain conscientious but could only assume a vague moral position:

> The unspeakable anger toward the "system" and toward myself, who had failed to establish [critical] subjectivity, was still smoldering in me. Yet I could not envision the ways the society and myself ought to be; and I resented everything [around me]. Especially I hated those who put their hearts into something at the universities, acting as if they owned the future. Being aware that I don't belong wherever I am—that is the posture, if I can call it that, that I assumed in stepping into tomorrow, where I have no sure purchase.[38]

In his confusion and disappointment, the only place he saw for himself was neither in the present nor in the future but in a nowhere land. Gone was the earlier aspiration to change the "system" through political action. He could only aspire to be a free and conscientious being.

As broad support for the movements on college campuses waned, radical groups escalated their use of violence to maximize their effect and appeal. Their targets were not limited to political authorities; hundreds of activists fell victim to factional violence.[39] Some were even killed. What little optimism remained was dashed by the gruesome purges committed by the United Red Army (URA), a militant group that sought to realize their revolutionary vision through armed conflict with the state. When members of the group barricaded themselves in a Karuizawa lodge with a hostage in February 1972, the general public still felt a considerable degree of support for revolutionary causes. The arrests of its core members, however, led to the revelation that the URA had killed fourteen of its own for reasons ranging from treason to deficient revolutionary spirit (I discuss these cases in more detail in chapter 8). Public opinion turned against the group, and violent leftist protests became something to be feared. Under these circumstances, it would be disingenuous for an audience to indulge in fantastic narratives in which violence revealed a way out of contradictions, even in the dark space of a movie theater. Once media reports of the brutality of radical groups surpassed in gruesomeness the aestheticized violence of yakuza film, the genre lost its power to offer a fantasy resolution. By 1972 yakuza film could no longer count on its faithful following, and Toei ceased production of its long-running series. The genre's decline was only temporarily halted by the success of the *Battles Without Honor and Humanity* series (1973–1974), which reinvented the yakuza hero and offered a new stance toward contemporary society.

## Transforming the Yakuza Film

For many yakuza film fans, Tōei's *Battles Without Honor and Humanity* series was a departure from the cinematic conventions of the genre. Fans and critics hailed its refreshing visual style. The jerky movements of a hand-held camera brought audiences closer to the site of violence, while monochrome still frames and voice-overs marking key events added a documentary aesthetic. An assassination scene was shot on a train platform and in busy shopping areas without a permit or rehearsal, as if it were a happening staged by a performance collective.[40] The reactions of the unsuspecting bystanders were incorporated into the shots. Many viewers were shocked by the mechanical treatment of deaths: the victims' bodies appear on frozen frames, with on-screen text denoting their names and the times of their deaths.[41] Body parts are graphically severed, and blood gushes in abundance. A group of young characters inhabited the film as realistic figures caught in a complex web of gang rivalry. The film is attentive to the lesser characters, whose desperate struggle for survival underscores the inhumanity of the yakuza world. Actors in minor roles offered serious performances in violent scenes, disregarding the possibility of injuries. The director, Fukasaku Kinji (1930–2003), tapped into their energies by giving them creative latitude. He listened intently to their ideas and let them act in the way they believed best suited the scenes.[42]

Tōei marketed the film as a work of *jitsuroku* (factual recording), a realistic portrayal of the actual yakuza world. (While it is a work of fiction, the film was indeed based on the memoirs of a retired yakuza don, Mino Kōzō, and the scriptwriter Kasahara Kazuo conducted extensive research for the screenplay.)[43] Toei hastily began producing a sequel, anticipating the original film's commercial success even before its theatrical release.[44]

The stylistic singularity of *Battles* becomes evident when its opening sequence is compared with that of *Brutal Tale of Chivalry* (*Shōwa zankyōden*), the eponymous film for the subsequent series (1965, dir. Saeki Kiyoshi). Both films portray a black market in the immediate postwar period, but in contrasting manners. *Brutal Tale of Chivalry* introduces a few central characters, using stationary camera positions and long takes. Although a fight breaks out in the scene, its overall aesthetic is static and stylized. By contrast, chaos rules the scene in *Battles*. In the establishing crane-shot, the camera zooms into the bustle of the black market. The rest of the sequence is shot with a hand-held camera in natural light. Numerous characters are introduced as they run through the black market. Here and throughout the film, *Battles* stylistically departed from the banal conventions of yakuza film. To viewers accustomed to the Toei yakuza film's visual style, the scene appeared dizzyingly dynamic.

But the techniques used in *Battles Without Honor and Humanity* were not new to contemporary Japanese filmgoers. Fukasaku had already used them in similar fashion in films such as *Under the Flag of the Rising Sun* (*Gunki hatameku motoni*, 1972), *Street Mobster* (*Gendai yakuza: Hitokiri Yota*, 1972), and *Outlaw Killer: Three Mad Dog Killers* (*Hitokiri Yota: Kyōken sankyōdai*, 1972). Furthermore, Fukasaku could not claim originality with regard to the graphic depiction of violence, which included the severing of arms in the opening sequence: Kurosawa Akira had already included such visceral shots in *Yojimbo* (1961). By this time, too, the unsteady images produced by a hand-held camera were not a novelty to Japanese film viewers. (As discussed in chapter 2, even Yamada Yōji—a director known for his stable camerawork—used them in *Where Spring Comes Late*.) Although Fukasaku used those techniques effectively and extensively, the new look of *Battles* does not solely account for its popularity.

The cinematographer Yoshida Sadaji approached the film from another vantage point:

> I had seen some of Mr. Fukasaku's works and thought they were full of "movements." I thought then, on my own, that his film was not a box office hit because it lacked "quiet" [parts] to enhance the impact of "motions" by contrast. When I worked with Mr. Fukasaku, I believed that if we paid attention to the contrast, his film would be a lot more appealing. That is why, in shooting scenes that resembled those from a domestic drama, I strove for stable images like those in period films.[45]

The dynamic images shot with a hand-held camera have been recognized as a notable idiosyncrasy of *Battles,* but, as Yoshida notes, the "movements" have maximum impact when viewed against the "quiet" parts shot from stable camera positions.

The theory that the fans—who seemingly had grown tired of fantastic tales—were attracted to *Battles'* depictions of actual yakuza rivalries and fights cannot explain its wide appeal, given that not just yakuza film fans but audiences in general were enthralled by the film. The scriptwriter, Kasahara Kazuo (1927–2002), was not merely replicating real-life violence. Describing the plot as "factual recording" was Toei's marketing ploy: in fact, Kasahara completely transformed the original turf wars in Kure into a complex drama of machination and intrigue.

This creative collaboration almost did not happen because of Kasahara's misgivings about the director. Fukasaku was famous for changing scripts at the shooting sites.[46] Although Fukasaku readily agreed to stick to the script, Kasahara was outraged when he first saw the final cut and stormed out of the preview room. Fukasaku's excessive use of a hand-held camera, Kasahara believed, destroyed "the rich story of men and the pathos of the youths in a bombed-out city." Only after watching the film for the second time on a big screen in a crowded theater was he able to appreciate what Fukasaku had accomplished.[47] The key to understanding the film's success in the Japanese society of 1973 lies in the creative tensions between Fukasaku's directing style, Yoshida's camerawork, and the tight, complex narrative that Kasahara offered. In the following section we turn our attention to Kasahara's contribution, which is often underappreciated by the film's fans.[48]

### Narrative Structure of *Battles Without Honor and Humanity*

There is a curious paradox in *Battles Without Honor and Humanity*. Its hero, Hirono Shōzō (played by Sugawara Bunta, 1933–2014), appears more realistic than his counterparts in earlier yakuza films, not because he behaves more violently, but because he fails to act in key scenes. Although Hirono is endowed with a strong sense of justice, like the traditional yakuza heroes who appeared on the screen before him, he is unable to express his ethical stance through an act of violence—quite unlike his cinematic predecessors. He serves only as a witness—a seer par excellence—to the gruesome crimes. Ultimately, though, his perspective holds the narrative together. This new hero is suited to the political reality of Japan in 1973, where violence had lost its allure as a means for political reform and had become merely the subject of television spectacle.

In contrast to the conventional yakuza film, the narrative of *Battles* consists of a complex web of actors and actions. Multiple viewings are required to fully comprehend the dynamically shifting gang alliances and rivalries, in which violence alone does not assure survival. It is often necessary for individual yakuza to compromise, setting aside the Manichean vision of "us against them." In this world of scheming and realignment of power, the protagonist alone maintains his integrity.

The film opens with a scene of a black market in Kure City, Hiroshima Prefecture. Hirono Shōzō is introduced as a man who, despite his proclivity for violence, maintains an old-fashioned sense of justice within the chaos of postwar society. For example, after saving a woman from an attempted rape by a group of American GIs, Hirono listens to a military song on the record player in an eatery. The woman who runs the place stops the music, chiding him: "Hey, you, turn off that corny song." Hirono, however, puts the music back on and continues to listen to it. Just then the woman that he rescued in the previous scene walks into the eatery with another woman and two GIs: her makeup, dress, and mannerisms plainly reveal that she has become a prostitute. On spotting Hirono there, she feels awkward and leaves hastily with her American companion. Hirono, dressed in an

Imperial Japanese Navy uniform, witnesses moral decay in front of his own eyes. The opening sequence establishes that he is a man who holds on to traditional values—much like his idealized predecessors on the screen—amid radically changing social conditions. That he beat American soldiers and rescued the woman suggests that he will live as a man of principle without kowtowing to the new authorities of postwar Japan.[49] His listening to military songs implies that his sense of justice is rooted in the Japan that existed before the foreign occupation.

But the new hero's valor and virility are not constrained by the conventions of yakuza film. Killing a drunken yakuza in the black market is his first step toward becoming a full-fledged member of a yakuza gang. The scene also announces the death of yakuza film as fans know it, upending cinematic conventions. The young hoodlums who control the market are unable to subdue the drunken yakuza, who is dressed in kimono and wielding a long Japanese sword. Hirono summarily takes care of him with a handgun. (That the gun initially misfires and Hirono pulls the trigger several times connotes the nature of his work in the yakuza world: he is literally a troubleshooter.) The traditional—once the source of moral rectitude in yakuza film—is invoked in degraded form, only to be destroyed by the hero. Using a Western weapon, Hirono recovers his masculine self in the world of the black market, the chaotic space ruled by capitalist desire. Although his conscience may be anchored in traditional values, Hirono is not imprisoned by them.

Hirono never gets entangled in disputes over economic interests; he takes action only out of loyalty toward the Yamamori family, to which he pledges his allegiance. By contrast, Boss Yamamori, who is wrapped up in greed, involves himself in the political intrigues of the Kure City Council. Yamamori's men kidnap a council member in order to break a tie in the council chair election to tip the race in his coconspirator's favor. At stake is control over a huge amount of materials that the army and navy had stashed away in preparation for the mainland battle. Departing from the conventions of first-wave yakuza film, *Battles* forthrightly identifies politicians as key members of the corrupt system.[50]

Most important, the subsequent infighting within the Yamamori family breaks out in Hirono's absence. Imprisoned for the second time—for murdering Doi Kiyoshi, the don of a rival family—Hirono is spared from taking a side in the Yamamori's internal disputes. Thanks to Hirono's sacrifice, the Yamamori family expands its market and thrives through the wide sale of methamphetamine (Philopon).[51] The profits from the meth distribution business undermine family unity, however. Dissatisfied with their meager share, young family members start selling meth on their own. Once the young defectors are purged from the family, a deeper fissure develops between the don and his deputy, Sakai Tetsuya, who holds significant power in the family. Sakai tries to force Yamamori into retirement. Yamamori in turn tells Hirono, who has just been released from prison, to kill Sakai. Although Hirono accepts Yamamori's command, he still tries to mend relations between the two men. Sakai promises to honor Hirono's wish for reconciliation but actually uses Yamamori's murderous scheme to continue to pressure the don to retire.

Hirono then makes the most enigmatic decision in the film. Realizing that Sakai broke his trust and plotted to slay one of the founding members of the Yamamori gang, Hirono swears to kill Sakai this time. Even when he discovers that Yamamori betrayed his own men to protect himself, Hirono does not direct his anger toward his boss. Finally disgusted with Yamamori's inability to lead the family, Hirono heads to Sakai's hideout to kill him. Why does he not kill Yamamori instead of Sakai? In *Big Gambling Ceremony*, whose script Kasahara also wrote, the protagonist feels morally justified in killing the patriarch for his wretched behavior. (Kaneko Nobuo plays the patriarch in both films.) Why would it be more acceptable for Hirono to kill his sworn brother Sakai than his boss? The audience never has to face these questions, however, because Hirono fails to commit the fratricide: Yamamori informs Sakai of Hirono's intent in order to set up a deadly trap.[52]

Within this tight-knit matrix of evil intentions and organizational mandates, the protagonist struggles to maintain his integrity, only to be totally frustrated in the end. In this sense, the characters in *Battles* are no more realistic than those in the conventional yakuza films. Like pieces on a chessboard, they are manipulated by larger forces and engage in futile battles. Caught in their own fear, they express their anguish and emotions only in stereotypical fashion. Kasahara's comments about the series' factual-recording style attest to its opportunistic use of historical elements:

> The "factual recording" style might sound like a work of nonfiction. But from the get-go I understood it as an "alternative form of fiction." . . . Representing things as they really are is realism's basic requirement. But the "factual-recordings" style puts emphasis on

the baroque: by exaggerating the "toxicity" of the material, I will bring to the fore the hidden aspects of the reality. Therefore, the basic format of the work must be comedy.[53]

While some scenes are humorous, *Battles* as a whole is not a comedy. Kasahara uses the word "comedy" to underscore the ways in which he dramatizes the "'toxicity' of the material," or incredible behaviors of real-life yakuza that he came across in his research.[54] The factual-recording style allowed him to highlight the characters' fallibility: instead of "the best of the men" that the conventional yakuza film portrayed ad nauseam, Kasahara created "men who were not the best of the men."[55]

Kasahara's departure from the conventions of yakuza film is most evident in *Battles'* anticlimactic ending, where, though Hirono expresses his frustration and acts out his anger, his weapon fails to find a living target. Two gunmen have ambushed Sakai. Hirono shows up in the middle of his funeral, which is attended by the major yakuza leaders in Hiroshima and Kure, including Yamamori, the man who ordered Sakai's killing. Approaching the altar uninvited, Hirono looks intently at Sakai's picture and asks the deceased if he is happy to be given such a grand funeral. After stating that he is as unhappy as Sakai is, Hirono pulls out a handgun and starts shooting at the nameplates attached to the dedicated flowers—surrogate targets rather than the dons themselves. Through shooting, he expresses his allegiance to his sworn brother without completely dishonoring the code of behavior in yakuza society. Hirono's symbolic act affirms that he is not an impotent figure. Yet the ejaculation of his violence fails to impregnate the final scene with moral catharsis.[56]

*Battles* thus rewrites the conventional yakuza film by prohibiting the final resolution through violence. Sugawara Bunta, the actor who plays Hirono Shōzō, never embodies justice as Takakura Ken and Tsuruta Kōji (1924–1987) do in earlier films. The protagonist strives to maintain an ethical stance in a yakuza world filled with suspicion, betrayal, and revenge—a world manipulated by the powerful. Director Fukasaku Kinji had already portrayed men in a similar situation in *Street Mobster* and *Outlaw Killer: Three Mad Dog Killers*. The protagonists in these films (also played by Sugawara) are transitional figures in the evolution of yakuza heroes. They struggle in vain to maintain their integrity against the mandates of powerful underground organizations, and both meet violent ends, departing from the traditional image and fate of the yakuza hero. By contrast, the figure of

Hirono is distinctive in that he does not engage in a self-destructive battle against the powerful but remains unharmed in most of the series and serves as a witness to intricate political rivalries.[57] (He lops off the tip of the left pinky in order to express remorse for a mistake in the first film and is stabbed only at the very end of *New Battles Without Honor and Humanity: Boss's Last Days* [1976], the final film of the second series.) Hirono's mostly unscathed body represents a man who remains constant even as he engages in dangerous political scheming. He is the antithesis of the yakuza heroes who get wounded as they engage in a final battle.

By withdrawing from the site of violence at key scenes and refraining from a self-destructive act in the final sequence, Hirono offers a stable, continuous perspective that maintains a distance from the political dynamics of yakuza society even while ensconced in it. In other words, in the *Battles Without Honor and Humanity* series, the yakuza hero returns to the movie screen not necessarily as a doer within the violent drama, but as a viewer par excellence. The yakuza hero is reduced to an inactive agent who holds the narrative structure together. As Kasahara appropriately describes the role: "In [*Battles Without Honor and Humanity*], [the character of Sugawara] Bunta is the least developed character, but without him the story falls apart."[58] Takada Kōji, who wrote the script for *Battles Without Honor and Humanity: Final Episode (Jinginaki tatakai: Kanketsu-hen)*, expresses a similar view: "Although *Battles Without Honor and Humanity* left a huge impression on me, honestly, I had many problems with it. The protagonist Hirono is not terribly interesting because he is just a character that helps drive the story. The secondary characters, including Don Yamamori, have real human qualities. But it is hard to see who Hirono really is."[59] Hirono must be transparent—his motives must always border on naïveté—in order to provide a stable perspective from which the audience can appreciate the whirlwind of plotting and compromise.

## The End of Radical Activism and the Birth of a New Yakuza Hero

Although the series takes its theme from the postwar history of Hiroshima yakuza organizations, *Battles*' relationship to its larger historical context is precarious and in some ways opportunistic. It incorporates the historical conditions of postwar Hiroshima to explain the motives for the yakuza gangs' escalating violence, but only in the most general terms, invoking the confusion and chaos of a social space in which yakuza members strove for financial success and struggled to maintain an advantage amid bloody gang rivalries. The opening scenes, for example, attest that historical authenticity was not Fukasaku's primary concern. Even though more than a year had passed since the end of the war (the story begins in late 1946), Japanese were still suffering from a dire shortage of daily essentials. Many veterans, lacking alternative clothing, kept wearing their filthy and, in some cases, thread-bare military uniforms. Hirono shows up to the black markets, however, in his crisp navy uniform, with no traces of a past struggle for survival. History is invoked only as an abstract idea, not as lived experiences.[60]

The mandate to keep production costs down also eliminated some historical elements. Toei spent a large amount of money recreating the black market in the opening scenes of the first film, but the company could not afford to reproduce it for the sequel, *Battles Without Honor and Humanity: Deadly Fight in Hiroshima*, and Kasahara Kazuo was forced to change the film's chronological setting by a few years. This change blurred the connection between war experiences and the protagonist's inclination toward violence, a connection that Kasahara originally intended to foreground. Fragments of history are selectively imported into the sequels, as when the dire poverty of the atomic bomb slum offers a motive for a murder in *Battles Without Honor and Humanity: Police Tactics*. Yet these attempts to introduce the historical conditions of the larger postwar society remain largely external and incidental to the narrative development of the films.[61]

*Battles* should rather be understood as Toei's response to the political climate of Japan in the early 1970s, when political action had failed to break through to a new horizon of social criticism. The yakuza film of the late 1960s rejected the status quo, while *Battles* emulates the pessimistic outlook of its time. Even in the style and degree of violence, the films lagged behind what contemporary radical sects administered. Trapped in their own failure, the radical groups merely turned their attention to internal and interfactional politics. They became the object of their own criticism and violent struggle, which eventually culminated in bloody sectarian rivalries and internal purges. Gone were the aspirations of the late 1960s for social change and popular support for radical movements. As the revolutionary political movements became further radicalized, even their sympathizers, including those who frequented rundown movie theaters to watch their favorite yakuza stars, distanced themselves from political activism, transforming themselves into voyeuristic bystanders who witnessed the activists' violent confrontation with authority on the television screen.

Fukasaku was shocked by the United Red Army's bloody purges, made known to the public in 1972. He condenses the five-year development of Japan's student protest movements into a few sentences:

> The student movements had evolved at a rapid pace to the point where the participants began using staves. I was envious of them but was not sure where the movements were heading. Then hell broke loose—so many dead bodies. I was thinking: "Hey, is this it?" Their behavior was beyond any logic, though logic was supposedly at the base of the members' self-criticism [which led to the internal violence]. All of that hit me when I was writing the script for *Street Mobster*.[62]

While reeling from the gruesome outcomes of radical politics, Fukasaku produced the hopeless story of *Street Mobster*, whose protagonist—a personification of violence—challenges a powerful yakuza organization and is easily eliminated.

*Battles* recasts the political conditions of 1973 with its own drama of internal conflict and rivalry within yakuza society. Hirono Shōzō's situation could easily be read as parallel. His action, though motivated by his righteous anger, only worsens the conditions he finds abhorrent. His attempt to reconcile Yamamori and Sakai ends with Sakai's murder. The final scene of the film demonstrates Hirono's dire predicament: even if he managed to kill a few yakuza dons, his act would only create maneuvering room for the other bosses and thus serve the "system." The harder he struggles to free himself from the system's hold, the more he becomes entangled in it. Much like the demise of radical politics in the early 1970s, *Battles* announces that no one can maintain autonomous subjectivity, even in oppositional politics.

As a depiction of yakuza life, *Battles Without Honor and Humanity* is not the radical departure from the conventional yakuza films that Toei claimed it to be. By rejecting violence as a means to render the final resolution, the film complicates the hero's anguish. Despite its anticathartic ending, the film still negotiates the conventions of yakuza film. While the series throws the yakuza hero into a state of existential angst, its carefully constructed narrative safeguards his fall. *Battles* makes Hirono simultaneously naïve and self-reflective about his relationship to larger social and political conditions. Perhaps this contradictory portrayal allowed the hero to remain an attractive individual even though he is deeply mired in the ugly reality of yakuza society.

These tensions within the film reflect the filmmakers' divergent intentions. Fukasaku wished to create images that would destabilize viewers' understanding of social reality. By contrast, Kasahara tried to accommodate yakuza film fans' expectations while writing a screenplay in the new factual-recording style. Kasahara claims that the film was not meant to be a complete departure but rather a "half-step forward" from what the audience was accustomed to. While incorporating elements from yakuza members' quotidian life to enhance the film's realistic feel, Kasahara still structured the narrative around the binary between the traditional and the modern. The traditional yakuza drama with rules and honor therefore comes to the surface amid what otherwise appears to be total chaos—yakuza battles without honor and humanity.[63] Kasahara's "half-step forward" guided the audience through Fukasaku's dynamic and at times disorienting images.

The success of the *Battles* series temporarily rekindled fans' interest in yakuza film. In the subsequent works in the series, Hirono continues his existential quest for autonomous agency by participating in political struggles within yakuza society. Although he attains temporary success by outmaneuvering the big players, defeat is inevitable. In the final episode, which brings the narrative up to 1970, almost contemporary with the film's production, he is forced to retire.

Toei demanded the sequels in order to capitalize on the success of the first film, but the series failed to maintain the original level of intensity. In particular, the three episodes produced under the title of *New Battles Without Honor and Humanity* (*Shin jinginaki tatakai*, 1974–1976) suffered from the departure of screenwriter Kasahara Kazuo.[64] (Yoshida Sadaji served as the cinematographer for the first series and the first film in the second series.) The atavistic return to the image of the lone hero who embodies justice deprives the new series of the moral struggle found within the original one. With the demise of *New Battles Without Honor and Humanity*, yakuza film entered a long period of marginal success, much like the Japanese film industry in general. Most of the yakuza films produced in the following decades appealed only to a diminishing circle of hardcore fans. Many of them were released straight to the VHS and DVD markets.[65] The modest "half-step" that *Battles* added to yakuza film proved to be a vast distance that nobody else managed to emulate commercially.[66]

The contrast between the two types of yakuza hero—the protagonist of a conventional yakuza film and Hirono Shōzō—is not as striking as many film fans and critics believed. Both stoically struggle to maintain their integrity while dealing with the tension between the traditional and the modern. They differ from each other only in the degree to which they reject the system they inhabit. The conventional yakuza hero breaks away from all social constraints, albeit temporarily, while Hirono is aware of the futility of such an act.[67] What their difference reveals is the effect of mass socialization on their fans in the Japan of the late 1960s and early 1970s. Deep anxiety, accompanied by a degree of euphoria stemming from the uncertainty of the transition, was displaced by the realization that there was no way out of what the future had wrought.[68] Yet, as we witness in the next two chapters, this realization did not spell an end to the romantic notion of violence as a means to gain critical distance from contemporary Japanese society. As it loses clear external targets, violence turns inward: mass consumer society that purportedly exists inside each individual becomes a new object of popular criticism.

CHAPTER VII

## Jō and Hyūma

*Kajiwara Ikki's Manga Heroes and Their Violent Quest for Historical Agency*

> Finally, let us reconfirm. We are Tomorrow's Jō.
> —TAMIYA TAKAMARO, RED ARMY FACTION LEADER, IN A HIJACKED JAPAN AIRLINES JETLINER, 1970

By the late 1960s, manga weeklies had become an integral part of Japanese youth culture.[1] As their target audience, the Japanese baby boomers, grew up, the weeklies evolved to cater to this more mature audience as well as to juvenile readers.[2] Among the scores of manga magazines introduced to the market in the 1950s and 1960s, *Weekly Shonen Magazine* (*Shūkan shōnen magajin*: hereafter referred to as *Magazine*) not only boasted the largest circulation of any manga magazine—over one million in 1967—but also enjoyed an iconic status in youth culture.[3] The cliché was that the students on the street and the college campuses walked with two weeklies in their hands: *Magazine* in their left hand and the highbrow, left-leaning *Asahi Journal* in their right.[4] In a survey of University of Tokyo undergraduates in 1970, *Magazine* and *Journal* ranked second and first on the list of their most popular periodicals.[5]

The writer Kajiwara Ikki (1936–1987) played an essential role in *Magazine*'s growth in the 1960s and 1970s. In the early 1960s, to relieve artists from the relentless pressure of weekly production, *Magazine* introduced a division of labor between scriptwriter and artist. Kajiwara was one of the weekly's early writing recruits, a new breed of storyteller.[6] He subsequently produced original scripts for a number of successful works. *Star of the Giants* (*Kyojin no hoshi*) was serialized in *Magazine* (1966–1971) and produced as a television anime program (1968–1971); *Tomorrow's Jō* (*Ashita no Jō*) was also serialized in *Magazine* (1968–1973) and produced as a television anime program (1970–1971, 1980–1981), an animated film (1980, 1981), and a live-action film (1970, 2011).[7] Both works, the focus of this chapter, received enthusiastic support from contemporary readers and audiences and have since been touted as classics of Japanese manga and television animation.[8]

Endowed with exceptional physical abilities, Kajiwara's young heroes reject the middle-class comfort and happiness that many in Japan pursued during the high-growth period. Striving for "genuine" self-realization, these fictional characters endure extreme physical and mental hardship. Through their extraordinary bodily performance, they confirm their working-class, masculine identity against a society filled with passive consumption. Their perseverance also liberates their bodies from the conformity that undergirded the regime of high growth. Yet the works' heroes stand as antitheses of each other in many respects, as illustrated by their choice of sports. While Hoshi Hyūma struggles for glory as a member of a professional baseball team, the Yomiuri Giants, Yabuki Jō strives to maintain his independent spirit by defying social conventions, including those of the boxing world. The two heroes, furthermore, fight two different kinds of "war" in the postwar era. A war injury cut short the baseball career of Hyūma's father. By living his father's dream, Hyūma continues to fight the Asia Pacific War, working through the devastating loss that his father's generation suffered. By contrast, Jō's war against social norms is in the present, and he wages it for himself alone, against any constraints placed on his free spirit.

The same scriptwriter gave birth to these two contrasting protagonists, and both became iconic figures in Japanese society in the final years of the high-growth era. This chapter foregrounds the contrary masculine ideals presented in the two works and proposes that the heroes' divergent behavior patterns attest to conflicting desires that ran deep in late 1960s and early 1970s Japan. Hyūma is ensconced in the postwar optimism that undergirded Japan's radical socioeconomic transformation. Jō wants to stand outside it. The popularity of both ultimately demonstrates the urgency with which their contemporary audience sought a critical purchase on their drastically changing society.

The production system of the Japanese manga weeklies involved intricate collaboration among weekly editors, scriptwriters, manga artists, artists' assistants, and even readers. This partnership was essential to the success of both titles. The names of Kajiwara Ikki and the two artists—Kawasaki Noboru and Chiba Tetsuya—may have been the most recognizable, but the phenomenal success of *Star of the Giants* and *Tomorrow's Jō* owed much to a production system that combined many exceptional talents. Weekly editors took a strong interest in fostering young artists' talent while establishing close personal and work relations with them. They spent countless hours working with them, deeply involved in aspects of production ranging from devising plots to figuring out the composition of individual frames.[9]

For *Star of the Giants*, editor Miyahara Teruo and the rest of *Magazine*'s editorial team were instrumental in its production. (As discussed in chapter 2, they also recruited Mizuki Shigeru in the mid-1960s.) The basic themes of the popular baseball manga serial emerged from intense discussions among Miyahara and other members of the staff. Believing in Kajiwara's ability to produce the unconventional drama that the editorial team wanted, Miyahara chose him as scriptwriter.[10] While Kajiwara's scripts would amaze even Miyahara, the team's groundwork was essential for his successful writing. Miyahara also gave careful consideration to the choice of a manga artist for each title. Kawasaki Noboru (b. 1941) made critical contributions to the popularity of *Star of the Giants* by his skill in graphically dramatizing the characters' emotional turmoil.[11]

Of the scores of manga artists with whom he worked, Kajiwara developed the closest relationship with Chiba Tetsuya (b. 1939), his collaborator on *Tomorrow's Jō*. The exceptional quality of the work is widely credited to the creative tension between the two men. Chiba was already an established manga artist, one capable of producing sophisticated plots for his own works, when he began working on *Tomorrow's Jō*. Recognizing Chiba's talent, Kajiwara, who typically refused to allow artists to change a single line in his scripts, gave him more creative latitude than he normally tolerated. Yet this arrangement did not necessarily ease the tensions between them. Kajiwara was initially frustrated when Chiba set aside his original scripts for the first several episodes introducing Jō and other characters. Miyahara intervened, encouraging Kajiwara to appreciate Chiba's artistic vision.[12] At a relatively early stage of serialization, Chiba's interpretation of one particular character could have jeopardized Kajiwara's overall story design, although the two subsequently repaired the potentially disastrous situation and even turned it into a creative advantage. When working on a scene where the protagonist Yabuki Jō encounters his archrival, Riki'ishi Tōru, for the first time in a reformatory, Chiba misunderstood Kajiwara's intent and portrayed Riki'ishi as an imposing figure, far larger than Jō. In Kajiwara's original plan, however, Jō and Riki'ishi were destined to meet in the boxing ring, meaning that their physiques needed to be evenly matched. In the subsequent discussions between Chiba and Kajiwara, a new plotline emerged: in order to accept Jō's challenge, Riki'ishi must endure severe weight reduction, which would ultimately contribute to his death in the match with Jō.[13]

While Kajiwara Ikki was a talented and celebrated scriptwriter, his authorship was deeply anchored in the collective process of manga production, open to the other participants' creative interventions—at least until he grew more arrogant as a result of the success of his work.[14] The popularity of the works serialized in *Magazine* stemmed from the collaborative efforts of exceptional talents, in which Kajiwara was a key contributor. In the following discussion of *Star of the Giants* and *Tomorrow's Jō*, his name stands for the most visible part of the dynamic manga production process.[15]

The manga industry, particularly the major publishing houses, is and has been sensitive to reader responses.[16] Unpopular serials are quickly terminated, while the popular ones continue for years, even decades.[17] To expand the weekly's circulation, *Magazine*'s editors have tried to find connections between their manga and the world the readers inhabit, paying close attention to social trends.[18] Consequently, Kajiwara's two best-known works resonated with contemporary social and political concerns. As the sociologist Hashimoto Kenji has observed, for example, class tensions constitute a central theme of both.[19] *Star of the Giants* and *Tomorrow's Jō* deal with class issues differently, however, as their heroes demonstrate contrasting attitudes toward the class structure.

Although Kajiwara started his serialization of *Star of the Giants* in the second half of the 1960s with rather retrograde concepts of real men, he drastically complicated them in *Tomorrow's Jō*. The two heroes stand for contrasting ideals of manhood and independent agency, yet both ideals had tremendous appeal in contemporary Japanese society. The two sets of images stand for two separate discursive strategies through which to rupture the smooth surface of consumer society. Hyūma works from within; Jō from outside.

### *Star of the Giants*: Corporate Culture, Class, and Gender

*Star of the Giants* is a *Bildungsroman* deeply rooted in the socioeconomic conditions of 1960s Japan. The young hero, Hoshi Hyūma, realizes his dream of becoming an ace pitcher on a professional baseball team, the

Yomiuri Giants.[20] While making heroic efforts to perfect his pitching, the protagonist establishes his individuality within the team. To achieve his own glory, Hyūma must first learn to trust his teammates and earn their trust. His efforts to defeat his rivals are acceptable only insofar as they contribute to his team's victories. Like the corporate "warriors" who dedicated their lives to constant technological innovation at the expense of their personal lives, Hyūma ultimately sacrifices his baseball career for perfecting new and revolutionary pitches. By articulating the liberatory meaning of self-discipline, *Star of the Giants* captured the hearts of millions.

The Yomiuri Giants are an actual team that belong to the Nippon Professional Baseball organization and are by far the most popular among its twelve organizations, thanks to their heavy television exposure. The team's parent company, Yomiuri Shinbun, controlled the Nippon Television Network, which televised all the Giants' home games until the early 2000s. When *Magazine* began serializing *Star of the Giants*, the team was at the start of a long stretch of successful seasons: beginning with the 1965 season, the Giants won nine consecutive national titles. It appears natural, therefore, that *Magazine*'s editors and Kajiwara chose the team as the stage for their fantastic tale, in which Hyūma and his rivals interact with real-life star players.[21] The Giants readily collaborated with *Magazine*, embracing the opportunity to expand their fan base to younger age groups.[22] The team was also attractive for another reason: their success derived from the disciplinary regime imposed on the players by Kawakami Tetsuharu (1920–2013), manager from 1961 to 1974. Japanese baseball culture used to valorize individual talent over teamwork, giving players more latitude on and off the field. Nagashima Shigeo, the Giants' star third baseman, joined the team in 1958 and was unimpressed by his first spring training. Daily practice ended around noon so that the team members could play mahjong in the afternoon.[23] In 1961, after witnessing the Los Angeles Dodgers' training methods up close in Vero Beach, Florida, Kawakami began training his own team, to the players' consternation, according to the systematic principles detailed in Al Campanis's *Dodgers' Way to Play Baseball*.[24] The media strongly reacted to Kawakami's philosophy that each athlete should fulfill his own part for the sake of achieving success for the whole team, calling it *kanri yakyū* (managed baseball) because it dovetailed perfectly with the corporate culture that had begun to dominate contemporary Japan.[25] Hyūma and his rivals were admitted into the corporatized, regimented world of Japan's professional baseball, not to critique it but to augment and perfect it with their virility.

To maintain his independent existence, Hyūma must transcend the historical conditions of postwar Japan, manifested first and foremost as class relations. While his rivals on other teams may suffer the adverse effects of class, Hyūma remains unaffected by his family's lowly status. He is presented as a figure of noble origin—a baseball aristocrat—temporarily lost in the sordid world but, thanks to his exceptional talent, destined to rise above challenges and social constraints.[26] Hyūma's and his rivals' bodies exist as privileged material with which to realize ideal masculine selves. By enduring impossibly difficult physical training, the male characters show off their virility and distance themselves from feminine qualities. Without the slightest hint of irony or embarrassment, Hyūma embraces his lower-working-class background. In his high school admission interview, he proudly announces: "My father is the best day laborer (*ninpu*) in Japan" (*Star of the Giants* [hereafter *SG*], 2:24).[27] Although he now works as a day laborer, Hyūma's father, Hoshi Ittetsu, was a legendary third baseman for the Yomiuri Giants before the end of the war. Because of a wartime injury, he was unable to make a comeback as a professional baseball player in the postwar years.[28] He has poured his passion for baseball into his son, subjecting him to rigorous training from an early age. The poverty in which Ittetsu and Hyūma find themselves is external to the innate identity of the father-son dyad. Their elite status will be confirmed, not through their material possessions but through their ability to dedicate their lives solely to the game of baseball.

Although each of Hyūma's archrivals stands on one side or the other of the great class divide, class is ultimately a minor inconvenience that each player must overcome in order to find his true calling in baseball. Hanagata Mitsuru is the heir of a powerful industrialist, the president of a car manufacturing company. With every need instantaneously met, Hanagata struggles to find a purpose in his early life. Only baseball, and his irreducible struggles in the game, allow him to overcome the upper-class upbringing that stifles his spirit. His baseball rivalry with Hoshi Hyūma awakens his passion (though his father constantly presses him to quit baseball and to pursue a business career). By contrast, Samon Hōsaku fails to transcend his class origins. He is the oldest son of a poor farm family in Kumamoto, burdened with the responsibility of taking care of five young siblings after their parents' deaths. Samon is confident that he too could crush Hyūma's signature pitches if only he could immerse himself in baseball training to the same degree that Hanagata has done. Samon's foremost concern is to protect the life he shares with his siblings in what appears to be a one-room apartment. He could not possibly jeopardize his career just for the sake of momentary glory.

*Star of the Giants* is also a drama of homosocial bonds from which women—symbolic or biological—are excluded. Samon Hōsaku embodies a feminine quality, and for that he is eventually excluded from the male drama. Facing reporters' blunt questions about why Hanagata, not he, first successfully hit Hyūma's signature pitch, Samon explains his familial obligations and embraces his sisters and brothers (SG 6:260–65). The scene transforms him into a maternal figure, whose masculine yet rounded features are appropriate for a tough mother holding the family together at all costs. There is no place for biological women in the male bond either. Hyūma's mother is long dead, while his rivals' mothers are unmentioned. Although his older sister, Akiko, plays a motherly role, taking care of Hyūma's everyday material as well as emotional needs, she eventually leaves him to avoid interfering with his masculine battle (SG 15:194). Her disappearance also shields his rival, Hanagata, from distraction, since he is in love with her. Despite finding his true love in Mina, Hyūma resolves to leave her in order to focus on his professional career—although he is ultimately spared from choosing baseball over her when her death from malignant melanoma releases him to return to his calling (SG 12:88–171).[29] Heterosexual relations are a nascent form of domesticity that must be avoided because they interfere with the homosocial bond among the male characters. Kajiwara introduces and subsequently eliminates the female characters to highlight the masculine drama staged by the baseball heroes.

### Hyūma: A Japanese Hero

Through the rivalry between Hyūma and the African American player Armstrong Ozuma, *Star of the Giants* reenacts the war that the two nations fought more than two decades before. The story inverts the popular narrative that the United States was victorious thanks to its overwhelming material power: the Japanese hero and his exceptional willpower triumph over Ozuma, the product of American material wealth. Three characters—Hyūma, Hoshi Ittetsu (his father), and Ozuma—represent, respectively,

Japan, Japan's wartime past, and the United States. Together they stage a secondary drama through which Hyūma works through their tension-filled relations. While burdened with the weight of history—his father's frustrated dream—Hyūma overcomes it by accepting it as his own. By contrast, Ozuma is unable to escape the fetters of historical conditions, which may have made him a physically superb athlete but ultimately deprived him of the capacity for independent thinking.

Ozuma's career uncannily mirrors Hyūma's. The St. Louis Cardinals discover his exceptional talent while he is still in an orphanage. In a parallel to Hyūma's early training, Ozuma is given special coaching by the Cardinals' staff. After fifteen years of baseball education, he debuts as a Cardinals player in an exhibition game against the Yomiuri Giants. His impressive physique represents what American material conditions can produce out of the least advantaged in society. When he faces the Japanese pitcher for the first time, Ozuma instinctively recognizes his double (SG 11:133). Later, when given the opportunity to talk to Hyūma directly, Ozuma declares to him that Hyūma is a mere baseball robot, just like himself: neither of them has a life outside baseball. The American athlete thus presents himself as a mirror on which Hyūma—for the first time—critically reflects on himself. To Hyūma's insistence that he happily embraces baseball, Ozuma offers a point-by-point rebuttal demonstrating how limited their lives have been (SG 11:166). Ozuma's critical voice shakes Hyūma to the core and drives him into a spiritual abyss and a period of deep soul searching.[30]

Hyūma eventually overcomes Ozuma's questioning by finding a new passion in baseball (fig. 7.1). Although he initially tries to find a life outside baseball by consuming the material benefits brought by his success, this renders him the subject of media gossip, thoroughly consumed by the audience. His relationship with (and loss of) Hidaka Mina eventually helps him rediscover the spiritual aspect of baseball. By choosing baseball again of his own volition, Hyūma asserts his willpower and establishes his genuine agency. By contrast, his dark-skinned double fails to achieve a genuine self. Whereas Hyūma is able to work through Japan's traumatic past, Ozuma is completely weighed down by the dark history of slavery in the United States: cast as the racial other, he is portrayed as incapable of working through the historical trauma. Ozuma questions but is unable to overcome the condition in which he finds himself.

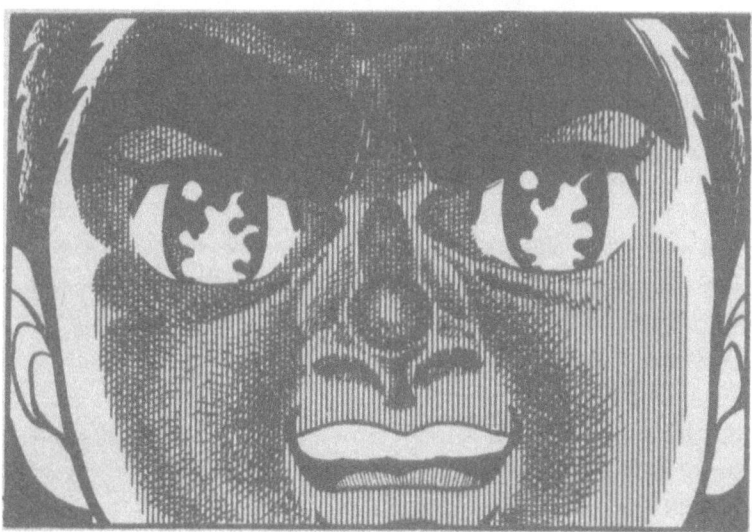

*Figure 7.1* Flames in Hyūma's eyes: after much soul searching, he rediscovers passion for baseball. This is one of the over-the-top techniques that Kawasaki Noboru uses to dramatize the narrative. SG 13:61.

Before reaching his ultimate goal, however, Hyūma must overcome his father, Hoshi Ittetsu, who set him on his path. Determined to make Hyūma a star player for the Giants, Ittetsu mercilessly trained him from an early age, forcing him to wear a homemade tension-resistance device on his upper body even when not training (SG 1:55–62). The father's will is physically enforced on his young son's body, resisting every move he makes. Only when the device becomes like a part of him can Hyūma free himself from it. He remains in the world that his father imposed on him until the conversation with Ozuma shatters this father-son dyad, propelling Hyūma to a search for his genuine self.

Having lost Hyūma, Ittetsu is now determined to become his son's biggest rival, while Ozuma must be punished for undermining his fatherly authority. Ittetsu leaves his impoverished neighborhood to accept a coaching job with a rival team, the Chūnichi Dragons, on one condition: the Dragons must acquire Armstrong Ozuma from the Cardinals. Once he joins the team, Ozuma serves as a medium for Ittetsu's determination to crush his son and is subjected to a training regime reminiscent of the one Ittetsu once forced on Hyūma. Recognizing their shared desire to defeat

Hyūma, Ozuma grudgingly accepts Ittetsu's authority and subjugates himself to the abusive training regime.

Reminiscent of earlier Japanese representations of colonial subjects, images of Ozuma oscillate between childlike and animalistic.[31] Although he may no longer feel like a robot, his Japanese coach sees few signs of intelligence in him. When they try to figure out the secret of Hyūma's new pitch, Ittetsu calls Ozuma's explanation "kindergarten-level guess work" and declares him a simpleton (SG 14:154). When the American player reacts emotionally to his provocation, Ittetsu cracks a bat down on home plate like a whip (SG 14:154). Although Ozuma had earlier managed to hit Hyūma's signature pitch out of the park, he is intimidated by Hyūma's new pitch, which disappears over home plate (SG 14:185). Facing its magical effects for the first time, Ozuma shows a visceral reaction, portraying him like a wild creature fearing the unknown. By reinscribing racial stereotypes through Ittetsu's and Ozuma's behavior, Kajiwara imprisons the African American player in the historical legacies of slavery. Although he may be able to question his state, Ozuma does not possess enough self-awareness to attain genuine agency. It is Hyūma's role to inherit his rival's self-doubt and address it satisfactorily. Ozuma's superior material support and education fail to produce a comparable subjectivity in him. He appears, therefore, only as a foil to Hyūma's exceptional (read: Japanese) accomplishment. It is Hyūma's quintessentially Japanese identity that allows him to resist and eventually overcome historical conditions, including baseball's American identity.[32]

By transcending historical conditions manifested in the form of class, gender, race, and nationality, Hyūma achieves his genuine subjectivity. Using a magical new pitch, he pitches a perfect game—the third and last in his career—against the Dragons, defeating his father and a former teammate, Ban Chūta.[33] When Ittetsu admits defeat, the son finally achieves his father's dream. However, the price for this accomplishment is high. The physical stress from repeatedly throwing the new pitch destroys his left arm, prematurely ending his baseball career at the age of nineteen, in the middle of his third season. In realizing his father's dream, Hyuma replicates his father's career: a legendary player whose career ends because of an injury.[34] Yet there is a key difference between them: while Ittetsu's injury was caused by external forces—the war—Hyūma has continued to throw his new pitch with the full knowledge that it will cause him serious injury.

Hyūma's body thereby serves as a medium through which to overcome the historical conditions of postwar Japan, where frustrated dreams still haunted the war generation. He exorcises the shadows of the past and of a former enemy nation through reenacting the war in which his father was injured. By fulfilling his father's dream, Hyūma finally liberates himself from its weight. In other words, he offers his throwing arm—the symbol of his masculine identity—as a payment to settle the account with his father and the past that he represents, and he thus gains the freedom to enjoy his (and Japan's) new life with no sense of guilt.[35] Although Hyūma in effect inherits an injured masculine identity from his father, he is able to live as a winner by restoring the masculine regime before sending it back to where it rightfully belongs: the past. Japan's problematic history is tamed and exorcised thanks to Hoshi Hyūma's heroic efforts.

*Star of the Giants* strives to establish an autonomous subjectivity through Hyūma's body in a society that was celebrating an unprecedented economic prosperity. The story posits the body as a possible site of resistance against consumer culture. The protagonist's body, however, is ultimately sacrificed to prove the supremacy of the human spirit, a theme inspired by Kajiwara's seemingly unquestioning belief in willpower. This confirmation of human agency was consistent with the optimism of Japanese society at the peak of the high-growth era. While still working on *Star of the Giants*, the writer began producing the script of *Tomorrow's Jō*, which would eventually take the tension between body and spirit in a far bleaker direction. In the new script, Jō's spirit never achieves liberation, though he too sacrifices his body in his struggle to achieve a genuine agency of action.

## *Tomorrow's Jō*: A Battle Against Self

Unlike Hyūma, Yabuki Jō, the fifteen-year-old protagonist of *Tomorrow's Jō*, does not directly grapple with the embodiment of the past, although he struggles, literally and figuratively, with his own class. There are few traces of the past in Jō's life. He grew up in an orphanage and has no family. One day he turns up from nowhere on the skid row on the outskirts of Tokyo. Lacking familial and geographic ties, Jō is a liminal figure throughout the story. Much like Hyūma, he exercises self-discipline in order to excel in his sport of choice: boxing. In *Tomorrow's Jō*, however, excellence in sports bears a radically different meaning. Hyūma realizes his individuality only as part of the team and in reaction to his father's masculine intervention. Familial and social institutions do not define this star baseball player, who effectively transcends all social ties and reaches the pinnacle of stardom. They are merely part of the setting, a backdrop against which to dramatize his ascendance. By contrast, Jō constantly strives to free himself from all social constraints. Trapped in the nexus of institutional conventions, nevertheless, he can only seek freedom within the socioeconomic network that he loathes.[36] Only through self-destructive bouts does he protect his liminal identity, or the ultimate autonomy of his self.

There was a paradigmatic shift in early postwar Japanese boxing. When Shirai Yoshio (1923–2003) won the Japanese fly weight title in 1949 and then the world title three years later under the tutelage of the American coach Alvin Cahn (1892–1971), the media touted the modern, scientific, American methods of training and fighting that Cahn administered to the new champion.[37] This media valuation was consistent with the contemporary popular narrative that attributed the U.S. victory over Japan to the former's scientific power.[38] Japanese pugilism thus became a showcase where the new scientific regime supersedes the old and irrational, setting Japanese society on a proper path of modernization. By the time *Magazine* began serializing *Tomorrow's Jō* in January 1968, Japan had produced several boxing world champions, proving that it had successfully adapted to the new global standards. Yet, finding inspiration in the legendary boxer Piston Horiguchi (1914–1950), Kajiwara focuses on the dark destructive impulse of the sport, the excess that refused to be subsumed under the scientific discourse.[39] Horiguchi represented the old style of boxing, which made light of footwork and defense: his reckless fighting style was popularly called "*gyokusai* [shattering of a jewel] *senpō*," after the mass suicide attacks that the Japanese Imperial Army troops carried out in the South Pacific.[40] *Tomorrow's Jō* resists, at least initially, the modernization of boxing, lingering a while longer in the space between the old and the new regimes.

Boxing—a legalized form of violence—is well suited to underscore Jō's marginal existence. When he finds a man who is stronger than he is, and when he discovers that the man has trained himself to box, Jō, who prides himself on being an excellent street fighter, takes an interest in the sport and ultimately embraces the world of pugilism. Through this physical performance that renders violent exchanges comprehensible, Jō for the first time establishes genuine connections with others. By embracing boxing's inherent violence, he finds a space where he truly belongs, yet this sense of belonging takes a toll on his physical being.

The story introduces Jō as a young man who instinctively resists authority and its demands for conformity. He dreams of an antiestablishment utopia and commits petty crimes to realize it. This rebellious character strongly appealed to the participants in and sympathizers of antiestablishment movements in contemporary Japan. In March 1970, for example, a nine-member team of the radical Red Army faction hijacked a commercial jetliner and forced it to fly to North Korea. The group's leader, Tamiya Takamaro, famously concluded a manifesto with the enigmatic statement: "Finally, let us reconfirm. We are tomorrow's Jō."[41] While it is not clear exactly what he meant to communicate by these sentences, the popular cultural reference attested to the radical message that the Red Army faction members found in the first half of *Tomorrow's Jō*. At the most obvious level, Jō's affinity for the residents of his poor neighborhood and his hostility toward upper-class characters make him an iconoclastic figure in class society. It is not difficult to see why Jō's physical struggle against his archrival Riki'ishi to maintain his autonomous agency apart from materialist society appealed to the Red Army faction members, who also tried to reclaim the body as a site of political resistance[42] and, like the two fictional boxers, wagered their bodies in their battle against political power. (Chapter 8 offers a more detailed discussion of the United Red Army, which was created in 1971 through a merger between the Red Army faction and the Revolutionary Left.)

Once he settles into skid row, Jō shares with neighborhood children his grandiose vision of building them an amusement park, a general hospital, a nursing home, a nursery, a large-scale market, and a factory (*Tomorrow's Jō* [hereafter *TJ*] 1:119–20). He turns the children into accomplices in the crimes he commits to realize his socialist dream. To achieve his goal more expeditiously, he uses the children to commit fraud, feeding newspaper reporters a false story claiming that he has been taking care of the orphans on his own. Once the story appears in the newspaper, many readers send money, which he simply pockets. Pursued by the police, Jō and the children run into the abandoned building that Jō has been using as a base of operation and throw rocks at the police officers (*TJ* 1:140–41). This scene, which appeared in the February and March 1968 issues of *Magazine*, was soon replicated on streets and college campuses, where activists and sympathizers hurled rocks at the riot police (they also used staves and threw

Molotov cocktails).[43] There were reports that the story of Jō was read like "scripture" on the campuses closed down by student activists.[44]

Many of the students who barricaded themselves within administrative and academic buildings entertained ideals of social reform that were as lofty as Jō's, if not as concrete. Yet, just as in the radical youth movements, Jō's romantic visions are never realized and soon recede into the background. His utopian dreams illustrate his defiant attitude toward the period's social and political conventions. In the rest of the story, however, Jō turns his attention to himself and never talks about them again. His violent self is co-opted into the disciplinary "regime" of boxing, and his battle becomes more introspective.

## The Education of Jō

Jō's criminal offenses and defiant attitude land him in a reformatory—an embodiment of the state's disciplinary power. There he meets the two characters key to his awakening as a boxer: Shiraki Yōko and Riki'ishi Tōru. Yōko is a granddaughter of a powerful businessman and a benefactor of the institution. She convinces the guards of the educational benefits of boxing and thus lays the ground for the intramural match between Jō and Riki'ishi, a former professional boxer. Jō has rudimentary knowledge of boxing, but only inside the reformatory does he truly begin to be drawn to the sport. Being boxed into the state correctional institution was a prerequisite for his discovery of boxing.

While Jō is confined, Tange Danpei, a trainer who had discovered Jō's talent back on skid row, sends him postcards that prove instrumental in his boxing renaissance. The postcards are entitled "For tomorrow" and carry some basic technical instructions. When the first card reaches Jō in a solitary cell right after his arrest, he immediately tears it up. Yet later, out of boredom, he puts the torn pieces together, reads Danpei's instructions on jabbing, and begins to practice, unwittingly accepting the disciplinary regime of boxing (*TJ* 1:165–76). He begins metaphorically forming a new self by reassembling the torn pieces of the card. As the poet and playwright Terayama Shūji laments, "Jō loses his top-class wildness [*yasei*] in order to acquire second-class technique."[45] Once he embraces and subjects himself to the sport, he allows his "wildness"—the source of his free spirit—to be systematically domesticated.[46] Riki'ishi hand-delivers the second postcard to Jō in the reformatory, inadvertently serving as a messenger for the world of boxing (*TJ* 2:102).

The contrast between Jō and Riki'ishi highlights Jō's wildness. Jō has no intention of staying in the correction facility until he completes his term; Riki'ishi is a model inmate and does not tolerate Jō's rebellious behavior. With the prospect of returning to his boxing career with financial support from Shiraki Yōko's grandfather, Riki'ishi has little reason to challenge the authorities. He even forcibly stops Jō's escape attempt. It is nevertheless possible to detect complex feelings in Riki'ishi. Jō's defiance of authority sows seeds of doubt in Riki'ishi's conformist thinking and reawakens Riki'ishi's own wildness, which has been thoroughly domesticated. Riki'ishi is determined to fight Jō to prove that he has chosen the right path and to soothe the wildness that has begun to raise its head. Just as Riki'ishi takes a step toward Jō, Jō also steps toward Riki'ishi by embracing boxing. The first half of *Tomorrow's Jō* portrays an ardent dialogue between the two men, made possible through the physical language of boxing.[47] Their exchange of punches enacts bodily dialectics: their contest—Riki'ishi as thesis and Jō as antithesis—appears to find a synthesis in the boxing ring. This dialectical utopia, however, is only an impossible dream whose pursuit eventually costs Riki'ishi his life.

### Class Struggle

The conditions of economic class are intertwined with heterosexual love in *Tomorrow's Jō*. The relationship between the two men is mediated by Shiraki Yōko, a feminine incarnation of the capitalist system. Riki'ishi identifies with Yōko, less from cold calculation than from his desire for her and what she represents. By contrast, while Jō may be attracted to her, he instinctively senses the danger of getting too close to her and thus maintains a nonchalant attitude. Under her feminine appearance, Yōko is a strong-willed capitalist who tries to control Jō's boxing career. To maintain his freedom—his independence from all social forces—Jō must not fall for her. Yet his wildness, the essence of his free existence, is steadily channeled into pugilism through Yōko's careful planning.

The two characters' rivalry is cast in contrary images of modern versus retrograde. Riki'ishi trains at the Shiraki Boxing Gym, established by Yōko's grandfather. Housed in a modern building, the gym features a team of top coaches and medical staff. Among its talented trainees, Riki'ishi is treated as a star athlete (*TJ* 5:168–79). After a successful boxing career, it appears, he is promised a second career in the business world. By contrast, Jō upholds boxing as an extension of street fighting by choosing Danpei as his coach, despite the latter's expulsion from the boxing world for his alcoholism and bad temper (*TJ* 5:179–81). The owners of other major boxing gyms call him a throwback to the days when pugilism was associated with "scoundrels," and he is visually marked as such, carrying deep scars on his face and dressing like a day laborer (*TJ* 5:139). Danpei's anachronistic attitude is best illustrated by his use of the word *kentō* for the sport, a term from the pre–World War II era (*TJ* 1:50).[48] The "gym" that he prepares for Jō is initially an illegal structure under a bridge on the periphery of skid row.[49] By teaming with Danpei—a loser—Jō protects his marginal identity.

Riki'ishi must crush Jō and keep him from enjoying the freedom that Riki'ishi has sacrificed for his successful career. He must accept Jō's challenge in order to prove that he himself has made the right decision. When a match against Jō is finally arranged, Riki'ishi must clear a final obstacle: he needs to reduce his weight drastically in order to fight in Jō's bantamweight class, with its 118-pound limit. Although Riki'ishi normally fights in the featherweight class (limit 126 pounds), his weight can jump to the welterweight class (limit 147 pounds) if he is not careful (*TJ* 7:154). An irrational urge to compete drives Riki'ishi into a torturous weight reduction program. When Yōko's grandfather urges him to stay in the featherweight class and enjoy the meal, Riki'ishi answers: "I am going to fight a man who rejected an offer from the Shiraki Gym, which boasts the best, most modern facilities in the nation, a man who has risen from a crummy gym built underneath a bridge. If I mind this little hardship, I might as well already be defeated" (*TJ* 7:171–72). Jō's humble class identity is both a threat and an inspiration to his rival. To fight him, Riki'ishi decides to drop to Jō's class, in both weight and economic status, albeit temporarily. He attempts an excessive weight reduction and sacrifices material comfort, as if to symbolically shed his association with the upper class.

For Riki'ishi the fight starts with the battle against himself. To reduce his weight to the bantamweight limit, he imposes on himself an extraordinary regimen of practice and self-denial. By sheer willpower, he clears this obstacle. If he can prove that his free will is superior to Jō's free spirit, all the choices he has made will be justified. Jō awakens Riki'ishi's wildness, and Riki'ishi tries to control it by imposing extraordinary discipline on himself. In doing so, he finds genuine free will within an existence bound by the rules and conventions of the modern capitalist regime.

### Riki'ishi's Death and Shiraki Yōko's Gaze

Riki'ishi's heroic efforts end in tragedy, which radically alters the nature of Jō's quest. Although he knocks Jō out in the sixth round, the price for his victory is high. Riki'ishi dies shortly after the match (*TJ* 8:215–16): a punch in the head from Jō is the direct cause, but Riki'ishi's radical pre-bout weight reduction and striking the back of his head on a rope after Jō's punch are also contributing factors (*TJ* 8:175–77). His death forever suspends the tension between free will and free spirit. Defeat would have proven that his sacrifices were meaningless; victory should have proven his superior willpower. Yet according to Terayama Shūji, by eliminating the source of his inspiration, Jō, victory also deprives him of tomorrow. Riki'ishi's free will exists only as an antithesis to Jō's free spirit. Only in death can he escape the problematic ramifications of his victory. Riki'ishi may exist merely as a reaction to Jō's action; without a reaction, Terayama intimates, there will be no action by Jō either.[50]

Riki'ishi's death haunts Jō's subsequent boxing career, condemning him to an abject state of defeat. Jō will never have an opportunity to break free from what his archrival has defended with his life—the hegemony of free will. Riki'ishi's willingness to forgo his associations with the upper class and material comfort for the sake of fighting Jō had brought him closer to Jō's side. Jō's trauma derives from the fact that his violent quest has inadvertently killed the man who best understood the nature of that quest. For the two men, boxing is more than an exchange of violent blows; it is a physical art through which to communicate one's whole being with another. Their dialogue ends with Riki'ishi's demise, which also concluded the first half of *Tomorrow's Jō* in late January 1970. This fictional event affected Chiba Tetsuya as well. Shortly after this episode, he interrupted the serial for several weeks because of illness. He later acknowledged that the stress from drawing the dark scenes leading to and following Riki'ishi's death effectively led to his physical breakdown.[51] *Magazine* readers were saddened by Riki'ishi's departure: Terayama Shūji and two theater groups jointly staged his funeral at Kōdansha, *Magazine*'s publisher. As many as seven hundred fans attended.⁵²

The tone of the story changes completely in its second half. Without Riki'ishi's presence to triangulate the relationship, Jō is forced to form a dyad with Yōko, who translates pugilism into the language of capitalism. When the fighter contemplates giving up his career, she insists that he carries "sacred debts to the two boxers" (Riki'ishi and another rookie champion whose jaw he has crushed). The only way to repay these debts is to die in the ring, as Riki'ishi did. Identifying with Jō's rivals, Yōko admonishes him: "Right here, you should realize that you must die in the ring for the sake of Riki'ishi or Wolf [the rookie]. . . . Neither man would allow you to give up boxing. I would not allow that either" (*TJ* 9:125). Yōko turns herself into a debt collector on behalf of the two men destroyed by Jō's punches, demanding that he pay back in kind the moral debts he has accumulated while pursuing his project. He continues fighting despite the difficulties that he faces, attesting that he has accepted Yōko's logic. Jō easily pays back his debt to the rookie by taking revenge on the gangster who crushed Wolf in a street fight (*TJ* 9:162–63). However, it takes the rest of Jō's life to repay the debt to Riki'ishi. Until the moment he destroys himself, he must continue to make his payments.

Riki'ishi's death devastated Jō in another way, and Yōko is again instrumental in restoring Jō's boxing career. Suffering from serious psychological trauma, Jō is no longer able to deliver a decisive blow to his opponent's head. He suffers three consecutive losses as a result and is shunned in the boxing world. Yet he continues to fight Riki'ishi's ghost by joining a seedy local boxing league. Yoko eventually orchestrates a scheme to bring Jō back. Her grandfather lost interest in boxing after Riki'ishi's death. Assuming her new responsibilities as chairperson of the Shiraki Boxing Club, Yōko begins her career as a promoter with the goal of reigniting Jō's passion for boxing. Managing his career, she also hones her talent as a capitalist. Jō expends his energy in the space that she has carefully prepared for him. In a match arranged by Yōko, Jō regains his ardor and ability to land punches on his opponent's head.

Readers are constantly reminded of the presence of the shrewd capitalist Shiraki Yōko. Jō continues to climb into the boxing ring to repay his debt to Riki'ishi, while, by marketing his personal battles as spectacles, Yōko builds her prominent career as a successful promoter. As she discusses Jō's comeback fight, Yōko is reduced to a cool gaze—the right

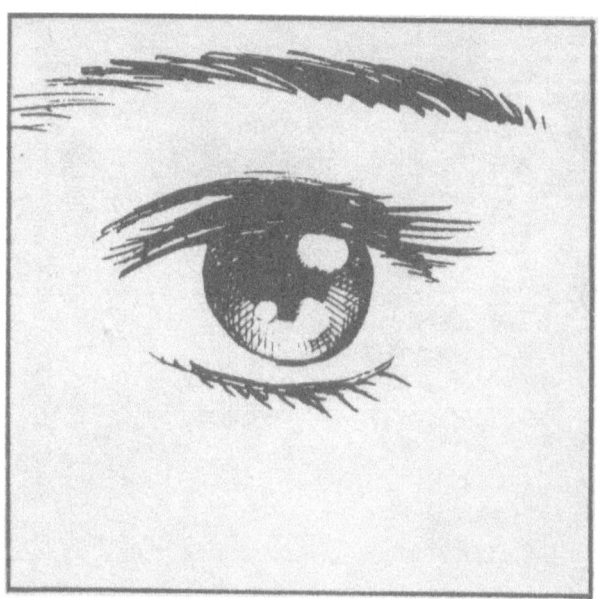

*Figure 7.2* Yōko's eye. *TJ* 12:148.

eye in an extreme close-up—which communicates her determination to see her plan through to the end (figure 7.2). Her eye dissociated from the body—an organ without the body[53]—represents capitalism as transparent power that stages but remains unaffected by the boxers' bodily performance. Yet Yōko turns her gaze away from the embattled bodies at two key moments. Right after Riki'ishi's death, his body rests on the bench inside the locker room (figure 7.3). Chiba drew the scene in such a way that Riki'ishi's body appears to be the sole source of light in the room. In the bottom of the frame, Yōko looks away, filled with regret for having failed to prevent his death. She also looks as if she cannot take the glow that his body emits. Yōko turns away for the second time when Jō violently vomits in a comeback match after hitting his opponent in the head (figure 7.4). On the ringside, momentarily shocked, she quickly turns and leaves the venue amid the flood of flashes (figure 7.5). While their bodies are subjugated to the capitalist machination (their bodily performances are consumed as spectacles), the two boxers still maintain independent stances through their self-destruction: the abject status of Riki'ishi's death and Jō's vomit may be dramatized, but they ultimately bear no value in the world of production and consumption. When Yōko

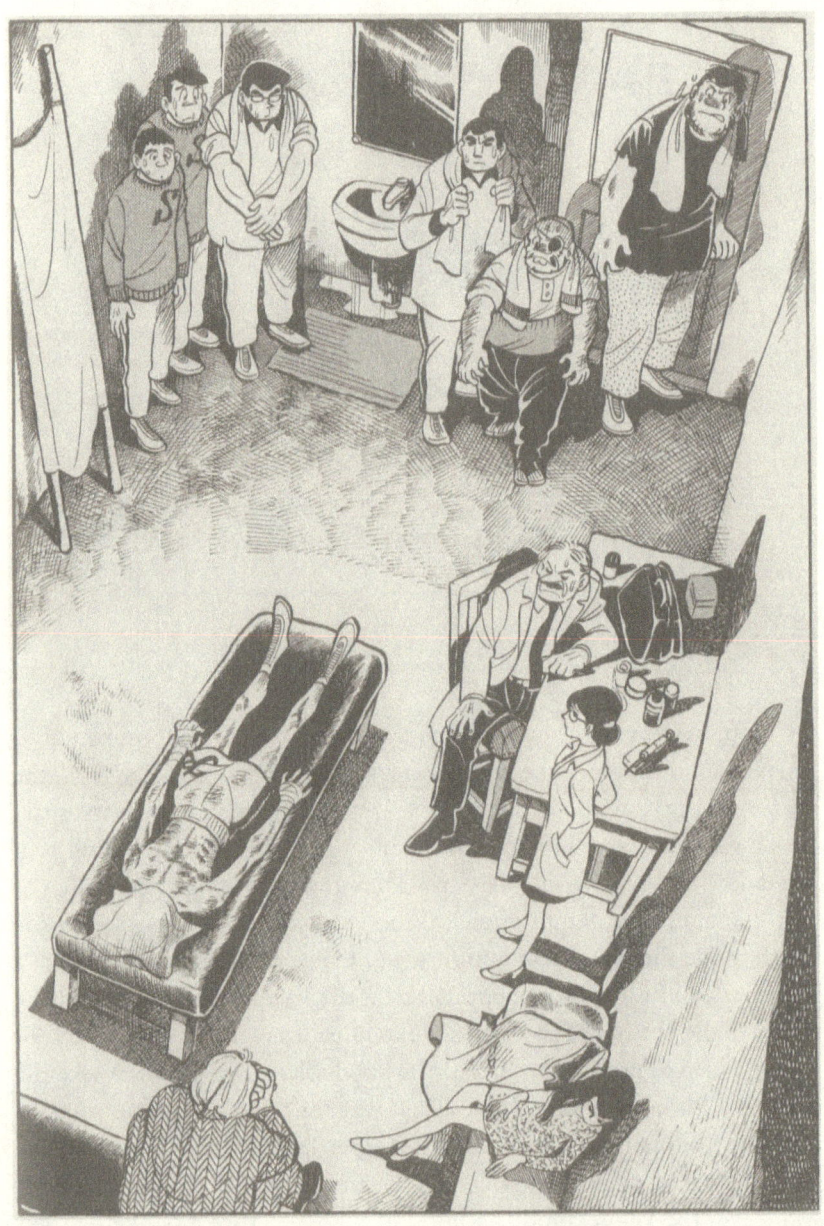

*Figure 7.3* Riki'ishi Tōru's glorious death. In the frame, his body appears to be the source of light. Yōko, sitting at the bottom of the frame, looks away. *TJ* 9:10.

*Figure 7.4* Jō falls into the depth of darkness. He throws up after hitting his opponent's head in a subsequent match. *TJ* 10:228–29.

*Figure 7.5* Yōko turns her back to the ring. "Let's head back, Robert. I am getting sick too." Robert is a manager for Venezuelan boxer Carlos Rivera. Yōko subsequently arranges a match between Jō and Rivera. *TJ* 10:234.

recognizes her inability to consume the masculine drama enacted through their bodies and the excess they "produce," she averts her eyes from the scene of violence.

Yōko's eye makes a stark contrast with Hoshi Hyūma's burning eyes that Kawasaki Noboru draws in *Star of the Giants* (figure 7.1). His burning—internally energized—gaze announces that Hyūma engages ultimately in a solipsist project to realize his potential: Hyūma's eyes are on the prize. Jō similarly flares with passion for boxing, but his flames are carefully stoked by Yōko's business acumen, embodied in her cool gaze. To counter the powerful gaze, he tries to take his burning to a logical end. Jō confides his friend Noriko of his desire: "I have had burning satisfaction many times in the ring . . . in the bloody ring. I am not like the ordinary guys, who are smoldering, barely keeping their fire alive. Even if just for a moment, I flare up bright red. Then there will be just white ashes left. There will be absolutely no cinders, just white ashes" (*TJ* 14:104).

Jō will soon have what he wishes for. Before that, however, he must first intensify the internal flame by internalizing Riki'ishi's death.

### Yabuki Jō's Philosophical Awakening

The writer Sano Mitsuo observes that "after Riki'ishi's death, *Tomorrow's Jō* story becomes metaphysical and less compelling."[54] Following Riki'ishi's final bout, the circulation of *Magazine* dropped precipitously, suggesting that for many readers the story culminated with Riki'ishi's demise.[55] Although the manga maintained its original intensity and subsequently recovered its popularity, the tenor of the story changed radically.[56] Building on Sano's cryptic observation, I argue that Jō's fight becomes metaphysical in the sense that he exchanges punches not to prove his ultimate outsider status—his wildness—but to gain philosophical insight into Riki'ishi's endeavor. By accepting his rival's fight as his own, Jō now struggles to demonstrate his free spirit within a regime where boxing and capitalism collude.

To exorcise Riki'ishi's ghost, Jō must overcome a Korean War survivor and formidable boxer, Kim Yong Bi. Jō's victory, however, is not precisely a "liberation." He escapes from Riki'ishi's spell only by completely identifying with him, and this identification finalizes Riki'ishi's triumph. Kim is a thinly disguised substitute figure for Japan's war generation, who experienced extreme deprivation during the Asia Pacific War. Jō's philosophical awakening in the match repudiates the guilt that the postwar generation is supposed to feel toward the elders who experienced wartime hardships. By positing their own bodies and everyday lives as sites of political contest and struggle, student activists sought to wage a war of their own while questioning the moral authority with which the war generations spoke of their war experiences. Their claim was that the elders were a mere product of, and therefore enslaved by, historical conditions. By denying the war generations their moral ground, the postwar youths tried to prove their own independent agency. This intergenerational conflict over war experiences was an undertone of youth protest movements in the late 1960s and early 1970s and the match between Jō and Kim.[57]

To stand in the same ring as Kim, Jō first denies the material comfort of postwar Japan and his own body that benefited from it. As he prepares for the match against Kim, bantam-class Asia champion, Jō reenacts the agony of the weight reduction that Riki'ishi experienced. Although he has grown 6 centimeters (2.36 inches) over the past year and his weight has increased to the featherweight range—the class in which Riki'ishi used to fight—Jō declares that he will continue to fight as a bantamweight.[58] When Danpei insists that Jō fight in the featherweight category, the boxer retorts: "Just because it is a little bit tough, there is no way I can leave the historic battlefield I shared with this lifelong enemy and lifelong friend" (*TJ* 15:82). Jō becomes Riki'ishi, in a sense, in his pursuit of the world bantamweight title. He fails to pass the first weigh-in, misled by Danpei, who does not wish to see Jō die like his rival. Later reduced to an emaciated state by taking laxatives and shutting himself in a steam bath, he barely passes the second weigh-in (*TJ* 15:183).

Witnessing Jō's struggle, Kim Yong Bi feels only contempt. His ghastly childhood experiences during the Korean War forever changed his relationship with food. Desperate and starving, he once killed a man for food. Later, learning that the man was actually his father, who had deserted the army to deliver rations to his family, he vomited up everything he had eaten.[59] Kim explains that he has never eaten his fill since the incident—he cannot. To a man who has committed patricide for a bit of sustenance, weight reduction is a luxury (*TJ* 15:198–212). Hearing this story from Kim, Jō loses his motivation to fight and, physically and psychologically exhausted, becomes vulnerable to his opponent's punches. Yet each time he is knocked down to the mat, he stands up, wondering to himself why he even keeps fighting. Kim's coach, Captain Hyun, uses an appropriate metaphor to describe Jō's condition: "Yabuki should be done for already. But he [comes right back up] like a puppet suspended by strings. . . . Almost all the strings are cut off. What's left, at best, is one last, almost severed string" (*TJ* 16:98). Jō is a puppet hanging on to that last string—his allegiance to his late rival, Riki'ishi.

Upon hearing Riki'ishi's name from Shiraki Yōko, who has shown up at ringside, Jō gains a philosophical insight (*TJ* 16:98–99).[60] Against Kim's historical trauma, Jō recalls the suffering that Riki'ishi chose to endure: "Kim 'was not able to eat.' But Riki'ishi 'did not drink' or 'eat' of his own volition! . . . Life-threatening hunger is not absolute. There was a man who willingly jumped into and overcame the hell!" (*TJ* 16:106–8). With this realization, Jō begins to hit back. Unlike Riki'ishi, Kim Yong Bi is merely a product of historical conditions, devoid of his own will. Even his calculated fighting style, which is compared to the precision of a computer, attests to his machinelike existence.

Kim's signature move is keeping an opponent on his feet while connecting punches—he wins by knockout. No boxer has ever staved it off until Jō, who continues to fight as if he is possessed. Witnessing Jō's ghastly state, Kim, visibly shaken, whispers, "[He is] a monster" (*TJ* 16:96–97). (In a later match, the fighter Jose Mendoza is similarly frightened to see Jō, who "should be long dead," standing up. Mendoza loses his composure and starts showering him with illegal punches. When the match is over, Mendoza's hair has turned white out of fear [*TJ* 20:259].) It is impossible to knock Jō out. Riki'ishi's spirit has taken over Jō's body and continues to fight, regardless of the damage that the body sustains. Jō the puppet goes on fighting toward the destruction of his body. In other words, only by destroying his own body can he stop fighting.

In the fierce fight against Kim, the philosophical contest between free will and free spirit seems to be resolved. Genuine free spirit emerges when free will prevails. The corollary is that Riki'ishi, who embodied both free will and free spirit, stands as the final victor. Jō must humbly accept his rival's success. That is, in order to achieve perfect freedom, Jō must fight like Riki'ishi and die in the ring. Jō embraces this moral and philosophical imperative, which Yōko, using the language of capitalism, once called a "sacred debt." By completely identifying with his dead rival, Jō severs the last string that externally controlled him. Although it appears that Jō has gained genuine agency, it is a far cry from the "wildness" that he had originally treasured. Jō, who rejected all social conventions, including boxing, now locates freedom within those conventions and the regime of boxing. Inside the boxing ring, the meaning of freedom has turned upside down.

Thereafter Jō has morphed into one of the living dead—a zombie—who continues to fight until his body crumbles. Using the term "zombie" here invokes the literary critic Suga Hidemi's discussion of the ideological struggles of the United Red Army, whose members privileged the revolutionary will to overcome the material conditions of consumer culture in contemporary Japan (see chapter 8). Through their desperate training at their "mountain bases," they began to valorize death as a litmus test for unconditional commitment: only in death could members claim the genuine revolutionary subjectivity that transcends the material conditions of contemporary society. Even as they stoically tried to deny themselves material comforts, the fact that they were alive showed that they lacked the agency to act—they were living dead in the materialist world.[61] In the end, both the URA members and Jō sacrificed their tomorrows in order to pay back what they believed they owed to the regime that they defied. It is noteworthy that the publication in February and March 1972 of the issues featuring Jō's fight with Kim Yong Bi coincided with the media spectacle of the URA's clash with the police and the subsequent revelation of the group's bloody internal purges.

After the match with Kim Yong Bi, Jō begins to show symptoms associated with chronic traumatic encephalopathy (CTE).[62] For example, he blacks out at his gym just as he hangs his hat and coat on a wall peg (*TJ* 16:144–48). The fighting style that he has practiced since his reformatory days deemphasizes defense and thus exposes him to the opponents' punches. He is perfectly aware of what has been happening to his body, and he also seems to know that only when his body is destroyed will he be able to repay all his moral debts and be freed from everything. One might call such a condition perfect "freedom." Ironically, however, Jō does not have the freedom to reject this particular form of "freedom." He has come a long way from the state of wildness that he was in when he first showed up on skid row.

### *Does Jō Die?*

The challenging task of devising a satisfactory ending for *Tomorrow's Jō* became the sole responsibility of Chiba Tetsuya and his assistants.[63] Although Kajiwara provided a narrative, Chiba was dissatisfied and told Kajiwara that he was going to change it.[64] Well past the deadline, Chiba completed the last installment, in which Jō, having fought a punishing match with the world champion Jose Mendoza, sits in his corner, motionless, looking down with a hint of a smile.

The story's ending is visually ambiguous, and readers fiercely debated whether Jō dies after losing to Mendoza. The writer Asaine Hideo (b. 1945) portrays in his fictional work the ways in which young male *Magazine* readers convinced themselves of Jō's death, unable to bear the idea that he would continue to live as an "invalid."[65] The manga critic Murakami Tomohiko (b. 1951), writing seven years after the final installment of *Tomorrow's Jō*, assigns the readers a more active role in Jō's demise: "These seven years were more like a process through which the "tomorrow" in *Tomorrow's Jō* gradually faded. If Jō had survived, he would have had to marry Shiraki Yōko and build a happy, middle-class family in those seven years. That is why, with our own hands, we killed the Jō who was burnt out and could be dead or alive. We tried to spare him from such an ugly fate."[66] These contemporary readers correctly saw no tomorrow for Jō once he was no longer able to fight for himself. Jō meets his end when he finally repays all his sacred debts, at the end of the championship match with Jose Mendoza. Only through his death can he free himself from moral duties and gain perfect freedom.

Right before the championship match begins, Yōko, wanting to preserve what she and Jō have accomplished together, tries to talk him out of fighting. She even promises to absorb the penalty payment that cancellation would incur. Seeing that her words have no effect, Yōko offers her love as compensation: "I love you, Jō. I have always loved you! I was not aware [of my own feelings] until recently. Please . . . for my sake. For my sake, do not climb into that ring!"[67] (*TJ* 19:213–14). Her feelings may be genuine, but she seems oblivious to the fact that she has always expressed them through boxing. Her relationship with Jō has been nothing more than a business arrangement between a capitalist and a boxer. She has expressed her love in the language of capitalism, while Jō has understood it in the language of boxing. But as she senses that his boxing career is nearing an end and thus their relationship is ending as well, Yōko tries to invite Jō into the new realm of heterosexual love. If he gives up the championship match, he loses the opportunity to repay his sacred debts, and his relationship with the debt collector, Yōko, will forever remain fixed.

Her physical performance—she blocks the locker room door as she confesses her love—is summarily rejected by Jō, who is thinking only about expending his last remaining energies in the men's world of the ring and paying his debts. Yōko's heterosexual love is incompatible with his homosocial bonds with other fighters: accepting would betray the men he has fought and Jose Mendoza, who awaits him. Unable to change his mind, Yōko leaves the arena but soon returns to complete her part in the drama. She is the "instigator," after all, who has the responsibility of collecting the debt that Jō has accrued.[68] She returns to ringside at the end of the twelfth round, this time urging Jō to fight to the end. When the final round is over, Jō seeks her with his unfocused eyes and asks her to keep his sweat-soaked boxing gloves (*TJ* 20:257). With this symbolic transaction (figure 7.6), he completes the payment of his moral debts and quietly and

*Figure 7.6* Jō's final payment: "I want you to keep these." *TJ* 20:257. Clad in a high-collared black tunic, Yōko stands at the ringside as the high priestess of capitalism, receiving Jō's final payment.

peacefully expires in his corner.[69] By destroying his body, Jō gains ultimate freedom and is finally liberated from the historical conditions of postwar society. Only in death can such a goal be achieved: there is no tomorrow for Yabuki Jō. He has refused to live a snug, comfortable life in postwar Japan. His struggle is a process of shaving off the time that belongs to the future and using it to erase the traces of the life that he has lived. By literally crushing with his body the myth of a better future that postwar Japan has embraced, Jō finally, irrevocably, becomes unfettered by historical forces.

## Hoshi Hyūma, Yabuki Jō, and Postwar Japanese Society

In the immediate postwar years the unprecedented catastrophe of the Asia Pacific War prompted Japanese intellectuals to search for political agency untethered to their particular historical conditions. Some envisioned revolutionary subjectivity, while others sought a universal philosophical basis for freedom of action.[70] As Japan regained independence and began to recover economically, however, philosophical questions about political subjectivity seem to have been displaced gradually by the more practical concern of how best to act in given political contexts. Subjectivity nevertheless remained a key concept in Japan's leftist discourse and was widely recognized as a sine qua non for revolutionary change in the 1960s political movements.[71]

*Star of the Giants* and *Tomorrow's Jō*, with their singular focus on genuine agency of action, powerfully engaged with the contemporary political concerns of Japanese youth. Hyūma and Jō find themselves in the socioeconomic conditions of contemporary Japan—conditions that the intellectuals of an earlier era could never have imagined. Mass consumer society, in the midst of an era of high economic growth, made the project of producing autonomous subjectivity far more complex and challenging. The contrasting conclusions of *Star of the Giants* and *Tomorrow's Jō* reflect the drastic transformation of postwar Japan: while Hyūma's triumphant spirit represents the country's powerful postwar optimism,[72] *Tomorrow's Jō* drastically shifts its tone after Riki'ishi's death, turning from a relatively buoyant *Bildungsroman* to an introspective philosophical exploration. Jō's inability to break free from socioeconomic constraints (except through death) attests to a more somber reality of the early 1970s.

The genius of the two stories is that they literally flesh out the concept of subjectivity against the conditions of contemporary Japan. The heroes' bodies become sites of contest between individual will and socioeconomic forces. Through their bodily performance, the two heroes express their individuality and agency, but their bodies are always and already caught in the nexus of socioeconomic forces. Only the destruction of bodily functions assures the ultimate triumph of their spirits over external conditions. As we will see in chapter 8, the members of the United Red Army acted out the same dead-end scenario in their remote mountain bases in 1971 and 1972. *Star of the Giants* and *Tomorrow's Jō* are essential texts through which to better understand the logic that drove the URA's deadly internal struggles.

## CHAPTER VIII

## Dead Bodies and Living Guns

*The United Red Army and Its Deadly Pursuit of Revolution*

In order to strengthen our unity and to gain genuine communist subjectivity, you must begin the battle of annihilation. Only then will you transform yourself into a revolutionary soldier who fights the battle of annihilation. The gun does not change you; you change the gun. For that, you need to transform yourself into a revolutionary soldier who can engage in the battle of annihilation.

—MORI TSUNEO, 1971

I am compelled to think about the bizarreness of televising such a bizarre situation as this to your living room.

—NHK REPORTER HIRATA ETSURŌ, 1972

On the evening of February 28, 1972, 89.2 percent of Japanese television sets (roughly 60 million viewers) were tuned in to coverage of the end of a hostage situation in Karuizawa carried out by five members of a militant leftist organization, the United Red Army (map 2.1).[1] After a nine-day stand-off, riot police units raided Asama-sansō, a mountain lodge where armed URA members had taken a caretaker hostage. To neutralize the hostage-takers' rifles and shotguns, the police used a wrecking ball to make an opening in a wall and then sprayed water and shot tear-gas shells through it. The URA members resisted by shooting guns and throwing explosive devices. Although what went on inside the lodge was not clear from the outside, the police operation provided exciting images for the television screen. Indeed, the Japanese media had a field day at the site. The hundreds of media crews who had been covering the event in freezing temperatures were rewarded with a newsworthy situation.[2] After eight hours of battle, the police brought the hostage to safety and arrested all the hostage-takers. Two of their own officers were killed and scores more injured in the rescue operation.

At the closing of this media event, a wide array of viewers harbored sympathy for the hostage-takers, who appeared to have engaged in a courageous battle against state authority. For example, a male college student quoted in a weekly magazine said: "Although I am, if anything, right wing, I understand the United Red Army members' feelings. . . . Whichever way you look at it, Japan resembles a police state. In challenging the system, their battles have to take such [combative] forms."[3] This student depicted the URA members' conflict with the police as a genuine act of resistance. From the opposite end of the political spectrum, the film director Wakamatsu Kōji expressed his total support, similarly claiming that violence was the only way to fight state authority.[4]

But the URA activists' image as heroic resisters did not hold up long after their arrests. Through interrogations, the police soon learned the gruesome details of the URA's purges conducted in the mountain hideouts. Between December 1971 and February 1972, ten of the original twenty-nine participants in the group's military training camp were killed in the name of *sōkatsu* (self-criticism), while two were executed for their alleged antirevolutionary behavior. Two more activists had been killed for their desertion from a mountain base in August 1971 by the Revolutionary Left, the militant group that later merged with the Red Army faction to form the United Red Army. Once the media reported these acts, whatever sympathy the public had afforded the group immediately dried up. Even those who had defended—or perhaps celebrated—the armed confrontation with the police could not support those bloody purges.

The so-called Asama-sansō incident gained iconic status as the event that announced the end of Japan's postwar new left movements. The dramatic contrast between the spectacular conflict with the police and the dark secrets exposed afterward symbolized the culmination and subsequent collapse of political activism in the late 1960s and early 1970s. In the minds of many who had participated in or sympathized with new left activism, the shock of learning about the URA's crimes was inseparably linked with their own decisions to distance themselves from their prior political commitments. The gruesomeness of the crimes appeared to accentuate the depth of loss felt at the time—the loss of revolutionary hopes throughout Japanese society.

This media event also exposed the chilling reality that the drastic transformation of Japanese society had outpaced the radicals' revolutionary visions. The establishment of mass consumer society, a direct outcome of the high-growth economy, transformed political dynamics in the 1960s and early 1970s. Japan's economic success afforded greater access to information and consumer goods. The all-consuming economy and its leveling effects posed a challenge to those on the left who attempted to criticize the existing political system from an external position in order to envision an alternative system that would replace it. By the late 1960s, when consumerism permeated postwar Japan, the social critic Yoshimoto Taka'aki and others had already identified the conceptual challenge that the new consumer society posed to the left: there was no longer any safe, external position from which to critique postwar society.[5] Everyone was complicit with the political and economic mechanisms that produced social injustice, insofar as individuals took advantage of them. It was impossible to make a stand outside the "system."

Political activists may not have been fully cognizant of the nature of the newly emerging society; nevertheless, they felt a deep anxiety about drastic social change and tried in various ways to formulate a way out of mass consumer society and its symptoms. Some of these attempts took extreme forms, as in the case of the radical student movements. The extremity of these responses mirrored the degree of social transformation that Japan experienced during this period. Violence was the mark of a society desperately trying to make sense of the drastic changes that roiled it during the late 1960s and early 1970s.

The paradigmatic shift caused by Japan's high-growth economy demanded a new theory and practice of political engagement. The URA, however, merely wished to evade the effects of economic development, literally seeking to establish a critical foothold outside the existing system. They physically distanced themselves in mountain bases, while valorizing violence as a means to achieve alternative political conditions. This antiquated vanguardism proved completely inadequate in fighting the revolutionary battles of early 1970s Japan.

Insisting on a clean break, the URA possessed no effective means to analyze or fight consumer society, which they claimed perpetually privileged the class interests of the bourgeoisie. Their fight against consumerism was eventually displaced by their desperate efforts to transcend their own "bourgeois propensities" through self-discipline. When they found the "enemy" within—in the form of members who needed assistance in overcoming their bourgeois propensities—the result was deadly. Their final battle at Asama-sansō was less a radical act than entertainment eagerly consumed by the media. In the face of intense and merciless media coverage, URA members were not radical activists but instead silent and powerless pawns.

With their fall, the prospect of mounting a heroic battle in which revolutionary agents could transcend contemporary society was lost. On the crudest level of observation, a revolution was a hard sell in a nation where the majority of people eagerly consumed the fruits of the leading party's economic policy. More fundamentally, the radical change that society was experiencing under the regime of a high-growth economy rendered many of the new left's visions infeasible. The rise and fall of the URA, eagerly disseminated by the media, confirmed rather than challenged the effects of consumerism on Japanese society.

## The Birth of the United Red Army

The United Red Army was the product of a rare merger between two radical organizations—the Red Army faction of the Second Communist League (Kyosanshugisha dōmei) and the Revolutionary Left (Kakumei saha)—that shared the desire to create revolutionary conditions in Japan through militant confrontations with the state.[6] To be precise, the merger involved the two organizations' "military" units; their fundraising and propaganda units remained independent. The organizations were strange bedfellows in many ways. Under the ideological leadership of Shiomi Takaya (b. 1941), the Red Army faction called for militant proletarian uprisings as the sine qua non for a simultaneous global revolution. They saw national struggles as a transitional step toward the envisioned global transformation. On the other hand, the Revolutionary Left embraced nationalistic anti-U.S.-patriotism, aspiring to revolution on the national level under a Maoist ideology. The groups' different organizational characteristics reflected their ideological disagreements. The Red Army faction maintained a vertical command structure, headed by a central committee. The Revolutionary Left was more horizontally organized and continually recruited workers as activists. Whereas the Red Army faction was dominated by male members, the Revolutionary Left boasted a number of female activists. Despite this ideological and organizational incongruence, the leaders of the two groups agreed to merge in order to carry out their revolutionary plans. As many pundits and former members have suggested, the rivalry between the groups subtly affected the ways in which the members interacted with each other in their "military" bases, exacerbating the need for ideological policing.[7]

In 1969 the Red Army faction formally split off from the Second Communist League ("the Bund") after two years of interfactional struggle. During the ongoing debate within the Bund about the proper revolutionary path, Shiomi Takaya's essay, "Katoki sekai ron" (A thesis on the transitional phase of the world, 1967), had introduced a stage theory that envisioned a global revolution as the end goal of all revolutionary movements, transcending local differences. By combining the geographic exterior (the world) and the teleology of revolutionary time, Shiomi envisioned a millenarian resolution to the local economic and political conditions that activists faced in Japan.[8] With his increasing promotion of militancy, Shiomi's ideas appealed to those within the Bund who were seeking a major breakthrough for Japan's radical movements. The question of whether to call for militant action provoked fierce debate within the factions. The Kansai faction, under the leadership of Shiomi Takaya and Tamiya Takamaro (1943–1995), formed a military committee within the Bund and, in July 1969, took a decisive step toward breaking away from the majority by beating and forcing a self-criticism on the Bund chairman, Saragi Tokuji (1929–2003).[9]

The majority group outnumbered and outmaneuvered the Kansai faction, taking key Kansai leaders hostage and using them to pressure the faction to abandon its militant policy. The captured members eventually got away (one accidentally died from a fall during the escape) and rejoined the Kansai faction to rebuild the organization. In August 1968 the Kansai faction sent Yamada Takashi (who would later be killed in a URA mountain camp) to the Bund's fourth central committee meeting to declare the faction's independence. Formally adopting the name Kyōsandō Sekigunha (Communist League, Red Army faction), the leaders scrambled to recruit "soldiers." Thanks to their forceful recruitment tactics, membership grew from about fifty to three hundred by the time the group held its inaugural meeting on September 4, 1969.[10]

Immediately following its formation, the Red Army faction began to implement its plans for insurgency. Members would raid police boxes in Osaka in order to obtain handguns for use in the next set of assaults, planned for Tokyo in October. The leaders' final goal was to arouse the general public by attacking government offices and police stations and killing the bureaucrats and police officers who worked there. They called the first stage the Osaka War and the second the Tokyo War. The plans were ill-conceived and hazardously executed. Participants managed to torch a few police boxes with the help of non–Red Army activists on September 22 but failed to acquire any handguns.[11] Eight days later the Tokyo War was carried out in a drastically scaled-down form as activists threw Molotov cocktails at a police station. Both attacks not only fell far short of their professed goal of creating mass unrest but also undermined the incipient organization by leading to the arrest of thirty-six members.[12]

Undaunted, the Red Army faction continued its disastrous "military" operations. With each failure—and even with its one success—it lost members. Perhaps the most damaging failure of all was the arrest of fifty-three members on November 5, 1969. In preparation for a planned attack on the prime minister's residence two days later, members had gathered at a mountain cottage in Yamanashi Prefecture. The security police had learned of the plot in advance and raided the site.[13] After this bungle, the Red Army leaders desperately embraced the idea of establishing international bases outside Japan, where faction members could safely prepare for revolutionary struggles at home in the near future. Facing the encroaching circle of state surveillance, the Red Army faction's desire to produce a vanguard position—an ideological outside position—metamorphosed into seeking a temporary refuge in the geographic exterior. They would make up for the mistakes of 1969 by using international bases to strike back in the fall of 1970.[14] The leaders initially wished to send their members to Cuba, but, mindful of the distance to cover and the frequent refueling stops they would have to make, they changed their destination to North Korea. In March 1970 a nine-member team led by Tamiya Takamaro hijacked a Japan Airlines plane to defect to North Korea. While the hijacking itself was a spectacular success, the members were never able to fulfill their revolutionary dreams in Japan.[15]

The leadership of the Red Army faction continued to shrink. The highest commander, Shiomi Takaya, was arrested by the police two weeks before the hijacking. Of the original seven members of the central committee, only one was still active in April 1970. To fill the void, six other members were promoted to the central committee. Among these six was Mori Tsuneo (1944–1973), who later led the Red Army faction to a disastrous end in the mountain bases. Attrition among the leadership as well as the membership never abated. The constant arrests devastated the organization, while a number of members became disillusioned with its revolutionary visions and dropped out. In this period of confusion, Mori emerged as a new leader determined to further militarize the Red Army faction.[16] His pursuit of armed action eventually devolved into a series of robberies, further alienating other leaders and members. The merger in 1971 with the Revolutionary Left, which possessed much coveted firearms, was part of Mori's efforts to realize a revolutionary army.

The Revolutionary Left took a different path to arrive at the point of merging. In April 1969 some twenty members of the Japanese Communist Party Left (established in 1966 by China sympathizers who had been expelled from the Japan Communist Party) formed a splinter organization, the Japanese Communist Party Revolutionary Left Kanagawa Committee.[17] Under the banner of anti-American patriotism, the Revolutionary Left members chose U.S. bases in the Tokyo metropolitan area as the targets for their militant actions. As Kawashima Tsuyoshi (1941–1990) emerged as the organization's sole leader, his strong advocacy of guerrilla-style attacks defined the Revolutionary Left's maneuvers over the next two years. In September 1969 a five-member team led by Sakaguchi Hiroshi (b. 1946) reached Haneda Airport despite heavy police protection. (Sakaguchi later became a member of the URA and was arrested in the Asama-sansō incident.) Before their arrest, they threw Molotov cocktails and sang "The Internationale" on a runway in an effort to prevent the foreign minister's departure for the Soviet Union and the United States.[18] Three other members were arrested after failed attempts to hurl Molotov cocktails into the Soviet and U.S. embassies on the same day.[19]

The group soon began to use dynamite stolen from quarries to build timer-triggered explosive devices and plant them at U.S. bases. All the explosives placed in 1969 were discovered before they were detonated. Information given to the police by the lone member apprehended for the dynamite attacks led to Kawashima Tsuyoshi's arrest in December 1969. Yet even from his prison cell, Kawashima sent directives to members of the Revolutionary Left. Inspired by the Red Army faction's success in hijacking a commercial jet to North Korea, Kawashima began to promote guerrilla-style militant actions, not merely as political demonstrations but as a way to incite widespread uprisings. (His directives also included a command to rescue him from incarceration.)[20] In his absence, Nagata Hiroko (1945–2011) assumed the role of leader in September 1970. She would work dutifully to implement his instructions.

In the second half of 1970 the Revolutionary Left drew up various plans for Kawashima's release. They abandoned the idea of kidnapping foreign diplomats in favor of a scheme to rescue him on his way to court, using firearms. To obtain the needed guns, three members attacked a police box in Tokyo on December 18, 1970. Armed only with homemade weapons—lead sticks encased in garden hoses—they were easily gunned down by one of the policemen stationed in the box. Shibano Haruhiko died from the wounds he received. Seeing Shibano's death as evidence of police brutality, the Revolutionary Left grew more determined than ever to fight state authority through violent means.[21] On February 17, 1971, three members robbed a gun shop in Tochigi Prefecture, obtaining ten shotguns, an air rifle, and 2,380 rounds of ammunition. Although two members were arrested afterward, the remaining six action group members managed to get away with the weapons.[22]

Their sudden success put the police on such high alert that the group was forced to stay in a hideout in Sapporo for a month and a half, with their guns buried in the nearby mountains.[23] Unable to take meaningful action, and with monetary support waning, Nagata and the other members toyed with the idea of defecting to China to establish an overseas base for revolutionary struggle. Much like the Red Army faction, members of the Revolutionary Left yearned for a space, a safe distance away, from which to strike back. On April 20 Nagata and Sakaguchi Hiroshi left Sapporo for Tokyo in order to establish hideouts in the capital and explore possible means to defect.[24] There they contacted the Red Army faction leader, Mori Tuneo, to discuss each organization's future course of action and perhaps forge a relationship of mutual support. Although Mori shot down Nagata and Sakaguchi's proposal for bases in China, the Red Army faction provided them with money and shelter.

The two organizations found themselves in need of each other. The Revolutionary Left had weapons but hardly any cash, while the Red Army faction had raised funds by robbing financial institutions during the months when the remaining six members of the Revolutionary Left were hibernating in Sapporo. The Red Army faction had learned how to produce homemade explosive devices, yet despite repeated attempts had never succeeded in obtaining firearms by force. The guns that the Revolutionary Left owned but could not use would complete the Red Army faction's preparation for armed uprisings. In late April or early May 1971, money and guns changed hands between the two groups. In return for ¥300,000 ($833), the Revolutionary Left provided the Red Army faction with two shotguns (these guns would later be confiscated by the police when one of the faction's armed robbery units was arrested).[25] From this exchange, it was only a short distance to discussions of a merger.

Around the time this exchange took place, Sakaguchi Hiroshi suggested that the Revolutionary Left establish a mountain base to evade police scrutiny. Acting immediately on Sakaguchi's idea, Nagata and other members relocated in late May to an abandoned hut in the Yamanashi mountains. They discarded that base in a matter of days, fearing that the police would learn about it through a defector. Another member deserted a new base in July, forcing the group to keep moving, constantly seeking a more secure location. While in the mountains, the members of the Revolutionary Left were shocked to learn that President Richard Nixon had scheduled a visit to China the following year. Chairman Mao Zedong, who only a year before had urged the world to stand up against the United States, would accept the U.S. president's visit. Though they tried to analyze the political context for Mao's move, the situation was beyond their comprehension.[26]

Meanwhile the Revolutionary Left dealt with a more immediate issue. Believing that the two defectors would endanger their group, the leaders decided to execute them. The first was killed on August 3, the second on August 10. According to Nagata's recollections, she announced a plan to kill the defectors, to which Mori acquiesced.[27] Sakaguchi, however, insists in his memoirs that he decided to carry out the executions because of Mori's strong urging.[28] Nagata's version appears closer to reality, given Mori's visceral disgust at the news of the executions: Red Army faction member Bandō Kunio recalls that upon hearing of the second execution, Mori blurted: "What, they did it again? They are not revolutionaries any longer! Have they gone mad?"[29]

Yet Nagata's version does not completely contradict Sakaguchi's. Mori had actually ordered some members to murder a Red Army faction defector in August 1971, but they decided to let her go.[30] It is possible that Mori urged the Revolutionary Left members to kill the defectors, as he had ordered his own men, without expecting his advice to be carried out. His incendiary rhetoric may have been meant to dramatize his dedication to the cause, until the Revolutionary Left carried out his command literally. When the deed caught up to his rhetoric, he was confronted with the effects of his words.

The violent means used to discipline members of the Revolutionary Left would come to haunt the future of the URA. The Revolutionary Left's determination to act, even against its own members, forced Mori to internalize violence as the foundation of revolutionary organizations. Days after learning of the second execution, Mori lectured the four Red Army faction members who had failed to kill their defector, saying that they should be as resolute as the Revolutionary Left in conducting their revolutionary battles.[31]

As the leader of an organization that advocated the use of violence, Mori Tsuneo had no choice but to accept the Revolutionary Left's merciless application of it. The way in which he had reached his leadership position further encouraged him to accept the sudden growth of internal violence. Fearful of being hurt in the 1969 infighting within the Bund, Mori defected from the group right before the Kansai faction abducted and beat up its chairman.[32] Although the Red Army faction took him back because of severe attrition in the ranks, he had to prove his loyalty. The guilt he felt about his defection made him strongly embrace the faction's advocacy of violent acts: backing down from violence was no longer an option.[33]

A few weeks before the executions of the Revolutionary Left defectors, the two organizations began serious talks about a merger. Despite multiple points of contention, the leaders of the Revolutionary Left and the Red Army faction agreed on July 13 to integrate their military units into the Unified Red Army (Tōitsusekigun).[34] A month later the name was changed to the United Red Army (Rengōsekigun).[35] Yet the two organizations operated independently until they began joint military training in December 1971—except for Red Army faction member Uegaki Yasuhiro, who visited the Revolutionary Left's mountain camp for bomb-building instruction in October.[36] In November the Red Army faction relocated to a mountain base in Yamanashi Prefecture in preparation for the coming joint training. After completing the training session in December, the Red Army faction members moved to the Revolutionary Left's Mt. Haruna base in Gunma Prefecture to finalize the merger.

## A Death Camp for the Dedicated

The new organization was born in December 1971 at a mountain base in Gunma Prefecture, where members stayed until they moved to another location in the same prefecture in late January 1972. The URA added the element of violence to the Japanese new left's commitment to self-reform and self-denial. Willingness to resort to violence—to kill the enemy—became the litmus test for members' unconditional commitment to the revolutionary cause. Only by facing the extreme condition of "kill or be killed," the argument went, could one gain proper revolutionary subjectivity.[37]

During his police interrogation on April 21, 1972, for example, Uegaki recalls his feelings as he watched other members bury the body of Kojima Kazuko, who had died in the mountains:[38]

> At that time the death did not exist as somebody else's business in another world. Death and life were two sides of a coin in the process of carrying out a revolutionary war. It was not simply an idea like the "battle of kill or be killed" that Shiomi [Takaya] advocated, but it was ingrained into my experience. Having faced imminent death, [I realized that] revolution and death always coexisted. Judging from my own experience, I never felt particularly strange and accepted without the slightest compunction that some comrades failed in the self-transformation needed for the communist revolution and died. Actually I felt that was a natural outcome. I thought they deserved to be despised because they failed to contribute to our revolution.[39]

In the "battle of kill or be killed," members would be ordered either to go kill a policeman or die trying. By putting their own lives on the line, URA members struggled to transform themselves into killing machines devoid of human concerns and fears. They managed to dehumanize not only their target—a policeman—but also themselves, denying all emotional and physical needs. Uegaki's recollection attests to the degree to which their deadly ideology had taken hold.

Within their revolutionary struggle, there was no longer any room for living. Even their bodies—as the media of emotional and physical activities—became sites of ideological battle. Desire for bodily comfort was equated with propensity toward bourgeois pleasure: the militants considered the body an enemy territory littered with capitalist traps. Bodies merely belonged to the conditions that must be overcome in order to reach the higher goal of revolution.

In contrast to the denigration of bodies, guns acquired life in URA training sessions. Mori Tsuneo provided a rather dubious theoretical basis for the necessity of instilling life into guns, arguing that their use assisted members in embracing the extreme condition of kill or be killed.[40] Nagata Hiroko, the leader of the Revolutionary Left, quotes Mori's rather "theatrical" explanation of the "war of annihilation with guns" during a joint training session:

> Namekata [Masatoki, of the Red Army faction], think about the rifle that you are holding right now. What kind of a gun was that? It was just a dead gun, which was originally displayed at a gun shop and later used to shoot a bird for pleasure. However, once it was snatched away by our hands, this dead gun began to grow and became a gun we forcefully gained control over. However, if one possessed it as a mere weapon or hid it in the attic, its growth would stop, and it would not serve our struggle in strengthening our unity and gaining genuine communist subjectivity. It would be pitiful for the gun. In order to strengthen our unity and gain genuine communist subjectivity, you must begin the battle of annihilation. Only then will you transform yourself into a revolutionary solider who fights the battle of annihilation, while the gun in your possession will transform itself into a gun for the battle of annihilation. The gun does not change you; you change the gun. For that, you need to transform yourself into a revolutionary soldier who can engage in the battle of annihilation.[41]

The argument appears to be a bad caricature of Marx's theory of commodity fetishism. The gun, the industrial product, rhetorically gained life, while twelve URA members were literally deprived of it. Namekata Masatoki later became the sixth member killed at the hands of his comrades for his allegedly insufficient commitment to the revolutionary cause. The fetish object of the gun was material evidence of the ways in which violence would rule the URA camps, demanding deadly commitment from each member.

Under the joint leadership of Mori Tsuneo and Nagata Hiroko, the URA began to conduct military training and self-criticism (*sōkatsu*) at the "base"—a shack that they constructed in the mountains of Gunma Prefecture in December 1971.[42] Katō Yoshitaka and Kojima Kazuko (Revolutionary Left) were the first members subjected to the brutal process of sōkatsu. The group's second-level leaders, who later formed a seven-member central committee, sanctioned Mori's high-handed demand, made on rather trivial and arbitrary grounds, for Katō and Kojima to perform self-criticism. Katō was accused, among other things, of paying attention to his clothes and hairstyle and of chatting with the interrogator while in police custody following his earlier arrest.[43] Kojima was criticized for her unwillingness to fight her own bourgeois thinking.[44]

Mori Tsuneo initiated the use of beating as a means to facilitate self-critique. By beating the member unconscious, he claimed, other members could bring him or her to a higher level of sōkatsu. On regaining consciousness, he or she will be ready to accept genuine communist subjectivity.[45] Yet inflicting violence on one of their own was not an easy decision. In a later account, Nagata Hiroko recalls that her hands were shaking uncontrollably even after she accepted Mori's reasoning.[46] Sakaguchi Hiroshi (Revolutionary Left), a member of the central committee, recounts the situation he and the others faced: "Many of us hesitated to beat Katō. Therefore, once we participated in the beating, we were haunted by the idea that we had to self-critique ourselves even harder. This [moral disguise] gave the brutal and merciless beating a scrupulous appearance. To beat a man in order to carry out one's own self-critique. What a perverted logic!"[47] Once directed toward one's fellow members, violence became a tool to police one's own ideological correctness. To hesitate to beat a comrade, in turn, demonstrated inadequate commitment to the cause. As Nagaka has aptly observed, through this boomerang effect Mori managed to maintain his hegemonic role while avoiding the potentially explosive issue of ideological discord within the organization.[48]

In the early hours of December 27, 1971, the beating sessions began. On this occasion Katō was the prime target of the "guidance" (shidō).[49] Even Kojima and Katō's two teenage brothers were forced to participate.[50] There was, however, a miscalculation about how the human body responds to blows. Katō did not lose consciousness as they initially expected, despite various attempts to knock him out. Although he had not been given proper rations for several days as part of his comprehensive self-critique, he withstood bodily assault without collapsing. This was held against him. Mori concluded that Katō had not lost consciousness because he was not truly committed to his self-criticism.[51] Mori's ideology subsumed Katō's battered body because a body that did not conform to self-criticism and the political program was not revolutionary enough. In the meetings that followed the bloody sessions, the other members confirmed the beating as "comradely assistance" (dōshiteki enjo). Katō remained tied up, initially inside the mountain base but later outside, exposed to the frigid weather. Although

Mori and Nagata finally recognized his commitment to self-criticism and brought him indoors, he died on January 4, 1972.[52]

Meanwhile, the "assistance" was extended to other members, one by one. Ozaki Michio (Revolutionary Left) was the first to die directly from sōkatsu, or the perceived insufficiency of his efforts toward it. On the evening of December 28, Ozaki became the target of collective criticism in a meeting. As a consequence, he was forced to remain sitting in the *seiza* position with his buttocks on top of his ankles until the middle of the following day, concentrating on his self-criticism. Ozaki was accused of cowardice for failing to participate in the Revolutionary Left's assault on a local police box in December 1970, an incident in which Shibano Haruhiko was shot to death. As part of his sōkatsu, Ozaki was assigned to play the role of one of the assailants, while Sakaguchi Hiroshi volunteered to represent the policeman who had shot Shibano. Reenacting the bloody fight against the police was supposed to help Ozaki overcome his "defeatism." Sakaguchi was better built, and Ozaki was exhausted from earlier self-criticism sessions, so the outcome of their contest was never in doubt. The URA's revolutionary ideas were reduced to a rather farcical reenactment in which the participants merely reproduced the identical outcome— the attacker's defeat.[53]

Already beaten to a pulp, Ozaki was tied up and then beaten again on December 30. A few hours later he died. He had been allowed no food since the beginning of the sōkatsu on the night of December 28. Facing the grave consequences of their role as ideological accomplices, central committee members and eventually the rest of the membership accepted Mori's characterization of Ozaki's death as a casualty of the revolutionary struggle: he died because he failed in his self-criticism. According to Sakaguchi, Mori announced to the central committee: "Because Ozaki did not try to attain genuinely communistic subjectivity, his spirit was defeated, leading to the corporeal defeat. If one were serious about becoming a revolutionary soldier, one would not die. The defeat of a revolutionary soldier means his death."[54] Once the death was blamed on the victim's own failure in the ideological battle, there was no longer an agent of violence. Violence ceased to be a form of assistance among comrades and became the evidence of the victims' own guilt.

The disappearing agency of violence was clearest in the case of Tōyama Mieko (Red Army faction), whom Mori ordered to beat herself on January 3, 1972. Surrounded by the other members, Tōyama repeatedly hit her face with her own fists for about thirty minutes until it was a swollen, bloody mess.[55] There was no way out of the situation in which she found herself. Refusing to beat herself would surely be construed as evidence of her unwillingness to subject herself to sōkatsu. On the other hand, accepting the organization's command of "self-assistance" proved that she needed it. Having helped construct this inescapable regime of violence, Tōyama dutifully applied the ideological assistance to herself. Yet her self-critique was deemed insufficient, and the others offered helping hands in her deadly endeavor, hitting her, cutting her hair, and finally leaving her tied up until her death on January 7.

Tōyama's case further demonstrates that, as the cultural critic Ōtsuka Eiji has cogently argued, the repression of femininity was an integral part of the group's critique of bourgeois identity.[56] Tōyama's concern about her appearance had been an earlier point of tension. At a joint training session of the Revolutionary Left and the Red Army faction in early December 1971, Nagata insistently criticized Tōyama for wearing her hair long, using makeup, and refusing to dispose of her ring.[57] Nagata's criticism was perhaps retaliation for the Red Army faction's criticism of Revolutionary Left members for another trivial matter (not bringing water bottles to the training camp), but subsequent criticisms also targeted victims' feminine qualities.

In the critical retrospective that Mori wrote in police custody, he described what was at stake in Tōyama's self-criticism:

> The demand for a sōkatsu on Miss Tōyama derived from various issues raised at the joint military training session—specifically, once at the mountain bases, she lacked independence, autonomy, and vitality in comparison with the female members of the Revolutionary Left, and this problem manifested itself through her clothes, makeup, and attitude. While this issue was criticized, another criticism was offered: the problem [the lack of independence, autonomy, and vitality] demonstrated that she had not been engaging in the process of transforming women into soldiers by fostering an independent mind and active and independent behavior. It only attested to her habitual, constant reliance on and obsequious attitude toward men. From these criticisms, we [Mori and Nagata] concluded that the production of women soldiers required self-transformation of the bourgeois, feminine constitution [*taishitsu*] for the sake of the struggle.[58]

In Mori's report, the feminine is paired with bourgeois identity as a condition that needed to be transcended for the revolutionary struggle. His strong misogynistic attitudes may have defined the terms of these criticisms.[59] Yet the characterization of revolutionary struggle as a male activity found support from other members, including Tōyama herself. To fend off Mori's criticism, Tōyama claimed that she had participated in political activities thinking that she was a "man-woman," denying her feminine qualities.[60] Her desperate rebuttal merely confirmed the correctness of the conceptual framework through which the criticisms were made.

There is some evidence suggesting that *Tomorrow's Jō* provided a critical framework through which Red Army faction members articulated personal struggles. In a letter dated November 25, 1971, which Tōyama addressed to Takahara Hiroyuki—her partner and Red Army faction leader in prison—she wrote: "I just followed Riki'ishi Tōru, without finding a proletarian politics through which to live or clearly understanding the dialectical relations between Jō and Riki'ishi. Because I assumed that I would die in fall, I wanted to embrace even for once the feminine part that I had abandoned [for the sake of revolutionary struggles]."[61] As we saw in the previous chapter, while Riki'ishi dies shortly after the match against Jō, the latter's struggle continues and takes a dark turn after Riki'ishi's death. Regardless of what the Red Army faction members understood by "the dialectical relations between Jō and Riki'ishi," there is clearly no place for women in their male bonds. At the mountain base, it appears that Tōyama was instructed to eliminate her femininity symbolically by reenacting Jō's and Riki'ishi's deathly bout by herself.

Shortly after Nagata's death in 2011, the feminist activist Tanaka Mitsu reiterated her own long-held opinion of the gender dynamics within the URA. In fall 1971 Nagata tried to recruit Tanaka to the Revolutionary Left and invited her to their mountain base. Out of curiosity, Tanaka visited the base and immediately saw through the unreality of the struggle there. After recalling their real-life encounter, Tanaka offers a forceful analysis of what drove Nagata to deadly action:

> [After Tanaka's visit], the Revolutionary Left merged with the macho Red Army faction—top-heavy with ideas—creating the United Red Army. Just because she wished to be recognized by the self-proclaimed revolutionary men of the former Red Army faction, Nagata tried to behave perfectly in political and revolutionary terms. She tried to live

as a "perfect, impossibly unrealistic woman." Therefore, she was compelled to purge the woman who was eight months pregnant and the woman who showed her attachment to accessories—those who embodied "woman who exists here." Yes, Nagata was too much of a woman to aspire to be in the men's world. She killed her own avatars.[62]

The focus of Tanaka's criticism is not Nagata's allegedly fraudulent personality but the larger patriarchal structure that forced her to abandon the bodily reality of here and now in the hopes of reaching the abstract goal of the revolutionary future.

In late January the news of a former Red Army faction member's arrest and the defection of a current member forced the URA leaders to move their base to another location in Gunma Prefecture.[63] Eight members had been killed by then; nine were dispatched to build a hut at the new base. In their absence, Mori and Nagata began to hurl criticisms at two female members, Ōtsuki Setsuko and Kaneko Michiyo (both Revolutionary Left). Ōtsuki was interrogated about the pants and coat that she had bought with money supplied by a supporter and was also accused of having her hair cut at a beauty parlor.[64] The feminine was coupled with the sin of finding pleasure in consumption. The act of self-criticism had become a deadly ritual through which to exorcise the social forces that had found their way into the revolutionary organization.[65] Ōtsuki and Kaneko were tied up, carried to the new base, and left outside underneath the hut. Despite Ōtsuki's efforts at self-criticism, she fell short of transforming herself into a genuine revolutionary soldier. On January 30 she became the tenth member to die at the camps (a male member, Yamamoto Jun'ichi, who was simultaneously going through a sōkatsu, died shortly before her). Mori declared that her death stemmed from the shock she suffered on learning of the members' determination to continue her self-critique.[66]

Mori's condemnation of Kaneko initially focused on her alleged antagonism to Nagata and her opportunistic associations with men—using them as a means to establish her hegemony in the organization.[67] Even her husband, Yoshino Masakuni, following Mori's lead, criticized her for taking an active role in their sexual intercourse.[68] As fears of detection by the authorities deepened, the feminine came to be identified not only as a negative condition to be overcome but as a threat that could undermine the whole revolutionary movement. Mori later defined Kaneko's body as a site of ideological battle. Kaneko was pregnant with Yoshino's child at the time, and their fetus was construed as a future revolutionary solider whose custody belonged to the organization. Mori denounced her for treating it like private property, and for assuming that she would not be killed as long as she was pregnant. The demand for her sōkatsu was transformed into a struggle to transfer the fetus into the URA's possession. Mori seriously contemplated delivering the baby prematurely by caesarean section (he ordered Aoto Mikio [Red Army faction], a former medical student, to purchase books on obstetrics).[69] Kaneko's body was reduced to its reproductive functions, mobilized for the revolutionary future. Nagata embraced Mori's stance and announced to the other members: "Kaneko's child [is not her private property, but] belongs to our organization, and we must reclaim our control over it. The central committee are discussing C-section as an option [in case Kaneko fails in her sōkatsu]."[70] However, the opportunity for the operation never came. Kaneko died on February 4, along with the eight-month-old fetus.[71]

Under the guise of the revolutionary struggle against capitalist society, bodies were subject to constant policing. The revolutionary subjectivity that the members strived for was tantamount to believing in the superiority of will over material conditions. Expressions of bodily concerns and desires were seen as evidence of bourgeois propensities. Sexual desires in particular were problematized because undisciplined sexual practices were deemed to be mere reflections of bourgeois gender relations.[72] A number of victims were accused of improper sexual conduct in the past. In this repressive atmosphere, even hygienic concerns became a target of criticism. The final victim, Yamada Takashi (Red Army faction), was denounced because he took another member to a public bath while they were on mission in town. Later, in police custody, Bandō Kunio recalled that "[Yamada's] behavior became an issue [because the members thought] it is a bourgeois individualistic attitude to take a bath and be clean while the other members were wholeheartedly engaging in a battle at the mountain base."[73] Seeking bodily cleanliness was construed as deadly betrayal of their revolutionary ideal.

The sense of liberation gained from being in the radical oppositional movements—especially in the mountains, away from official surveillance—was displaced by the lifeless, drab regimen of the bases.[74] Sakaguchi

TABLE 8.1
Revolutionary Left and United Red Army members killed in intrafactional violence, 1971–1972

| Date of Death | Name | Gender | Age at Death | Original Affiliation |
|---|---|---|---|---|
| 8/4/1971 | Sakisaka Yasuko | Female | 22 | Revolutionary Left |
| 8/10/1971 | Mukōyama Shigenori | Male | 21 | Revolutionary Left |
| 12/31/1971 | Ozaki Michio | Male | 22 | Revolutionary Left |
| 1/1/1972 | Shindō Ryūzaburō | Male | 21 | Red Army faction |
| 1/1/1972 | Kojima Kazuko | Female | 22 | Revolutionary Left |
| 1/4/1972 | Katō Yoshitaka | Male | 22 | Revolutionary Left |
| 1/7/1972 | Tōyama Mieko | Female | 25 | Red Army faction |
| 1/9/1972 | Namekata Masatoki | Male | 25 | Red Army faction |
| 1/17/1972 | Teraoka Kōichi | Male | 24 | Revolutionary Left |
| 1/19/1972 | Yamazaki Jun | Male | 21 | Red Army faction |
| 1/30/1972 | Yamamoto Jun'ichi | Male | 28 | Revolutionary Left |
| 1/30/1972 | Ōtsuki Setsuko | Female | 23 | Revolutionary Left |
| 2/4/1972 | Kaneko Michiyo | Female | 24 | Revolutionary Left |
| 2/12/1972 | Yamada Takashi | Male | 27 | Red Army faction |

Hiroshi's writing on his involvement in the Revolutionary Left and later in the URA testifies to this change. Where he discusses his early career as a radical activist, his account is filled with descriptions of his bodily sensations. For example, in the section that explains how he and his coconspirators managed to get to Haneda Airport on the night of September 3, 1969, defying heavy police protection, Sakaguchi provides a full account of his bodily experiences. Of the decision to cross a canal that separated the airport from the surrounding area, he wrote:

> We stuck a stick in the water, and realized it was less than a meter deep. We decided to walk in the water [instead of swimming]. The bottom of the water was covered by sludge. Every step we took, our feet sank into the sludge, which clung to our soles. It was very gross.... [Once he began to swim], my whole body was slimy and extremely uncomfortable. The smell did not bother me much, but it was a far cry from the fragrance of my hometown sea. The width of

the canal was about 200 meters. It felt much longer than when we had observed it during the day.

Sakaguchi's struggle was registered by his bodily senses and even connected to past sensations. Although it was not necessarily pleasant to wade through the heavily polluted water in Tokyo Bay, the richness of Sakaguchi's sensory imagery attests to his heightened awareness of the environment as well as his sense of excitement in the dark water.[75]

The descriptions of bodily sensations, however, disappear from his account when he begins to describe his relations with the Revolutionary Left. The only subsequent reference to sensory perceptions is about the putrid smell of dead bodies. In the early morning of August 4, 1971, greeting four members who have just returned from murdering another member in order to ensure her silence, he is shocked by the strong stench:

> As soon as everyone entered the room, a peculiar smell filled it. It was a mixture of the odor of alcohol and the smell of the dead body. Later, when we beat Ozaki Michio to death, I smelled the same odor. It was a rotten stench that was strongly disagreeable. Back then, I did not clearly understand that it was the smell of the dead body. I just thought it seeped into their clothes when they killed her.[76]

The smell of the dead bodies became the only sensory marker strong enough, momentarily, to cut open the regime of corporeal repression; and even to that, and to their own body odor, the members eventually grew desensitized.[77]

The bodies appear to have had their revenge, so to speak. On February 16, 1972, after realizing that the police were closing in on them, the remaining members abandoned the mountain cave at Mt. Myōgi in Gunma Prefecture to which they had moved a few days earlier. To outwit the police search teams, they decided to take a treacherous mountain route to reach the Nagano Prefecture part of the Japan Alps. They initially walked along streams in order to leave no traces for the police canine team. Mori and Nagata, who had dispatched themselves to Tokyo to raise money, were arrested at the foot of the mountain where the cave was located, while attempting to rejoin the group. Although the nine members managed to cross the prefectural border after hours of trekking, they wandered into a new resort development that was not on their map. Among the plots for sale in the upscale resort—the epitome of Japan's consumer society—the revolutionary soldiers were totally disoriented. Uegaki Yasuhiro, Aoto Mikio, Terabayashi Makie, and Itō Kazuko thought they were heading for a nearby town to procure food and supplies, but they ended up in the city of Karuizawa. They were arrested at the Karuizawa Station while trying to take a train on February 19. Their bedraggled appearance, filthy hands, and strong stench caught the attention of a kiosk clerk, who immediately alerted the station supervisor.[78] The URA members' stoic efforts to transform themselves into revolutionary soldiers by transcending their corporeal needs were eventually frustrated by their own unhygienic bodies. Uegaki was bitterly disappointed that he had let down the other members, yet he was simultaneously relieved that he could finally rest his hurt and fatigued body in the prison cell.[79] Their neglected bodies finally insisted on being included in the revolutionary dream.

## Television Worth Watching

The URA's struggles against what they called bourgeois propensities took the most conservative form possible. Away from police surveillance, members tried to break away from contemporary society by exorcising all the things they associated with consumer society. The police, on the other hand, emphasized visual surveillance, saturating the public space with photographs of the suspects. While hiding in Niigata in February 1971, Sakaguchi was shocked to find out that the police were using television to their advantage by leaking key information to the media.[80]

Only three years earlier, television had captured police violence against the student radicals protesting the arrival of the USS *Enterprise*—a nuclear-powered aircraft carrier equipped with nuclear weapons—in the Sasebo Port.[81] These graphic images powerfully undermined the official narrative that denigrated the protesters as a violent mob, turning viewers into the radicals' sympathizers. Sakaguchi too watched the confrontations on television: on January 17, 1968, he recalled, the student activists "confronted the riot police on the Hirase Bridge leading to the U.S. base in Sasebo. It was moving to watch the students charge into the wall of the riot police, defying water cannons and gas shells."[82] A cadre member of the National Police Agency dispatched to deal with the situation in Sasebo, seeing the citizens' sympathetic reactions, mourned afterward: "If only we had not had television right there."[83] Sakaguchi was not exaggerating when he stated that for six months after the large-scale violent protest at Haneda Airport on October 8, 1967, "television, newspaper, and radio covered the new left's street actions almost every day. Japanese society was in a kind of excited state."[84] This euphoric period did not last long. The new left groups failed to take media relations seriously and were outmaneuvered by Liberal Democratic Party leaders, who, through unofficial channels, pressured the television stations to rectify their "biased" coverage.[85]

In the early 1970s the police focused on community relations, mobilizing a massive number of officers in order to extend its searches into neighborhoods with the help of citizens.[86] The police hunted down radical activists and their sympathizers, searching more than 350,000 buildings during the two separate campaigns from December 29, 1971, through February 29, 1972, and from March 1 through April 30, 1972.[87] The URA's retreat to the mountains was an attempt to escape the tightening circle of surveillance and the nearly ubiquitous presence of the media and erase from themselves all traces of society before engaging in a "war of annihilation." It is deeply ironic (and perhaps appropriate) that their efforts ended with the hostage-taking in Karuizawa, which was so extensively covered by the Japanese media. For nine days in the mountain lodge, the remaining five members—Bandō Kunio, Sakaguchi Hiroshi, Yoshino Masakuni, and the two younger brothers of Katō Yoshitaka—made no contact with the outside world, hiding away from the cameras' merciless gaze.

Yet for the first three days of the nine-day siege, until the police cut off their electricity, they spent many hours watching television. On February 22 the five witnessed a shocking scene on the television screen: Richard Nixon making a historic visit to Beijing to normalize U.S.-China relations. The event completely undermined the Maoist and anti-American ideology of the former Revolutionary Left. The members were unable to process the information and merely stared at the screen.[88] Their situation aptly attests to the failure of their attempt to distance themselves from consumer society. While the television coverage of Nixon's visit to China debunked their ideological premises, their hostage-taking—the long-waited opportunity to launch the war of annihilation—became a source of visual entertainment for the television audience (figure 8.1). The

*Figure 8.1* Line of telephoto lenses at Karuizawa, February 22, 1972. Courtesy of Mainichi Newspapers.

remaining five members could do nothing about the assault of visual images but sit in front of the television and dutifully consume them.

On February 28 the police made their move to rescue the hostage by force. The battle lasted almost eight hours, with some interruptions. Although two of their own were shot to death, the police carefully avoided killing any suspects, lest they make martyrs out of them. In the end, the hostage was brought to safety after 218 hours of captivity, while the five URA members were arrested. The URA's violent protest against capitalist society ended as a television spectacle, thoroughly consumed by tens of millions (figure 8.2). The feminist writer Tanaka Mitsu recalls how an NHK reporter repeatedly commented during the Asama-sansō hostage situation: "I am compelled to think about the bizarreness of televising such a bizarre situation as this to your living room."[89] The reporter's self-reflective gesture cunningly supplanted the extraordinary nature of the event itself with the extraordinary power of the media that rendered everything to viewers' living rooms.

*Figure 8.2* The crowd watches the battle between United Red Army members and police on a television at the Dōjima Underground Concourse in Osaka, February 28, 1972. Courtesy of Mainichi Newspapers.

## Postscript

Soon after the remaining members' arrests, the public learned about the killings that took place at the URA's mountain bases. For many sympathizers, that dark revelation spelled the end of the new left movement.[90]

As early as March 5, Okuzawa Shūichi, one of the first members to be arrested (while transporting camp gear in a car), confessed to the violent purging of a fellow activist. The next day the youngest of the Katō brothers (age sixteen at the time of his arrest) began talking to the police interrogators about the deaths of twelve members.[91] His testimony prompted his brother and those who were arrested at the Karuizawa Station to describe the gruesome events at the mountain camps. On March 8 Mori Tsuneo confessed (in writing to the Maebashi district court) his involvement in the killings.[92] A few days later he informed police interrogators of the executions of two Revolutionary Left members—the two killings before the two organizations' merger. Police recovered the bodies of all fourteen victims by March 25. On April 11 Nagata began to talk about the killings. On January 1, 1973, unable to bear the burden of his own self-criticism, Mori Tsuneo hanged himself from an iron bar on the door of his jail cell.

The Red Army faction members who had moved to Lebanon in 1971 in order to establish an overseas base for revolutionary struggle (known as the "Arab branch") broke away from the URA after witnessing its spectacular failure.[93] Shigenobu Fusako, who later led the faction, has acknowledged that frustration with their colleagues' missteps in Japan drove the Arab branch members into radical action.[94] In May 1972 their organization (then named the Arab Red Army, later renamed the Japanese Red Army)[95] made its international "debut" at Lod Airport, where three of its members killed twenty-four passengers and airport staff and injured more than eighty, purportedly to render support for the Palestinian struggle against Israel—and advance the global revolution advocated by Shiomi Takaya.[96] The Arab Red Army posited Palestine as the "forefront of world revolution," a strategic site from which to launch their attack on imperialism.[97] In August 1975 five Japanese Red Army members occupied the American and Swedish Embassies in Kuala Lumpur, taking the United States consul and fifty-two other embassy employees hostage. In exchange for the hostages' release, the hostage-takers demanded that seven of their fellow revolutionaries in Japanese prisons be immediately allowed to join them. Two URA members were on the list. Sakaguchi Hiroshi refused to leave prison because he no longer believed in armed struggle and wanted to complete the legal process, notwithstanding his anticipated death sentence.[98] Bandō Kunio, however, left Japan to join the Japanese Red Army.[99] In September 1977 five Japanese Red Army members, including Bandō, hijacked a Japan Airlines plane in Dhaka and demanded a $6 million ransom and the release of Uegaki Yasuhiro and eight other prisoners. Uegaki refused release because he believed it was more important to confront his past actions in court.[100]

The younger of the two surviving Katō brothers was released from a juvenile correction facility in 1974 and resumed life as a high school student. In 1977 the middle brother, Katō Michinori, decided, with Yoshino Masakuni, to break away from the other defendants and have separate court proceedings. In March 1979 Yoshino was sentenced to life in prison, and Michinori to thirteen years. The latter was released on parole in 1987.[101] In 1982 the key members of the URA, who had chosen to be tried as a group, were sentenced at Tokyo district court. Nagata Hiroko and

Sakaguchi Hiroshi were sentenced to death, while Uegaki Yasuhiro received a twenty-year term. The presiding judge, Nakano Takeo, displayed deep-seated misogyny in his judgment on Nagata, characterizing her as "an extreme attention-seeker, who has an overly emotional and aggressive character as well as strong suspicion and jealousy. Personality was plagued by numerous problems, including the relentlessness particular to women, spitefulness, and a grim sadistic tendency."[102] In 1993 the Supreme Court rejected their appeals, confirming their death sentences. At that point Nagata's and Sakaguchi's contacts with the outside world were limited to their immediate family members. Sakaguchi, who still awaits execution, has since expressed deep remorse through his *tanka* poems, some of which have been published in the newspaper and later as several collections.[103] After serving his full term, Uegaki was released from prison in 1998. He has frequently and publicly discussed his experiences as a member of the URA. When he had an opportunity to talk to an executive of Kawai Musical Instruments, which used to own Asamasansō, he apologized on behalf of his former colleagues for the disturbance they had caused at the lodge. The executive responded that Kawai pianos sold well thanks to the event itself and the attendant media exposure. That the URA's revolutionary struggle would have boosted the sales of a quintessential middle-class symbol would indeed be a heavy irony.[104] Nagata died in prison in 2011 from complications caused by a brain tumor.[105]

# Epilogue

*Legacies of 1972*

By every substantial measure, Japan's high-growth era came to a close in 1973. Pressing domestic and international issues forced the government to revise its economic strategies, and the economy's survival, rather than its growth, became the nation's central focus, at least in the short term. For the vast majority of Japanese people, who had assumed that the high-growth era would continue indefinitely, the tumults of 1973–1974 announced a seismic shift in the postwar economic regime. Many citizens feared that their modern lives stood on precarious ground. In the end, however, Japan's economy adjusted to floating exchange rates and higher oil prices and maintained a respectable rate (4.2 percent) of annual growth for the next decade and a half. Optimism soon returned. The country's ability to ride out unprecedented challenges and return to steady growth gave rise to a nationalistic pride in the form of *nihonjin-ron* (discourse of Japanese uniqueness). But these dramatic turns in Japan's economic fortune were culturally and experientially less cataclysmic than the paradigm shifts of the high-growth era. Metavisuality and mass consumerism—the conditions constitutive of the decades of growth—continued to shape everyday life in post-1972 Japan.

It is instructive to examine how three prominent Japanese men, all deeply invested in and benefiting from mass consumer society, responded to the time of economic panic. Tanaka Kakuei (1919–1993), who led the nation as the prime minister during the turbulent period from 1972 to 1974, was acutely conscious of how far Japan's rural areas lagged behind the rest of the country in economic development and access to media. Although he tried to perfect and perpetuate the conditions of 1972 by permanently extending those benefits, his very efforts contributed to the demise of the high-growth regime.

The television commercial director Sugiyama Toshi and the writer Komatsu Sakyō responded in more artistic and personal ways. Sugiyama desired to maintain an autonomous, creative self outside mass consumerism and the media gaze, yet his suicide in December 1973 and the cryptic message he left behind intimated that he had ultimately surrendered to them. Komatsu's doomsday scenario attested not only to the deep confusion and uncertainty that Japan faced in 1973 but also to the popular desire to escape the effects of mass consumerism. Instead of looking for a way out of the conditions of 1972, the writer used his literary imagination to destroy the entire "inside" by sending the country to the bottom of the Pacific. As divergent as the three men's responses were, they were all firmly predicated on the conditions of 1972. In this epilogue we return briefly to the year 1972 to contemplate how its legacies continue to define Japanese society today.

## The Rise and Fall of Tanaka Kakuei

On July 5, 1972, after receiving a majority vote in the second round of the Liberal Democratic Party leadership election, Tanaka Kakuei was declared the party president. Two days later, as the leader of the majority party, he replaced Satō Eisaku as prime minister and formed a new cabinet. The drama of Tanaka's extraordinary ascent—a man of humble origins achieving the highest political office in Japan—resonated with the optimism of the period. The media portrayed Tanaka as a sort of folk hero, a leader who instinctively understood ordinary people's needs and sentiments, and his long-held political stances gave credence to that image. His political vision was anchored in his formative experience of growing up in a rural community. Having witnessed the hardships of life in Niigata, Tanaka made it his lifelong project to extend economic benefits to those who lived outside the major urban centers.

Even though residents of the countryside enjoyed increasing access to the new media and mass consumerism during the high-growth era, they also saw the rural economy erode relative to the exponential growth of urban areas. Agricultural income had to be supplemented by earnings from other forms of labor, including seasonal *dekasegi* (chapter 2). The lack of economic opportunity in the countryside especially affected young people, many of whom left their hometowns to seek jobs in large cities. In the mid-1960s middle school teachers in Amakusa, Kyushu, bade farewell to teenagers destined to work in the big cities as if they were sending them off to war.[1] Those cities overflowed with young migrants, while the countryside was left with a steadily shrinking and graying population.[2] Tanaka aspired to bridge the growing city-country gap by radically transforming Japan's industrial structure through a massive infrastructure expansion campaign.

The new prime minister had been known for his efforts to extend economic benefits to the countryside, notably his active role in the expansion of television networks. In 1957, as the minister of post and telecommunications, he granted licenses to seven NHK stations and thirty-six commercial television stations (owned by thirty-four companies), to the consternation of many officials and bureaucrats in his own ministry who believed that Japan still lacked the technological and economic base to support television culture.[3] Tanaka also used his political clout to secure the construction permit for Tokyo Tower, a 333-meter (1,093-foot) broadcasting tower that became an icon of the high-growth era.[4] He subsequently exerted power over the television industry, whose expansion he personally oversaw. His political maneuvers in the late 1950s helped bring the new media—an essential ingredient for the explosive expansion of mass consumerism—to millions of rural residents. Improved media access was required to convert them into consumers, but they then needed the economic basis to support their new purchasing habits. While the LDP's agricultural policies modestly increased rural households' income, they did little to slow the flood of people from country to city.

In 1972 Tanaka tried to realize his political vision by forcefully altering Japan's economic landscape. The premiership offered him the opportunity to implement his bold vision for the nation, which he had published a month before the LDP election: *Building a New Japan: A Plan for Remodeling the Japanese Archipelago* (*Nippon rettō kaizōron*).[5] It was not an easy read—it was most likely ghostwritten by bureaucrats—but Tanaka's popularity pushed it up the bestseller list.[6] The book proposed an expansion of the existing high-speed railway and highway networks in order to facilitate the transfer of economic functions to midsize cities. In theory, the new infrastructure would allow the government to tackle both overpopulation in the major cities and depopulation in the countryside. In the conclusion of his manifesto, Tanaka wrote: "I am motivated by a strong desire to rebuild the hometown [*kyōri*] of the Japanese people, which has been lost and destroyed and is declining today but which, once restored, will again give to our society a sense of tranquility and spiritual enrichment."[7] Tanaka did not elaborate on what Japanese society would look like once it recovered its "tranquility and spiritual enrichment," but clearly his focus was on further economic development.

Commenting on Tanaka's political style, Hosaka Masayasu characterizes him bluntly as an enabler of the masses:

> What Tanaka consistently pursued throughout the thirty years of his political career is the translation of Japanese people's desires into his policies. The straightforward desire for sufficient food, an affluent and convenient life, and [a concern for] pragmatism rather than ideals and beliefs constituted the backbone of his policies. The slogan "building a new Japan" was typical of his political style.[8]

Tanaka unconditionally embraced the materialist cravings that drove Japan's high economic growth and aspired to build a new Japan that could better accommodate popular desires. In doing so he intended to take the economy to the next level, where all citizens would have an equal footing in both the production and the consumption of wealth. In reality, however, he contributed to the process that effectively ended Japan's high-growth era.

Tanaka believed his plan was well within the realm of possibility and practicality; he did not expect blowback. His bold initiatives to address pressing national issues, however, led some associates to begin purchasing land in the areas where new large-scale development was expected. As the journalist Tachibana Takashi's investigations later revealed, land speculation had also been Tanaka's regular way of rewarding his loyal supporters.[9] Tanaka had in turn relied on their monetary contributions to outmaneuver his political rivals in the LDP, right up to the party leadership election in 1972. The specific identification of some target cities and areas for development in Tanaka's book encouraged property speculation and fueled inflation.[10] Rumor had it that exorbitant amounts of money changed hands in each election, but the media and public seemed willing to turn a blind eye to the practice as long as the political system produced the desired outcomes.

This time it was different. Inflation reached a dangerous level following the oil crisis of 1973. Soon after the Yom Kippur War of October 1973, the Arab members of the Organization of Petroleum Exporting Countries raised prices and threatened to terminate exports to nations deemed pro-Israel. Although the Japanese government secured its oil imports—albeit at higher prices—by taking a pro-Arab stance, the crisis in the Middle East exposed the shaky ground on which Japan's post–World War II system stood. In November 1973, to fight inflation, Tanaka rescinded his plan for national remodeling and appointed his political rival, Fukuda Takeo (1905–1995), an advocate of steady economic growth, as the minister of finance.[11] The next year, however, the inflation rate reached 23.2 percent and the growth rate turned negative (−0.5 percent) for the first time in the postwar period.

Even Tanaka's spectacular success in diplomacy had little effect on the precipitous decline of his approval rating. As soon as he became prime minister, he took steps to normalize Japan's relationship with the People's Republic of China.[12] Bolstered by strong popular support, he overrode opposition from pro-Taiwan members of the LDP and achieved his goal in September 1972.[13] Yet that month's 62 percent approval rating plummeted to 12 percent in a little over two years.[14] On November 26, 1974, Tanaka resigned from the premiership. In July 1976 he was arrested for allegedly receiving bribes from the Lockheed Corporation. Three weeks later the Tokyo District Public Prosecutors Office indicted him on charges of bribery and violations of the Foreign Exchange Management Act. Tanaka proclaimed his innocence and engaged in a prolonged legal battle until his death in 1993. Even after his resignation and arrest, he remained the leader of the largest faction within the LDP and continued to exert influence over national politics. Tanaka's fall, nonetheless, marked an end to the ascendancy of the persona he projected: hyper-driven, burning with naked ambition, epitomizing the ethos of the high-growth era.[15]

## Death of a Television Commercial Director

On December 13, 1973, a well-known director of television commercials, Sugiyama Toshi (1936–1973), was found dead in his posh Tokyo apartment. Two weeks later, a newspaper article reproduced in its entirety the suicide note he had left:

> Since I am not rich
> I would not understand a rich world.
> Since I am not happy
> I would not be able to portray a happy world.
> Since I have no "dreams"
> Selling "dreams" is just . . .
> Lies will eventually be exposed.[16]

Sugiyama's death at the height of his success shocked people in the industry who had witnessed his creative power and drive up close, as well as members of the public who had enjoyed his commercials. In his short career he received numerous domestic as well as international awards for the advertisements he directed.

Although Sugiyama was perhaps best known for his stylish Shiseidō commercials, his ad for Mobil Oil in 1971 became one of the most iconic of the period.[17] In the minute-long spot, two casually dressed young men push a small, boxy, antique car (it appears to be a DATSUN 16 from the late 1930s) on a country road.[18] They have obviously run out of gas but do not seem flustered. They make casual stops along the way and appear to enjoy their journey. On the soundtrack, a male voice sings in a folky style, accompanied by a guitar: "Let's take it slow. / It would be all the same even if we rushed. / Let's take it slow. / Somehow things will work out in this world. / Let's take it slow. / Let's take it easy."[19] As the two men slowly walk into a town, a voiceover makes the obvious point that "cars run on gasoline," and the blue-and-red Mobil logo appears. The casual, easygoing message should not be taken at face value, since the main point of the advertisement was to sell Mobil products. As the advertisement calls viewers' attention to gasoline distribution systems, it naturalizes Mobil against the bucolic scenery. The classic car on the screen translates the modern lifestyle into an aesthetic choice: Mobil will be there to help maintain the viewers' beautiful life. The ad is less advocacy for the slow life than a celebration of Japan's economy, which has finally reached the stage where its participants can afford to be self-reflective and playful about their achievements.

Sugiyama was keenly aware of the underlying dilemma in the Mobil ad. In his book about the first twenty-five years of Japanese television, Shiozawa Shigeru reports the following exchange he had with Sugiyama right after its production work was completed:

SHIOZAWA: Rather than just imploring us to save gas, I wanted you to go so far as to abandon automobiles altogether.
SUGIYAMA: I was tormented by that point. But I could not do that. I am weak. At this point, as long as one continues to make television commercials, one is not allowed to deny the high-growth economy. I wanted to deny it but stopped a step short—that was my limit.
SHIOZAWA: That's why the ad highlights gas as an essential product though it begs us to save gas.
SUGIYAMA: Please don't corner me like that. Television commercials are scary because they expose the lies. As a commercial producer, I am always troubled by that. I hate this profession.[20]

Sugiyama's thoughtful responses to Shiozawa's queries prefigured the sentiments expressed in his suicide note.

Sugiyama's close friends and associates, many of whom were established figures in the advertising industry and the media, contributed their recollections to a retrospective volume five years after his death. They attested to his exceptional stature as a creator of television commercials. As Yamada Shōji points out, however, Sugiyama's name was largely unknown outside the industry even at the peak of his career. Only after his death was he extolled as an auteur of television commercials. His death and suicide note contributed to the posthumous veneration of his talent.[21] Sugiyama's intense lifestyle, with its long work hours, copious alcohol consumption, and string of affairs with women, was then reconstituted as a sign of his exceptional drive.

Photographer Kurigami Kazumi, one of the contributors to the retrospective volume, sees in Sugiyama's death the end of an era: "The creators of television commercials engage in the task of crafting and communicating a message. He himself in the end became a message. The man called Sugiyama Toshi, his existence, was the message. He completed the cycle [of becoming the message] with his own hands. I felt, when he died, that a trend in television commercials was over."[22] According to Kurigami, Sugiyama completely wove himself into his television commercials. He existed only as the message that he crafted and communicated. Kurigami discusses the freedom that existed in commercial production in earlier years, implying that a short-lived sense of openness disappeared as the industry matured.[23] Sugiyama stepped into the new territory of television commercial production at the right time, while it was still young, and left his indelible mark on it. Having intertwined himself with that world, however, he was unable to escape when its openness disappeared. Sugiyama's suicide note hermetically sealed the world of television commercials: his death effectively denied that his authentic—happy and rich—self could exist outside his message. He dissolved into the very world of consumption that he had helped carry into the innermost private sphere of everyday life.

The journalist Tahara Sōichirō shares the observation of one of Sugiyama's associates that the director was "madness. It was frightening to watch him work. He was running full throttle. [His attitude was that] 'I am the television commercial.' It felt like you would get burnt if you got too close to him."[24] The unnamed associate went on to make a surprising connection to a contemporary news event: "It was January 1973. Sugi-san was reading a newspaper. When I peeked at it, he hastily folded the paper and gave me a grin. After a while, he just muttered, 'They freaking lost. Idiots.' I actually knew what Sugi-san was reading. He was reading an article about Mori Tsuneo, the URA leader, hanging himself in a prison cell."[25] Who would expect a man completely absorbed in his work at the cutting edge of mass consumerism to harbor sympathies for self-proclaimed fighters against capitalist hegemony (chapter 8)? A single-minded devotion to weaving himself into commercial messages was perhaps the only way for Sugiyama to ground himself in mass consumer society. In the end, however, both the professional revolutionary and the television commercial director decided to exit that society in the same year and through an identical method—by hanging themselves.[26]

## Sinking Japan to the Bottom of the Pacific

The 1973 oil shock and its aftermath created deep anxiety and disquiet in Japan. What had appeared to be solid ground began to shift, and the nation's optimism receded, exposing a ragged subterranean realm of complex emotions. Capturing the fear of and fascination with the global turmoil, Komatsu Sakyō's disaster novel, *Japan Sinks* (Nihon chinbotsu, 1973) quickly climbed to the top of the bestseller list.[27] Komatsu imagines an exit from the regime of the high-growth economy by annihilating the geopolitical entity of Japan. Rather than conceiving an outside, he destroys the inside—what postwar Japan has built—and forces all the inhabitants of Japan to live as diasporic outsiders.

The story is built around a series of natural disasters of unprecedented scale. Hitherto unknown geophysical mechanisms cause the entire Japanese archipelago to sink to the bottom of the ocean, while the Japanese government secretly orchestrates the resettlement of the islands' 110 million inhabitants. Trying for verisimilitude, Komatsu extensively researched the latest findings in geophysics, seismology, and volcanology, offering detailed discussions of the science behind Japan's imaginary demise. *Japan Sinks* is not an inviting text. Its narrative is disjunctive, focused on the geological processes through which the nation physically falls apart, complete with detailed numerical data. Despite their good intentions and determination, the human characters, overpowered by nature, are the least memorable part of the story. The transitional paragraphs that connect one natural phenomenon to another are filled with banal criticisms of Japan's obsession with shallow economic prosperity. Had there not been an oil crisis, it is likely that the book would have appealed only to a handful of diehard science fiction fans.

The actions and thoughts of a young Japanese man, Onodera Toshio, form the thread connecting the human aspects within the story of outsized catastrophe. As the pilot of a deep-sea exploratory submersible vessel, he gathers data vital to the nationally organized research team, observing the signs of large-scale seismic activity on the sea floor, up close and earlier than anybody else. His vision, however, is limited to the reach of the light beam cast by his tiny vessel. At the end of the story, Onodera's status as a powerless witness is confirmed: though he survives the physical perils, he suffers from dementia and struggles to recall who he is. There is no narrative resolution in the first installment of the story, published in two parts in 1973, which ends as Onodera gradually awakes in unfamiliar surroundings. He is being nursed by a young woman whom he does not recognize on a Siberian railway train running, presumably, away from what was once Japan.

By sending the entire Japanese archipelago to the bottom of the Pacific, Komatsu tried to shake his readers out of their complacency and forcefully ask what it meant to be Japanese. The destructive impulse behind *Japan Sinks* resonated with a country in the throes of the oil crisis, thrust into the rough and uncharted waters of international politics. Readers were urged to imagine the physical destruction of their nation as an opportunity to reinvent it. Unmoored from geography and history, national identity appears in a more malleable form. Yet the author was less interested in imagining a new Japan than in exposing the fragility of what postwar Japan had accomplished. The destruction of the homeland that he had witnessed as a teenager in the final phase of the Asia Pacific War colored his view of postwar Japan's economic success and eventually motivated him to write the disaster novel:

> The [Asia Pacific] War was the motive for writing *Japan Sinks*. Although Japan was supposed to perish with the final battle on the mainland and suicide attacks by one hundred million Japanese, it survived because it accepted the defeat. Only twenty years later, Japan successfully reconstructed itself, held the Olympic Games, climbed the steps of high economic growth, and held Expo '70. Japan became a developed nation. I too ran through that maelstrom and benefited from the newfound affluence, but I always felt wary and anxious at the back of my mind. I thought the Japanese people were intoxicated and infatuated with high growth. . . . I began writing the story to make the Japanese, who were unconcerned and happy, face a crisis, albeit fictional, in which they lose their country.[28]

To the author, who had witnessed firsthand the war's devastation, what he experienced in the "maelstrom" of Japan's high-growth era appeared unreal. To register the ephemeral nature of Japan's prosperity, Komatsu thoroughly destroys Japan in his imaginary world. The commercial success of *Japan Sinks* suggests that many in contemporary Japan—from both the war generation and the postwar one—shared Komatsu's sentiment that the material wealth of postwar Japan was perhaps too good to be true.[29]

In 1973, as the Japanese were thrown into the difficult terrain of international politics with little warning, Komatsu's novel gave shape to their fear and anxieties, which powerfully resonated with memories of past destruction. But these were not the only emotions that accompanied the country's unprecedented situation. There was also the sense of an opening. It was exciting to imagine a radically different path for Japan, even though it was terrifying to picture the loss of what the nation had accomplished in recent decades. (Some considered the destruction to be worth it in order to be liberated from the shackles of a regimented, high-consumption lifestyle.) Komatsu's doomsday scenario allowed his readers to exit the contemporary regime of the high-growth economy, even though it failed to offer any concrete image of life outside the current arrangements.[30]

## Legacies of 1972

In closing, we circle back to this book's opening premise that Japan experienced a major paradigmatic shift circa 1972. While the upheavals of 1973 and 1974 forced adjustments on the economic system, they had limited effects on Japanese society as such. The development of mass consumerism began in the 1920s and accelerated during the high-growth era, reaching a critical point in the several years leading up to 1972. The transition at the tail end of this process was so explosive and expansive that Japan morphed into a completely different place. Yet we have failed to register the year 1972 as a turning point in modern Japan's history because there have been few effective ways to measure the impact of this unprecedented transition. No dramatic regime change occurred, as in 1868.[31] Nor did millions die, as in the case of the Asia Pacific War. The transition of 1972 occurred quietly, but the social ramifications were enormous. Endowed with a new self-reflective vision—metavision—individuals redefined their relationship with the material world and the larger society. Even their temporal perception changed. With vague hopes for future revolutionary changes dashed, they were resigned to live in the homogeneous time of mass consumer society.

This book has been an effort to historicize a new self-reflective form of vision by examining the struggles of imaginary male characters and United Red Army members against the socioeconomic conditions of contemporary society. The records of their ardent and yet hopeless battles are valuable materials with which to analyze and illustrate Japan's radical transformation in this period. Their resistance, whether imaginary or real-life, helped give shape to—and make visible—the attendant effects of mass consumerism, including the new visual experience.[32] The cultural heroes and would-be revolutionaries struggled to transcend the deleterious effects and thus restore their masculinity. Their failure on both accounts effectively debunked the myth of autonomous and independent masculine agency.

The heroic narratives of circa 1972 proved to be attractive fodder for media consumers although their impact declined with each iteration. Yet as long as there is discomfort about mass consumerism in Japanese society or elsewhere, the memories of cultural and political resistance in the late 1960s and early 1970s remain relevant. To cast a critical, self-reflective gaze on the socioeconomic arrangements of the contemporary world, one must start by staring back at the narratives' protagonists as they battle the conditions of Japan circa 1972.

# Notes

## Introduction

1. Suntory Group corporate information, http://www.suntory.co.jp/company/history/timeline/ (accessed February 10, 2020).
2. Lyrics, Tōjō Tadayoshi; music and vocals, Kuni Kawachi.
3. Ōki Minoru, *Ōki Minoru zen shishū* (Tokyo: Chōryūsha, 1984), 514.
4. In 1948, for example, Ōki published two free-verse poems under the same title, "Sanrinsha" (A tricycle). In both he laments that he is unable to buy a tricycle for his son and hopes that "when he [grows up and] no longer needs one, he will realize there are so many children who do not have a tricycle." Ōki, *Ōki Minoru zen shishū*, 260–62.
5. Tsubouchi Yūzō, *1972: "Hajimari no owari" to "owari no hajimari"* ("The end of a beginning" and "the beginning of an end") (Tokyo: Bungeishunjū, 2003), posits the year 1972 as a key turning point in postwar Japan's historical consciousness. From his personal interactions with the generations born before and after 1972, Tsubouchi submits there is a generational chasm in terms of their understanding of Japan's history. This chasm stems from the cultural shift that occurred at the tail end of Japan's high growth: "A large-scale cultural transformation began in 1964, peaked in 1968, and completed in 1972. 1972 was 'the end of a beginning' and 'the beginning of an end' for a new era" (13). Tsubouchi, however, offers no explanation as to what caused this transformation. He surveys popular magazines (mostly weeklies and some monthlies) published in 1972 in chronological order, juxtaposing the year's media events with his own personal experiences in the year (he was born in 1958). Throughout the book, Tsubouchi remains close to the ground, so to speak, to recuperate the ambience of the society experiencing the dramatic transformation. In his fascinating

recounting of the period, however, his initial claim of 1972 as a watershed year recedes into the background.

6. In discussing the relationship between war experiences and postwar Japan's work ethic, the sociologist Hazama Hiroshi emphasizes the diverse ways in which Japanese people responded to those memories. Hazama Hiroshi, *Keizai taikoku o tsukuriageta shisō* (Tokyo: Bunshindō, 1996), 13–29.

7. Miyadai Shinji, *Owarinaki nichijō o ikiro: Ōmu kokufuku kanzen manyuaru* (Tokyo: Chikuma shobō, 2018).

8. Female artists were an essential part of the growing manga industry, but the publishing houses that published their works rarely had women on their staffs.

9. Hamano Sachi, *Onna ga eiga o tsukurutoki* (Tokyo: Heibosha, 2005), 16.

10. In the 1970s, Year 24 Group (24 nengumi)—a cluster of female manga artists who were born around Shōwa 24, or 1949—began publishing the works that revolutionized shōjo manga (manga catering to teenage female audience) through their daring themes and aesthetic styles. Some are notable for featuring psychological—often overtly homoerotic—dramas of young male characters. In 1974 Hagio Moto published "Tōma no shinzō" (The heart of Thomas), which features same-sex romance in a boarding school in Germany. Takemiya Keiko serialized "Kaze to ki no uta" (The poem of wind and tree) from 1976 and 1984, which depicts homoerotic relations between two teenage boys. Yamagishi Ryōko casts the revered historical figure Prince Shōtoku as a homosexual male in "Hino izuru tokoro no tenshi" (Prince of the Land of the Rising Sun, 1980–1984).

11. Amano Masako, "Toraianguru (kazoku—gakkō—kigyō) no seiritsu to yuragi," in *Sengo keiken o ikiru*, ed. Amano Masako, Ōkado Masakatsu, and Yasuda Tsuneo (Tokyo: Yoshikawa kōbunkan, 2003), 165.

12. Oguma Eiji, *1968 1: Wakamonotachi no hanran to sono haikei* (Tokyo: Shin'yōsha, 2009) and *1968 2: Hanran no shūen to sono isan* (Tokyo: Shin'yōsha, 2009).

13. Oguma's indifference to culture stems from his highly mechanistic understanding of history, which renders invisible the youths' internal struggles. He insists: "With the landscape and lifestyle rapidly changing and the familiar scenery from their early ages disappearing, this generation felt alienation and discomfort with respect to the entire society" (1:101). This sense of "alienation and discomfort" is, in his estimation, the primary cause of the youth revolt. His *1968* makes sure the reader will not miss this point by repeating it with slight variations: "When they faced the mass consumer society that the high-growth economy realized, the generations that grew up in rural hamlets and urban back alleys felt anxious and tensed up" (1:103). Labeling historical phenomena with terms like "alienation" or "contemporary unhappiness" (*gendaiteki fukō*) reveals little about the complex processes that produced them, while it reduces the participants in these political movements to automata merely reacting to changes in their socioeconomic environment. Their internal struggles become invisible in Oguma's inquiry, which reduces the historical dynamics of the high-growth era to a simple cause-and-effect scheme. With the common culture destroyed, Oguma implies, the youths acted destructively. Oguma replicates the static vision of society that the sociologist Harold Garfinkel criticizes using the term "cultural dope":

a person who "acts in compliance with preestablished and legitimate alternatives of action that the common culture provides." Harold Garfinkel, *Studies in Ethnomethodology* (Englewood Cliffs, N.J.: Prentice-Hall, 1967), 68. For a more detailed critique of Oguma's study, see Yoshikuni Igarashi, "'Ano jidai' no hanran wa wareware ni nani o oshieru noka: Oguma Eiji cho *1968* jō-ge," *Cultures/Critiques*, no. 2 (2010): 129–44.

14. Miryam Sas, *Experimental Arts in Postwar Japan: Moments of Encounter, Engagement, and Imagined Return* (Cambridge, Mass.: Harvard University Asia Center, 2011).
15. Bruce Baird, *Hijikata Tatsumi and Butoh: Dancing in a Pool of Gray Grits* (New York: Palgrave, 2012).
16. William Marotti, *Money, Trains, and Guillotines: Art and Revolution in 1960s Japan* (Durham, N.C.: Duke University Press, 2013).
17. Yuriko Furuhata, *Cinema of Actuality: Japanese Avant-Garde Filmmaking in the Season of Image Politics* (Durham, N.C.: Duke University Press, 2013).
18. Reiko Tomii, *Radicalism in the Wilderness: International Contemporaneity and 1960s Art in Japan* (Cambridge, Mass.: MIT Press, 2016).
19. Other works that focus on avant-garde art in 1960s Japan include Doryun Chong, ed., *Tokyo 1955–1970: A New Avant Garde* (New York: Museum of Modern Art, 2012); Peter Eckersall, *Performativity and Event in 1960s Japan: City, Body, Memory* (New York: Palgrave Macmillan, 2013); Steven C. Ridgely, *Japanese Counterculture: The Antiestablishment Art of Terayama Shūji* (Minneapolis: University of Minnesota Press, 2010); and Maureen Turim, *The Film of Oshima Nagisa: Image of a Japanese Iconoclast* (Berkeley: University of California Press, 1998).
20. Isolde Standish, *Politics, Porn and Protest: Japanese Avant-Garde Cinema in the 1960s and 1970s* (New York: Continuum, 2011).
21. Alexander Zahlten, *The End of Japanese Cinema: Industrial Genres, National Times, and Media Ecologies* (Durham, N.C.: Duke University Press, 2017).
22. Nagai Katsuichi, *"Garo" henshūchō* (Tokyo: Chikuma shobō, 1987), 293.
23. Kaikō's novel *Natsu no yami* (Tokyo: Shinchōsha, 1972) went through ten printings in less than two years after the original publication. According to the National Diet Library catalog, this novel has been issued in at least nine different formats and anthologized in several other collections.
24. For more detailed discussion on this topic, see Yoshikuni Igarashi, *Bodies of Memory: Narratives of War in Postwar Japanese Culture, 1945–1970* (Princeton, N.J.: Princeton University Press, 2000).
25. Yamamoto Akira, *Sengo fūzokushi* (Osaka: Osaka shoseki, 1986), 111.
26. Many more American television programs were aired in Japan. The following is a partial list of such shows aired in the early years of Japanese television: *77 Sunset Strip* (1960–1963), *87th Precinct* (1962–1963), *The Adventures of Rin Tin Tin* (1956–1960), *Alfred Hitchcock Presents* (1957–1963), *The Alfred Hitchcock Hour* (1962–1963), *Annie Get Your Gun* (1957), *Ben Casey* (1962–1965), *Bronco* (1961–1962), *Combat!* (1962–1967), *Cowboy G-men* (1956), *The Donna Reed Show* (1959–1963), *Father Knows Best* (1958–1964), *The Fugitive* (1964–1967), *Gunsmoke* (1959–1962?), *Heckle and Jeckle* (1957–1958), *Highway Patrol* (1956–1960), *I Love Lucy* (1957–1960), *Laramie* (1960–1963), *Lassie* (1957–1966),

*The Mickey Rooney Show* (1957–?), *Lone Ranger* (1958–1959), *Perry Mason* (1957–1966), *Rawhide* (1959–1965), *Sheriff of Cochise / U.S. Marshal* (1958–1961), *Route 66* (1963), *Superman* (1956–1960), *The Untouchables* (1959–1963), *The Twilight Zone* (1961–1967), *Wanted Dead or Alive* (1959–1961, 1966). Nishii Kazuo, ed., *Sengo 50 nen* (Tokyo: Mainichi shinbunsha, 1995), 175–78; Iyota Yasuhiro et al., eds., *Terebishi hando bukku* (Tokyo: Jiyūkokuminsha, 1996).

27. Kōno Hiromi. "Kōno Hiromi (35 sai)," in *Jinsei dokuhon terebi* (Tokyo: Kawade shobō-shinsha, 1983), 213.
28. The historian Arima Tetsuo offers a detailed account of Shōriki's close and clandestine relations with the CIA in *Nippon Terebi to CIA: Hakkutsu sareta "Shōriki fairu"* (Tokyo: Shinchōsha, 2006).
29. Kunihiro Yōko, "Dankai no sedai: Terebi to seichō o tomonishi, oini mukau," in *Terebi to iu kioku: Terebi shichō no shakaishi*, ed. Hagiwara Shigeru (Tokyo: Shin'yōsha, 2103), 88–92.
30. Jayson Makoto Chun, *"A Nation of a Hundred Million Idiots"? A Social History of Japanese Television, 1953–1973* (New York: Routledge, 2007), 258, 264.
31. For example, Yoshimi Shunya locates "techno-nationalistic sentiments" in ad campaigns run by Japanese appliance companies in the 1960s. Yoshimi Shunya, "Consuming America, Producing Japan," in *The Ambivalent Consumer: Questioning Consumption in East Asia and the West*, ed. Sheldon Gardon and Patricia L. Maclachalan (Ithaca, N.Y.: Cornell University Press, 2006), 80.
32. Yamamoto, *Sengo fūzokushi*, 180–81.

# 1. Reflections on the Consuming Subject: The High-Growth Economy and the Emergence of a New National Community

1. Satō's grandnephew, Abe Shinzō, became the longest-serving prime minster on November 20, 2019, during his second tenure. He broke Satō's single-tenure record on August 24, 2020.
2. "Naite, waratte, okotte: Saru Satō san 'ato' o nigosu," *Mainichi shinbun*, June 17, 1972, evening 4th ed.
3. Satō's retirement announcement is printed in its entirety on the front page of the *Asahi shinbun*, June 17, 1972, evening 3rd ed.
4. Satō's approval rating steadily dropped to the mid-20s by the end of his second year in office but soon recovered to the high 30s and remained at around 40 until a year before his retirement. *Asahi shinbun*, December 8, 1974, 13th ed.
5. *Asahi shinbun*, August 19, 1965, evening 3rd ed.
6. "Naite, waratte, okotte." See also Nishii Kazuo, ed., *Rengōsekigun: "Ōkami" tachi no jidai, 1969–1975*, Shiriizu 20 seiki no kioku (Tokyo: Mainichi shinbunsha, 1999), 222.
7. Nishii, *Rengōsekigun*, 222.

8. In 1968, for example, several LDP members pressured the popular television news anchor Den Hideo (1923–2009) to resign because of his alleged anti-U.S. stance. Den claimed that he quit in protest against LDP's political intervention. Ogimoto Haruhiko, Muraki Yoshihiko, and Konno Tsutomu, *Omae wa tadano genzai ni suginai: Terebi ni naniga kanōka* (Tokyo: Asahi shinbun shuppan, 2008), 209–10.
9. Matsumoto Hideo, "Sasebo jiken to terebi hōdō," *Gendai no riron* (April 1968): 115.
10. Satō's assessment was right, though the print media sympathetically covered the protest as well. For the details of this event, see William Marotti, "Japan 1968: The Performance of Violence and the Theater of Protest," *American Historical Review* 114, no. 1 (February 2009): 112–28.
11. Ōsaka Iwao, "Nihon ni okeru tere porittekusu no tenkai," *Sekai* 956 (December 2003): 194–95.
12. One can find eight of those commentators in "Shinbun kisha wa deteike!" *Shūkan asahi*, June 30, 1972, 15–20.
13. The president of Nippon Television, Shōriki Matsutarō, placed 220 receivers at fifty-five locations. Iyota Yasuhiro et al., *Terebi shi handobukku* (Tokyo: Jiyūkokuminsha, 1996), 14.
14. Even between the wars, the Japanese government allocated large portions of the national budget for the expansion and maintenance of its military forces. For annual military budgets from 1875 to 1945, see "Tōkei shiryō: gunji hi," available at Teikoku-shoin's website, https://www.teikokushoin.co.jp/statistics/history_civics/index05.html (accessed April 2, 2020).
15. As scholars have rightly insisted, however, the economic disparity between the populations inside and outside the circle never disappeared, even at the height of Japan's economic glory in the 1970s and 1980s. As we will see in this chapter, wage differentials persisted between big and small businesses in postwar Japan. Workers in small business worked longer hours in more hazardous conditions for lower wages. Hashimoto Kenji, *Kakusa no sengoshi* (Tokyo: Kawade shobō-shinsha, 2009), 145. If figure 1.3 could be rendered three-dimensionally, the center part would bulge slightly, like the surface of a cathode-ray tube, to represent the persistent social stratification: the closer to the center, the higher one's socioeconomic status. The economic disadvantages of some received little attention amid the excitement of the nation's drastic transformation; the bulge grew less pronounced as Japan's economy rapidly expanded, but inequality remained a fundamental attribute of Japanese society.
16. Kase Kazutoshi, "Nōson to chiiki no henbō," in *Sengo Nihon ron*, Nihonshi kōza 10, ed. Rekishigaku kenkyūkai and Nihonshi kenkyūkai (Tokyo: Tokyo Daigaku Shuppankai, 2005).
17. Noguchi Yukio, *Sengo keizaishi: Watashitachi wa dokode machigaeta noka* (Tokyo: Tōyō Keizai Shinpōsha, 2015), 105.
18. Iino Ryūichi, *Sengo Nihon nōgyōshi* (Tokyo: Shinnihon shuppansha, 1996), 35.
19. Noguchi Yukio, *Shinpan 1940 nen taisei* (Tokyo: Toyō Keizai Shinpōsha, 2002), 67–69.
20. Noguchi, *Sengo keizaishi*, 44–45.
21. Bureau of Statistics, Office of Prime Minister, *Japan Statistical Yearbook 1972* (Tokyo: Japan Statistical Association, 1972), 491; *Japan Statistical Yearbook 1975*, 489.

22. In relation to the 2005 consumer price index, the 1958 and 1973 figures were 18.2 and 40.7, respectively. Cabinet Office, Government of Japan, *Heisei 24 nendo nenji keizaizaisei hōkoku*, "Chōki keizai tōkei mokuji," http://www5.cao.go.jp/j-j/wp/wp-je12/h10_data05.html (accessed November 27, 2017).
23. Teranishi Jūrō, *Nihon no keizai shisutemu* (Tokyo: Iwanami shoten, 2003), 136.
24. Hashimoto Kenji sets the poverty line at 50 percent of the median household equivalent income (total household income divided by the square root of the number of household members). Hashimoto, *Kakusa no sengoshi*, 108, 122, 143. Wada Yumiko and Kimura Mitsuhiko suggest a more dramatic drop in postwar Japan's poverty level. According to their study, the proportion of households below the poverty line was as high was 30 percent but decreased to 17 percent in 1960, 5 percent in 1965, and 1 percent in 1970. Asai Yoshio, "Gendai shihonshugi to kōdoseichō," in *Sengo Nihon ron*, Nihonshi kōza 10, ed. Rekishigaku kenkyūkai and Nihonshi kenkyūkai (Tokyo: Tokyo daigaku shuppankai, 2005), 203.
25. The economist Tachibanaki Toshiaki observes that Marxist economics was a mainstream academic discipline at Japan's top universities until the 1970s. It was therefore common for graduates trained in Marxist economics to become corporate executives or senior government officials. Tachibanaki submits that their academic background gave them an egalitarian outlook. Tachibanaki Toshiaki, "Marukei to kinkei: Kaikyū masatsu herashita 'mujun' no jinzai ikusei," *Asahi shinbun*, August 1, 2006, evening ed.
26. Domestic models of washers and refrigerators were introduced into the Japanese market in 1930 and 1933, respectively, but they were prohibitively expensive for most families. Yamaguchi Masatomo, "Dōgu," in *Kōdo seichō to Nihonjin* 2, ed. Kōdo keizaiseichō o kangaeru kai (Tokyo: Niho editaasukūru shuppanbu, 1985), 71–72.
27. Watanabe Osamu, "Kōdoseichō to kigyōshakai," in *Kōdoseichō to kigyōshakai*, ed. Watanabe Osamu (Tokyo: Yoshikawa kōbunkan, 2004), 107; Kase, "Nōson to chiiki no henbō," 240.
28. Ino, *Sengo Nihon nōgyōshi*, 33, 56, 125.
29. Kase, "Nōson to chiiki no henbō," 238. Mechanization also added to the overall cost of farm production. Simon Partner succinctly characterizes the issue: "The cost of machinery was almost always greater than the labor saved on the tiny average farm, and the more sophisticated the machinery adopted, the more pronounced this trend became." Simon Partner, "Brightening Country Lives: Selling Electrical Goods in the Japanese Countryside, 1950–1970," *Enterprise & Society* 1, no. 4 (December 2000): 781.
30. Kase, "Nōson to chiiki no henbō," 101. From 1960 to 1967 the official price of rice rose at an average rate of 9.5 percent annually. Sekizawa Mayumi, "Kōdo keizaiseichō to chiikishakai," in *Kōdo keizaiseichō to seikatsu kakumei*, ed. Kokuritsu rekishi minzoku hakubutsukan (Tokyo: Yoshikawa kōbunkan, 2010), 43.
31. Watanabe, "Kōdoseichō to kigyōshakai," 65–66, 106.
32. Kase Kazutoshi, "Kōdo keizai seichō no shojōken to nōgyōbumon no ichi," in *Kōdo keizai seichō to seikatsu kakumei*, ed. Kokuritsu rekishi minzoku hakubutsukan (Tokyo: Yoshikawa kōbunkan, 2010), 99–100.

33. Ino, *Sengo Nihon nōgyōshi*, 448.
34. Ino, *Sengo Nihon nōgyōshi*, 146–47.
35. Watanabe Osamu lists three specific disincentives: the lack of social welfare, the lack of steady employment, and the rise of land values. Watanabe, "Kōdoseichō to kigyōshakai," 106.
36. Sekizawa, "Kōdo keizai seichō-ki to chiikishakai," 43.
37. Uchiyama Takashi, *Nihonjin wa naze kitsune ni damasarenaku nattanoka* (Tokyo: Kōdansha, 2007), 11–12.
38. Uchiyama suggests seven reasons for the demise of foxes' magical power: (1) changing lifestyles under the high-growth economy; (2) more scientific thinking; (3) improved communications; (4) higher education; (5) changing views about death; (6) changing relations with nature; and (7) loss of foxes' magical power (as human activities heavily affected their habitat). Uchiyama, *Nihonjin wa naze kitsune ni damasarenaku nattanoka*, 34–70.
39. Hazama Hiroshi, *Keizai taikoku o tsukuri ageta shisō* (Tokyo: Bunshindō, 1996), 61–62.
40. Hazama, *Keizai taikoku o tsukuri ageta shisō*, 113–14.
41. Ishikawa Akihiro, "Misekake no chūryū ishiki," in *Hirogaru chūryū ishiki, 1971–1985*, Riidingusu Sengo Nihon no Kakusa to fubyōdō 2, ed. Hara Junsuke (Tokyo: Nihon toshosentaa, 2008), 143. In prewar and wartime Japanese corporations, blue-collar workers were even treated with suspicion. They could be subjected to frisking or searches of their personal items, practices from which white-collar workers were exempted. Hashimoto, *Kakusa no sengoshi*, 86.
42. Ishikawa, "Misekake no chūryū ishiki," 144. In his case study of Nippon Kōkan, Andrew Gordon documents the union's strong early postwar interest in discrimination against blue-collar workers. Andrew Gordon, *The Wages of Affluence: Labor and Management in Postwar Japan* (Cambridge, Mass.: Harvard University Press, 1998), 27–29.
43. Hazama, *Keizai taikoku o tsukuri ageta shisō*, 57, 184.
44. Teranishi, *Nihon no keizai shisutemu*, 237; Gordon, *The Wages of Affluence*, 34–35.
45. Gordon reminds us that corporations did not adopt new titles solely out of altruism: more than two-fifths of Japanese businesses made the shift in the first seven years of the 1960s "to combine the nominal equality of a single status, sought by workers, with more rigorous programs, sought by managers, to differentiate employees by ability." Gordon, *The Wages of Affluence*, 162.
46. Ishikawa, "Misekake no chūryū ishiki," 144.
47. Endō Kōshi, "Rōdōkumiai to minshushugi," in *Sengo minshushugi*, ed. Nakamura Masanori et al. (Tokyo: Iwanami shoten, 1995), 68.
48. Hazama, *Keizai taikoku o tsukuri ageta shisō*, 113.
49. Watanabe, "Kōdoseichō to kigyōshakai," 55–56.
50. Japan had low official unemployment rates also in the 1950s, but many people were actually underemployed or discouraged from seeking employment. The agricultural sector absorbed a large labor force that might otherwise have been unemployed. As a result, the wage level in agriculture was depressed. Hashimoto Kenji, "Gekihensuru shakai no tayōna shūgyōkōzō," in *Kazokuto kakusa no sengoshi*, ed. Hashimoto Kenji (Tokyo: Seikyūsha, 2010), 54–55.

51. Asai, "Gendai shihonshugi to kōdoseichō," 211.
52. A minimum wage was legislated for the first time in 1959. See http://www.japaneselawtranslation.go.jp/law/detail/?id=2420&vm=04&re=02 (accessed August 1, 2020).
53. Asai, "Gendai shihonshugi to kōdoseichō," 212. Foreign residents were not eligible for the benefits. Tessa Morris-Suzuki, *Exodus to North Korea: Shadows from Japan's Cold War* (Lanham, Md: Rowman & Littlefield, 2007), 67.
54. Endō, "Rōdōkumiai to minshushugi," 71–72; Morris-Suzuki, *Exodus to North Korea*, 67; Kikuchi Yoshiaki, *Kitachōsen kikoku jigyō: Sōdaina rachi ka tsuihō ka* (Tokyo: Chūōkōron, 2009), 150.
55. Some neighborhoods have been traditional homes for Burakumin communities, and individuals' connections with them are easily traceable through the family registry (*koseki*). The personal information on the family registry remained publicly accessible until 1976. Christopher Bondy, *Voice, Silence, and Self: Negotiations of Buraku Identity in Contemporary Japan* (Cambridge, Mass.: Harvard University Asia Center, 2015), 20–21.
56. When the manga artist Satō Masa'aki (1937–2004) searched for a job in the final year of junior high school (the ninth grade), he found that one of the standard requirements for potential employees was that "both parents must be in good health." He angrily reacted to his discovery: "This one line badly hurt my fragile ego. Having lost my father when I was in the first grade, and mother in the eighth grade, I was not able to attend high school and was even denied job opportunities. I hated the society that discriminated against me just because I did not have parents." Satō Masa'aki, *Gekiga shishi 30 nen* (Moroyamamachi, Saitama: Tōkōsha, 1984), cited in Kashihon manga kenkyūkai, ed., *Kashihon manga returns* (Tokyo: Popurasha, 2006), 106.
57. Endō, "Rōdōkumiai to minshushugi," 70–72.
58. The International Committee of the Red Cross, the Japanese and North Korean governments, the General Association of Korean Residents, and the Japan-Korea Association collaborated on the project to "repatriate" Korean residents and their Japanese spouses to North Korea. The first repatriation ship left for North Korea in December 1959, carrying 957 people. Although the active phase ended around 1962, the project lasted until 1984. During the twenty-five years, 93,339 people, including 6,679 Japanese citizens, "returned" to North Korea. Lee Young-Chea, "Sengo Nicchō kankei no shoki keiseikatei no bunseki: Zainichi Chōsenjin kikoku undō no tenkaikatei o chūshin ni," *Ritsumeikan hōgaku*, no. 333 and 334 (2010): 33–34. The LDP supported the repatriation project, believing that it was the most cost-effective way to deal with the Resident Korean communities that suffered from high crime rates and economic malady. Morris-Suzuki, *Exodus to North Korea*, 152. The major Japanese dailies supported the Japanese government's decision as a humanitarian action. Kikuchi, *Kitachōsen kikoku jigyō*, 107.
59. Simon Partner, *Assembled in Japan* (Berkeley: University of California Press, 1999), 207–19, 221–24.

60. "Ūman ribu mo taji taji 'joshi jakunen teinen-sei' no kabe," *Shūkan asahi*, March 24, 1972, 115–16.
61. Andrew Gordon, "Managing the Japanese Household: The New Life Movement in Postwar Japan," *Social Politics* 4–2 (Summer 1997): 260–61; Andrew Gordon, "Nihon katei keieihō: Sengo Nihon ni okeru 'Shin seikatsu undō,'" in *Sengo to iu chiseigaku*, ed. Nishikawa Yūko (Tokyo: Tokyo daigaku shuppankai, 2006), 103–18.
62. Miura Atsushi, *Kazoku to kōfuku no sengoshi: Kōgai no yume to genjitsu* (Tokyo: Kōdansha, 1999), 128.
63. Amano Masako, "Sōron: Otoko de arukoto no sengoshi," in *Otoko rashisa no gendaishi*, Danseishi 3, ed. Abe Tsunehisa, Amano Masako, and Obinata Sumio (Tokyo: Nihon keizai hyōronsha, 2006), 17.
64. Amano Masako, "Torai anguru (kazoku–gakkō–kigyō) no seiritsu to yuragi," in *Sengo keiken o ikiru*, ed. Amano Masako, Ōkado Masakatsu, and Yasuda Tsuneo (Tokyo: Yoshikawa kōbunkan, 2003), 165.
65. The sociologist Ochiai Emiko lists three historical conditions that created what she calls the "Postwar Family System," which became widely accepted as a social norm in postwar Japan. First, a large portion of women became housewives. This was an outcome of the fact that more women chose to marry white-collar workers. Second, the majority of women had two to three children. Finally, postwar families were supported by the transitional generation. In the process of shifting from a high birthrate/high mortality situation to a low birthrate/low mortality one, Japanese society experienced a transitional phase of high birthrate/low mortality. The generation that grew up in this transitional period had more surviving siblings than other generations, and their siblings became the basis of a familial support network. Ochiai Emiko, *The Japanese Family System in Transition: A Sociological Analysis of Family Change in Postwar Japan* (Tokyo: LTCB International Library Foundation, 1997), 9–72.
66. The ratio of female temporary and daily employees steadily increased after the early 1970s, reaching 21 percent in 2000.
67. Yoshimi Shunya, "Terebi o dakishimeru sengo," in *Taishū bunka to media*, ed. Yoshimi Shunya and Tsuchiya Reiko (Kyoto: Mineruba shobō, 2010), 186–87.
68. In 1955, on average, food and beverages accounted for 46.9 percent of household living expenditures. The percentage dropped to 41.6 in five years. See Statistics Bureau of Japan, "Issetai atari nen heikin ikkagetsu no shishitsu (zensetai): zentoshi (Showa 21–37)," https://warp.da.ndl.go.jp/info:ndljp/pid/2931932/www.stat.go.jp/data/chouki/20.htm (accessed August 1, 2020).
69. Statistics Bureau of Japan, "Tatami-sū oyobi hitori Atari tatami-sū," http://www.e-stat.go.jp/SG1/estat/GL08020103.do?_toGL08020103_&tclassID=000001027434&cycleCode=0&requestSender=search (accessed April 2, 2020).
70. Kokumin seikatsu kenkyūjo, *Shōwa 42 nendo-ban: kokumin seikatsu tōkei nenpō* (Tokyo: Shiseidō, 1967), 134–35.
71. Kase, "Nōson to chiiki no henbō," 241.
72. Satō Takumi, *Terebi teki kyōyō: Ichioku sō hakuchika eno keifu* (Tokyo: NTT shuppan, 2008), 137.

73. Sano Shin'ichi, *Karisuma: Nakauchi Isao to Daiei no sengo* (Tokyo: Nikkei BP-sha, 1998), 318, 418.
74. Nakauchi Isao, *Waga yasu'uri tetsugaku* (Tokyo: Nihon keizai-shinbunsha, 1969).
75. The set was sold for ¥59,800 under Daiei's own private label, Bubu. Other companies' products were priced at ¥99,800. Tateishi Yasunori, *Matsushita Kōnosuke no Shōwa-shi* (Tokyo: Nanatsumori shokan, 2011), 231. Consumers, however, did not leap to acquire these products because it was not clear how long production and product support would continue. Sano, *Karisuma*, 409–10. As Sano notes, it was extremely ironic that Daiei began selling the television sets on November 25, the day Mishima Yukio killed himself in protest against the spiritually unresponsive state of Japan under conditions of economic prosperity. Mishima lamented in his manifesto: "We have witnessed postwar Japan becoming infatuated with economic prosperity, forgetting about the nation's essential values, losing the national spirit, fixating on trivialities without rectifying the foundation, resorting to stopgap measures and deception, and falling into a spiritual vacuum." Mishima Yukio, *Mishima Yukio zenshū 36* (Tokyo: Shinchōsha, 2003), 402.
76. "Daiei no mise wa shōhisha no 'kaihōku' ya," *Shūkan asahi*, October 27, 1972, 27–28.
77. By contrast, the Seibu department store met new consumer needs by first establishing small-scale department stores and then the Seiyū supermarket chain. Yui Tsunehiko, Yanagisawa Asobu, and Tatsuki Mariko, *Sezon no rekishi* 1 (Tokyo: Libro Port, 1991), 134–42, 379–404.
78. Noriko Aso provides a concise and insightful history of the Mitsukoshi department store from its inception to the end of the Asia Pacific War in *Public Properties: Museums in Imperial Japan* (Durham, N.C.: Duke University Press, 2014), 169–202.
79. Jinno Yuki, *Shumi no tanjō* (Tokyo: Keisōshobō, 1994), 7.
80. Nakauchi casts his business persona as supermasculine against the "naked girls" on display and effeminate Kabuki actors, who impersonate female characters on the stage. Nakauchi, *Waga yasu'uri tetsugaku*, 97.
81. Kagaku gijutsu chō shigen chōsa kai, "Shokuseikatsu no taikeiteki kaizen ni shisuru shokuryō ryūtsūtaikei no kindaika ni kansuru kankoku," in *Kōrudo chein chōsa hōkoku kenkyū taisei* 1, ed. Science and Technology Agency (Tokyo: Sōwa shuppan, 1976), 1–189.
82. "Tonai ni 15 ten ga kimaru," *Asahi shinbun*, August 13, 1966, 13th ed.
83. "1 gatsu kara Kantō de jisshi," *Asashi shinbun*, December 23, 1970, 12th ed. It appears that Nakauchi was initially not too enthusiastic about cold chains: he expresses his distaste for frozen food in his book *Waga yasu'uri tetsugaku* (1969), 192.
84. Endō Tetsuo, *Taishū meshi gekidō no sengoshi: Ii mono kutterya shiawaseka?* (Tokyo: Chikuma shobō, 2013), 42.
85. The first frozen food—frozen strawberries—had appeared in the Japanese market in 1930, coinciding with the rise of consumer society in the prewar period. *Asahi shinbun*, November 2, 2016, evening 3rd ed.
86. "Gakkō kihon chōsa, nenji tōkei: Singakuritsu," https://www.e-stat.go.jp/stat-search/files?page=1&query=%E9%80%B2%E5%AD%A6%E7%8E%87&layout=dataset (accessed August 1, 2020).

87. For example, between 1961 and 1970 the number of students in science and engineering at four-year institutions grew from 118,443 to 344,150 (a 191 percent increase), while the total figure in the humanities and social sciences combined increased from 451,161 to 912,905 (a 102 percent increase). *Japan Statistical Yearbook 1962*, 466; *Japan Statistical Yearbook 1972*, 555.
88. Bureau of Statistics, Office of Prime Minister, *Japan Statistical Yearbook 1975*, 556.
89. Takano Etsuko, *Nijussai no genten: Joshō* (Tokyo: Shinchōsha, 1979), 23, 32, 39. Takano Etsuko committed suicide at age twenty. Her diaries were posthumously published in three volumes and became national bestsellers.
90. Daigaku hakusho sakusei shōiinkai, *Ritsumeikan daigaku kyōgaku hakusho* (Kyoto: Ritsumeikan Daigaku kokkofutan ni kansuru iinkai, 1973), 38, 35, 32–33. The actual number of students at Ritsumeikan was about 15 percent higher than the official figure. Adjusted, the actual campus-wide student-faculty ratio was as high as 79.6 to 1. The figures for the Economics and Literature Departments are based on the number of registered students.
91. Takano, *Nijussai no genten*, 63.
92. Hamashima Akira, "Chūryū ishiki no kōzō to dōtai," in *Hirogaru chūryū ishiki, 1971–1985*, Riidingusu Sengo Nihon no kakusa to fubyōdō 2, ed. Hara Junsuke (Tokyo: Nihon toshosentaa, 2008), 166. It has been argued that this trend carries little significance since similar results have been reported in other countries. An international study that used the same question format found that 93.8 percent of U.S. subjects claimed they belonged to the middle stratum, as did 89.4 percent in South Korea, 94.3 percent in Singapore, 92.6 percent in the Philippines, 86.1 percent in Italy, and 91.2 percent in India. Hashimoto, *Kakusa no sengoshi*, 139. Japan should certainly not be exceptionalized, but the changes observed there over the eighteen years during the high-growth era deserve attention.
93. Murakami Yasusuke, "Shin chūkankaisō no genjitsusei," *Asahi shinbun*, May 20, 1977, evening 3rd ed.
94. Murakami, "Shin chūkankaisō no genjitsusei."
95. Tada Michitarō, "The Glory and Misery of My Home," in *Authority and the Individual in Japan: Citizen Protest in Historical Perspective*, ed. J. Victor Koschmann (Tokyo: University of Tokyo Press, 1978), 212. Tada's essay appeared originally in Japanese in 1971.
96. Aoki Toshiya, *Saigen Shōwa 30 nendai: Danchi 2DK no kurashi* (Tokyo: Kawade shobō-shinsha, 2001), 24.
97. Murakami, "Shin chūkankaisō no genjitsusei."
98. Kishimoto Shigenobu, "Shin chūkankaisō-ron wa kanōka," *Asahi shinbun*, June 9, 1977, evening 3rd ed.; Kishimoto Shigenobu, *Chūryū no gensō*, excerpted in Hara Junsuke, *Hirogaru chūryū ishiki, 1971–1985*, 138.
99. Tominaga Ken'ichi, "Shakai kaisōkōzō no genjō," *Asahi shinbun*, June 27, 1977, evening 3rd ed.
100. Mamada Takao, quoted in Tominaga Ken'ichi, *Nihon no kindaika to shakai hendō* (Tokyo: Kōdansha, 1990), 251–52.
101. Sudo Naoki, *Nihonjin no kaisō ishiki* (Tokyo: Kōdansha, 2010), 184, 186.

## 2. Circular Vision: The Metavisuality of Television

1. Benedict Anderson, *Imagined Communities* (London: Verso, 2006), 36.
2. People in the film industry called television "electric *kamishibai*." *Kamishibai* is a form of street-corner entertainment for children in which men use picture panels to narrate stories as a way to sell cheap confections. The implication is that television programs, being cheaply made, are not worthy of serious adult attention. Kitamura Mitsufumi, *Terebi wa Nihonjin o "baka" ni shitaka?* (Tokyo: Heibonsha, 2007), 55–56.
3. The University of Tokyo student, Kanba Michiko, died in a disturbance outside the National Diet building on June 15, 1960. Although police violence was strongly suspected to be the cause of her death, the medical examination was inconclusive. Esashi Akiko, *Kanba Michiko: Seishōjo densetsu* (Tokyo: Bungeishunjū, 2010), 224–40.
4. Quoted in Tsuji Ichirō, *Watashi dake no hōsōshi* (Tokyo: Seiryūshuppan, 2008), 253–54.
5. Esashi, *Kanba Michiko*, 219.
6. In May 1960 the price for a 14-inch television ranged from ¥56,500 to ¥62,000 (see table 1.1), while the average monthly farm household income for fiscal year 1959 (from April 1, 1959, to March 31, 1960) was ¥44,813. Bureau of Statistics, *Japan Statistical Yearbook 1962*, 106.
7. Miyamoto Tsuneichi, *Miyamoto Tsuneichi Chosakushū* 2 (Tokyo: Miraisha, 1967), 200.
8. Miyamoto, *Miyamoto Tsuneichi Chosakushū* 2, 199–200.
9. Miyamoto, *Miyamoto Tsuneichi Chosakushū* 2, 196.
10. For example, popular scriptwriter Hashida Sugako (b. 1925) wrote that she often received letters claiming that her television dramas were based on the viewers' family situations and asking how she learned about them. Hashida Sugako, "Hōmu dorama no ennoshita," in *Jinsei dokuhon: Terebi* (Tokyo: Kawade shobō-shinsha, 1983), 188.
11. Koyama Ken'ichi, "Yama no bunkō no kiroku," *Hōsō bunka* 15, no. 6 (June 1960): 54.
12. In the evening the television was made available for community viewing. NHK Aakaibusu bangumi purojekuto, *Yamano bunkō no kiroku* (Tokyo: Futabasha, 2004), 42.
13. Test scores improved for Japanese and science, while there were no significant changes in math and social studies. Koyama, "Yama no bunkō no kiroku," 57–58.
14. This part is not included in the abridged version, which is available at http://www.nhk.or.jp/school/yamanobunkou/ (accessed August 2, 2020). This episode about the kitchen update is found in the printed descriptions of the program. Koyama, "Yama no bunkō no kiroku," 55.
15. *Dawn Over the Mountains* exemplifies the didactic perspective by highlighting television's educational effects on the Dorobu children. The narrator, for example, initially describes them in uncomplimentary terms: they are "always timid and show no enthusiasm in doing anything"; "there are many children who can pay attention only for a

short time and show no response to what the teachers say." Images of bored-looking children accompany the voiceover. After the introduction of the television, the narration takes a more positive tone: "The children's eyes became more lively." "Their pictures used to be dark, but they now use more bright colors. There are some that show more originality, like this one."

16. NHK Aakaibusu bangumi purojekuto, *Yamano bunkō no kiroku*, 49–50, 61–67.
17. For example, in 1960 the Ministry of Education provided financial assistance for 208 elementary schools and 92 middle schools in remote regions to acquire a television set. Ōta Shizuki, "Hekichi no terebi chōsa," *Hōsō kyōiku kirokushū* 7 (1961): 85.
18. A number of accounts in *Jinsei dokuhon: Terebi* (Tokyo: Kawade shobō-shinsha, 1983) describe the writers' emotional encounters with television. See, for example, the contributions of Fujita Hideko, 42–43; Nankō Shigenobu, 48–49; Katayama Yasuo, 50–51; Obara Sayoko, 212–13; Kōno Hiromi, 213–14.
19. Fatimah Tobing Rony, *The Third Eye: Race, Cinema, and Ethnographic Spectacle* (Durham, N.C.: Duke University Press, 1996), 4.
20. Television resembles Bentham's panopticon as discussed by Michel Foucault in *Discipline and Punish* in that some early viewers assumed the other's gaze through it, but it differs from the eighteenth-century invention in many other aspects. For example, the gaze that these early television viewers experienced was less disciplinary than emotional, as shown by the cases cited in this chapter. Michel Foucault, *Discipline and Punish: The Birth of the Prison* (New York: Vintage Books, 1979), 200–228. Tony Bennett's discussion of exhibitionary space, in which he tries to historicize the Foucaultian panoptic theory, is better suited to cultural analysis of television viewing. Bennett explains the dynamic of seeing and being seen: "The exhibitionary complex [namely, museums, expositions, and department stores in the nineteenth century] . . . perfected a self-monitoring system of looks in which the subject and object positions can be exchanged, in which the crowd comes to commune with and regulate itself through interiorizing the ideal and ordered view of itself as seen from the controlling vision of power—a site of sight accessible to all." Tony Bennett, *The Birth of the Museum: History, Theory, Politics* (New York: Routledge, 1995), 69. The twentieth-century technological development realized such "a site of sight accessible to all" in living rooms, further complicating the relationship between the subject and object of the gaze.
21. Tsuchiya Yuka, "Senryōki no CIE eiga (Natoko eiga)," in *Fumikoeru dokyumentarii*, Nihon eiga wa ikiteiru 7, ed. Kurosawa Kiyoshi, Yoshimi Shunya, Yomota Inuhiko, and Lee Bong-ou (Tokyo: Iwanami shoten, 2010), 155–56.
22. There were 7,067 movie theaters in Japan in 1958, with a total of 1.127 billion tickets sold for the year. Bureau of Statistics, *Japan Statistical Yearbook 1962*, 479.
23. First-run theaters typically showed imported films as single features, while Japanese features were combined with a shorter film to be shown as double features.
24. NHK hōsōbunka kenkyūjo, *Terebi shichō no 50 nen* (Tokyo: Nihon hōsō shuppan kyōkai, 2001), 142.
25. Konno Tsutomu, "Terebiteki shisō towa nanika," *Eiga hyōron* 24, no. 3 (1967): 44.
26. NHK Aakaibusu bangumi purojekuto, *Yamano bunkō no kiroku*, 59.

27. Poem by Watanabe Tokiko quoted in NHK Aakaibusu bangumi purojekuto, *Yamano bunkō no kiroku*, 57–59.
28. Amarume-machi merged with Tachikawa-machi, thereby creating the larger municipality, Shōnai-machi, in July 2005. Shōnai-machi, "Shōnai-machi no rekishi," https://www.town.shonai.lg.jp/gyousei/gaiyou/tyouseiyouran/rekishi.html (accessed January 31, 2020).
29. Miyamoto, *Miyamoto Tsuneichi Chosakushū* 2, 196–97.
30. The film also references a typical danchi apartment in a concrete building. Satō Dai and Hayami Kenrō argue that *Good Morning* is an homage to Jacques Tati's *Mon Oncle* (1958). Ōyama Ken, Satō Dai, and Hayami Kenrō, *Danchi dan* (Tokyo: Kinemajunpōsha, 2012), 186–87.
31. This mistake was a common occurrence in actual danchi. The literary critic Akiyama Shun, for example, recalls a similar episode involving his neighbor's relative. Hara Takeshi and Akiyama Shun, "Danchi to bungaku," *Gunzō* (November 2008): 142.
32. As if to underline the sense of threat, a high-pressure salesman with an unkempt appearance goes around the neighborhood, visiting homes and trying to intimidate housewives into buying his shoddy merchandise. Right after he makes his rounds, his accomplice makes another pass through the neighborhood selling security buzzers. The team preys on the middle-class families' sense of vulnerability.
33. For more detailed discussions of Ōya's warning, particularly the historical context from which it emerged, see Satō Takumi, *Terebi teki kyōyō* (Tokyo: NTT Shuppan, 2008), 109–15, and Jayson Makoto Chun, *"A Nation of a Hundred Million Idiots"? A Social History of Japanese Television, 1953–1973* (New York: Routledge, 2007), 160–68. *Ichioku sō hakuchika* was one of the most popular phrases of 1957. Kitamura Mitsufumi traces the genealogy of Ōya's phrase, noting that the media's focus on television became clearer over several years in the mid-1950s. Kitamura, *Terebi wa Nihonjin o "baka" ni shitaka?* 35, 80–122.
34. In 1959 a 14-inch set, which the Hayashis eventually purchase, cost more than one and a half times as much as the average monthly household income of urban working households (see table 1.1).
35. Shintani Takanori, "Denki sentakuki no kioku," in Kokuritsu rekishi minzoku hakubutsukan, *Kōdo keizai seichō to seikatsu kakumei* (Tokyo: Yoshikawa kōbunkan, 2010), 113. The women who directly benefited from owning the washers must have had a different opinion. For example, the writer Shigekane Yoshiko was so grateful for her first washing machine that she "wanted to offer a prayer of thanks to it." Shigekane Yoshiko, *Nyōbo no yuriisu* (Tokyo: Kōdansha, 1984), 12.
36. Iyota Yasuhiro et al., *Terebi-shi handobukku* (Tokyo: Jiyū Kokumin-sha, 1996), 13.
37. Ozu's attitude strongly contrasts with Ōshima Nagisa's portrayal of television in his debut film, *A Town of Love and Hope* (*Ai to kibō no machi*, 1959), where television serves as a prop that symbolizes the vast and irreconcilable class differences in Japanese society. The fifteen-year-old boy protagonist almost achieves a life inside the high-growth regime through a chance encounter with an upper-class girl. He is promised a job at the company where her father is an executive—a company that produces

television sets. His hopes are dashed, however, when it is discovered that he has been engaging in petty crimes: repeatedly selling two pigeons that escape their new owners and return to him. The pigeons both bring hope to the boy (he meets the girl through a transaction involving the pigeons) and take it away (they mark him as a criminal). At the end of the film, the protagonist embraces his criminal self, declaring that he will continue to sell his sole remaining pigeon. The girl purchases the pigeon from him and has her brother kill it with a shotgun. Now that the tie between them is destroyed, the rich person and the poor one go their separate ways. The boy is entrenched in his poverty, and the girl gives up her illusion that she could do something for the poor. Ōshima refuses any easy compromise between the two classes. In his critical vision, class resentment is a necessary condition for class struggle.

38. The hopeful ending of the other film that Ozu directed in 1959—*Floating Weeds* (*Ukigusa*)—also attests that the director did not take the threat of television too seriously. A traveling theater troupe settles in a small coastal town for a performance. The troupe, however, incurs a large loss because it fails to attract locals and its manager runs away with its cash fund. The leader dissolves the group, only to decide later to build a new one. It is obvious that television is the cause of the troupe's demise, effectively driving the itinerant performers out of a job. Contrary to the optimistic tone of the closing sequence, the troupe leader would have little to no hope of reestablishing himself in the actual world of 1959 Japan. *Floating Weeds* is a remake of the film *A Story of Floating Weeds* (*Ukigusa monogatari*, 1934), in which the poor attendance is blamed on rain.

39. Hayashi Nozomu, *Tsui konoaida atta mukashi* (Tokyo: Kōbundō, 2007), 136; Okazaki Takeshi, *Shōwa 30 nenndai no nioi* (Tokyo: Gakken, 2008), 114; Miyamoto, *Miyamoto Tsuneichi Chosakushū*, 2, 195.

40. *Jinsei dokuhon: Terebi*, 57–58.

41. An article in the child psychology journal *Jidō shinri* in 1961 discusses issues particular to this transitional phase. The author was an elementary school teacher in Gunma Prefecture who struggled to avoid a division in his classroom between those who had a television set at home (53 percent) and those who did not (47 percent). The students in the second category often felt inferior to those in the first. The author's strategies to reduce tensions around television included suggestions about how television-owning parents should deal with their children's televisionless friends. Furusawa Kiyoshi, "Terebi no aru kodomo to nai kodomo," *Jidō shinri* (April 1961): 502–7.

42. Yoshikawa Hiroshi, *Kōdoseichō: Nihon o kaeta 6,000 nichi* (Tokyo: Yomiuri shinbunsha, 1997), 53–54.

43. Yoshimi Shunya, "Terebi ga ie ni yattekita: Terebi no kūkan, terebi no jikan," *Shisō*, no. 956 (December 2003): 42. A housewife in Yokohama wrote in 1991 that she experienced little family life in the war and postwar period, and her images of it came from television. "Terebi no omoide," in *Kaden seihin ni miru kurashi no sengoshi*, ed. Kubo Masataka (Tokyo: Mirion shobō, 1991), 109.

44. While publishing "TV Boy" in its quarterly version, *Shōnen magajin* carried three episodes of *Gegege no Kitarō* as a trial run in its weekly version. Miyahara Teruo, *Jitsuroku! Shōnen magajin meisaku manga henshū funtōki* (Tokyo: Kōdansha, 2005), 101–2.

45. Mura Nunoe, *Gegege no nyōbo* (Tokyo: Jitsugyō no nihon-sha, 2008), 121–22.
46. Tōei anime, "Anime *Gegege no Kitarō* 50 shūnen kinen," http://www.toei-anim.co.jp/kitaro/50th/ (accessed December 9, 2019). In total, six separate Kitarō animation series were produced and aired: 1968–1969, 1971–1972, 1985–1988, 1996–1998, 2007–2009, 2018–2020.
47. Muramatsu Takeshi, "Terebi, kono shiseikatsu eno shinryakusha," *Taiyō* (September 1968): 127.
48. According to the studies conducted by Nihon risaachi centaa sōgō kenkyūjo, a Japanese person received 99 percent of his or her information through the mass media in 1985, and 90 percent of that came from television. Weeklies were responsible for only 0.88 percent of the total information delivered. Asahi shinbun sha, *Shūkanshi no subete* (Tokyo: Kokusai shōgyō shuppan, 1975), 28.
49. Takahashi Gorō, *Shūkanshi fūunroku* (Tokyo: Bungeishunjū, 2006), 70.
50. The following major weeklies started in the 1950s: *Shūkan sankei* (1952–1988), *Shūkan yomiuri* (1952–2000), *Shūkan Tokyo* (1955–59), *Shūkan shinchō* (1956–), *Asahi geinō* (1956–), *Shūkan josei* (1957–), *Shūkan taishū* (1958–), *Shūkan myōjō* (1958–1991), *Josei jishin* (1958–), *Shūkan jitsuwa* (1958–), *Shūkan gendai* (1959–), *Shūkan bunshun* (1959–), *Shūkan heibon* (1959–), and *Asahi journal* (1959–1992). Takahashi, *Shūkanshi fūunroku*, 194.
51. Sakamoto Hiroshi, *Heibon no jidai: 1950 nendai no taishū gorakushi to wakamono tachi* (Kyoto: Shōwadō, 2008), 148.
52. Kōgo Eiki, "Kōdo keizaiseichō to media: Terebi no kakudai," in *Media shi o manabu hito no tameni*, ed. Ariyama Teruo and Takeyama Akiko (Kyoto: Sekaishisōsha, 2004), 336.
53. In 1959 the total circulation numbers for the weeklies and monthlies were 520 million and 465 million, respectively. Kōgo, "Kōdo keizaiseichō to media," 336.
54. Shūkanshi kenkyūkai, ed., *Shūkanshi* (Tokyo: San'ichi shobō, 1959), cited in Motoki Masahiko, *Shūkanshi wa shinazu* (Tokyo: Asahi shinbun shuppan, 2009), 81.
55. Katō Hidetoshi, "Terebiteki bunmei no tenbō," *Chūōkōron* (February 1958): 212; Marshall McLuhan makes a similar point. Television actors and actresses are treated as "one of our own" by viewers, while film stars exist in a world beyond viewers' reach. Marshall McLuhan, *Understanding Media: The Extension of Man* (Cambridge, Mass.: MIT Press, 1994), 319–20. Takahashi Keizō, a well-known television personality, reported an episode that concisely demonstrates this point. When he was walking on New York's Fifth Avenue with Mifune Toshiro, the actor who appeared in numerous films directed by Kurosawa Akira, the Japanese tourists who happened to recognize them talked in a friendly way solely to Takahashi. He strongly felt that being on television means being in somebody's living room (and Mifune was not too happy about the whole episode). Hayasaka Akia, *Terebi ga yattekita* (Tokyo: Nihon hōso shuppan kyōkai, 2000), 236.
56. Asashi shinbunsha, *Shūkanshi no subete*, 119.
57. Of course, some weeklies were more gossipy than others, but, generally speaking, even the newsweeklies associated with political and economic topics were inclined to print behind-the-scenes, insider stories—gossip of a different sort.
58. Amakasu Akira quoted in Sakamoto, *Heibon no jidai*, 155.

59. Kurosaki Isao, "Doshirōto 'teinen' kara no shuppatsu," *Shuppan kurabu dayori*, October 1, 2002, quoted in Ueda Yasuo, *Zasshi wa miteita: Sengo jaanarizum no kōbō* (Tokyo: Suiyōsha, 2009), 221.
60. The media scholar Sakamoto Hiroshi emphasizes the transitional role that the monthly *Heibon* played in postwar Japan's media development: "Before the popularization of television, *Heibon*'s photo pages made it possible to see the lively figures of movie stars and singers in their everyday lives." Sakamoto, *Heibon no jidai*, 83.
61. Iyoda Yasuhiro et al., *Terebishi handobukku*, 17.
62. Tsutsui Yasutaka highlights the arbitrary nature of celebrity status in his short story "Ore ni kansuru uwasa" (Rumors about me, 1972). One morning the protagonist wakes up to find that he—a man of no distinction—has become the focus of intense media coverage. Trivial matters in his life clutter the media space until he shows up in the editorial office of a weekly, thereby bringing media attention to the media itself. Print media and television stations promptly shift their focus to another random person. Tsutsui Yasutaka, *Tsutsui Yasutaka zenshū* 13 (Tokyo: Shinchōsha, 1984), 104–18.
63. Ishida Ayuu, *Micchii būmu* (Tokyo: Bungeishunjū, 2006), 182.
64. "Naitei shita!? Kōtaishihi: sonohito Shōda Michiko san no egao," *Shūkan myōjō*, November 23, 1958, 10.
65. Matsushita Kei'ichi, "Taishū tennōsei ron," *Chūōkōron* (April 1959): 33.
66. Yoshimi Shunya, "Media ibento toshiteno Goseikon," in *Sengo Nihon no media ibento, 1945–1960*, ed. Tsuganesawa Toshihiko (Kyoto: Sekaishisōsha, 2002), 269.
67. Takahashi Tōru et al., "Terebi to 'kodoku na gunshū,'" *Hōsō to senden: CBC repōto* 3–6 (June 1959): 5–6.
68. From the households that were located close to the parade route and that owned a television, 598 were randomly selected for two rounds of interviews (one before and one after the wedding). Takahashi et al., "Terebi to 'kodoku na gunshū,'" 4–5.
69. Takahashi et al., "Terebi to 'kodoku na gunshū,'" 5.
70. The film director Shinoda Masahiro once declared in a public setting that he had had a chance to give a personal lecture to Akihito when he was still crown prince. When Akihito asked why the Japanese film industry had declined, Shinoda answered: "Because the honorable crown prince got married." How Akihito responded to the director's answer is unknown. Tanikawa Kenji, "Sengo eiga ni okeru kanshū," in *Taishū bunka to media*, Sōsho gendai no media to jaanarizumu 4, ed. Yoshimi Shunya and Tsuchiya Reiko (Kyoto: Mineruba shobō, 2010), 160–61.
71. Ueda Yasuo, *Zasshi wa miteita* (Tokyo: Suiyōsha, 2009), 208–9.
72. Nagao Saburō, *Shūkanshi keppūroku* (Tokyo: Kōdansha, 2004), 60; Ishida, *Micchii būmu*, 222.
73. *Asahi shinbun*, April 8, 1959, 8; *Mainichi shinbun*, April 8, 1959, 10.
74. See, for example, "Happyōgo tōkakan," *Shūkan shinchō*, December 15, 1958, 28–34.
75. Matsushita, "Taishū tennōsei ron," 35.
76. Even when the new media tried to focus on the shiny image of the royal wedding of 1959, one weekly's chosen title inadvertently revealed the underlying sexual dimension of the event. The words *josei jishin* (the Japanese title of *Women's Self*) have come to connote female genitalia.

77. Iyoda et al., *Terebishi handobukku*, 86–87.
78. The three major photo exposé weeklies are *Fōkasu* (Focus, 1981–2001), *Furaidei* (Friday, 1984–), and *Furashu* (Flash, 1986–). Kamei Jun argues that there was nothing new in the exposé weeklies' voyeuristic practices. He locates an early example of the genre in an August 1972 issue of *Shūkan shinchō*, which carried photos, taken with an infrared camera, of young couples' outdoor rendezvous in the darkness of hot summer nights. Kamei Jun, *Shūkan shi no yomikata* (Tokyo: Hanashi no tokushū, 1985), 180.
79. Fujitake Akira, *Terebi media no shakairyoku* (Tokyo: Yūhikaku, 1985), 151–52.
80. McLuhan, *Understanding Media*, 189.
81. Cecelia Tichi discusses the erotic associations of solitary television watching as well as discursive strategies to suppress them in U.S. television culture, in *Electronic Hearth: Creating an American Television Culture* (New York: Oxford University Press, 1992), 70–83.
82. Fujitake, *Terebi media no shakairyoku*, 151.
83. In the second half of the 1960s and the early 1970s, the fictional works of Tsutsui Yasutaka addressed many of the media-related issues that Fujitake would raise in the 1980s.
84. Jean-Paul Sartre, *Being and Nothingness* (New York: Philosophical Library, 1956), 260.
85. An interdisciplinary study group offered its definition of *danchi* in 1963 (since then repeated by many dictionaries and encyclopedias): It is "a cluster of living units constructed on a plot of land according to a planned layout. It is equipped with such facilities as roads, water works, sewers, and green space. It also houses such public facilities essential for the residents' everyday living as a store, meeting room, nursery, and elementary school depending on its scale. . . . *Danchi* is constructed and maintained by local public organizations, Japan Housing Corporation (Nihon jūtaku kōdan), private companies (for their employees), and private developers." Seikatsu kagaku chōsakai, *Danchi no subete* (Tokyo: Seikatsu kagaku chōsakai, 1963), 239. Laura Neitzel explores the cultural and social meanings of danchi in her book *The Life We Longed For: Danchi Housing and the Middle Class Dream in Postwar Japan* (Portland, Me.: MerwinAsia, 2016).
86. Tada Michitarō, "Tsukiai no arachi, danchi seikatsu," *Fujin kōron* (February 1961): 71, quoted in Neitzel, *The Life We Longed For*, 63.
87. Hara Takeshi and Shigematsu Kiyoshi, *Danchi no jidai* (Tokyo: Shinchōsha, 2010), 79. Hara also argues that the sequence of the royal couple's visits to Hibarigaoka danchi and the United States underscored the idea that danchi embodied American-style living. To 1960s Japan, however, the United States was more of an abstract concept than a concrete geographical entity. Contemporary accounts of danchi life tended not to make explicit connections with the United States.
88. Akiyama Shun, *Hoseki no shisō* (Tokyo: Ozawa shoten, 1997), 28, 29.
89. The television antenna, which was normally installed outdoors, was a sign that somebody owned a television set. Ida Emiko, "Terebi to kazoku no 50 nen: 'Terebiteki' ikkadanran no hensen," *NHK hōsōbunka kenkyūjo nenpō* 2004, 116.
90. Manabe Hiroki, "Kōgai no 60 nen," *Asahi shinbun*, October 31, 2005, 13th ed.

91. Surveys from the early 1960s discovered that danchi residents actually did not have much interaction with their neighbors. Ochiai Emiko, *The Japanese Family System in Transition* (Tokyo: LTCB International Library Foundation, 1996), 68. At Akiyama's danchi, the "happiness race" was a form of communication among the residents.
92. While recognizing danchi's homogenizing effects on Japanese family life, sociologist Watanabe Daisuke observes that blue-collar workers living in danchi tended to live closer to their workplaces and hence enjoyed more time with their families than their white-collar neighbors. Aizawa Shinichi and Watanabe Daisuke, "Hajimeni," in *Sōchūryū no hajimari: Danchi to seikatsu jikan no sengoshi*, ed. Watanabe Daisuke, Aizawa Shin'ichi, and Mori Naoto (Tokyo: Seikyūsha, 2019), 12; Watanabe Daisuke, "Futsū no jikan no sugoshikata no seiritsu to sono henyō," in *Sōchūryū no hajimari*, 34.
93. Hara Takeshi, *Danchi no kūkan seijigaku* (Tokyo: NHK bukkusu, 2012), 49–53.
94. In writing an alternative political history of postwar Japan, Hara Takeshi situates political affiliation within the particular geographical and spatial conditions associated with the different railway lines in Tokyo. Hara Takeshi, *Reddo arō to Sutaa hausu: Mōhitotsu no sengo shisōshi* (Tokyo: Shinchōsha, 2012), 388–96.
95. Hara and Shigematsu, *Danchi no jidai*, 72.
96. As a *Shūkan posuto* article discusses the allegedly prevalent prostitution at danchi, it focuses only on housewives' prurient behavior. By pathologizing female psychology, the article exonerates male readers. "Shufu kōrugaaru ga ichiban ōitoiu kōgai danchi," *Shūkan posuto*, September 25, 1970, 38–39.

## 3. Japan on the Move, a Family on the Run: Yamada Yōji's Countervision of Contemporary Japan

1. Yamada Yōji, "Synopsis: *Kazoku*" (Tokyo: Shōchiku Ōtake Library, n.d.).
2. I reconstructed the Kazamis' itinerary using some clues in the film and the train schedules I found in *Kōtsūkōsha no jikokuhyō* (April 1970). This itinerary, however, is not necessarily consistent with the diegetic time. Yamada departed from the actual train schedules in some key scenes in order to dramatize the family's emotions in an unfamiliar environment.
3. A sizable number of residents in the Nagasaki region secretly continued their practice of Catholicism, despite the Tokugawa shogunate's strict ban on Christianity. In the early Meiji years many of them rejoined the Catholic Church, while some continued to practice an indigenized form of Catholicism. Gonoi Takashi, *Nihon Kirisutokyō shi* (Tokyo: Yoshikawa kōbunkan, 1990), 215–43.
4. Cheap imported coal and oil began to expand their shares of Japan's energy market in the second half of the 1950s. The Japanese government's embrace of oil as the main energy source in the late 1960s rendered a deadly blow to the domestic coal industry. Yomiuri shinbun Shōwa jidai purojekuto, *Shōwa jidai sanjū nendai* (Tokyo: Chūōkōron shinsha, 2012), 293; Gotō Keinosuke and Sakamoto Dōtoku, *Gunkanjima no isan*

(Nagasaki: Nagasahi shinbunsha, 2005), 26. In 1957 Japan employed 298,000 full-time workers at 864 coal mines; by the mid-1970s these numbers declined to 48,000 and 76, respectively. Iwata Masami, *Hinkon no sengoshi: Hinkon no katachi wa dō kawattanoka* (Tokyo: Chikuma shobō, 2017), 145.

5. Many small- and medium-scale coal mines remained in operation for a time by disregarding the welfare and safety of their workers. Ueno Eishin provides vivid accounts of coal workers in late 1950s Kyushu in *Oware yuku kōfutachi* (Tokyo: Iwanami shoten, 1960).

6. In direct response to these labor disputes, the Japanese government subsequently extended financial assistance to the former coal miners. Laura Hein, *Fueling Growth: The Energy Revolution and Economic Policy in Postwar Japan* (Cambridge, Mass.: Harvard East Asia Monographs, 1990), 326.

7. The coal mines on nearby Hashima (commonly known as Gunkanjima) and on Takashima were closed in 1974 and 1986, respectively. Nagasaki-shi shi hensan iinkai, *Shin Nagasaki shi* 4 (Nagasaki: Nagasaki-shi, 2013), 454.

8. Ueno Eishin, *Shutsu Nippon ki* (Tokyo: Shakai shisōsha, 1995), 37.

9. As a member of the government-affiliated organization that promoted emigration, Wakatsuki Yasuo struggled to improve Japanese migrants' living conditions in Bolivia in the late 1950s but was frustrated by most Japanese officials' callous attitudes toward their plight. Wakatsuki documents his experiences working both in the headquarters in Japan and in Bolivia, with a short discussion of the fate of the Japanese migrants in subsequent years. Wakatsuki Yasuo, *Hatten tojōkoku eno ijū no kenkyū: Boribia ni okeru Nihon imin* (Tokyo: Tamagawa Daigaku shuppanbu, 1987); Wakatsuki Yasuo, *Gaimushō ga keshita Nihonjin* (Tokyo: Mainichi shinbunsha, 2001).

10. The families that moved to the Dominican Republic in the 1950s experienced extreme hardship. They were given only about one-third of the land that the Japanese government promised them. The land was filled with rocks and gravel, and some areas had high levels of salt. They often experienced water shortages because of limited access to the irrigation system. Furthermore, after the assassination of President Rafael Trujillo in 1961, the Japanese immigrants faced fierce local anti-Japanese sentiments. (Trujillo had forcefully taken away some land from Dominican farmers to redistribute to the Japanese immigrants.) For more detailed accounts about Japanese settlers' hardship and their struggles with the Japanese officials and the immigration agency, see Takahashi Yukiharu, *Karibu kai no "rakuen": Dominika imin 30 nen no kiseki* (Tokyo: Ushio shuppansha, 1987).

11. To put this another way, Sei'ichi's family relocates to an area where they can still watch television, whereas many emigrants to Latin America did not even have access to electricity. According to Ueno Eishin, the instructor at the emigration training center told the trainees not to bother bringing their television receivers, since many of them were migrating to areas without electricity. *Shutsu Nippon ki*, 39.

12. Nihon nōritsu kyōkai sōgō kenkyūjo, *Kurashi to keizai no deeta sōran 2005* (Tokyo: Seikatsu jōhō sentaa, 2005), 176–177.

13. "*Kazoku* to Yamada Yōji," *Kinema junpō*, October 15, 1970, 7.

14. "*Kazoku* to Yamada Yōji," 5.

15. Takaha Tetsuo, "Satsuei hōkoku: *Kazoku,*" *Eiga Satsuei,* no. 39 (1970): 10.
16. "*Kazoku* to Yamada Yōji," 4–5.
17. Abuno Katsuhiko, "Terebi wa chiiki o gyōshisuru," in *Nihon no dokyumentarii* 3, ed. Satō Tadao (Tokyo: Iwanami shoten, 2010), 84–85.
18. In his *Man Vanishes (Ningen jōhatsu,* 1967), Imamura Shōhei relentlessly questions the boundaries between fiction and reality. Takeshige Kunio, who participated in the shooting of the film, offers an insider's account on the planning and production process in "*Ningen Jōhatsu*: The World of Imamura Shōhei," http://www.cinemanest.com/imamura/home.html (accessed September 17, 2017).
19. Yoshida Naoya, "Eiga to terebi dokyumentarii," in *Nihon eiga no mosaku*, Kōza Nihon eiga 6, ed. Imamura Shōhei et al. (Tokyo: Iwanami shoten, 1987), 393.
20. Bertolt Brecht, "On Chinese Acting," *Tulane Drama Review* 6, no. 1 (September 1961): 130–36.
21. Wolfgang Schivelbusch, *Railway Journey: The Industrialization of Time and Space in the 19th Century* (Oakland: University of California Press, 1977), 61.
22. Yamada Yōji and Miyazaki Akira, "Kazoku," *Kinema junpō,* November 15, 1970, 102.
23. His car and house cost ¥360,000 ($1,000) and ¥3,600,000 ($10,000), respectively. He pays ¥28,000 for them each month and makes extra payments in summer and winter.
24. In 1970 a bottle of Torys cost ¥340, while the Kakubin and Old whiskies in the cupboard cost ¥1,450 and ¥1,900, respectively. I thank Suntory's customer service department for providing this information (email response May 25, 2009).
25. The factory in the scene belonged to Nihonon Kokan (NKK). With the construction of a fifth blast furnace (completed in 1972), NKK's Fukuyama facility boasted the world's largest production capacity. Fukuyama-shi shi henshū kai, *Fukuyama-shi shi* 2 (Fukuyama-shi: Fukuyama-shi shi henshū kai, 1978), 1158–59.
26. The lead actress Baishō Chieko describes shooting the scene in the following way: "I stand with bags in one hand, holding the boy's hand in the other hand, and the baby on the back. Igawa Hisashi, who plays my husband, and Ryū Chishū, my father-in-law, are waiting in a store for the cue to begin. The cinematographer is there with a camera under his jacket. He is also with an assistant. We are all scattered, discreetly watching the director Yamada who stands at a distance. When he raises a rolled-up script, we casually gather, and the lighting technician throws light on us. The scene is quickly shot, and we nonchalantly scatter into the crowd again." Baishō Chieko, *Baishō Chieko no genba* (Tokyo: PHP, 2017), 162.
27. They do this against the advice of a passerby: "There are a plenty of places to eat underground."
28. Uryū Yoshimitsu, "Shōshitsu suru Banpaku, Shōhi sareru toi—1970 nen, Osaka Banpaku nitsuite," in *Cultural Politics 1960/70,* ed. Kitada Akihiro, Nogami Gen, and Mizutamari Mayumi (Tokyo: Serika shobō, 2005), 159.
29. Yoshimi Shunya, *Banpaku to Sengo Nihon* (Tokyo: Kōdansha, 2011), 58.
30. Lily Franky, "Expo 70 Diary," in *Expo 70 densetsu: Unofficial guidebook,* ed. Hobara Shunji, Saitō Satoko, and Matsuhisa Atsushi (Tokyo: Media waakusu, 1999), 195.

31. Sadakane Hiroyuki, "Shōshitsu suru Banpaku, shōhi sareru toi—1970 nen, Osaka Banpaku ni tsuite," in *Cultural Politics 1960/70*, 166–70; and Kitada Akihiro, *Zōho, kōkoku toshi, Tokyo* (Tokyo: Chikuma shobō, 2011), 185–87.
32. This figure is likely dozens short of the true number of projectors on site. There were also projection systems that used 35mm or 16mm film projectors. Ogi Masahiro, "Banpaku eizō sōhihanron V," *Kinema junpō*, September 15, 1970, 44.
33. Ogi, "Banpaku eizō sōhihanron V," 44.
34. Hirano Akiomi, *Osaka Banpaku: 20 seiki ga yumemita 21 seiki* (Tokyo: Shōgakukan, 2014), 138. The screen area was as large as 2,000 square meters (about half an acre).
35. Kushima Tsutomu, *Maboroshi bankoku hakurankai* (Tokyo: Shōgakukan, 1998), 171.
36. Kushima, *Maboroshi bankoku hakurankai*, 170–71.
37. Ogi, "Banpaku eizō sōhihanron V," 45.
38. "Banpaku shōnen to 90-nendai no kimi no taiwa," in *Expo 70 densetsu*, 189.
39. Yamada Yōji, *Eiga wa omoshiroika* (Tokyo: Junpōsha, 1999), 122.
40. In 1967 the Ministry of Health presented a plan to strengthen the nation's emergency care system in response to the public outcry over the acute shortage of emergency care facilities, but the situation remained dire even in the early 1970s. "Sukuwarenu kyūkyū kanja," *Asahi shinbun*, September 2, 1971, evening 3rd ed. On October 7, 1969, *Mainichi shinbun* (7th ed.) ran an editorial that described the dismal state of emergency medical services in Japan and strongly urged the national government to establish an effective system.
41. Quoted in Horikiki Naoto, *Atsumi Kiyoshi: Asakusa, wagei, Tora-san* (Tokyo: Shōbunsha, 2007), 139.
42. Atsumi Kiyoshi and Yamada Yōji, "Taidan, otoko wa tsuraiyo," *Nihon eiga no genzai*, Kōza Nihon eiga 7, ed. Imamura Shōhei et al. (Tokyo: Iwanami shoten, 1988), 165.
43. In the planning stages of *It's Tough Being a Man*, concern was voiced that the main character's identity as a huckster was inappropriate for a television drama. Kiridōshi Risaku, *Yamada Yōji no sekai: genfūkei o otte* (Tokyo: Chikuma shobō, 2004), 114.
44. Yamada directed two more films under the title *It's Tough Being a Man* after the death of the lead actor Atsumi Kiyoshi in 1996 (1997 and 2019), using stock footage and computer graphics. I do not include them in the series because, simply put, they are more about Torajirō's absence.
45. Yamada Yōji, *100 nen intabyū Yamada Yōji*, NHK BShi, November 15, 2007; DVD (Tokyo: NHK Enterprises, 2009).
46. When shooting the first installment of *It's Tough Being a Man*, Yamada confided to a journalist that he would quit Shōchiku Studios if it turned out to be a bust. Shirai Yoshio, "Torasan kantoku Yamada Yōji no kenkyū," *Chūōkōron* (September 1978): 175. In 1965 Shōchiku Studios closed its Kyoto and Ōfuna studios. Nitta Masao, *Yamada Yōji: Naze kazoku o egaki tsuzukerunoka* (Tokyo: Daiyamondosha, 2010), 86.
47. Torajirō also becomes seasick in the television version of *It's Tough Being a Man*: on a ferry bound for Amamiōshima, the character experiences nausea and, it is suggested, throws up all night long. The difference between his experience and that of the passenger in *Where Spring Comes Late* is significant: Torajirō's inability to control nausea foreshadows his subsequent death from a snake bite.

48. The film's opening credits, for example, list Kazami Tamiko's name first and then identify Sei'ichi as Tamiko's husband. I would like to thank Yuka Kanno for calling my attention to this gender reversal.
49. Yamada received complaints from local farmers about the welcoming party scene, in which male and female members of the community sit at separate tables. The locals denied that there was any gender divide in their dairy farm community, where everybody participated in all tasks. Yamada Yōji et al., "Yamada Yōji kantoku o kakomu *Kazoku* tōron," *Kinema junpō*, October 15, 1970, 33.
50. Yamada et al., "Yamada Yōji kantoku wo kakomu *Kazoku* tōron," 34.
51. Kaikō Takeshi's *Robinson no matsuei* (Robinson's descendants, 1960) is a novel about destitute families that move from Tokyo to Hokkaido to settle at the foot of Mount Daisetsu in the immediate postwar period. As soon as they arrive at their destination, they realize that nobody has resources to help them. Promises of assistance from the settlement office in Tokyo turn out to be empty. They are left on their own to survive on barren land. The story ends with descriptions of the settlers dropping out one by one. Kaikō Takeshi, *Kaikō Takeshi zenshū*, vol. 3 (Tokyo: Shinchōsha, 1991–1993), 255–511 (hereafter cited as *KTZ*). Komatsu Sakyō visited the community on which Kaikō had based his story and learned that all the settlers from Tokyo had left by the mid-1960s. Komatsu Sakyō, *Yomu tanoshimi kataru tanoshimi* (Tokyo: Shūeisha, 1981), 169–71.
52. Nakashibetsu-chō 50 nen shi hensan iinkai, *Nakashibetsu-chō 50 nen shi* (Nakashibetsu: Nakashibetsu-chō, 1995), 406.
53. Yamada et al., "Yamada Yōji kantoku wo kakomu Kazoku tōron," 31–32.
54. The situation was already familiar to Japanese rice growers in 1970. In the previous year, facing overproduction, the national government began enforcing a rice acreage reduction policy. Ino Ryūichi, *Sengo Nihon nōgyōshi* (Tokyo: Shinnihon shuppansha, 1996), 171. In one scene in *Where Spring Comes Late*, a man refers to the policy, telling his fellow passengers: "We cultivated the land just for a year, and left it untouched this year."
55. For example, the number of households engaging in dairy farming in Nakashibetsu-chō peaked in 1960 at 979 and declined to 440 over the next thirty-seven years. In the same period the total number of cows there increased from 4,087 to 35,500. Nakashibetsu-chō 50 nen shi hensan iinkai, *Nakashibetsu-chō 50 nen shi*, 337.
56. The actors operated an actual rock-ferrying boat that was so old that the main mast broke in two during the shooting. Igarashi Keiji, *Tora-san no tabi* (Tokyo: Nihon Keizai shinbunsha, 1993), 104.
57. Statistics Bureau of Japan, "Motion Picture (1955–2005)," http://www.stat.go.jp/english/data/chouki/26.htm (accessed July 14, 2017).
58. Satō Tadao, *Nihon eigashi* 3 (Tokyo: Iwanami shoten, 1995), 107, 108. In 1964 Tōei established a separate company, Tōei Kyoto Television Production, and transferred to it many employees of the Tōei Kyoto Studios. Kasuga Taichi, *Jinginaki Nihon chinbotsu: Tōhō vs. Tōei no sengo sabaibaru* (Tokyo: Shinchōsha, 2012), 104.
59. Kasuga, *Jinginaki Nihon chinbotsu*, 242–43.
60. Shinoda, Ōshima, and Yoshida joined Shōchiku in 1953, 1954, and 1955, respectively.

61. Nitta, *Yamada Yōji*, 86.
62. Katsura Chiho, "Yamada Yōji no uragawa," *Eiga hyōron* (May 1974): 36.
63. Nitta, *Yamada Yōji*, 262.
64. Sei'ichi's yearning to keep his distance from the big thing is vicariously realized, albeit momentarily, by a family friend named Matsushita-san, played by Atsumi Kiyoshi. Much like Atsumi's character in *Where Spring Comes Late*, Matsushita is close to the family as it experiences a crisis. Although he is not originally from the area—he was born in Korea—he has settled on the island for the moment, peddling fish from his small truck. Living alone in an old, decrepit apartment, he seems to be attached to no particular social institutions. His livelihood is completely dependent on what he sells, and he does not show any concern about his future prospects. The fragmentary information about Matsushita suggests that he is unaffected by the forces that have swallowed the small island. He continues to be an outsider within—a liminal figure who inhabits the margins of the community.
65. Horikiri Naoto, *Atsumi Kiyoshi: Asakusa, wagei, Tora-san* (Tokyo: Shōbunsha, 2007), 183–84.
66. Kobayashi Nobuhiko, *Okashina otoko: Atsumi Kiyoshi* (Tokyo: Shinchōsha, 2003), 345. The sequence of the films' release—the sixth film in the *It's Tough Being a Man* series was released three months after *Where Spring Comes Late*—attests to Yamada's nostalgic turn in the early 1970s.
67. The Chisso Corporation discharged organic mercury into Minamata Bay in Kyushu. People in and around the town of Minamata suffered symptoms including tunnel vision, speech impediments, hearing loss, sensory disturbances, tremors, and ataxia. The most acute cases ended with the patient's death. The cause was identified in 1959, but Chisso did not stop dumping the effluent containing organic mercury until 1966. Some area residents continued to consume local sea products until 1973, when fishing was finally banned in Minamata Bay. Timothy S. George, *Minamata: Pollution and the Struggle for Democracy in Postwar Japan* (Cambridge, Mass.: Harvard University Asia Center, 2001); Jun Ui, "Minamata Disease," in *Industrial Pollution in Japan*, ed. Jun Ui (Tokyo: United Nations University Press, 1992), 103–32.
68. Costs associated with industrial production were externalized by dumping effluent into the water. The fact that the sea pollution cases finally gained the Japanese government's attention in the 1960s attests to the fact that the adjacent waters had been politically recognized as inside Japan. It is no accident that Japan extended its exclusive economic zone to 200 nautical miles from its coasts in 1977. *Gyogyō suiiki ni kansuru zantei sochi-hō*, May 2, 1977, http://www.shugiin.go.jp/internet/itdb_housei.nsf/html/houritsu/08019770502031.htm (accessed August 3, 2020).
69. Nihon zōsen shinkō zaidan, *Zōsen fukyō no kiroku: Daiichiji sekiyukiki ni taiōshite* (Tokyo: Nihon zōsen shinkō zaidan, 1982), 1–4.
70. The journalist Kamata Satoshi's investigation of labor relations within the shipbuilding industry in the 1970s supports this observation. Consider, for example, job losses at the Mitsubishi Shipyard in Nagsaki: 54 percent of workers at subsidiary companies lost their jobs, while the workforce at the parent company was reduced by

32.1 percent. Furthermore, those who remained at the subsidiary companies had their workloads increased. Kamata Satoshi, *Zōsen fukyō* (Tokyo: Iwanami shoten, 1993), 201–2.

## 4. Lost in Transition: Travel, Memory, and Nostalgia in Tsuge Yoshiharu's Travel Manga

1. Amasawa Taijirō, *Sakuhin kōiron o motomete* (Tokyo: Seidosha, 1985), 195.
2. Tsuge Yoshiharu, *Hinkon ryokōki* (Tokyo: Shōbunsha, 1991), 11–31.
3. Mura Nunoe, *Gegege no nyōbo* (Tokyo: Jitsugyō no nihon sha, 2008), 137–38.
4. Tsuge's father died in 1942, and his mother remarried in 1946. Tsuge Yoshiharu, *Tsuge Yoshiharu zenshū* (Tokyo: Chikuma shobō, 1993–1994), suppl.: 221–22. Hereafter cited in text and notes as *TYZ*.
5. He received ¥30,000 in royalties for a 128-page book in 1955. As a factory worker, he had earned ¥5,000–6,000, including overtime pay, each month. *TYZ* suppl.: 197–99.
6. His brother, Tadao, worked at a blood bank after he graduated from junior high school. Yoshiharu had often gone to the blood bank to sell his blood before Tadao gained employment there. *TYZ* suppl.: 183–85.
7. The initial diffusion of manga culture in the early postwar years owed much to the success of the so-called *akahon* (red book: they acquired the moniker because of their reddish covers). Tezuka Osamu's now legendary *Shin takarajima* (New Treasure Island [Tokyo: Ikuei shuppan, 1947]) was first published as an akahon. In the rapidly exploding book rental market of the 1950s, manga became a big draw for young readers of both genders, from school-age children to young blue-collar workers. The cheaply bound akahon that used to fill the shelves of rental shops, however, were replaced by the manga books (*kashihon manga*) designed especially for rental use (more pages and studier binding). Tsuge's early career was closely linked with the rise of kashihon manga. As the economy grew, books and magazines became something to purchase, and the big publishers' weekly manga magazines pushed the mom-and-pop shops that churned out rental manga out of business. Kashihon manga kenkyūkai, *Kashihon manga returns* (Tokyo: Popurasha, 2006), 12–34; Takeuchi Osamu, *Sengo manga 50 nen-shi* (Tokyo: Chikuma shobō, 1995), 18–30, 67–70; Naiki Toshio, "Kashihon manga," in *Manga no Shōwa shi: Shōwa 20-nen–55-nen* (Tokyo: Randamu Hausu Kōdansha, 2008), 44.
8. In the mid-1960s Tsuge worked as an assistant for Shirato Sanpei but found the work too demanding and quit in a week. Adachi Noriyuki, "Tsuge Yoshiharu to Mizuki Shigeru," in Rekishi to bungaku no kai, *Tsuge Yoshiharu no miryoku* (Tokyo: Bensei shuppan, 2001), 34; Tsuge Yoshiharu and Gondō Shin, *Tsuge Yoshiharu mangajutsu 2* (Tokyo: Waizu shuppan, 1993), 416–17.
9. Tsuge Yoshiharu, *Tsuge Yoshiharu, shoki kessaku tanpenshū 1* (Tokyo: Kōdansha, 2003), 283.

10. *Gensen* is transliterated in katakana, but the literary critic Shimizu Masahi reads it as 源泉, which means "source" or "fountainhead." Shimizu's inference is cogent in that it captures Tsuge's desire for a connection with the past, but his ancillary supposition that it is linked to the womb is just too schematic to have much analytical power. Shimizu Masahi, *Tsuge Yoshiharu o yome* (Tokyo: Chōeisha, 2003), 424.
11. Imagami Onsen in Yamagata was the model for the hamlet. Tsuge visited there in February 1968, five months before he published "Gensenkan Master." Tsuge and Gondō, *Tsuge Yoshiharu mangajutsu* 2, 140.
12. Shimizu Masahi criticizes Tsuge for abruptly ending his narrative with an encounter with a doppelganger: Shimizu argues that a complex tale of existential crisis (much like the one Dostoevsky offered in *The Double: A Petersburg Poem*) should unfold after this encounter. I argue that the story has no such deeper layer. Here, as in his later works, Tsuge was not allowed to escape into the inner realm of his self. For Shimizu's discussion of "Gensenkan Master," see his *Tsuge Yoshiharu o yomu* (Tokyo: Gendaishokan, 1995), 96–102.
13. Tsuge claims that he had not seen the film but felt affinities to the song. Tsuge and Gondō, *Tsuge Yoshiharu mangajutsu* 2, 160.
14. The text says that the man gets off the train at "N-ura Station" (*TYZ* 5:155). The actual location is Nagaura Station on the Uchibō line. Tsuge and Gondō, *Tsuge Yoshiharu mangajutsu* 2, 159.
15. This is a technique that Mizuki Shigeru often used in his work. He had his assistants draw detailed backgrounds, whereas Tsuge drew everything by himself.
16. As Shimizu Masahi points out, Tsuge revised the line in later editions, including *Tsuge Yoshiharu zenshū*. The first *Garo* version reads: "I was awake all night and left Yanagiya early next morning." It was changed to: "I was awake all night fantasizing, and left Yangiya early next morning." Shimizu, *Tsuge Yoshiharu o yomu*, 208. Relying on the *Garo* version, Shimizu suggests that the action takes place in the ambiguous boundaries between fantasy and reality. This reading is not sustainable, however, because, as Shimizu also notes, the beginning of the fantasy sequence is marked by the specific line: "I indulged in a daring fantasy."
17. "Ōba Electric Metal Plating Industry" (Ōba denki tokin kōgyōsho, 1973) is an early example of Tsuge's autobiographical work. *TYZ* 7:5–28.
18. A cursory internet search reveals that it is still a common taboo in twenty-first-century Japan.
19. Oyamada Tomokiyo, *Matsunoya hikki* (Tokyo: Kokusho kankōkai, 1908), quoted in Tsunemitsu Tōru, *Shigusa no minzokugaku: Jujutsuteki sekai to shinsei* (Kyoto: Mineruba shobō, 2006), 76.
20. Tunemitsu, *Shigusa no minzokugaku*, 77.
21. She is twenty-eight years old when she first appears in the story, if we assume that it takes place between 1969 and 1970. *TYZ* 5:164.
22. Tsuge and Gondō, *Tsuge Yoshiharu mangajutsu* 2, 159.
23. For example, "Umibe no jokei" (1967), "Chōhachi no yado" (1968), "Nejishiki" (1968), and "Komatsu misaki no seikatsu" (1978) all conclude with a frame that centrally features the sea.

24. Elsewhere Tsuge describes the special place that the sea occupies in his mind: "I believe the reason I still feel somehow excited when I see and smell the sea is that I spent my childhood in Ōshima, Izu, and a fishing village in Chiba. It may have something to do with my family line: most of the relatives on my mother's side make a living as fishermen or divers." *TYZ* suppl.:148.
25. Tsuge and Gondō, *Tsuge Yoshiharu mangajutsu* 2, 164.
26. My discussion of Discover Japan is informed by Marilyn Ivy's analysis in *Discourse of the Vanishing: Modernity, Phantasm, and Japan* (Chicago: University of Chicago Press, 1995), 40–48. In this section, I extend her argument by focusing on the visual aspect of Discover Japan.
27. Ōsaki Norio, "Hakken sareta Nihon," in *Disukabaa, Disukabaa Japan Tōku e ikitai*, ed. Nariai Hajime and Shimizu Hiroko (Tokyo: Tokyo Station Gallery, 2014), 188.
28. Fujioka's background was quite different from Tsuge's. In 1950 he graduated from the University of Tokyo, passed the national civil service exam, and was about to join the Ministry of Finance, following the established path for the elite; instead, he decided to join Dentsū. Fujioka Wakao, *Fujioka Wakao zenshigoto* 1 (Tokyo: PHP kenkyūjo, 1987), 235–37.
29. Tsuge and Gondō, *Tsuge Yoshiharu mangajutsu* 2, 140.
30. Of the sixty-four million who visited Expo '70, JNR transported twenty-two million. Fujioka Wakao, "'Byūtifuru' na sekai ni narunowa itsuno kotodarō," *Chōsajōhō* (March–April 2010): 9.
31. Fujioka, *Fujioka Wakao zenshigoto* 1, 36.
32. Fujioka, *Fujioka Wakao zenshigoto* 1, 22–23.
33. Fujioka Wakao, *Attu, purodyūsaa: Kaze no shigoto 30 nen* (Tokyo: Kyūryūdō, 2000), 37–45.
34. Fujioka, *Attu, purodyūsaa*, 47–48, 39–40.
35. Kawahara Shirō, who served as the art director for Discover Japan, explains the use of young women: "The predominant image of JNR then was a 'mass of iron.' Nobody saw it positively. Dubious and unsophisticated. Those negative associations must be busted in order for the passengers to enjoy railway travel. The top people of JNR were of the same opinion." Kawahara Shirō, "'Kuroi Kokutetsu' o karafuruni," in *Disukabaa, Disukabaa Japan Tōku e ikitai*, 61.
36. Fujioka uses condescending language to describe the moral deficiencies of women: "The women neither possess any rules to begin with nor enter a society with rules later in their lives. If they are always being spoiled and left alone, what kind of women will fill our society in the end? I have no idea." Fujioka Wakao, *Karei naru shuppatsu: Disukabaa Japan* (Tokyo: Mainichi shinbunsha, 1972), 32. At the base of his misogyny was a division of society into two spheres. Men were constantly subjected to regulatory forces as members of the productive regime; women were free from them because of their primary identity as consumers.
37. Fujioka, *Karei naru shuppatsu*, 40.
38. The primary function of other Japanese fashion magazines was to provide dressmaking patterns. The readers sewed the dresses by themselves or had them tailored using those patterns. Akagi Yōichi, who was a member of the team that created *an·an*, was

asked by the editor of another fashion magazine if *an·an* had proofreaders who could check patterns. Akagi does not say how he responded to the question, but there was of course no need to proofread nonexistent patterns. Akagi Yōichi, *"an·an" 1970* (Tokyo: Heibonsha, 2007), 41.

39. Fujioka, *Attu, purodyūsaa*, 74.
40. Fujioka, *Fujioka Wakao zen shigoto* 1, 111.
41. Nakano Midori, *Oyōfuku kuronikuru* (Tokyo: Chūōkōron shinsha, 1999), 182, quoted in Nanba Kōji, *Zoku no keifugaku* (Tokyo: Seikyūsha, 2007), 180.
42. Nakazawa Yuriko, "Ganso an-non zoku 2," in *Waga sedai, Shōwa 29 nen umare*, ed. Kawadeshobō shinsha henshūbu (Tokyo: Kawadeshobō shinsha, 1987), 231.
43. The three issues of *provoke* appeared in November 1968, March 1969, and August 1969. Takanashi Yutaka, Nakahira Takuma, Taki Kōji, and Okada Takahiko were the founding members of the magazine. Moriyama Daidō joined them for the final two issues.
44. Nakahira Takuma, *Naze shokubutsu zukan ka* (Tokyo: Chikuma shoten, 2007), 57.
45. Nakahira, *Naze shokubutsu zukan ka*, 57. According to Kawahara Shirō, the art director for Discover Japan, *provoke* was not the source of inspiration. He had used a blurry photo, to the consternation of the photographer, to emphasize the athletes' movement in an IBM advertisement during the 1964 Olympics, held in Tokyo. Kawahara Shirō, "'Kuroi Kokutetsu' o karafuruni," 59–60.
46. Yasumi Akihito, "Kaisetsu: Dantei no ronri," in Nakahira, *Naze shokubutsu zukan ka*, 300.
47. Fujioka Wakao, "Disukabaa Japan futatabi," *Shūkan daiyamondo*, May 5, 1999, 77.
48. A translation of Kawabata's lecture is available at the official Nobel Prize site, http://www.nobelprize.org/nobel_prizes/literature/laureates/1968/kawabata-lecture.html.
49. Ōe Kenzaburō critiqued Kawabata's vision of Japan in his 1994 Nobel Prize lecture, "Japan, the Ambiguous, and Myself." For the English version of his lecture, see http://www.nobelprize.org/nobel_prizes/literature/laureates/1994/oe-lecture.html. From its early phases, pundits argued that Discover Japan was a copy of the Discover America campaign, launched by the U.S. government in 1965. Sasaki Morio, "Disukabaa Japan wa kokumin eno marusei kōgeki," *Shakaishugi* (December 1971): 144; Ōmae Masaomi, "Discover Japan kyanpein uraomote kō," *Senden kaigi* (January 1972): 15; "Disukabaa Japan," *Asahi shinbun*, December 6, 1973, evening ed., 3. Marilyn Ivy also contends that "Discover Japan was in fact a direct transfer from Discover America. It copied not only the copy, but also the graphics of Discover America, transforming its trademark weather vane arrow into a stylized, foreshortened one." Ivy, *Discourse of the Vanishing*, 42. The similarities, however, stop there. Discover America targeted different segments of society—middle-aged and older males—and promoted specific geographic regions of the United States. Shimura Hiro'o, "Hen'yōsuru Discover America," *Senden kaigi* (January 1972): 42–49. Fujioka studied the American campaign, and did not find its "grandeur and patriotic style too helpful for his practices in Japan." Fujioka, *Fujioka Wakao zen shigoto* 1, 52.

50. Fatimah Tobing Rony, *The Third Eye: Race, Cinema and Ethnographic Spectacle* (Durham, N.C.: Duke University Press, 1996), 4–5.
51. This observation also applies to other travel manga that Tsuge published in 1968, including "Chōhachi no yado," "Futamata keikoku," and "Ondoru goya." The works in which a specific location is given tend to be more humorous and less contemplative.
52. Akutagawa Ryūnosuke, *Akutagawa Ryūnosuke zenshū* 3 (Tokyo: Iwanami shoten, 1996), 208–14; Akutagawa Ryūnosuke, "The Spider Thread," in *Rashōmon and 17 Other Stories*, trans. Jay Rubin (London: Penguin, 2006), 38–41.
53. Tsuge knew that "The Spider Thread" was in an elementary school textbook and decided to use the story to dramatize the final scene. Tsuge and Gondō, *Tsuge Yoshiharu mangajutsu*, ge, 206.
54. The photo was taken at Daikaku-ji temple in Ibaraki Prefecture. Fujioka, *Attu, purodyūsaa*, 75.
55. Mizuki Shigeru manufactured and marketed notions of the past in the form of ghosts and monsters, with huge success.
56. The psychiatrist Fukushima Akira observes that after peaking in the late 1960s, Tsuge's creative trajectory entered a phase of self-imitation and then, in subsequent years, one of psychic despondency. "Tsuge Yoshiharu sairon," *Yuriika* (March 1982): 127. While agreeing with Fukushima's general periodization, I would add that Tsuge's self-imitation is more a compulsion to reenact the drama of being forced out of his fantasy world.

## 5. The Ethics of Witnessing: Kaikō Takeshi's Vietnam War

1. Kaikō and Akimoto left for Vietnam on November 15, 1964, and returned to Tokyo on February 24, 1965. Kaikō Takeshi, *Kaikō Takeshi zenshū*, vol. 22 (Tokyo: Shinchōsha, 1991–1993): 565–66. Hereafter cited in text and notes as *KTZ*.
2. To take advantage of the fast-growing popular interest in Vietnam, the publisher pressured Kaikō to revise and publish his reports as a book immediately. As soon as he returned to Tokyo, he was ushered to a hotel room in Tokyo and then moved to an inn in Hakone. He finished the revisions in one week, turning them in on March 7. The official publication date on the book is March 20, 1965. *KTZ* 22:87.
3. Comparatively speaking, the Korean War had a larger economic impact on Japan than the Vietnam War did. The scale of Japan's economy had vastly increased by the mid-1960s, so it was far bigger in relation to the U.S. war effort. However, to borrow the economist Imura Kiyoko's expression, the "large-scale war that the United States forcefully carried out in Southeast Asia largely dictated, on a very basic level, Japan's high growth and its becoming an economic giant." Imura Kiyoko, *Gendai Nihon keizairon* (Tokyo: Yūhikaku, 1993), 226.

4. Thomas R. H. Havens chronicles Japan's movements against the Vietnam War in *Fire Across the Sea* (Princeton, N.J.: Princeton University Press, 1987).
5. For example, his wife, Maki Yōko, insists that witnessing the execution of a Vietnamese youth was a turning point in Kaikō's life: "Since then, whatever he did, he could not escape feelings of desolation." Maki Yōko and Koyama Tetsurō, "Kare wa ikinuku tsumori datta: Maki Yōko san ni kiku," *Bungakukai* 44, no. 2 (February 1990): 289.
6. *Into a Black Sun* won a Mainichi Shuppan Bunka prize in 1968.
7. Kotobukiya changed its corporate name to Suntory in 1963.
8. "Mainichi Design Awards, Kanendo jushōsha ichiran," http://macs.mainichi.co.jp/design/m/index.html#menu3 (accessed April 5, 2020).
9. Tsubomatsu Hiroyuki, *Kotobukiya kopii raitaa Kaikō Takeshi* (Osaka: Taru shuppan, 2014), 57.
10. When Torys was first introduced to the market in 1946, there were three tax brackets for whisky, with lower rates applied to lower-class whisky. Torys belonged to the lowest class (contents no more than 3 percent original malt whisky). Kita Yasutoshi, *Saji Keiji to Kaikō Takeshi: Saikyō no futari* (Tokyo: Kōdansha, 2015), 223, 304–5; Tsubomatsu, *Kotobukiya kopii raitaa Kaikō Takeshi*, 56.
11. The Japanese original reads: "Akaruku tanoshiku kurashitai. Sonna omoiga Torisu o kawaseru. Tegaruni yūge ni hana o soetai. Sonna omoiga Torisu o kawaseru." Tsubomatsu, *Kotobukiya kopii raitaa Kaikō Takeshi*, 104–5.
12. Yanagihara Ryōhei, "Torisu jidai no Kaikō-kun," in *Osaka de umareta Kaikō Takeshi*, ed. Nanba Toshizō et al. (Osaka: Taru shuppan, 2011), 38–9.
13. It was originally a bimonthly magazine with a circulation of 20,000. It soon became a monthly, with a circulation of almost 200,000. *KTZ* 21:427.
14. Tsubomatsu, *Kotobukiya kopii raitaa Kaikō Takeshi*, 108.
15. Literary scholar and Kaikō's personal friend Tanizawa Ei'ichi asserts that Kaikō's first bout of depression began several hours after he received the Akutagawa prize. Tanizawa Ei'ichi, "Kaikō Takeshi no utsu, *Nihon byōsekigaku zasshi*, no. 64 (August 2002): 3–5.
16. Tanizawa Ei'ichi, *Kaisō Kaikō Takeshi* (Tokyo: Shinchōsha, 1992), 178.
17. For example, he made frequent research trips to Hokkaido in 1959 as he prepared to write *Robinson's Descendants* (*Robinson no matsuei*), discussed in chapter 3.
18. Kaikō Takeshi, *Kako to mirai no kuniguni* (Tokyo: Iwanami shoten, 1961), and *Koe no Karyūdo* (Tokyo: Iwanami shoten, 1962).
19. Hino Keizō and Mukai Satoshi, "Kaikō bungaku no kagayakeru yami," *Bungakukai* (February 1990): 324.
20. Hino Keizō, "Tōgenkyō eno michi," in *Yūyū to shite isoge: Tsuitō Kaikō Takeshi*, ed. Maki Yōko (Tokyo: Chikuma shobō, 1991), 89.
21. Hino, "Tōgenkyō eno michi," 88.
22. Kaikō Takeshi, "Hinomaru katsuide senka no nakae," in *Aa, nijūgonen* (Tokyo: Ushio shuppansha, 1983), 317.
23. The serialization lasted from October 4, 1963, to November 6, 1964. For a discussion of Tokyo's transformation in the early 1960s, see Yoshikuni Igarashi, *Bodies of Memory:*

*Narratives of War in Postwar Japanese Culture, 1945–1970* (Princeton, N.J.: Princeton University Press, 2000), 146–53; Shunya Yoshimi, "1964 Tokyo Olympics as Post-War," *International Journal of Japanese Sociology*, no. 28 (2019): 80–95.

24. For example, in an installment that covered the Tokyo Olympics, all the foreign names and words were underlined and transliterated in *hiragana*. This unconventional method created a jarring effect, powerfully calling readers' attention to their foreignness—as if his writing were being invaded by foreign names and words. *KTZ* 12:443–51.

25. Ashida Terukazu, "Betonamu shuppatsu zengo," *Omoshiro hanbun*, November 1978, 142–43; *KTZ* 22:80–82. Tanizawa Ei'ichi claims that the idea was Kaikō's. *Kaisō Kaikō Takeshi*, 187–88.

26. Donald Keene attests to Kaikō's English-language skills, even wondering if Kaikō could have translated his own works into English, in "'Nihon rashisa' o koeta bungaku *Natsu no yami*," *Kotoba*, no. 17 (Autumn 2014): 29. When he was seventeen, Kaikō began to study French at a small school run by Morishita Tatsuo. *KTZ* 22:33–34.

27. Akimoto Kei'ichi, "Futatsu no kioku," *Omoshiro hanbun* 13, no. 7 (November 1978): 155. Akimoto's photos of the execution scene were printed in *Shūkan asahi*, February 12, 1965, 7–12.

28. Yoshimoto Taka'aki, *Yoshimoto Taka'aki chosakushū* 13 (Tokyo: Keisō Shobō, 1969), 324.

29. Yoshimoto, *Yoshimoto Taka'aki chosakushū* 13, 323–26.

30. Mishima Yukio, *Mishima Yukio zenshū* 39 (Tokyo: Shinchōsha, 2004), 529–30.

31. For example, Mishima created the character Yasunaga Tōru in *The Decay of the Angel* (New York: Vintage, 1990), the fourth volume of the Sea of Fertility tetralogy. Tōru is reduced to a pure gaze (as a signalman at a harbor, he spends the whole day gazing at ships), but he loses his sight at the end of the novel. For a more detailed discussion of the significance of vision in Mishima's tetralogy, see Igarashi, *Bodies of Memory*, 181–94. In Abe Kōbō's *The Box Man* (New York: Vintage, 2001), the protagonist become a voyeur par excellence by hiding himself inside a large cardboard box and observing the outside world through a small hole he makes in the box.

32. We can perhaps add the name of Tsutsui Yasutaka to this list, though he offers his criticism in the form of satirical short fiction and does not mention Kaikō's name. The protagonist of Tsutsui's "Betonamu kankōkōsha," set in the future, visits a Vietnam where war is staged for tourists. The story ends as he becomes an active participant in the war, blurring the boundaries between seeing and action. Tsutsui Yasutaka, *Tsutsui Yasutaka zenshū* 3 (Tokyo: Shinchōsha, 1983), 320–38.

33. Kaikō returned to Vietnam in 1968 and 1973.

34. The English excerpts from *Kagayakeru yami* and *Natsu no yami* are from Cecilia Segawa Seigle's translations, *Into a Black Sun* (Tokyo: Kodansha International, 1980) and *Darkness in Summer* (Tokyo: Kodansha International, 1973). The second parenthetical numbers refer to pages in the English versions. I have made a few modifications in Seigle's translations to better render nuances in the originals.

35. The term appears to be Kaikō's neologism. *Kōjien* starts listing it in the 2008 version. Niimura Izuru, ed., *Kōjien*, 6th ed. (Tokyo: Iwanami Shoten, 2008), 1203. It makes a first appearance in *Daijirin*, 3rd ed. (Tokyo: Sanseidō, 2006), 1077. Neither *Nihon kokugo daijiten*, 2nd ed. (Tokyo: Shōgakkan, 2000–2002), nor Morohashi Tetsuji's *Dai kanwa jiten*, 2nd ed. (Tokyo: Daishūkan, 1990), includes the term.
36. Abe Kōbō uses the term *shikansha* in *Hako otoko* (*The Box Man*, 1973), in *Abe Kōbō zenshū* 24 (Tokyo: Shinchōsha, 1999), 74. This is the earliest use of the term that I found outside of Kaikō's text.
37. Washida Koyata, *Shōwa shisōshi 60 nen* (Tokyo: San'ichi shobō, 1986), 396–404.
38. G. W. F. Hegel, *Phenomenology of Spirit* (Oxford: Oxford University Press, 1977), 19.
39. *Nagisa kara kurumono* was his attempt to render "what he learned in Vietnam, Korea, China, Indonesia, and other nations" in an allegorical story. Although he completed this work of considerable length, he decided not to publish it in book form for two reasons. First, even though he intended it to be a fictional work, many believed that it referred to actual conditions in Vietnam; second, he came to realize that the image of marching dead soldiers in the final scene was not especially original (*KTZ* 22:88). Kaikō did, however, eventually agree to publish the work as a book in 1980.
40. Kaikō Takeshi, *Nagisa kara kurumono* (Tokyo: Kadokawa Shoten, 1980), 188.
41. Mori Masato reminds us that since the mid-1960s Japanese men have participated in sex tourism in other Asian countries. Mori Masato, *Shōwa ryokōshi: Zasshi "Tabi" o yomu* (Tokyo: Chūōkōron shinsha, 2010), 180–81. Kaikō's protagonist uncritically engages in exploitative behavior for the sake of reaffirming his masculine identity.
42. The protagonist first hears an imaginary voice in a movie theater. The voice is connected to an earlier episode at the front and seems to have the power to invoke the specific conditions of the front lines: "And suddenly I thought I heard a whisper in Chinese. It was the same southern Chinese I'd heard at the front: harsh, guttural, dark, and energetic; the same voice that airwaves had carried across the scrub and rice fields that late afternoon on patrol" (*KTZ* 6:221/186). The protagonist's reaction to the voice appears to be visceral: he stiffens and looks around in the theater.
43. In an early scene the protagonist pays the bar madam a large amount of money for a night with To-nga. "In her faultless French she murmured an exorbitant price, then picked the money from my palm with elaborate disdain, as though picking a feather off her clothes. She was a study in how to dignify vulgarity" (*KTZ* 6:70/52). The focus on her manner offsets his vulgar act of buying a woman for the night. Referring to the madam's connection with French education as perhaps the source of her dignified vulgarity further helps to conceal the man's own role in the colonial power structure.
44. Even To-nga's brother Tran serves as a character witness for the protagonist in the story. Tran works as "an interpreter and assistant at the Saigon office of a Japanese newspaper" (*KTZ* 6:79/58). Right before joining the military, he chopped off two of his fingers, not to avoid military service but to show that he has no intention of killing, in case he became a prisoner of the National Liberation Front (*KTZ* 6:116/92). This act of self-mutilation seems to open him up to the protagonist. But when the protagonist and Yamada—Tran's employer—visit the Vietnamese youth to bid him

farewell on his induction into the army, Kaikō has him say: "I misunderstood you people. . . . I thought you were just having fun. Foreign journalists are all like that. They pretend to sympathize, but they're all here for the thrill of it. . . . I know you gave me some medicine that helped get rid of my fever, and you talked with me a lot. But I thought the medicine was because you didn't want to see anything that might upset you. No one really seriously sympathizes with us, because if they did they couldn't bear this country for another day. But you people [care about me and my country]" (KTZ 6:181/151). Tran initially accuses the protagonist of being one of the callous journalists but eventually recognizes his sincerity. The native finally expresses his appreciation and approval of the colonial master.

45. "Kaikō Takeshi shi no janguru senki," *Asahi shinbun*, February 17, 1965, 12th ed.
46. While he does not disclose the full information, Kaikō never claims that only seventeen of the original two hundred *survived*. The corresponding passage in *Vietnam War Report* reads: "When we counted the soldiers scattered around sitting in daze at the tree roots, the 200-man First Battalion was now only 17 men" (KTZ 11:150). Several pages later, he provides the precise casualty figures. Critics have long misread the scene and assumed that more than 90 percent of the battalion members died in combat. For examples, see Tono'oka Akio, "Kansatsusha no hihyōsei: Betonamu sensō yori," *Kokubungaku: Kaishaku to kyōzai no kenkyū* 27, no. 15 (November 1982): 49; Kikuya Kyōsuke, *Kaikō Kakeshi no iru fūkei* (Tokyo: Shūeisha, 2002), 65; and Yoshioka Ei'ichi, *Kaikō Takeshi no bungakusekai: Kōsakusuru Ōeru no kage* (Tokyo: Alpha Beta Books, 2017), 242.
47. Yoshida Haruo, *Kaikō Takeshi: Tabi to hyōgensha* (Tokyo: Sairyūsha, 1992), 116–18.
48. Kaikō, *Nagisa kara kurumono*, 335.
49. A comparable scene in *From the Shores* makes it clear that the protagonist's pride carries an imprint of Japan. The bag that the Japanese journalist clings to is a complimentary gift from Japan Airlines. He also carries a Japanese flag in his pocket, hoping that the guerrillas will refrain from shooting at him if they recognize that he is Japanese. He expects a bubble of national identity to protect him from hostile fire. Kaikō, *Nagisa kara kurumono*, 342–43.
50. The body is also an important connection to the past. Bruce Suttmeier offers a cogent reading of the final scene in which the clinging hand of a Vietnamese solider harks back to Japan's unresolved memories of the Asia Pacific War. Bruce Suttmeier, "Seeing Past Destruction: Trauma and History in Kaikō Takeshi," *positions* 15, no. 3 (Winter 2007): 473–77.
51. Kaikō Takeshi and Yamazaki Masakazu, "Genseki to hōseki," *Kokubungaku: Kaishaku to kyōzai no kenkyū* 27, no. 15 (November 1982): 28.
52. Ishihara Bunyō used a telephoto lens to shoot the scene. He also claims that at another location he captured a scene where Vietnamese soldiers killed a prisoner of war, excised his liver, and ate it raw for good luck. Ishikawa Bunyō, "*Minami betonamu kaihei daitai senki* satsuei ki," in *Nihon no dokyumentarii* 3, ed. Satō Tadao (Tokyo: Iwanami shoten, 2010), 134–35.
53. "Kūzen no zankoku shiin kōkai no uchimaku," *Shūkan manga sandei*, June 2, 1965, 22.

54. The following night, Chief Cabinet Secretary Hashimoto Tomisaburō called the president of Nippon Television to protest against the scenes of cruelty. "Konwaku suru kenryokushasō," *Tosho shinbun*, May 29, 1965, 1. Most of the calls and letters that reached the station soon after the show were positive. "Kūzen no zankoku shiin kōkai no uchimaku," 22. An abridged version of the three-part documentary was available for viewing at the Kawasaki City Museum. In this version the scenes with the decapitated head have been edited out. *Betonamu Kaihei daitai senki*, Nippon TV, 50:00, May 9, 1965. The museum, however, sustained heavy damage due to the October 2019 flooding and has been closed to the public for an indefinite period. An anonymous person uploaded a low-resolution recording to YouTube. See https://www.youtube.com/watch?v=fkivla5zjdk (accessed April 5, 2020).
55. The story was first published in *Shinchō* (October 1971): 6–139 and then appeared in book form the following year (Tokyo: Shinchōsha, 1972).
56. Literary scholar Yoshioka Eiichi describes the shock of reading *Darkness in Summer* for the first time as a college student: "Until then, I was not an avid reader of Kaikō, but *Darkness in Summer*'s fulgent language, daring sexual descriptions, the protagonist's confessional monologues overwhelmed me. It was also refreshing to see the story set in European cities like Paris. It appealed to me because it offered something that I had not found in the traditional novels imbued with Japanese sentiments and lyricism." Yoshioka, *Kaikō Takeshi no bungaku sekai*, 3.
57. Jürgen Berndt, the German translator of *Darkness in Summer* [*Finsternis eines Sommers*] (Berlin: be.bra edition q, 1993), was initially reluctant to work on the translation because he deemed, given the heavy sexual content of the book, it would be impossible to obtain a permission in the German Democratic Republic (East Germany). Jürgen Berndt, "Naze ima Kaikō Takeshi nanoka," *Shinchō* (December 1991): 128.
58. For a detailed discussion of the Nikkatsu staff's reaction to the studio's decision to start producing softcore porn films, see Matsushima Toshiyuki, *Nikkatsu roman poruno zenshi* (Tokyo: Kōdansha, 2000), 18–50.
59. The whisky that he drank in the commercials was upgraded over the years, from a midlevel product (Kakubin) to a high-grade one (Royal).
60. The incomplete manuscript was posthumously published in 1990. "Hana owaru yami," *Shinchō* 87, no. 2 (February 1990): 6–88; *KTZ* 9:393–523. Kaikō emphasized the complementary quality of the first two volumes of the trilogy: "If *Into a Black Sun* is a male screw, *Darkness in Summer* is a female screw. It must be. I carried everything out on that premise" (*KTZ* 22:345).
61. With some detective work, the writer Kikuya Kyōsuke identified the model for the female character in *Darkness in Summer*. She died in a car accident in January 1970, and Kikuya attributes Kaikō's inability to complete the trilogy to her premature death. Kikuya, *Kaikō Takeshi no iru fūkei*, 125–28. Kaikō was indeed devastated by the loss, as he confided to Yoshiyuki Junnosuke. Quoted in Hosokawa Fukuko, *Watashi no Kaikō Takeshi* (Tokyo: Shūeisha, 2011), 108. Kaikō completed the manuscript of *Darkness in Summer* while deeply mourning her death. However, the published text of *Darkness in Ending Flowers* suggests that his struggle was more about breaking out of the world he created through the first two works of the trilogy.

# 6. Heroes in Crisis: The Transformation of Yakuza Film

1. Satō Tadao, *Nihon eigashi 3: 1960–1995* (Tokyo: Iwanami shoten, 1995), 50; Aoyama Sakae and Shiba Tsukasa, *Yakuza eiga to sono jidai* (Tokyo: Chikuma shobō, 1998), 39, 67–68. Keiko Iwai McDonald singles out *Theater of Life: Hishakaku* as the film that established a new yakuza narrative formula that would be used in one variation or another in over three hundred films before the decade was out." Keiko Iwai McDonald, "The Yakuza Film: An Introduction," in *Reframing Japanese Cinema: Authorship, Genre, History*, ed. Arthur Nolletti Jr. and David Desser (Bloomington: Indiana University Press, 1992), 174.
2. In 2004 Home Vision Entertainment released a DVD box set of the series under the title *The Yakuza Papers: Battles Without Honor and Humanity*.
3. One finds this popular narrative uncritically reproduced in Richard Torrance's essay on *Battles Without Honor and Humanity*, "The Nature of Violence in Fukasaku Kinji's Jingi naki tatakai (War without a code of honor)," *Japan Forum* 17, no. 3 (2005): 389–406.
4. Outlaw gamblers and itinerant hucksters (*tekiya*) have typically been acknowledged as the ancestors of yakuza groups. Miyazaki Manabu distinguishes modern from premodern yakuza and argues that the modern yakuza emerged among the unskilled workers on urban industrial sites. Miyazaki Manabu, *Yakuza to Nihon: Kindai no burai* (Tokyo: Chikuma shobō, 2008), 55–56.
5. McDonald, "The Yakuza Film," 174.
6. Mishima Yukio, "Tsuruta Kōji ron: Sōchō tobaku to Hishakaku to Kiratsune no nakano," in *Mishima Yukio zenshū* 35 (Tokyo: Shinchōsha, 2003), 413.
7. Mishima and three Shield Society members sang "Karajishi botan," the theme song for the *Remnants of Chivalry in the Showa Era* series, in the car on their way to the Grand Self-Defense Force Ichigaya Base on November 25, 1970. Several hours later Mishima and one of the Shield Society members committed suicide there. Yasuda Takeshi, *Mishima Yukio "nichiroku"* (Tokyo: Michiya, 1996), 413.
8. Mishima himself played a yakuza character in the film *Karrakaze yarō* (1960, dir. Masumura Yasuzō).
9. The same rule applies to Kurosawa Akira's *Seven Samurai* (1954), in which four of the seven samurai fall to the bandits' muskets.
10. Takeda Izumo, Miyoshi Shōraku, and Namiki Senryū, *Kanadehon Chūshingura* (Tokyo: Iwanami shoten, 1937); Nogami Tatsuo, "Ninkyō eiga wa kabuki," *Kinema junpō*, August 30, 1971, 56.
11. Kasahara Kazuo, Arai Haruhiko, and Suga Hidemi, *Shōwa no geki: Eiga kyakuhonka Kasahara Kazuo* (Tokyo: Ōta shuppan, 2002), 45; Shundō Kōji and Yamane Sadao, *Ninkyō eigaden* (Tokyo: Kōdansha, 1999), 118.
12. Isolde Standish traces "tragic heroes" narratives, which are found widely in Japanese film, back to *Chūshingura*. Her book *Myth and Masculinity in the Japanese Cinema: Toward a Political Reading of the "Tragic Hero"* (London: Routledge, 2000) is an effort to historicize Japanese cinematic conventions.

13. Kasahara Kazuo claims that the primary goal of the *Bakuto* series (1964–1971) was to introduce the uninitiated to the world of yakuza. Kasahara et al., *Shōwa no geki*, 154. Contrary to the consensus among filmmakers and critics, the director Ozawa Shigehiro insists that *Bakuto* (1964) was the original yakuza film. Aoyama and Shiba, *Yakuza eiga to sono jidai*, 40. It should be noted that television first introduced the rituals of yakuza and *tekiya* (itinerant huckster) families to the general public. NHK broadcast the documentary *Nihonjin to Jirochō* on January 5, 1958. In it, about twenty yakuza bosses from the Tokyo area enacted a gambling scene for the program. Nihon hōsō kyōkai, *20 seiki hōsōshi* 1 (Tokyo: Nihon hōsō shuppan kyōkai, 2001), 379; Shindō Kaneto and Yoshida Naoya, "Terebi no hōhō," in *Nihon eiga no mosaku*, Kōza Nihon no eiga 6, ed. Imamura Shōhei et al. (Tokyo: Iwanami shoten, 1987), 378–79. The television camera allowed the viewers to engage in a voyeuristic exploration and appreciation of this forbidden realm from a safe distance. In real life, such access would have been unimaginable to most viewers.

14. Kusakabe Gorō, *Shinema no gokudō: Eiga purodyūsaa ichidai* (Tokyo: Shinchōsha, 2012), 53–54. The protocol among yakuza was actually so rigid that a self-introduction could take as long as forty minutes. Ide Hideo, *Yakuza gaku nyūmon* (Tokyo: Hokumei shobō, 1969), 145.

15. Before the final sequence was shot, an artist drew the tattoos on Takakura's back. Takakura was on his stomach during the entire process, which took as long as six hours. It was a genuine work of endurance. Yamadaira Shigeki, *Ninkyō eiga ga seishun datta* (Tokyo: Chikuma shobō, 2004), 79.

16. According to legend, *karajishi* is the mightiest of all animals but is vulnerable to parasitic insects. It sleeps underneath peony plants because the dew that collects on the flowers repels the insects from the *karajishi*'s body. Amamiya Kumi, "Nihon ni okeru botan to shishi bunka no keisei to yōkyoku 'Ishibashi,'" *Kokusai kankei kenkyū* 36, no. 1 (October 2015): 67–68.

17. I submit that the success of the six-part film *The Human Condition* (Ningen no jōken: 1959–1961, dir. Kobayashi Masaki) may have been the original inspiration for yakuza film in the 1960s. While situated in imperial Japan, the story offers the key elements of yakuza film. The protagonist Kaji struggles to maintain his conscience within the army and in the front—the space filled with violence. After witnessing and enduring the abuse administered by an opportunistic noncommissioned officer, Kaji finally explodes with anger and kills the man. For a discussion of the novel and film versions of *The Human Condition*, see Yoshikuni Igarashi, *Homecomings: The Belated Return of Japan's Lost Soldiers* (New York: Columbia University Press, 2016), 51–78. There is evidence to show the affinities between them: Kaneko Nobuo plays both the abusive and calculating NCO in *The Human Condition* and the rapacious dons in *Big Gambling Ceremony* and *Battles*. Furthermore, all-night showings of yakuza film in Tokyo's downtown theaters attracted young male audiences in the late 1960s and early 1970s. The practice of all-night showing began with *The Human Condition* (nine and a half hours long all together) in the late 1960s.

18. Saitō Ayako, "Takakura Ken no aimai na nikutai," in *Otokotachi no kizuna, Ajia eiga, homosōsharu na yokubō*, ed. Yomota Inuhiko and Saitō Ayako (Tokyo: Heibonsha,

2004), 63–120; Eve K. Sedgwick, *Between Men: English Literature and Male Homosocial Desire* (New York: Columbia University Press, 1985), 1–15.
19. Okabe Hiroyuki, *Hadaka no keizaigaku* (Tokyo: Shōkoten shobō, 1958), 115–16; Santō Kyōden and Miyazaki Shōzō, *Fukagawa Taizen* (Tokyo: Chinshokai, 1917), 15.
20. Abashiri Prison Museum website, http://www.kangoku.jp/kangoku_hiwa5.html (accessed April 5, 2020).
21. Though its facilities were dated, Abashiri Prison benefited from earlier efforts to modernize Japan's penitentiaries. Three years after the 1909 fire, the main building was rebuilt, modeled after the star-shaped structure of the Central Prison of Leuven in Belgium, which opened in 1860. In this semipanoptical structure, the gaze served as an important instrument through which to control the prison population effectively: while the prison guards were able to look into each cell, the prisoners could not see fellow inmates in other cells. Iso Tatsuo and Miyazawa Hiroshi, "Naibu ni hirogaru gaibu: Abashiri kangoku goyoku-hōshajō shabō (1912 nen)," *Nikkan aakitekuchaa*, August 25, 2014, 72–73.
22. The official term for "bangaichi" is *mubanchi* (land with no street numbers). *Mubanchi* is used often to designate nationally owned land, including rivers and roads. Abashiri Prison's actual address is Kanyū mubanchi, Aza Sanchō, Abashiri-shi (Offical land with no street number, Sanchō area, Abashiri City). Imao Keisuke, *Jūsho to chimei no daikenkyū* (Tokyo: Shinchōsha, 2004), 68–69.
23. Oguma Eiji, *1968 1: Wakamonotachi no hanran to sono haikei* (Tokyo: Shinyōsha, 2009), 117. Satō Tadao critically writes about yakuza film's "grotesquely anachronistic aestheticism" in *Nihon eigashi 3: 1960–1995*, 54.
24. Takada Fumio, *Tadashii dankai no sedai hakusho* (Tokyo: Kōdansha, 1993), 111.
25. It has been reported that at the peak of yakuza film's popularity, twelve to thirteen thousand fans attended Saturday all-night showings at the three Toei theaters in downtown Tokyo. Yamadaira, *Ninkyō eiga ga seishun datta*, 7.
26. Itō Katsuo et al., "Viva! Ninkyō eiga," *Kinema junpō*, August 30, 1971, 45; Takada, *Tadashii dankai no sedai hakusho*, 110; Aoyama and Shiba, *Yakuza eiga to sono jidai*, 16.
27. Yamadaira, *Ninkyō eiga ga seishun datta*, 78–79.
28. Ōshima Nagisa, *Waga Nihon seishin kaizōkeikaku* (Tokyo: Sanpō, 1972), 142–43.
29. Yamadaira, *Ninkyō eiga ga seishun datta*, 8.
30. In his conversation with Tsuruta Kōji, Sudō Hisashi similarly underscores the affinities between yakuza film and the student movements: "I have seen many cases in which students recharge their energy by watching yakuza films and participate in the radical demonstrations the following day. A student who was a Red Army sympathizer had a bunch of Tsuruta Kōji's posters and music records in his room. This is something that I saw with my own eyes, but he would cut out a photo of Yano Ryūko [the protagonist in the *Red Peony Gambler* series] and paste it inside his helmet when he went to participate in a demonstration." Sudō Hisashi, *Hajakensei no rōman* (Tokyo: San'ichi shobō, 1974), 26.
31. Aoyama and Shiba, *Yakuza eiga to sono jidai*, 18; Itō Katsuo et al., "Viva! Ninkyō eiga," 45; Takada, *Tadashii dankai no sedai hakusho*, 110; Ueno Kōshi, *Sengo saikō* (Tokyo: Asahi shinbunsha, 1995), 186.

32. Aoyama and Shiba, *Yakuza eiga to sono jidai*, 110.
33. Kasahara Kazuo admits that when he was writing for *Legends of Chivalry* (*Ninkyō retsuden otoko*, 1971), he could not come up with an original plot. Kasahara Kazuo et al., *Shōwa no geki*, 273. Both Takakura Ken and Tsuruta Kōji cautiously expressed their frustration with the genre in interviews in 1971. Takakura Ken and Wakita Takuhiko, "Eiga shinseikatsu, fan no koto," *Kinema junpō*, March 20, 1971, 78; Tsuruta Kōji, "Boku to ninkyō eiga," *Kinema junpō*, March 20, 1971, 87.
34. Kusakabe, *Shinema no gokudō*, 77.
35. Kobayashi Nobuhiko, *Gendai shigo nōto* (Tokyo: Iwanami shoten, 1997), 147.
36. On a symbolic level, the couple's gender dynamics were a bit more complicated. Fuji Junko married the kabuki actor Onoe Kikunosue IV, who was best known for his impersonation of female characters on stage. In real life, many fans and Toei executives were concerned about Fuji's standing in the highly exclusive kabuki world. In the short speech he gave at her wedding, Tōei president Okada Shigeru implored the attendees not to torment her even if she failed in her duties. "Kabuki no minasan Junko o ibiranaide hoshii!" *Shūkan josei*, April 22, 1972, 41.
37. Takazawa Kōji provides a list of colleges and high schools shut down by student activists in the late 1960s and early 1970s in *Zenkyōtō gurafitii* (Tokyo: Shinsensha, 1990), 55.
38. Saishu Satoru, "Hitotsu no kekki: Watashi no Zenkyōtō," *Asahi kuronikuru shūkan 20 seiki, 1969*, August 9, 1999, 8.
39. It is impossible to know the exact number of the victims because they were unlikely to report the assaults to authorities. Konishi Makoto estimates that 113 were killed and 4,600 were injured in intra- or interfactional violence from 1969 through 2001. Twenty-five of these deaths occurred between 1969 and 1972. Given the ratio of one death to forty injured (113/4,600), it is safe to assume that hundreds were injured in those four years. Konishi Makoto, "Naze ima uchigeba no kenshō ga hitsuyōka," in Iida Momo et al., *Kenshō uchigeba* (Tokyo: Shakaihihyōsha, 2001), 6.
40. Yamane Sadao and Yonehara Hisashi, *"Jinginaki tatakai" o tsukutta otokotachi* (Tokyo: NHK shuppan, 2005), 113–14.
41. *Nihon ansatsu hiroku* (1969) was the first film to use this style. According the film's director, Nakajima Sadao, the idea originally came from Kasahara Kazuo. Nakajima Sadao, "Nihon ansatsu hiroku no koto," in *Kasahara Kazuo: Hito to shinario*, ed. Shinario sakka kyokai (Tokyo: Shinario sakka kyōkai, 2003), 401.
42. Yamane and Yonehara, *"Jinginaki tatakai" o tsukutta otokotachi*, 46–48; Tatematsu Wahei, *Eiga shugisha, Fukasaku Kinji* (Tokyo: Bungeishunjū, 2003), 80–97.
43. Excerpts from Kasahara's voluminous research notes have been published under the title *"Jinginaki tataka" chōsa shuzairoku shūsei* (Tokyo: Ōta shuppan, 2005).
44. Kasahara Kazuo, *Jinginaki tatakai* (Tokyo: Tōgensha, 1998), 343.
45. Yonehara Hisashi and Yoshida Sadaji, "Manei, Uchida Tomu, soshite Fukasaku Kinji: Kikigaki kameraman Yoshida Sadaji," in Yamane and Yonehara, *"Jinginaki tatakai" o tsukutta otokotachi*, 116–17.
46. Kasahara Kazuo et al., *Shōwa no geki*, 283, 296; Kusakabe, *Shinema no gokudō*, 88–89.
47. Kasahara Kazuo, *Eiga wa yakuza nari* (Tokyo: Shinchōsha, 2003), 7–10.

48. The names of the producer Shundō Kōji and the former yakuza don and writer Minō Kōzō should be added to this list. Shundō chose Fukasaku as the director, and Minō's accounts of Hiroshima yakuza struggles inspired Kasahara's script. Kasahara, *Eiga wa yakuza nari*, 61–63, 66.
49. An incident in which a Japanese veteran beats up American GIs was more fantasy than reality, a product of the scriptwriter's resentment toward the U.S. occupation. Kasahara Kazuo, a navy veteran, silently endured humiliating encounters with American soldiers. When asked about the occupation in an interview, he replied: "You know, you get on a train. You are coming home from the countryside [where you got food]. You sit on a seat with a huge pack. Five or six American GIs get on the train car with prostitutes. They then pull out pistols and force us to get up on our feet. We have no choice but to stand up. On the empty seats, they sit, drink whisky, smoke, and neck with the girls. They can shoot us right there. That's them. I have often experienced things like that." Kasahara et al., *Shōwa no geki*, 534. Twenty years later Kasahara got revenge through his writing. In the original script, there was even a scene where the GIs suddenly changed their attitude and praised Hirono and Yamakata Shin'ichi (later Hirono's sworn brother) for their bravery. Fukasaku omitted the scene. Kasahara, *Jinginaki tatakai*, 12.
50. This episode is based on real-life events of 1949. Kasahara, *"Jinginaki tataka" chōsa, shuzairoku shūsei*, 63.
51. In the last phase of the Asia Pacific War, methamphetamine was distributed to workers on night shifts as well as to kamikaze pilots. Dainippon Seiyaku began its sale under the brand name Philopon in 1941. Following Japan's defeat, its use spread to the wider public, causing serious mental health issues. Its sale and use remained legal until 1951. Sasaki Takeshi et al., *Sengoshi Daijiten, 1945–2004* (Tokyo: Sanseidō, 2005), 783; Miriam Kingsberg, *Moral Nation: Modern Japan and Narcotics in Global History* (Berkeley: University of California Press, 2013), 181–99; Jeffrey W. Alexander, *Drinking Bomb & Shooting Meth: Alcohol and Drug Use in Japan* (Ann Arbor, Mich.: Association for Asian Studies, 2018), 99–114.
52. In the film's narrative, violence is not a function of individual subjectivity, except in Hirono's case; instead, it is a symptom of larger forces. The men act to realize the maximum gain for their organizations, and those who reject their organization's mandates are violently eliminated. Makihara Masakichi offers the only successful example of resistance when he evades Yamamori's command to kill Doi. A comical scene where Makihara tries to save his own life by pretending to weep for his pregnant wife is inserted to enhance his manipulative character; he later becomes Yamamori's right-hand man. The film's attention to details enhances the evil design of Yamamori, who pits his men against each other in order to assure maximum gain for himself.
53. Kasahara Kazuo, *Hametsu no bigaku: Yakuza eiga eno rekuiemu* (Tokyo: Tōgensha, 1997), 268.
54. Kasahara talks about a don, for example, who forced his subordinates to lop off their finger for minor infractions. He bottled them up in alcohol, treasuring them as his collection. Kasahara, *Hametsu no bigaku*, 268–72.

55. Kasahara, *Hametsu no bigaku*, 268.
56. The film's ending structurally resembles that of *The Scorching Sea* (*Taiyō no kisetsu*, dir. Furukawa Takumi, 1956), whose young protagonist, Tsugawa Tatsuya, shows up at his lover's funeral. Facing the altar, he throws a singing bowl at her picture and yells at the assembled elders, "You understand nothing!" The endings of the two films, however, offer a contrast: Tsugawa's act reaffirms his role as an iconoclastic destroyer of conventional morals, while Hirono's demonstrates his inability to break away from the world that the elders control.
57. Just like the tattoos that heroes of early yakuza films carry on their bodies, the severing of a body part serves as an initiation into the yakuza world. His left hand, however, is never displayed in subsequent scenes or in the rest of the series.
58. Kasahara et al., *Shōwa no geki*, 408.
59. Quoted in Itō Akihiko, *Eiga no naraku* (Tokyo: Kokusho kankōkai, 2015), 71.
60. Fukasaku's nonchalant attitude about historical authenticity contrasts with the meticulous care Kurosawa Akira took in representing black markets in *Stray Dog* (1949), in which the protagonist dons a thread-bare, patched-up army uniform to disguises himself as a destitute army veteran. When shooting *Seven Samurai* (1954), the crew prepared three sets of the same costume for the principal characters: they were asked to wear them at home every day to soil them naturally. Tsuchiya Yoshio, *Kurosawa saan! Kurosawa Akira tono subarashiki hibi* (Tokyo: Shinchōsha, 1999), 59. In *Battles*, the young male extras appear with long hair, a style of the early 1970s. In the early 1970s, with the whole film industry precipitously declining, no filmmakers could afford the level of care Kurosawa took in replicating historical settings.
61. Some critics of the film have pointed out that one cannot seriously portray yakuza society without addressing its strong ties with the Burakumin (a group that has historically been discriminated against) as well as resident Koreans. Yakuza society offered alternative forms of livelihood as well as an identity to members of these groups. Kasahara, *Jinginaki tatakai*, 346. Miyazaki Manabu reports on a yakuza boss's rough breakdown from the 1970s in which Burakumin, resident Koreans, and Japanese each constituted one-third of yakuza membership. Miyazaki agrees with the estimate, which he claims accurately describes the ratio in the Kansai area until the 1980s. Miyazaki Manabu, *Kindai yakuza kōteiron: Yamaguchi-gumi no 90 nen* (Tokyo: Chikuma shobō, 2007), 240–41.
62. Fukasaku Kinji and Yamane Sadao, *Eiga kantoku Fukasaku Kinji* (Tokyo: Waizu shuppan, 2003), 248–49.
63. Kasahara, *Jinginaki tatakai*, 341.
64. Although Kasahara did not write the script for *Battles Without Honor and Humanity: Final Episode*, the final film in the series, he shared his research notes and plot outline with the scriptwriter, Takada Kōji. Kasahara, *Eiga wa yakuza nari*, 81.
65. Alexander Zahlten offers a detailed discussion about the new generations of yakuza film that evolved as a subgenre of V-Cinema, or direct-to-video film, in *The End of Japanese Cinema: Industrial Genres, National Times, and Media Ecologies* (Durham, N.C.: Duke University Press, 2017), 178–85.

66. Some of the yakuza films that Kitano Takeshi directed broke out of the niche market and appealed to a wider audience.
67. The *It's Tough Being a Man* series was Shōchiku's answer to the demise of yakuza film. The boorish Torajirō was transformed into a lovable character as his ties with the shady *tekiya* world receded into the background (see chapter 3).
68. In real life, Fukasaku seemed to have lived a chauvinistic and far less complicated form of masculine ideal. Toward the end of his life, Fukasaku had an affair with the actress Oginome Keiko for nearly ten years (he was married to the actress Nakahara Sanae). Their relationship started, according to Oginome's accounts, with a rape. She was a lead actress in the film *Itsuka gira gira suru hi*, by Fukasaku. Oginome went to his hotel room to give him a massage and was assaulted by him. She was in a vulnerable state of mind: her former lover—another film director—committed suicide about a year before. She describes the rape in the following way: "Suddenly the director's body turned around. It was pressing my body down. I did not understand what was going on that moment. 'Is he kidding around? He must be drunk because he was drinking at dinner a moment ago. No, that's not it. I have no such intention. I've just come here [to Fukasaku's room] to give him a massage.' I tried to resist, but it was an awfully powerful force. I then became scared of his thick arms. I cried out 'Di-rec-tor.' When I heard my own strange voice, all my will to resist escaped my body. My own scream from the day when my former lover committed suicide returned and rendered my body powerless. 'Isn't he the one making this happen? Isn't he back here to bring me to his side, me who refused to follow him and am happily participating in the film shooting?' Such thoughts spun around in my head and I was no longer sure where I was. I could hardly speak. Then quiet returned to everything. The director gently rested my head on his arm and held me. I walked out of the room, stupefied." Oginome Keiko, *Joyū no yoru* (Tokyo: Tōgensha, 2002), 26–27. When Fukasaku discovered he had prostate cancer, he refused to go through hormone therapies, worrying that they would lower his male functions. He opted for more invasive treatments in order to maintain his sex life with Oginome. *Joyū no yoru*, 7–9.

## 7. Jō and Hyūma: Kajiwara Ikki's Manga Heroes and Their Violent Quest for Historical Agency

1. Anecdotal evidence suggests that the readership was not limited to youths. For example, visiting a Tohoku hot spring in 1969, Tsuge Yoshiharu was surprised to find manga weeklies among the reading materials that the elderly guests brought with them. Tsuge Yoshiharu, Ōsaki Norio, and Kitai Kazuo, *Tsuge Yoshiharu Nagare gumo tabi* (Tokyo: Ōbunsha, 1982), 58.
2. The Japanese boomers are commonly referred as *dankai no sedai* in Japanese. The writer Sakaiya Taichi coined the term to designate the explosive population growth from 1947 through 1949, in *Dankai no sedai* (Tokyo: Bungeishunjū, 2005), 38. Some writers use the term a bit more expansively. For example, Yuki Sōichi considers the

Japanese boomers to be those who were born from 1945 to 1950. Yuki Sōichi, *Dankai no sedai towa nandattanoka* (Tokyo: Yōsensha, 2003), 12.

3. In the late 1960s *Magazine* began to target older readers—high school students and young adults. Sakurai Tetsuo argues that this adjustment gave the weekly more creative latitude. Sakurai Tetsuo, *Haikyo no zanzō: Sengo manga no genzō* (Tokyo: NTT shuppan, 2015), 206.

4. The former editor of *Magazine*, Miyahara Teruo, recalls that the weekly was called "*Daigaku magajin* [College magazine]" on the streets in 1969 and 1970, at the height of the student radical movements. Miyahara Teruo, *Jitsuroku! Shōnen magajin meisaku manga henshū funtōki* (Tokyo: Kōdansha, 2005), 496–97.

5. Nagamine Hidetoshi, *Tōdaisei wa donna hon o yondekitaka: Hongō, Komaba no dokusho seikatsu 130 nen* (Tokyo: Heibonsha, 2007), 245–48.

6. Kajiwara Ikki, *Gekiga ichidai: Kajiwara Ikki jiden* (Tokyo: Shōgakkan, 2011), 53–55.

7. The story was also staged as a theatrical play (1971, 2016) and adapted for radio (1977). It inspired several video and computer games.

8. In 1992, based on survey responses from 174 celebrities and writers, the *Shūkan bunshun* editorial office named *Tomorrow's Jō* as the manga that left the deepest impression on contemporary readers. *Star of the Giants* ranked tenth in the same survey. Male subjects ranked both works higher than their female counterparts: *Tomorrow's Jō* and *Star of the Giants* ranked first and twelfth, respectively, among the male respondents, and twelfth and sixteenth among the female ones. There were also generational differences. Among the men who participated in the survey, those who were born between 1947 and 1956 ranked *Tomorrow's Jō* and *Star of the Giants* as first and tenth, while those who were born in and after 1957 ranked them second and first. Bungeishunjū, *Dai ankeito ni yoru shōnen shōjo manga besuto 100* (Tokyo: Bungeishunjū, 1992), 7–19, 66–67.

9. Their involvement can extend to finding housing for the artists and hiring assistants for them. Natsume Fusanosuke, "Sengo manga no nazo o tokukagi," in Miyahara, *Jitsuroku!*, 538. Sharon Kinsella observes that editor-artist relations can be acrimonious. Some artists see their editor's hands-on approach as encroachment on their creative freedom. Sharon Kinsella, *Adult Manga: Culture and Power in Contemporary Japanese Society* (Honolulu: University of Hawai'i Press, 2000), 8–9.

10. Miyahara, *Jitsuroku!*, 217–19, 223.

11. Natsume Fusanosuke discusses Kawasaki's dramatic drawing—some of which is even in the realm of experimental—in *Star of the Giants*. Natsume Fusanosuke, *Manga no fukayomi, otona yomi* (Tokyo: Iisuto puresu, 2004), 118–30.

12. Kajiwara, *Gekiga ichidai*, 80–81; Chiba Tetsuya, *Minminzemi no uta* (Tokyo: Nihon tosho sentaa, 2001), 136–37.

13. Chiba Tetsuya, *Dakara manga wa yamerarenai* (Tokyo: Popurasha, 1986), 176; Chiba Tetsuya, "*Ashita no Jō* to gensakusha," in *Ashita no Jō*, by Asamori Akio and Chiba Tetsuya (Tokyo: Kōdansha, 1989), 1:293–94.

14. Around 1975 Chiba tried to introduce a friend to Kajiwara in downtown Tokyo. Kajiwara pretended not to know Chiba and contemptuously walked away. Chiba was shocked by his arrogance. Saitō Takao, *Kajiwara Ikki den: Yūyake o miteita otoko*

(Tokyo: Bungeishunjū, 2005), 276–77. The quality of Kajiwara's work suffered as he began to demand deferential treatment from everybody around him.

15. Kajiwara's biographer, Saitō Takao, suspects that Kajiwara was jealous of Chiba's talent, and that he grew more protective of his scripts in later works. Saitō Takao, *Kajiwara Ikki den*, 209–10.

16. *Magazine*'s rival weekly *Weekly Shonen Jump* (*Shūkan shōnen janpu*) has always been hyper-responsive to readers, keeping only the most popular works on its roster. Saitō Jirō, *"Shonen janpu" no jidai* (Tokyo: Iwanami shoten, 1996), 12.

17. For example, Mizushima Shinji's baseball manga *Abu-san*'s serialization in *Big Comic Original* lasted from May 1973 to February 2014. The *Dokaben* series, also by Mizushima, appeared weekly in *Shōnen Champion* from April 1972 to June 2018. The action manga *Golgo 13* has been serialized in *Big Comic* from November 1968 to the present.

18. Miyahara, *Jitsuroku!*, 220.

19. Hashimoto discusses the two works along with *Love and Sincerity* (*Ai to makoto*, 1973–1976), another *Magazine* serial, for which Kajiwara also provided scripts. Hashimoto Kenji, *Kaikyū shakai: Gendai shakai no kakusa o tou* (Tokyo: Kōdansha, 2006), 74–92.

20. Kajiwara coined the name Hyūma from the English word "human" to highlight the human quality of the drama and thereby mark a departure from the fantastic tales that he had thus far produced. Miyahara, *Jitsuroku!*, 226.

21. Fujiki Kazuo discusses nine baseball manga, including *Star of the Giants*, that feature the Yomiuri Giants, in *Kyojin manga no keifu* (Tokyo: Suiseisha, 1998).

22. Ōno Shigeru, *"Sandei" to "Magajin"* (Tokyo: Kōbunsha, 2009), 209–10.

23. Sankei shinbun Sengoshi kaifū shuzai han, ed., *Sengoshi kaifū* 2 (Tokyo: Sankei shinbun nyūsu saabisu, 1995), 437.

24. Al Campanis, *Dodgers' Way to Play Baseball* (New York: Dutton, 1954). The Japanese translation was published three years later.

25. Ebisawa Yasuhisa, *Minna Jaiantsu o aishite ita* (Tokyo: Shinchōsha, 1983), 25–26.

26. Hyūma's story is reminiscent of the narrative pattern that Orikuchi Shinobu named *kishu ryūritan*: a person of noble birth condemned to life in a lower class. Although he or she suffers, the protagonist in the end rises above the challenges. In Orikuchi's characterization, noble birth can include divine origin. Furthermore, the stories do not necessarily end with the hero's or heroine's eventual triumph: they could die in total destitution. For a detailed commentary on the concept, see Nishimura Tōru, "Kishu ryūritan," in *Orikuchi Shinobu jiten*, ed. Nishimura Tōru (Tokyo: Daishūkan, 1988), 158–68.

27. For the 1995 version, the publisher, Kōdansha, deemed the designation *ninpu* (day laborer) derogatory and replaced it with *rōdōsha* (worker).

28. The television anime version further foregrounds the connections with the war. For example, in the scene where Kawakami Tetsuharu chases after the young Hyūma on the street, the background shows images of kamikaze planes diving at U.S. warships and Tokyo burning after the incendiary bombing. "Mezase eikō no hoshi," *Kyojin no hoshi* 1, DVD (Tokyo: Kōdansha and TMS, 2001).

29. On the basis of the information provided in the story, Eijun Itakura and Hisashi Uhara question whether Mina indeed has malignant melanoma and offer an alternative diagnosis of nail apparatus melanoma. Eijun Itakura and Hisashi Uhara, "Malignant Melanoma in Star of the Giants (Kyojin no Hoshi)," *Lancet* 12 (June 2011): 525.
30. The television version expresses their relationship more directly. In his dream, Hyūma looks into the mirror that Ozuma holds up. In it he sees Ozuma dressed in a Giants uniform. Furthermore, when he learns that Ozuma strongly desires to play in Japan, Hyūma's face suddenly metamorphoses into that of an African American man, with darker skin and thicker lips. "Oriawanu keiyaku," *Kyojin no hoshi* 92, DVD (Tokyo: Kōdansha and TMS, 2001).
31. This type of racial categorization is best represented by Shimada Keizō's illustrated story "The Adventures of Dankichi" (Bōken Dankichi), which was serialized from 1933 to 1939 in the monthly magazine *Shōnen kurabu*. Three chapters of the Dankichi story have been translated by Helen J. S. Lee and reprinted in *Reading Colonial Japan: Text, Context, and* Critique, ed. Michelle M. Mason and Helen J. S. Lee (Stanford, Calif.: Stanford University Press, 2012), 245–70. In the same volume, Kawamura Minato provides a concise commentary on Shimada's story and its historical context in "Popular Orientalism and Japanese Views of Asia," trans. Kota Inoue and Helen J. S. Lee, 271–98.
32. A popular manga serial from the late 1960s, Mochizuki Akira and Jinbo Shirō, *Sain wa V!*, featured another fictional character with African American heritage, Jun Sanders. Although she overcomes racial prejudice and becomes a star player on a corporate team, Tachiki Musashi, she dies from cancer right after the national championship game. *Sain wa V!*, 4 vols. (Tokyo: Shimanaka shoten, 2005).
33. The ball is pitched submarine style and evades the bat.
34. The legendary pitcher Sawamura Eiji (1917–1944) was the real-life inspiration for the story. Miyahara, *Jitsuroku!*, 218. It is possible to see a parallel between Hyūma and Sawamura in the way they change their arm slot from traditional overhand to submarine. Sawamura was forced to pitch from the side and eventually submarine because of shoulder injuries sustained while serving in the military. For the intertwining of Sawamura's career with Japan's war effort, see Dennis J. Frost, *Seeing Stars: Sports Celebrity, Identity, and Body Culture in Modern Japan* (Cambridge, Mass.: Harvard East Asian Monographs, 2010), 159–77.
35. Ōtsuka Eiji and Sasakibara Gō, *Kyōyō toshiteno manga, anime* (Tokyo: Kōdansha, 2001), 46.
36. In the planning stage for *Tomorrow's Jō*, the *Magazine* editors conceived the protagonist Jō as a nihilistic character who keeps his distance from both establishment and antiestablishment stances. Miyahara, *Jitsuroku!*, 240–41.
37. Norimatsu Suguru, *Bokushingu to Daitōa: Tōyō senshuken to sengo Ajia gaikō* (Tokyo: Bōyōsha, 2016), 223–25.
38. Yoshikuni Igarashi, *Bodies of Memory: Narratives of War in Postwar Japanese Culture, 1945–1970* (Princeton, N.J.: Princeton University Press, 2000), 69–70.
39. Takatori Ei, "Takamori Asao ni yoru *Ashita no Jō*," in *Ashita no Jō no jidai*, ed. Nerima kuritsu bijutsukan (Tokyo: Kyūryūdō, 2014), 154.

40. Norimatsu, *Bokushingu to Daitōa*, 224.
41. Tamiya Takamaro, "Shuppatsu sengen," in *Zōho Sekigun dokyumento—sentō no kōjiroku*, ed. Sashō henshū iinkai (Tokyo: Shinsensha, 1978), 101.
42. Although he stood on the opposite end of the political spectrum, Mishima Yukio sympathized with the antiestablishment youth movements and was also an avid fan of *Tomorrow's Jō*. Miyahara Teruo recalls that one day in 1969, Mishima showed up at *Magazine*'s editorial room late at night to obtain a copy of the weekly. Miyahara, *Jitsuroku!*, 251.
43. According to Takazawa Kōji, the 1969 campus shutdown spread to eighty-six public universities and seventy-nine private ones—almost half of all Japanese universities. Takazawa Kōji, *Zōho Zenkyōtō gurafitii* (Tokyo: Shinsensha, 1990), 48. The writer Tazawa Ryūji (b. 1953) recalls a scene he witnessed in March 1968, just as Jō is beginning to train himself in the reformatory. A group of student activists in their helmets were on a train heading for Narita. One of them happened to be reading *Magazine* and talked excitedly about the reformatory scene as a source of inspiration; other activists joined in the lively conversation. Tazawa Ryūji, "Chiba Tetsuya: Ashita no Jō ga watatta 1970 nen toiu hashi," in *Wakamono ga "Wakamono" datta jidai*, ed. Shūkan kinyōbi (Tokyo: Kinyōbi, 2012), 103–4.
44. *Sankei shinbun*, March 26, 1970, evening 2nd ed. Miura Atsushi discusses the report that copies of *Magazine* were everywhere in Yasuda Hall on the University of Tokyo campus when the riot police forcefully ended the campus strike. Miura Atsushi, *Dankai sedai no sengoshi* (Tokyo: Bungeishunjū, 2007), 53.
45. Terayama Shūji, *Shin sho o suteyo, machi e deyō* (Tokyo: Kawade shobō, 1993), 36–37.
46. The tensions between disciplining of the body and eventual release of wild energy existed already in early forms of pugilism. In writing about the ways in which legendary nineteenth-century bare-knuckle boxers Yankee Sullivan and Tom Hyer trained for a match, Elliott J. Gorn observes: "Just as prize fights created a meritocracy of violence, so the boxers' training regiments turned bourgeois and evangelical ideals on their heads, enlisting abstemiousness in the cause of wild pleasures." Elliott J. Gorn, *The Manly Art: Bare-Knuckle Prize Fighting in America* (Ithaca, N.Y.: Cornell University Press, 1986), 91.
47. Jō and his rivals freely exchange words in the ring. The words in the bubbles are only part of their dialogue. The rest of it is carried out through their physical exchange of punches.
48. *Nihon kokugo daijiten* lists an early usage of the term kentō from 1897.
49. It appears that Danpei later builds a more modern, legitimate gym near the original structure. *TJ* 16:126–27.
50. Terayama Shūji, "Darega Riki'ishi o koroshitanoka," *Nihon dokusho shinbun*, February 16, 1970, 8.
51. He was hospitalized for a duodenal ulcer. "Interview: Chiba Tetsuya," in *Ashita no Jō konpuriito bukku*, ed. Isshūkan henshūbu (Tokyo: Kōdansha, 2010), 55.
52. The ceremony was held on March 24, 1970. "Shōgeki no Riki'ishi To'oru kokubetsushiki fan 700 nin nekkyō no tsudoi," *Shōnen magajin*, April 19, 1970, 119–21; *Sankei shinbun*, March 26, 1970, 2nd evening ed. Steven Ridgely discusses Terayama's

reactions to Riki'ishi's death in *Japanese Counterculture: The Antiestablishment Art of Terayama Shūji* (Minneapolis: University of Minnesota Press, 2010), 92–97.

53. I am reversing Gilles Deleuze and Félix Guattari's concept "the body without organs" to highlight Yōko's essential identity as a capitalist. Gilles Deleuze and Félix Guattari, *Anti-Oedipus: Capitalism and Schizophrenia* (Minneapolis: University of Minnesota Press, 1983), 9–10.

54. Quoted in "Ashita no Jō ni kaketa Kajiwara Ikki, Chiba Tetsuya shi no tatakai no ato," *Shūkan taishū*, April 26, 1973, 36.

55. In early 1971, with *Star of the Giants* coming to its conclusion and *Tomorrow's Jō* interrupted because of Chiba Tetsuya's illness, *Magazine* faced a major challenge. Even after the serialization of *Tomorrow's Jō* resumed, *Magazine*'s circulation, which had reached 1.5 million, dipped below half a million for two issues. Miyahara, *Jitsuroku!*, 290–91, 337.

56. The writer Maki Hisao—Kajiwara's brother—insists that *Ashita no Jō* reached its climax with Riki'ishi's death, and what comes after that is redundant. Quoted in Saitō, *Kajiwara Ikki den*, 198.

57. For example, when the student activists at Ritsumeikan University in Kyoto dragged down the statue of Wadatsumi in May 1969, they were expressing their anger over the ways in which the war generations dominated and defined conversations about war. Since its creation in 1950, the slightly larger-than-life bronze statue of a young healthy man had been a symbol of the war generations' suffering as well as their aspirations for peace. By damaging the statue, the activists tried to assert their own subjective position, separate from that of the war generation, within the antiwar discourse of postwar Japan. They contended that the older generations had fallen into complacency, while the youth actively sought to confront Japan's wartime past. Ono Hiroshi, "Gūzōkashita 'Wadatsumi zō,'" *Sekai* (August 1969): 223–25; Ayuhara Rin, "Shishatachi no fukken: Wadatsumizō hakaisha tachi no shisō," *Asahi jaanaru*, February 8, 1970, 38–42. Like Riki'ishi and Jō, the activists at Ritsumeikan University and elsewhere insisted on the legitimacy of their struggle by rejecting the promise of "tomorrow"—an assured future in society under the high-growth economy. As it is impossible to transcend historical conditions completely, however, the activists could not claim perfect legitimacy for their actions. Unable to make a clean break with postwar society, they resorted to more direct actions—campus shutdowns, clashes with the riot police, and escalating violence.

58. Ōtsuka Eiji and Sasakibara Gō focus on the body that is unable to mature in *Astro Boy* and posit it as an important motif in Japan's postwar manga history. They extend their discussion and offer observations on *Star of the Giants* and *Tomorrow's Jō*: "Hyūma manages to grow only by exiting his father's narrative. By contrast, Jō tries to live as an 'eternal boy' like Astro Boy, with his youthful growing body." Ōtsuka and Sasakibara, *Kyōyō toshiteno manga, anime*, 35–36, 55. While the issue of physical growth is central to the two stories, Ōtsuka and Sasakibara do not say much about how it relates to specific historical conditions. Hyūma does not step out of his father's story but completely internalizes it, while Jō's growing body embodies the history of postwar Japan, particularly its economic growth.

59. After the conclusion of the Asia Pacific War, Chiba and his family repatriated from Manchuria. The difficult experience of repatriation, he recalls, resurfaced as he drew the scene leading to Kim's patricide: "Something that I had stored deep inside came out. . . . It's like, sometimes, an old wound opens and pus oozes out." Chiba Tetsuya, "Masshiro na hai ni natte moetsukiru made," in *Chiba Tetsuya*, ed. Nishiguchi Tōru and Anazawa Yūko (Tokyo: Kawadeshobō shinsha, 2011), 32.
60. Yōko's presence is instrumental to Jō's philosophical awakening in this scene. She strongly advises Danpei to throw in the towel to avoid repeating Riki'ishi's tragedy. Contrary to her intention, however, her words make Jō double down and fight to the end. This scene confirms that Yōko continues to mediate Jō and Riki'ishi's relationship.
61. Suga Hidemi, *Kakumei tekina amarini kakumei tekina: 1968 nen no kakumei shiron* (Tokyo: Sakuhinsha, 2003), 278. With the success of George Romero's *Dawn of the Dead* (1978, dir. George A. Romero), zombies have become a staple of popular culture. Fujita Naoya, *Shinseiki zonbi gaku* (Tokyo: Chikuma shobō, 2017), 16. In this film zombies are attracted and also controlled by consumer culture. It is possible to locate in this theme the fear of losing agency in a world of commodity fetishes. For a more detailed discussion of the connections between zombies and consumerism, see Stephen Harper, "Zombies, Malls, and the Consumerism Debate: George Romero's Dawn of the Dead," *Americana: The Journal of American Popular Culture* 1–2 (Fall 2002), http://www.americanpopularculture.com/journal/articles/fall_2002/harper.htm.
62. Although CTE today is most widely associated with American football, it was originally identified in boxers by H. S. Martland in 1928. In early medical discussions, such terms as *punch-drunk*, *dementia pugilistica*, and *psychopathic deterioration of pugilists* were used to describe the disorder now associated with CTE. Ann C. McKee et al., "Chronic Traumatic Encephalopathy in Athletes: Progressive Tauopathy After Repetitive Head Injury," *Journal of Neuropathology & Experimental Neurology*, 68, no. 7 (July 2009), https://academic.oup.com/jnen/article/68/7/709/2917002.
63. The publication of the final episode of *Tomorrow's Jō* was a much-anticipated event. A Kōdansha editor recalls a scene he witnessed: "When the *Shōnen magajin* with *Tomorrow's Jō*'s final installment came out, I happened to be at the Tokyo Station. Twenty to thirty young workers of the then–National Railways, dressed in work suits, were racing up the stairs to a platform, like a stampede. I was not sure what was going on. It turned out that they were scrambling to buy a copy of *Magajin* at the kiosk. I got goose bumps." Natsume, *Manga no fukayomi, otonayomi*, 199.
64. Chiba Tetsuya and his assistants created this famous scene. According to Chiba, Kajiwara's original script read: "Jose defeats Jō. Danpei comforts Jō, who is hanging his head in the corner: 'You lost the match but won the fight.' Jō is idly sunbathing with Yōko at the Shiraki mansion. It is not clear if he has lost his mental capacity. Yōko is smiling. They seem happy." Chiba informed Kajiwara over the phone that he would change this ending. Saitō, *Kajiwara Ikki den*, 206.
65. Asaine Hideo, *Ashita no Jō wa shindanoka* (Tokyo: Chikuma shobō, 1988), 153–54.
66. Murakami Tomohiko, "*Ashita no Jō* no kinō, kyō, ashita," *Kinema junpō*, February 1, 1980, 120.

67. According to Saito Takao, Kajiwara's biographer, this scene was not in Kajiwara's original script. Chiba added it on his own. Saito, *Kajiwara Ikki den*, 205.
68. This is a repeat of an earlier scene, which is revealed in a flashback. Yōko tried to leave the match between Jō and Riki'ishi in the reformatory. But Jō insisted that she, as the instigator, must watch the whole match (*TJ* 13:219–20).
69. While Chiba claimed that he made the final sequence intentionally ambiguous, he also admitted that he was thinking, as he drew the final scene, that Jō might have died completely burnt out. Toyohara Kikō and Chiba Tetsuya, *Chiba Tetsuya to Jō no Tatakai to seishun no 1954 nichi* (Tokyo: Kōdansha, 2010), 258. The editor Miyahara Teruo believed that because Riki'ishi died, Jō must die as well. Natsume, *Manga no fukayomi, otonayomi*, 222.
70. For detailed accounts and analyses of the debates on subjectivity in the early postwar years, see Victor Koschmann, *Revolution and Subjectivity in Postwar Japan* (Chicago: University of Chicago Press, 1996).
71. Kobayashi Toshiaki, *Shutai no yukue* (Tokyo: Kōdansha, 2010), 186–216.
72. In reality, Hyūma's future is not too bright. In exchange for his body, he gained access to "tomorrow." A former Giants pitcher who has destroyed his throwing arm would have no problem surviving the boom years. Yet to do so he would have to find a niche and ensconce himself in postwar Japan. In *New Star of the Giants* (*Shin Kyojin no hoshi*), serialized in *Weekly Yomiuri* from 1976 to 1979, Hyūma makes a comeback, pitching with his right arm. The sequel does not reveal how he survived in the intervening years. Kajiwara Ikki and Kawasaki Noboru, *Shin Kyojin no hoshi*, 6 vols. (Tokyo: Kōdansha, 1990).

## 8. Dead Bodies and Living Guns: The United Red Army and Its Deadly Pursuit of Revolution

1. Kunō Yasushi, *Asama-sansō jiken no shinjitsu* (Tokyo: Kawade shobō-shinsha, 2000), 265.
2. Fifty-two Japanese and a few foreign media companies were present at the daily press conferences held at the Karuizawa Police Headquarters. Kunō, *Asama-sansō jiken no shinjitsu*, 94. Commercial television stations sent nearly 340 people to Karuizawa to cover the event. Nihon hōsō kyōkai, *Hōsō 50 nenshi, shiryōhen* (Tokyo: Nihon hōsō shuppan kyōkai, 1977), 380.
3. "Asama jiken: Shōgakusei kara shufu made no uketomekata," *Shūkan sankei*, March 27, 1972, 133.
4. Wakamatsu Kōji, "Yonaoshi no kikkake," *Shukan gendai*, March 21, 1972, 122.
5. Yoshimoto Taka'aki, *Yoshimoto Taka'aki chosakushū* 13 (Tokyo: Keisōshobō, 1969), 87–101.
6. In the 1960s the new left groups splintered into scores of smaller factions, fighting over increasingly finer ideological points. Takagi Masayuki, "Shinsayoku keitō ryakuzu," in *Shinsayoku 30 nenshi* (Tokyo: Doyō bijutsusha, 1988), 255.

7. Patricia G. Steinhoff, *Shi eno ideorogii: Nihon-Sekigunha* (Tokyo: Iwanami shoten, 2003), 145–46; Oguma Eiji, *1968 2: Hanran no shūen to sono isan* (Tokyo: Shinyōsha, 2009), 610–12; Uegaki Yasuhiro quoted in Ōizumi Yasuo, *Asama-sansō jūgekisen no shinsō* (Tokyo: Shōgakukan, 2003), 366; Takazawa Kōji, *Rekishi toshiteno shinsayoku* (Tokyo: Shinsensha, 1996), 50–51; Yomiuri shinbun shakaibu, *Rengōsekigun: Kono ningen sōshitsu* (Tokyo: Ushio shuppan, 1972), 353–54; Maeno Tatsuyoshi quoted in Ōizumi, *Asama-sansō jūgekisen no shinsō*, 368–69; Shiomi Takaya, "Gokuchū no shidōsha Shiomi Takaya no shōgen," in *Shōgen Rengōsekigun*, ed. Rengōsekigin jiken no zentaizō o nokosukai (Tokyo: Kōseisha, 2013), 415–16; Bandō Kunio, *Nagata Hiroko san eno tegami* (Tokyo: Sairyūsha, 1984), 129–30.
8. The introduction and first section of Shiomi's "Katoki Sekai ron" are reprinted in Shiomi Takaya, *Sekigun-ha shimatsuki: Moto gichō ga kataru 40 nenn* (Tokyo: Sairyūsha, 2003), 232–49.
9. Shiomi, *Sekigunha shimatsuki*, 79–80, 81–82; Ara Taisuke, *Hatenkōden* (Tokyo: Ōtashuppan, 2001), 116. According to Shiomi Takaya's recollections, the Kansai faction began to use the name "Red Army" around June 1969.
10. Yomiuri shinbun shakaibu, *Rengōsekigun*, 142.
11. *Asahi shinbun*, September 23, 1969, 12th ed.
12. *Asahi shinbun*, October 1, 1969, 12th ed.
13. *Asahi shinbun*, November 5, 1969, evening, 3rd ed.; Biza henshū iinkai, ed., *Shinpen Sekigun dokyumento* (Tokyo: Shinsensha, 1986), 75–79.
14. Shiomi, *Sekigunha shimatsuki*, 101–2.
15. After intensive ideological training, the members embraced North Korea's official ideology and participated in a program designed to produce ethnic Japanese operatives for Pyongyang. They married Japanese women who had, for the most part, left Japan to deepen their understanding of North Korea; only after arriving there did the women realize that they had no choice but to marry a member of the Red Army faction. With their wives' help, faction members lured Japanese youths who were visiting Europe to North Korea. Takazawa Kōji, *Shukumei: Yodo-gō bōmeisha tachino himitsukōsaku* (Tokyo: Shinchōsha, 1998), 113–31, 214–22, 293–99. Of the nine activists who went to North Korea, the leader, Tamiya, and two others died there. Tanaka Yoshimi was arrested at the Cambodia-Vietnam border in 1996 and served a prison term in Japan; his sentence was suspended because of illness, and he died in 2007. Shibata Yasuhiro, the youngest of the hijackers (he was sixteen in March 1970), was arrested in Japan, served a prison term, and was subsequently freed; he died in 2011. The remaining four members still reside in North Korea. NHK hōdōkyoku Yodo-gō to rachi shuzaihan, *Yodo-gō to rachi* (Tokyo: NHK shuppan, 2004), 21–22.
16. Yomiuri shinbun shakaibu, *Rengōsekigun*, 288–89.
17. In the Japanese media, the name of a subgroup, Keihin Anpo Kyōtō, is often used to designate the Revolutionary Left because of the Japan Communist Party's repeated protests that the Revolutionary Left had no affiliation with the JCP. Shiino Reinin, ed., *Rengōsekigun o yomu nenpyō* (Tokyo: Sairyūsha, 2002), 27.
18. *Asahi shinbun*, September 4, 1969, 13th ed.
19. *Asahi shinbun*, September 4, 1969, 13th ed.

20. Nagata Hiroko, *Jūroku no bohyō* 1 (Tokyo: Sairyūsha, 1982), 146–51, 129–30.
21. The Red Army faction strongly supported this position. Biza henshū iinkai, *Shinpen "Sekigun" dokyumento*, 141–43.
22. Yomiuri shinbun shakaibu, *Rengōsekigun*, 326; *Asahi shinbun*, February 17, 1971, evening, 3rd ed. Ten days later the police recovered one shotgun and 1,500 rounds of ammunition that the group left at two hideouts in Tochigi and Gunma Prefectures. *Asahi shinbun*, February 28, 1971, 12th ed.
23. Nagata, *Jūroku no bohyō*, 1:183–89. Right after the incident, the police mobilized 45,000 officers and checked 250,000 locations. Sakaguchi Hiroshi, *Asama-sansō 1972*, 1 (Tokyo: Sairyūsha, 1993), 297–300.
24. Sakaguchi, *Asama-sansō 1972*, 1:303.
25. Nagata, *Jūroku no bohyō*, 1:219.
26. Sakaguchi, *Asama-sansō 1972*, 1:330.
27. Nagata, *Jūroku no bohyō*, 1:278.
28. Sakaguchi, *Asama-sansō 1972*, 1:337.
29. Bandō, *Nagata Hiroko san eno tegami*, 102–3.
30. Uegaki Yasuhiro, *Heishitachi no Rengōsekigun* (Tokyo: Sairyūsha, 2001), 220; Bandō, *Nagata Hiroko san eno tegami*, 104–5.
31. Uegaki, *Heishitachi no Rengōsekigun*, 223.
32. Yomiuri shinbun shakaibu, *Rengōsekigun*, 127.
33. Mori confided to Sakaguchi his determination to make up for the crime of defection by sacrificing his life for the cause. Sakaguchi, *Asama-sansō 1972*, 1:304.
34. Biza henshū iinkai, *Shinpen Sekigun dokyumento*, 196–99; Sakaguchi, *Asama-sansō 1972*, 1:324–25; Nagata, *Jūroku no bohyō*, 1:265–67.
35. Kawashima Tsuyoshi tried to exert his influence over the new organization from his prison cell by insisting that the new organization change its name to the United Red Army. His directive was largely symbolic, and other Revolutionary Left members were initially baffled by it, but they eventually accepted Kawashima's insistence that a new name was necessary to preserve the Revolutionary Left's original stance of anti-American patriotism. Nagata Hiroko, *Jūroku no bohyō*, 2 (Tokyo: Sairyūsha, 1982), 8; Takahashi Mayumi, *Katararezaru Rengōsekigun: Asama-sansō kara 30 nen* (Tokyo: Sairyūsha, 2002), 70.
36. Uegaki, *Heishitachi no Rengōsekigun*, 235–39.
37. Sakaguchi Hiroshi, *Asama-sansō 1972*, 2 (Tokyo: Sairyūsha, 1993), 210–12.
38. According to Uegaki, Tōyama Mieko and Namekata Masatoki carried Kojima's body to another location and buried it there as part of their self-critique sessions, while all the other members observed their every move. Ōtsuki Setsuko and another member helped dig a hole. Uegaki, *Heishitachi no Rengōsekigun*, 286–87.
39. Uegaki Yasuhiro, Written statement, Sasanoi Police Station, April 21, 1972, Takazawa Collection, University of Hawaii.
40. Sakaguchi, *Asama-sansō 1972* 2, 193–99; Uegaki, *Heishitachi no Rengōsekigun*, 265–67; Bandō, *Nagata Hiroko san eno tegami*, 139–41.
41. Nagata, *Jūroku no bohyō* 2, 111.

42. Although the Red Army faction and the Revolutionary Left began joint training in early December, the merger was not "official" until December 27, 1971.
43. Sakaguchi, *Asama-sansō 1972*, 2:257.
44. Mori Tsuneo, *Jūgekisen to shukusei* (Tokyo: Shinsensha, 1984), 32–33; Nagata, *Jūroku no bohyō*, 2:126; Sakaguchi, *Asama-sansō 1972*, 2:257.
45. Mori, *Jūekisen to shukusei*, 33; Nagata, *Jūroku no bohyō*, 2:164; Sakaguchi, *Asama-sansō 1972*, 2:255.
46. Nagata, *Jūroku no bohyō*, 2:165–66.
47. Sakaguchi, *Asama-sansō 1972*, 2:263.
48. Nagata, *Jūroku no bohyō*, 2:181.
49. Sakaguchi, *Asama-sansō 1972*, 2:259.
50. Although Katō Yoshitaka's two younger brothers hesitated to beat their sibling, the other members urged them on, defining the beating as "comradely assistance." Nagata brought the second brother's hand to Yoshitaka's face. Katō Michinori, *Rengōsekigun shōnen A* (Tokyo: Shinchōsha, 2003), 134–39.
51. Sakaguchi, *Asama-sansō 1972*, 2:263. Nagata recalls that Mori made these comments after beating Ozaki Michio. Nagata, *Jūroku no bohyō*, 2:204.
52. Mori, *Jūgekisen to shukusei*, 38–39; Sakaguchi, *Zoku Asama-sansō 1972*, 26–29.
53. Mori, *Jūgekisen to shukusei*, 115; Nagata, *Jūroku no bohyō*, 2:190–93; Sakaguchi, *Asama-sansō 1972*, 2:277–81.
54. Sakaguchi, *Asama-sansō 1972*, 2:287; see also Mori, *Jūgekisen to shukusei*, 49.
55. Mori, *Jūgekisen to shukusei*, 127; Sakaguchi, *Zoku Asama-sansō 1972*, 45–46. After this self-beating session, Nagata fetched a mirror to show Tōyama her battered face. Nagata, *Juroku no bohyō*, 2:234–36.
56. Ōtsuka Eiji, *Kanojotachi no Rengōsekigun: Sabu karuchaa to sengo minshushugi* (Tokyo: Bungeishunjū, 1996), 8–79.
57. Nagata, *Jūroku no bohyō*, 2:85–93; Sakaguchi, *Asama-sansō 1972*, 2:185–86.
58. Mori, *Jūgekisen to shukusei*, 60–61.
59. At one point, Mori made an explicit connection between his indifference to women's rights and his revulsion toward menstrual blood. Nagata, *Jūroku no bohyō* 2:128.
60. Quoted in Nagata, *Jūroku no bohyō* 2:109.
61. Nagata, *Jūroku no bohyō*, 2:93–94.
62. Tanaka Mitsu, "Nagata Hiroko shikeishū no shini: Onna de arisugita kanojo," *Asahi shinbun*, February 26, 2011, 13th ed.
63. Nagata, *Jūroku no bohyō* 2:289–90.
64. Mori, *Jūgekisen to shukusei*, 149; Nagata, *Jūroku no bohyō* 2:314.
65. The situation discussed here is reminiscent of the "great divide" between modernism and mass culture in nineteenth-century Europe that Andreas Huyssen discusses. While the self-conscious attitude of modernism was associated with the masculine, the amorphous nature of mass culture was associated with the feminine. The self-questioning required of each URA member was a thoroughly modernist act because it guarded the autonomy of revolutionary subjectivity by denigrating what takes place in the everyday life of the masses. Andreas Huyssen, "Mass Culture as

Woman: Modernism's Other," in *After the Great Divide: Modernism, Mass Culture, Postmodernism* (Bloomington: Indiana University Press, 1986), 44–62.
66. Mori, *Jūgekisen to shukusei*, 152; Nagata, *Jūroku no bohyō* 2:339.
67. Mori, *Jūgekisen to shukusei*, 85; Nagata, *Jūroku no bohyō* 2:315.
68. Nagata, *Jūroku no bohyō* 2:309.
69. Aoto objected to the idea on the grounds that the fetus would be too premature to survive out of utero. Aoto Mikio, Written statement, Nagano Police Station, April 10, 1972, Takazawa Collection, University of Hawaii.
70. Nagata, *Jūroku no bohyō* 2:343–44.
71. In a police interrogation, Aoto claimed that "when Kaneko died, Nagata beat her body bawling, 'You bastard.' The death of the fetus appeared to be a blow to her." Aoto, Written statement.
72. Mori, *Jūgekisen to shukusei*, 86.
73. Bandō Kunio, Written statement, Nakano Police Station, April 15, 1972, Takazawa Collection, University of Hawaii.
74. Although singing was one of the few forms of entertainment that participants in the training sessions initially enjoyed, it disappeared as an oppressive atmosphere of comprehensive self-criticism began to rule the group. Yukino Kensaku recalls his experiences at Revolutionary Left's mountain bases in the following way (he was arrested in August 1971 before the formation of the URA): "[Although the life at the camps was inconvenient in comparison to city life,] it was open and comfortable for those who were wanted by the police. When the weather is good, the sky is high and blue. We sometimes sang 'The Internationale' to our heart's content with candle light while drinking." Yukino Kensaku, "Waga seishun no shisōhenreki," in *Shōgen Rengōsekigin jiken*, ed. Shōgen Rengōsekigun jiken no zentaizō o nokosukai (Tokyo: Kōseisha, 2013), 344.
75. Sakaguchi, *Asama-sansō 1972*, 1:34.
76. Sakaguchi, *Asama-sansō 1972*, 1:344.
77. According to Nagata, Yoshino Masakuni realized Ozaki was dead because of the same odor that he recalled smelling at a member's execution. Nagata, Written statement, Matsuida Police Station May 6, 1972, Takazawa Collection, University of Hawaii.
78. "Rengōsekigun jōshin kokkyō yukino daihōisen," *Sandei mainichi*, March 5, 1972, 17.
79. Uegaki, *Heishitachi no Rengōsekigun*, 378.
80. Sakaguchi, *Asama-sansō 1972*, 1:296.
81. For a more detailed account of the event, see William Marotti, "Japan in 1968: The Performance of Violence and the Theater of Protest," *American Historical Review* 104, no. 1 (February 2009): 112–28.
82. Sakaguchi, *Asama-sansō 1972*, 1:113.
83. Quoted in Matsumoto Hideo, "Sasebo jiken to terebi hōdō," *Gendai no riron* (April 1968): 112.
84. Sakaguchi, *Asama-sansō 1972*, 1:116.
85. Matsumoto, "Sasebo jiken to terebi hōdō," 115.

86. Takigawa Hiroshi, *Kagekiha kaimetsu sakusen: Kōan kisha nikki* (Tokyo: San'ichi shobō, 1973), 64–65. The police expanded from a force of 128,000 to 177,612 in the ten years following the anti-U.S.-Japan Security Treaty demonstrations of 1960. Hoshino Yasusaburō, "Todōfuken keisatsu no jittai," *Toshi mondai* (June 1970): 5.
87. Takigawa, *Kagekiha kaimetsu sakusen*, 244–45.
88. Sakaguchi, *Asama-sansō 1972*, 2:90.
89. Tanaka Mitsu, *Inochi no onnatachi e* (Tokyo: Kawadeshobō shinsha, 1992), 198, quoting the reporter Hirata Etsurō. The recording of Hirata's comment is included in a television retrospective from 2012 on these events. *Asama-sansō jiken Media no genzai*, NHK, 70 min., February 26, 2012.
90. Yomota Inuhiko reports that many people believed "that the United Red Army's bloody purge was a reaction to Mishima Yukio's dramatic suicide." On November 25, 1970, Mishima and four members of the Shield Society (Mishima's private paramilitary group) went to the Ichigaya headquarters of the Eastern Command of the Ground Self-Defense Forces, took the commandant hostage, and demanded that Mishima be allowed to address the servicemen there. He implored them to rise up against the postwar constitutional system. Realizing their failure to incite the troops, Mishima and a Shield Society member committed ritual suicide by disembowelment. Yomota Inuhiko, "Kokuchi to genjitsu," in *1968 2, Bungaku*, ed. Yomota Inuhiko and Fukuma Kenji (Tokyo: Chikuma shobō, 2018), 49. In a murder mystery in 2017, Kasai Kiyoshi (b. 1948) has one of the characters articulate a theory relating the URA incident to the way Japan ended the Asia Pacific War: "The fact that the Japanese chickened out of the final battle in WWII begging for their lives and chose to become the United States' subject nation is the historical background of the URA's self-destruction." Another character elaborates: "The misfortunes of the postwar generations reside in the fact that Japan willingly accepted the status of a subject nation and was subsequently swallowed up by a shallow affluence. The slogan of 'revolutionary war' grabbed the hearts of many youths in 1969 because they consciously or unconsciously wished to complete the unfinished final battle with their own hands." Kasai Kiyoshi, *Tensei no ma: Shiritsu tantei Asukai no jikenbo* (Tokyo: Kōdansha, 2017), 250. While it is entirely possible that these two historical events cast dark shadows on the minds of politically active youths in early 1970s Japan, none of the participants in the URA purges ever acknowledged these historical connections.
91. Kunō, *Asama-sansō jiken no shinjitsu*, 282, 284. In his book, Kunō uses pseudonyms to protect the identity of low-ranking members.
92. Maruyama Teruo, "Mori Tsuneo to Rengōsekigun jiken," *Gendai no me* (January 1975): 196.
93. Shigenobu Fusako, "Saraba Rengōsekigun no dōshishokun: Beirūto yori aito kanashimi o komete," *Shūkan yomiuri*, April 15, 1972, 16–19.
94. Shigenobu Fusako, *Ringo no ki no shitade anata o umōto kimeta* (Tokyo: Gentōsha, 2001), 80–81.
95. Shigenobu Fusako, *Kakumei no kisetsu: Paresuchina no senjō kara* (Tokyo: Tōgensha, 2012), 161.

96. Patricia Steinhoff interviewed Okamoto Kōzō, the only surviving assailant in Israeli custody. A condensed version of the interview is included in her book *Shi eno ideorogii*, 25–43. The Japanese Red Army collaborated with the Popular Front for the Liberation of Palestine (PFLP) on other occasions. Fourteen months after the attack at Lod Airport, five Japanese Red Army members and four PFLP members hijacked a Japan Airlines 747 jetliner in Dubai. The plane was blown up in Benghazi by the hijackers minutes after they released 145 passengers and crew members. In January 1974 two Japanese Red Army members and two PFLP members attacked a Royal Dutch Shell oil refinery with explosives but failed to escape and took workers as hostages. Other militants from the two groups then raided the Japanese Embassy in Kuwait, took the ambassador and other diplomats hostage, and successfully negotiated the release of the first group.
97. Shigenobu Fusako, *Jūnenme no manazashi kara* (Tokyo: Hanashi no tokushū, 1983), 21.
98. Inoue Masaharu and Sakaguchi Hiroshi, "Watashi wa naze shakuhō o kyohishitaka," *Sandei mainichi*, August 24, 1975, 18–19.
99. Inoue and Sekiguchi, "Watashi wa naze shakuhō o kyohishitaka," 18–19; Sakaguchi, *Zoku Asama-sansō*, 250–54.
100. Uegaki Yasuhiro, "Kaisetsu ni kaete: Uegaki Yasuhiro rongu intabyū," in *Rengōsekigun jiken o yomu nenpyō*, ed. Shiino Reinin (Tokyo: Sairyūsha, 2002), 154.
101. Katō, *Rengōsekigun shōnen A*, 201.
102. "Rengōsekigun jiken (tōitsugumi) dai isshin hanketsu," June 18, 1982, *Hanrei jihō*, November 1, 1982, 50.
103. Sakaguchi Hiroshi, *Sakaguchi Hiroshi kakō* (Tokyo: Asahi shinbunsha, 1993), *Tokoshi eno michi* (Tokyo: Kadokawa shoten, 2007), and *Kashū ankoku seiki* (Tokyo: Kadokawa gakugei shuppan, 2015).
104. Asayama Jitsu, *Afutaa reddo: Rengōsekigun heishitachi no 40 nen* (Tokyo: Kadokawa shoten, 2012), 168. There is a popular theory that the police siege at Asama-sansō helped the subsequent sales of Cup O'Noodle, which was first introduced to the market in September 1971: televised scenes of policemen eating Cup O'Noodle in subzero temperatures gave the product household recognition. I suspect that this is largely an urban myth. The rising popularity of the product could well have been a delayed response to an aggressive advertising campaign.
105. "Nagata Hiroko shikeishū ga shibō," *Asahi shinbun*, February 7, 2011, 13th ed.

# Epilogue: Legacies of 1972

1. Sawamiya Yū, *Shūdan shūshoku: Kōdo keizai seichō o sasaeta kin no tamago tachi* (Fukuoka: Genshobō, 2017), 27–29.
2. LDP policy makers began to show concern about rural depopulation in the 1960s in large part because it would negatively affect their political base. The Diet passed *Kasochiiki taisaku kinkyūsochi hō*, an emergency bill to address issues associated with rural

depopulation, in 1970. http://www.shugiin.go.jp/internet/itdb_housei.nsf/html/houritsu/06319700424031.htm (accessed August 7, 2020).
3. Hayano Tōru, *Tanaka Kakuei: Sengo Nihon no kanashiki jigazō* (Tokyo: Chūōkōron shinsha, 2012), 146–47; Hosaka Masayasu, *Tanaka Kakuei no Shōwa* (Tokyo: Asahi shinbun shuppan, 2010), 153–56.
4. Japan's Building Standards Act set the height limit for buildings at 31 meters (101.7 feet). Tanaka argued that Tokyo Tower was an advertisement tower, not a building, and hence outside the purview of the act. Hayano, *Tanaka Kakuei*, 143.
5. Tanaka Kakuei, *Nippon rettō kaizōron* (Tokyo: Nihon kōgyō shinbunsha, 1972); *Building a New Japan: A Plan for Remodeling the Japanese Archipelago* (Tokyo: Simul Press, 1973).
6. Total sales reached 900,000 copies. Hayano, *Tanaka Kakuei*, 256.
7. Tanaka, *Nihon rettō kaizōron*, 216; *Building a New Japan*, 218. I translate *kyōri* as "hometown" here, although the published translation renders it as "home."
8. Hosaka, *Tanaka Kakuei no Shōwa*, 5.
9. Tachibana Takashi, "Tanaka Kakuei kenkyū: Sono kinmyaku to jinmyaku," *Bungeishunjū* (November 1974): 92–131.
10. Tanaka, *Nihon rettō kaizōron*, 84–85, 88, 92, 141.
11. Hayano, *Tanaka Kakuei*, 267.
12. Hattori Ryūji, *Tanaka Kakuei* (Tokyo: Kōdansha, 2016), 218.
13. Hattori Ryūji provides a detailed account of the negotiation process in *Nicchū kokkō seijōka* (Tokyo: Chūōkōron, 2012).
14. Hattori, *Tanaka Kakuei*, 218.
15. Tanaka actually had a number of health issues, including dry pleurisy in his early twenties and Graves' disease in later years. Extreme fatigue and stress also caused a facial nerve palsy, which lasted for several weeks in late 1973 and early 1974. Shiota Ushio, *Tanaka Kakuei shikkyaku* (Tokyo: Bugeishunjū, 2002), 105.
16. *Asahi shinbun*, December 26, 1973, 13th ed.
17. A collection of Sugiyama's fifty-nine award-winning television commercials was released in 2010. "Starting on a Journey" is included in the collection. *Sugiyama Toshi TVCM Works: ACC Awards 1961–1974*, DVD (Tokyo: Avex, 2010).
18. "Datsun Model 16 Sedan," https://www.toyota.co.jp/Museum/collections/list/data/0078_DatsunModel16Sedan.html (accessed on August 7, 2020).
19. Music and lyrics by Mike Maki (1971).
20. Shiozawa Shigeru, *Dokyumento terebi jidai: 25 nen no ningen dorama* (Tokyo: Kōdansha, 1978), 324.
21. Yamada Shōji, "CM sakka no shi: Sugiyama Toshi no shi to tanjō," *Nihon kenkyū* 29 (December 2004): 330. Sugiyama's life and death have been featured in two television dramas: *30 byō no sogekihei*, Terebi Asahi, 50 min., December 20, 1979; and *Messeiji: densetsu no CM direkutaa, Sugiyama Toshi*, TBS, 114 min., August 28, 2006.
22. Kurigami Kazumi, "Kare wa saigoniwa jibun ga messeiji ni natteshimatta," in *CM ni channeru o awaseta hi: Sugiyama Toshi no jidai*, ed. Baba Kei'ichi and Ishioka Eiko (Tokyo: PARCO shuppan, 1978), 88.
23. Kurigami, "Kare wa saigoniwa jibun ga messeiji ni natteshimatta," 87.

24. Tahara Sōichirō, "73 nen 12 gatsu 13 nichi nanika ga shinda," *Mondai shōsetsu* (November 1977): 345.
25. Tahara, "73 nenn 12 gatsu 13 nichi nanika ga shinda," 345.
26. A biographer of Sugiyama Toshi attributes his suicide to his depressive temperament. This pathographical interpretation may well be accurate, but it does not illuminate Sugiyama's creative struggle. Kawamura Ranta, *Densetsu no CM sakka: Sugiyama Toshi* (Tokyo: Kawadeshobō shinsha, 2012), 191.
27. Komatsu Sakyō, *Nihon chinbotsu*, 2 vols. (Tokyo: Kōbunsha, 1973); an abridged translation appeared as *Japan Sinks*, trans. Micheal Gallagher (New York: Harper & Row, 1976).
28. Komatsu Sakyō, *Komatsu Sakyō jiden* (Tokyo: Nihon keizaishinbun shuppansha, 2008), 76–77.
29. Kaikō Takeshi, born only four weeks earlier than Komatsu, also witnessed the war's devastation as a teenager (chapter 5). Kaikō similarly expressed discomfort with postwar Japan's reconstruction and subsequent economic success, albeit in a more nuanced way. A product of the war-torn land through and through, he had even found some comfort in the equilibrium between his traumatized mind and the ruinous landscape left by the conflict. The fast pace of change in postwar Japan left him mulling over what he had lost:

> The wilderness [*daishizen*] had a fleeting life. Before we realized that it had been a land of orange orchards, we'd lost it. In no time, man had covered the wasteland with a skin of asphalt and encrusted it with tiny matchbox-size houses and concrete buildings that looked like trash containers. Besieged, then parceled into tiny lots, the desert withdrew toward the sea and ultimately drowned. . . . And as I watched the wasteland being hunted down and driven out of sight, I found a hollowness in me that deepened day by day. Nothing will ever replace the vast and exhilarating feeling of that expanse, the things in it that gave my solitude and aimlessness external form. I lost an outer world that corresponded to the spreading void within, the growing alienation that I felt. One sees an object and becomes that thing oneself. (*KTZ* 6:209–10/176)

The "vast and exhilarating feeling" of the ruinous landscape defined Kaikō's postwar consciousness. It was both a terrifying and a liberating experience. Having lost it, he realized the value of what had disappeared: "a land of orange orchards." Kaikō went to Vietnam hoping to recover it, while Komatsu wrote his science fiction novel to re-present it in prosperous postwar Japan.

30. In November 1973, eight months after the publication of *Japan Sinks*, Gotō Ben's *Great Prophesy of Nostradamus* (*Nosutoradamusu no daiyogen*) hit the bookstands and became an instantaneous bestseller, creating synergetic effects with Komatsu's text. Gotō Ben, *Nosutoradamusu no daiyogen: Semarikuru 1999 nen no 7 no tsuki, jinrui metsubō no hi* (Tokyo: Shōdensha, 1973). The book introduced Japanese readers to the predictions of the astrologer Michel Nostradamus (1503–1566), who, the Japanese author claimed, predicted the destruction of Japan and the world in July 1999. Gotō

forcefully reads cryptic passages from the sixteenth-century text against historical and more recent events—from the death of Henry II of France in 1559 to environmental devastation in the contemporary world—arguing for the accuracy of Nostradamus's prophesies. Gotō even tries to lend some credence to Komatsu's vision: if not all of Japan, then at least the Kantō region (the Tokyo metropolitan areas and surrounding prefectures) could wind up underwater (*Nosutoradamusu no daiyogen*, 122–26).

31. This is not true of Okinawa, where the reversion to Japanese sovereignty in 1972 represented a regime change for its residents.
32. Although this book focuses exclusively on Japan, I do not intend to exceptionalize what happened there. Similar processes must have played out in other societies, at different rates and with different timings, as they embraced mass consumerism and television and other mass media. Building on the Lacanian concept of the "mirror stage," I would like to call the transformational moment that I discuss in this book the "television stage" of civilization. Jacques Lacan, *Écrits: A Selection*, trans. Bruce Fink (New York: Norton, 1977), 1–7.

# Bibliography

Abe Kōbo. *Abe Kōbō zenshū* 24. Tokyo: Shinchōsha, 1999.
——. *The Box Man*. Trans. Dale Saunders. New York: Vintage, 2001.
Abuno Katsuhiko. "Terebi wa chiiki o gyōshisuru." In *Nihon no dokyumentarii* 3, ed. Satō Tadao, 84–95. Tokyo: Iwanami shoten, 2010.
Adachi Noriyuki. "Tsuge Yoshiharu to Mizuki Shigeru." In *Tsuge Yoshiharu no miryoku*, ed. Rekishi to bungaku no kai, 33–35. Tokyo: Bensei shuppan, 2001.
Aizawa Shinichi and Watanabe Daisuke. "Hajimeni." In *Sōchūryū no hajimari: Danchi to seikatsu jikan no sengoshi*, ed. Watanabe Daisuke, Aizawa Shinichi, and Mori Naoto, 11–18. Tokyo: Seikyūsha, 2019.
Akagi Yōichi, *"an·an" 1970*. Tokyo: Heibonsha, 2007.
Akimoto Kei'ichi. "Futatsu no kioku." *Omoshiro hanbun* 13, no. 7 (November 1978): 153–55.
Akiyama Shun. *Hoseki no shisō*. Tokyo: Ozawa shoten, 1997.
Akutagawa Ryūnosuke. *Akutagawa Ryūnosuke zenshū* 3. Tokyo: Iwanami shoten, 1996.
——. "The Spider Thread." In *Rashōmon and 17 Other Stories*, trans. Jay Rubin, 38–41. London: Penguin, 2006.
Alexander, Jeffrey W. *Drinking Bomb & Shooting Meth: Alcohol and Drug Use in Japan*. Ann Arbor, Mich.: Association for Asian Studies, 2018.
Allen, Robert C., ed. *Channels of Discourse: Television and Contemporary Criticism*. Chapel Hill: University of North Carolina Press, 1987.
Amamiya Kumi. "Nihon ni okeru botan to shishi bunka no keisei to yōkyoku 'Ishibashi.'" *Kokusai kankei kenkyū* 36, no. 1 (October 2015): 67–78.
Amano Masako. "Sōron: Otoko de arukoto no sengoshi." In *Otoko rashisa no gendaishi*, Danseishi 3, ed. Abe Tsunehisa, Amano Masako, and Obinata Sumio, 1–32. Tokyo: Nihon keizai hyōronsha, 2006.

———. "Toraianguru (kazoku–gakkō–kigyō) no seiritsu to yuragi." In *Sengo keiken o ikiru*, ed. Amano Masako, Ōkado Masakatsu, and Yasuda Tsuneo, 148–77. Tokyo: Yoshikawa kōbunkan, 2003.

Amasawa Taijirō. *Sakuhin kōiron o motomete*. Tokyo: Seidosha, 1985.

Anderson, Benedict. *Imagined Communities*. London: Verso, 2006.

Aoki Toshiya. *Saigen Shōwa 30 nendai: Danchi 2DK no kurashi*. Tokyo: Kawadeshobō shinsha, 2001.

Aoto Mikio. Written statement. Nagano Police Station, April 10, 1972. Takazawa Collection, University of Hawaii.

Aoyama Sakae and Shiba Tsukasa. *Yakuza eiga to sono jidai*. Tokyo: Chikuma shobō, 1998.

Apter, David E., and Nagayo Sawa. *Against the State: Politics and Social Protest in Japan*. Cambridge, Mass.: Harvard University Press, 1984.

Ara Taisuke. *Hatenkōden: aru hanransedai no henreki*. Tokyo: Ōta shuppan, 2001.

Ara Taisuke et al. *Zenkyōtō sannjūnen: jidaini hangyakushita monotachi no shōgenn*. Tokyo: Jissensha, 1998.

Arima Tetsuo. *Nippon Terebi to CIA: Hakkutsu sareta "Shōriki fairu."* Tokyo: Shinchōsha, 2006.

———. *Terebi no yume kara samerumade: Amerika 1950 nendai terebi bunka shakaishi*. Tokyo: Kokubunsha, 1997.

*Asahi shinbun*. "Disukabaa Japan," December 6, 1973, evening ed.

———. "Kaikō Takeshi shi no janguru senki," February 17, 1965, 12th ed.

———. "Nagata Hiroko shikeishū ga shibō," February 7, 2011, 13th ed.

———. "Sukuwarenu kyūkyū kanja," September 2, 1971, evening 3rd ed.

———. "Tonai ni 15 ten ga kimaru," August 13, 1966, 13th ed.

Asahi shinbunsha. *Shūkanshi no subete*. Kokusai shōgyō shuppan, 1975.

Asai Yoshio. "Gendai shihonshugi to kōdoseichō." In *Sengo Nihon ron*, Nihonshi kōza 10, ed. Rekishigaku kenkyūkai and Nihonshi kenkyūkai, 197–226. Tokyo: Tokyo daigaku shuppankai, 2005.

Asaine Hideo. *Ashita no Jō wa shindanoka*. Tokyo: Chikuma shobō, 1988.

Asakura Kyōji. *Namida no shasatsuma: Nagayama Norio to 60 nendai*. Tokyo: Kyōdō tsūshinsha, 2003.

*Asama-sansō jiken Media no genzai*. NHK, 70 min. February 26, 2012.

Asamori Akio and Chiba Tetsuya, *Ashita no jō*, 20 vols. Tokyo: Kōdansha, 1993.

Asayama Jitsu. *Afutaa za reddo: Rengōsekigun heishitachi no 40 nen*. Tokyo: Kadokawa shoten, 2012.

Ashida Terukazu. "Betonamu shuppatsu zengo." *Omoshiro hanbun* (November 1978): 141–43.

Aso, Noriko. *Public Properties: Museums in Imperial Japan*. Durham, N.C.: Duke University Press, 2014.

Atsumi Kiyoshi and Yamada Yōji. "Taidan, otoko wa tsuraiyo." *Nihon eiga no genzai*, Kōza Nihon eiga 7, ed. Imamura Shōhei, Satō Tadao, Shindō Kaneto, Tsurumi Shunshuke, and Yamada Yōji, 158–77. Tokyo: Iwanami shoten, 1988.

Ayuhara Rin. "Shishatachi no fukken: Wadatsumizō hakaisha tachi no shisō." *Asahi jaanaru*, February 8, 1970, 38–42.

Baird, Bruce. *Hijikata Tatsumi and Butoh: Dancing in a Pool of Gray Grits.* New York: Palgrave, 2012.

Baishō Chieko. *Baishō Chieko no genba.* Tokyo: PHP, 2017.

Bandō Kunio. *Nagata Hiroko san eno tegami.* Tokyo: Sairyūsha, 1984.

———. Written statement. Nakano Police Station, April 15, 1972. Takazawa Collection, University of Hawaii.

"Banpaku shōnen to 90-nendai no kimi no taiwa." In *Expo 70 densetsu: Unofficial guidebook,* ed. Hobara Shunji, Saitō Satoko, and Matsuhisa Atsushi, 165, 189. Tokyo: Kadokawa shoten, 1999.

Benjamin, Walter. *Reflections: Essays, Aphorisms, Autobiographical Writings.* Ed. Peter Demetz, trans. Edmund Jephcott. New York: Schocken Books, 1978.

Bennett, Tony. *The Birth of the Museum: History, Theory, Politics.* New York: Routledge, 1995.

Berndt, Jürgen. "Naze ima Kaikō Takeshi nanoka." *Shinchō* (December 1991): 120–29.

*Betonamu Kaihei daitai senki.* Nippon TV, 50:00, May 9, 1965. https://www.youtube.com/watch?v=fkivla5zjdk.

Betts, Raymond F. *A History of Popular Culture: More of Everything, Faster and Brighter.* New York: Routledge, 2004.

Biza henshū iinkai, ed. *Shinpen Sekigun dokyumento.* Tokyo: Shinsensha, 1986.

Bondy, Christopher. *Voice, Silence, and Self: Negotiations of Buraku Identity in Contemporary Japan.* Cambridge, Mass.: Harvard University Asia Center, 2015.

Brecht, Bertolt. "On Chinese Acting." *Tulane Drama Review* 6, no. 1 (September 1961): 130–36.

Bungeishunjū. *Dai ankeito ni yoru shōnen shōjo manga besuto 100.* Tokyo: Bungeishunjū, 1992.

Bureau of Statistics, Office of Prime Minister. *Japan Statistical Yearbook 1962.* Tokyo: Japan Statistical Association, 1962.

———. *Japan Statistical Yearbook 1972.* Tokyo: Japan Statistical Association, 1972.

———. *Japan Statistical Yearbook 1975.* Tokyo: Japan Statistical Association, 1975.

Cabinet Office, Government of Japan. "Chōki keizai tōkei mokuji." In *Heisei 24 nendo nenji keizaizaisei hōkoku.* http://www5.cao.go.jp/j-j/wp/wp-je12/h10_data05.html.

Campanis, Al. *Dodgers' Way to Play Baseball.* New York: Dutton, 1954.

Chiba Tetsuya. "Ashita no Jō to gensakusha." In *Ashita no Jō,* by Asamori Akio and Chiba Tetsuya, 1:293–94. Tokyo: Kōdansha, 1989.

———. *Dakara manga wa yamerarenai.* Tokyo: Popurasha, 1986.

———. "Interview: Chiba Tetsuya." In *Ashita no Jō konpuriito bukku,* ed. Isshūkan henshūbu, 54–59. Tokyo: Kōdansha, 2010.

———. "Masshiro na hai ni natte moetsukiru made." In *Chiba Tetsuya,* ed. Nishiguchi Tōru and Anazawa Yūko, 10–40. Tokyo: Kawadeshobō shinsha, 2011.

———. *Minminzemi no uta.* Tokyo: Nihon toshosentaa, 2001.

———. *Yaneura no ehonkaki.* Tokyo: Shinnihon shuppansha, 2016.

Chong, Doryun, ed. *Tokyo 1955–1970: A New Avant Garde.* New York: Museum of Modern Art, 2012.

Chun, Jayson Makoto. *"A Nation of a Hundred Million Idiots"? A Social History of Japanese Television, 1953–1973.* New York: Routledge, 2007.

Cross, Gary. *An All-Consuming Century: Why Commercialism Won in Modern America*. New York: Columbia University Press, 2000.

Daigaku hakusho sakusei shōiinkai. *Ritsumeikan daigaku kyōgaku hakusho*. Kyoto: Ritsumeikan Daigaku kokkofutan ni kansuru iinkai, 1973.

"Datsun Model 16 Sedan." https://www.toyota.co.jp/Museum/collections/list/data/0078_DatsunModel16Sedan.html. Accessed August 7, 2020.

*Dawn Over the Mountains*. Abridged version. NHK, 47:41. http://www.nhk.or.jp/school/yamanobunkou/.

Deleuze, Gilles, and Félix Guattari. *Anti-Oedipus: Capitalism and Schizophrenia*. Minneapolis: University of Minnesota Press, 1983.

Dienst, Richard. *Still Life in Real Time: Theory After Television*. Durham, N.C.: Duke University Press, 1994.

Ebisawa Yasuhisa. *Minna Jaiantsu o aishite ita*. Tokyo: Shinchōsha, 1983.

Eckersall, Peter. *Performativity and Event in 1960s Japan: City, Body, Memory*. New York: Palgrave Macmillan, 2013.

Endō Kōshi. "Rōdōkumiai to minshushugi." In *Sengo minshushugi*, ed. Nakamura Masanori, Amakawa Akira, Yun Kŏn-ch'a, and Igarashi Takeshi, 65–96. Tokyo: Iwanami shoten, 1995.

Endō Tetsuo. *Taishū meshi gekidō no sengoshi: Ii mono kutterya shiawaseka?* Tokyo: Chikuma shobō, 2013.

Esashi Akiko. *Kanba Michiko: Seishōjo densetsu*. Tokyo: Bungeishunjū, 2010.

Etō Fumio et al. "Discover Japan kyanpein uraomote kō." *Senden kaigi* (January 1972): 14–23.

Foucault, Michel. *Discipline and Punish: The Birth of the Prison*. New York: Vintage Books, 1979.

Franky, Lily. "Expo 70 Diary." In *Expo 70 densetsu: Unofficial guidebook*, ed. Hobara Shunji, Saitō Satoko, and Matsuhisa Atsushi, 195. Tokyo: Media waakusu, 1999.

Frost, Dennis J. *Seeing Stars: Sports Celebrity, Identity, and Body Culture in Modern Japan*. Cambridge, Mass.: Harvard East Asian Monographs, 2010.

Fujiki Kazuo. *Kyojin manga no keifu*. Tokyo: Suiseisha, 1998.

Fujioka Wakao. *Attu, purodyūsaa: Kaze no shigoto 30 nen*. Tokyo: Kyūryūdō, 2000.

———. "'Byūtifuru' na sekai ni narunowa itsuno kotodarō." *Chōsajōhō* (March–April 2010): 8–11.

———. "Disukabaa Japan futatabi." *Shūkan daiyamondo*, May 5, 1999, 76–77.

———. *Fujioka Wakao zenshigoto 1*. Tokyo: PHP kenkyūjo, 1987.

———. *Karei naru shuppatsu: Disukabaa Japan*. Tokyo: Mainichi shinbunsha, 1972.

Fujita Naoya. *Shinseiki zonbi gaku*. Tokyo: Chikuma shobō, 2017.

Fujitake Akira. *Terebi media no shakairyoku*. Tokyo: Yūhikaku, 1985.

Fukushima Akira. "Tsuge Yoshiharu sairon." *Yuriika* (March 1982): 126–29.

Fukuyama-shi shi henshū kai. *Fukuyama-shi shi 2*. Fukuyama-shi: Fukuyama-shi shi henshū kai, 1978.

Furuhata Yuriko. *Cinema of Actuality: Japanese Avant-Garde Filmmaking in the Season of Image Politics*. Durham, N.C.: Duke University Press, 2013.

Furusawa Kiyoshi. "Terebi no aru kodomo to nai kodomo." *Jidō shinri* (April 1961): 502–7.

"Gakkō kihon chōsa, nenji tōkei: Singakuritsu." http://www.e-stat.go.jp/SG1/estat/List.do?bid=000001015843.

Garfinkel, Harold. *Studies in Ethnomethodology*. Englewood Cliffs, N.J.: Prentice-Hall, 1967.

George, Timothy S. *Minamata: Pollution and the Struggle for Democracy in Postwar Japan*. Cambridge, Mass.: Harvard University Asia Center, 2001.

Gonoi Takashi. *Nihon Kirisutokyō shi*. Tokyo: Yoshikawa kōbunkan, 1990.

Gordon, Andrew. "Managing the Japanese Household: The New Life Movement in Postwar Japan." *Social Politics* 4, no. 2 (Summer 1997): 245–83.

——. "Nihon katei keieihō: Sengo Nihon ni okeru 'Shin seikatsu undo.'" In *Sengo to iu chiseigaku*, ed. Nishikawa Yūko, 95–136. Tokyo: Tokyo daigaku shuppankai, 2006.

——. *The Wages of Affluence: Labor and Management in Postwar Japan*. Cambridge, Mass.: Harvard University Press, 1998.

Gotō Keinosuke and Sakamoto Dōtoku. *Gunkanjima no isan*. Nagasaki: Nagasahi shinbunsha, 2005.

Gorn, Elliott J. *The Manly Art: Bare-Knuckle Prize Fighting in America*. Ithaca, N.Y.: Cornell University Press, 1986.

Gotō Ben. *Nosutoradamusu no daiyogen: Semarikuru 1999 nen no 7 no tsuki, jinrui metsubō no hi*. Tokyo: Shōdensha, 1973.

*Gyogyō suiiki ni kansuru zantei sochi-hō*, May 2, 1977. http://www.shugiin.go.jp/internet/itdb_housei.nsf/html/houritsu/08019770502031.htm.

Hamano Sachi. *Onna ga eiga o tsukurutoki*. Tokyo: Heibosha, 2005.

Hamashima Akira. "Chūryū ishiki no kōzō to dōtai." In *Hirogaru chūryū ishiki, 1971–1985*, Riidingusu Sengo Nihon no Kakusa to fubyōdō 2, ed. Hara Junsuke, 165–79. Tokyo: Nihon toshosentaa, 2008.

*Hanrei jihō*. "Rengōsekigun jiken (tōitsugumi) dai isshin hanketsu," June 18, 1982, November 1, 1982, 24–53.

Hara Junsuke, ed. *Hirogaru chūryū ishiki, 1971–1985*, Riidingusu Sengo Nihon no Kakusa to fubyōdō 2. Tokyo: Nihon toshosentaa, 2008.

Hara Takeshi. *Danchi no kūkan seijigaku*. Tokyo: NHK bukkusu, 2012.

——. *Reddo arō to Sutaa hausu: Mōhitotsu no sengo shisōshi*. Tokyo: Shinchōsha, 2012.

Hara Takeshi and Akiyama Shun. "Danchi to bungaku." *Gunzō* (November 2008): 138–49.

Hara Takeshi and Shigematsu Kiyoshi. *Danchi no jidai*. Tokyo: Shinchōsha, 2010.

Harper, Stephen. "Zombies, Malls, and the Consumerism Debate: George Romero's Dawn of the Dead." *Americana: The Journal of American Popular Culture* 1, no. 2 (Fall 2002). http://www.americanpopularculture.com/journal/articles/fall_2002/harper.htm.

Harvey, David. *The Condition of Postmodernity*. Oxford: Blackwell, 1990.

Hashida Sugako. "Hōmu dorama no ennoshita." In *Jinsei dokuhon: Terebi*, 186–91. Tokyo: Kawadeshobō shinsha, 1983.

Hashimoto Kenji. "Gekihensuru shakai no tayōna shūgyōkōzō." In *Kazokuto kakusa no sengoshi*, ed. Hashimoto Kenji, 49–77. Tokyo: Seikyūsha, 2010.

——. *Kaikyū shakai: Gendai shakai no kakusa o tou*. Tokyo: Kōdansha, 2006.

——. *Kakusa no sengoshi*. Tokyo: Kawadeshobō shinsha, 2009.

Hattori Ryūji. *Nicchū kokkō seijōka*. Tokyo: Chūōkōron shinsha, 2012.

———. *Tanaka Kakuei*. Tokyo: Kōdansha, 2016.
Haug, W. F. *Critique of Commodity Aesthetics: Appearance, Sexuality and Advertising in Capitalist Society*. Minneapolis: University of Minnesota Press, 1986.
Havens, Thomas R. H. *Fire Across the Sea*. Princeton, N.J.: Princeton University Press, 1987.
Hayano Tōru. *Tanaka Kakuei: Sengo Nihon no kanashiki jigazō*. Tokyo: Chūōkōron shinsha, 2012.
Hayasaka Akira. *Terebi ga yattekita*. Tokyo: Nihon hōsō shuppan kyōkai, 2000.
Hayashi Nozomu. *Tsui konoaida atta mukashi*. Tokyo: Kōbundō, 2007.
Hazama Hiroshi. *Keizai taikoku o tsukuri ageta shisō*. Tokyo: Bunshindō, 1996.
Hegel, G. W. F. *Phenomenology of Spirit*. Oxford: Oxford University Press, 1977.
Hein, Laura. *Fueling Growth: The Energy Revolution and Economic Policy in Postwar Japan*. Cambridge, Mass.: Harvard East Asia Monographs, 1990.
Hino Keizō. "Tōgenkyō eno michi." In *Yūyū to shite isoge: Tsuitō Kaikō Takeshi*, ed. Maki Yōko, 87–90. Tokyo: Chikuma shobō, 1991.
Hino Keizō and Mukai Satoshi. "Kaikō bungaku no kagayakeru yami." *Bungakukai* (February 1990): 318–35.
Hirano Akiomi. *Osaka Banpaku: 20 seiki ga yumemita 21 seiki*. Tokyo: Shōgakukan, 2014.
Horikiki Naoto. *Atsumi Kiyoshi: Asakusa, wagei, Tora-san*. Tokyo: Shōbunsha, 2007.
Hosaka Masayasu. *Tanaka Kakuei no Shōwa*. Tokyo: Asahi shinbun shuppan, 2010.
Hoshino Yasusaburō. "Todōfuken keisatsu no jittai." *Toshi mondai* (June 1970): 3–14.
Hosokawa Fukuko. *Watashi no Kaikō Takeshi*. Tokyo: Shūeisha, 2011.
Huyssen, Andreas. *After the Great Divide: Modernism, Mass Culture, Postmodernism*. Bloomington: Indiana University Press, 1986.
Ida Emiko. "Terebi to kazoku no 50 nen: 'Terebiteki' ikkadanran no hensen." *NHK hōsōbunka kenkyūjo nenpō* (2004): 111–44.
Ide Hideo. *Yakuza gaku nyūmon*. Tokyo: Hokumei shobō, 1969.
Igarashi Keiji. *Tora-san no tabi*. Tokyo: Nihon Keizai shinbunsha, 1993.
Igarashi, Yoshikuni. "'Ano jidai' no hanran wa wareware ni nani o oshieru noka: Oguma Eiji cho '1968' jō-ge." *Cultures/Critiques*, no. 2 (2010): 129–44.
———. *Bodies of Memory: Narratives of War in Postwar Japanese Culture, 1945–1970*. Princeton, N.J.: Princeton University Press, 2000.
———. *Homecomings: The Belated Return of Japan's Lost Soldiers*. New York: Columbia University Press, 2016.
———. "Mothra's Giantic Egg: Consuming the South Pacific in 1960s Japan." In *Godzilla's Footsteps: Japanese Pop Culture Icons on the Global Stage*, ed. William Tsutsui and Michiko Ito, 83–102. New York: Palgrave Macmillan, 2006.
Imamura Shōhei, Satō Tadao, Shindō Kaneto, Tsurumi Shunshuke, and Yamada Yōji, eds. *Nihon eiga no mosaku*, Kōza Nihon eiga 6. Tokyo: Iwanami shoten, 1987.
Imao Keisuke. *Jūsho to chimei no daikenkyū*. Tokyo: Shinchōsha, 2004.
Imura Kiyoko. *Gendai Nihon keizairon*. Tokyo: Yūhikaku, 1993.
Ino Ryūichi. *Sengo Nihon nōgyōshi*. Tokyo: Shinnihon shuppansha, 1996.
Ishida Ayuu. *Micchii būmu*. Bungeishunjū, 2006.

Ishikawa Akihiro. "Misekake no chūryū ishiki." In *Hirogaru chūryū ishiki, 1971–1985,* Riidingusu Sengo Nihon no Kakusa to fubyōdō 2, ed. Hara Junsuke, 142–51. Tokyo: Nihon toshosentaa, 2008.

Ishikawa Bunyō. *"Minami betonamu kaihei daitai senki* satsuei ki." In *Nihon no dokyumentarii 3,* ed. Satō Tadao, 131–40. Tokyo: Iwanami shoten, 2010.

Ishikawa Hiroyoshi. *Yokubō no sengoshi: Shakai shinrigaku karano apurōchi.* Tokyo: Taihei shuppan, 1981.

Iso Tatsuo and Miyazawa Hiroshi. "Naibu ni hirogaru gaibu: Abashiri kangoku goyokuhōshajō shabō (1912 nen)." *Nikkan aakitekuchaa,* August 25, 2014, 72–75.

Itakura, Eijun, and Hisashi Uhara. "Malignant Melanoma in Star of the Giants (Kyojin no Hoshi)." *Lancet* 12 (June 2011): 525.

Itō Akihiko. *Eiga no naraku.* Tokyo: Kokusho kankōkai, 2015.

Itō Gō. *Tezuka izu Deddo: Hirakareta manga hyōgenron e.* Tokyo: NTT shuppan, 2005.

Itō Katsuo, Kofujida Eiko, Saeki Toshio, Shindō Nanao, and Watanabe Takenobu. "Viva! Ninkyō eiga." *Kinema junpō,* August 30, 1971, 43–52.

Ivy, Marilyn. *Discourse of the Vanishing.* Chicago: University of Chicago Press, 1995.

Iwata Masami. *Hinkon no sengoshi: Hinkon no katachi wa dō kawattanoka.* Tokyo: Chikuma shobō, 2017.

Iyota Yasuhiro, Kohtaki Tetsuya, Tamura Minoru, Noda Yoshito, and Susumago Isao. *Terebi shi handobukku.* Tokyo: Jiyūkokuminsha, 1996.

Izeki Tadahisa. *Doitsu o kaeta 68 nen undō.* Tokyo: Hakusuisha, 2005.

Jameson, Fredric. *Postmodernism, or, the Culture of Late Capitalism.* Durham, N.C.: Duke University Press, 1991.

Jinno Yuki. *Shumi no tanjō.* Tokyo: Keisōshobō, 1994.

*Jinsei dokuhon: Terebi.* Tokyo: Kawadeshobō shinsha, 1983.

Jōkyō shuppan henshūbu. *Zenkyōtō o yomu.* Tokyo: Jōykō shuppan, 1997.

Kagaku gijyutsu chō shigen chōsa kai. "Shokuseikatsu no taikeiteki kaizen ni shisuru shokuryō ryūtsūtaikei no kindaika ni kansuru kankoku." In *Kōrudo chein chōsa hōkoku kenkyū taisei* 1, ed. Science and Technology Agency. Tokyo: Sōwa shuppan, 1976.

Kaikō Takeshi. *Aa, nijūgonen.* Tokyo: Ushio shuppansha, 1983.

———. *Betonamu senki.* Tokyo: Asahi shinbunsha, 1990.

———. *Darkness in Summer.* Trans. Cecilia Segawa Seigle. Tokyo: Kodansha International, 1973.

———. *Finsternis eines Sommers.* Trans. Jürgen Berndt. Berlin: be.bra edition q, 1993.

———. *Into a Black Sun.* Trans. Cecilia Segawa Seigle. Tokyo: Kodansha International, 1980.

———. *Kaikō Takeshi zenshū.* 22 vols. Tokyo: Shinchōsha, 1991–1993.

———. *Nagisa kara kurumono.* Tokyo: Kadokawa shoten, 1980.

Kaikō Takeshi and Yamazaki Masakazu. "Genseki to hōseki." *Kokubungaku: Kaishaku to kyōzai no kenkyū* 27, no. 15 (November 1982): 11–33.

Kajiwara Ikki. *Gekiga ichidai: Kajiwara Ikki jiden.* Tokyo: Shōgakukan, 2011.

Kajiwara Ikki and Kawasaki Noboru. *Kyojin no hoshi.* 19 vols. Tokyo: Kōdansha, 1970–1972.

———. *Shin Kyojin no hoshi*. 6 vols. Tokyo: Kōdansha, 1990.
Kamata Satoshi. *Zōsen fukyō*. Tokyo: Iwanami shoten, 1993.
Kamei Jun. *Shūkan shi no yomikata*. Tokyo: Hanashi no tokushū, 1985.
Karakida Ken'ichi. *1968 nen niwa naniga attanoka: Tōdai tōsō shishi*. Tokyo: Hihyōsha, 2004.
Kasahara Kazuo. *Eiga wa yakuza nari*. Tokyo: Shinchōsha, 2003.
———. *Hametsu no bigaku: Yakuza eiga eno rekuiemu*. Tokyo: Tōgensha, 1997.
———. *Jinginaki tatakai*. Tokyo: Tōgensha, 1998.
———. *"Jinginaki tatakai" chōsa shuzairoku shūsei*. Tokyo: Ōta shuppan, 2005.
Kasahara Kazuo, Arai Haruhiko, and Suga Hidemi. *Shōwa no geki: Eiga kyakuhonka Kasahara Kazuo*. Tokyo: Ōta shuppan, 2002.
Kasai Kiyoshi. *Tensei no ma: Shiritsu tantei Asukai no jikenbo*. Tokyo: Kōdansha, 2017.
Kase Kazutoshi. "Kōdo keizai seichō no shojōken to nōgyōbumon no ichi." In *Kōdo keizai seichō to seikatsu kakumei*, ed. Kokuritsu rekishi minzoku hakubutsukan, 93–106. Tokyo: Yoshikawa kōbunkan, 2010.
———. "Nōson to chiiki no henbō." In *Sengo Nihon ron*, Nihonshi kōza 10, ed. Rekishigaku kenkyūkai and Nihonshi kenkyūkai, 227–51. Tokyo: Tokyo daigaku shuppankai, 2005.
Kashihon manga kenkyūkai. *Kashihon manga returns*. Tokyo: Popurasha, 2006.
*Kasochiiki taisaku kinkyūsochi hō*, no. 31 (April 24, 1970). http://www.shugiin.go.jp/internet/itdb_housei.nsf/html/houritsu/06319700424031.htm.
Kasuga Taichi. *Jinginaki Nihon chinbotsu: Tōhō vs. Tōei no sengo sabaibaru*. Tokyo: Shinchōsha, 2012.
Katō Hidetoshi. "Terebiteki bunmei no tenbō." *Chūōkōron* (February 1958): 207–15.
Katō Michinori. *Rengōsekigun shōnen A*. Tokyo: Shinchōsha, 2003.
Katō Utako. *Ichijō Sayuri no shinjitsu: Kyojitsu no hazama o ikita onna*. Tokyo: Shinchōsha, 2001.
Katsura Chiho. "Yamada Yōji no uragawa." *Eiga hyōron* (May 1974): 35–40.
Kawabata Yasunari. "Japan, the Beautiful and Myself." Nobel Lecture, December 12, 1968. http://www.nobelprize.org/nobel_prizes/literature/laureates/1968/kawabata-lecture.html.
Kawahara Shirō. "'Kuroi Kokutetsu' o karafuruni." In *Disukabaa, Disukabaa Japan Tōku e ikitai*, ed. Nariai Hajime and Shimizu Hiroko, 59–63. Tokyo: Tokyo Station Gallery, 2014.
Kawamoto Saburō. *Jidaigeki kokoni ari*. Tokyo: Heibonsha, 2005.
Kawamura Minato. "Popular Orientalism and Japanese Views of Asia." In *Reading Colonial Japan: Text, Context, and* Critique, ed. Michelle M. Mason and Helen J. S. Lee, 271–98. Stanford, Calif.: Stanford University Press, 2012.
Kawamura Ranta. *Densetsu no CM sakka: Sugiyama Toshi*. Tokyo: Kawadeshobō shinsha, 2012.
Keene, Donald. "'Nihon rashisa' o koeta bungaku *Natsu no yami*." *Kotoba*, no. 17 (Autumn 2014): 26–31.
Keisatsu Bunka Kyōkai. *Rengōsekigun Asama Sansō hitojichi jiken*. Tokyo: Keisatsu Bunka Kyōkai, 1973.
Kermore, Frank. *The Sense of an Ending: Studies in the Theories of Fiction*. Oxford: Oxford University Press, 2000.

Kikuchi Yoshiaki. *Kitachōsen kikoku jigyō: Sōdaina rachi ka tsuihō ka.* Tokyo: Chūōkōron shinsha, 2009.
Kikuya Kyōsuke. *Kaikō Takeshi no iru fūkei.* Tokyo: Shūeisha, 2002.
*Kinema junpō.* "*Kazoku* to Yamada Yōji," October 15, 1970, 3–8.
Kingsberg, Miriam. *Moral Nation: Modern Japan and Narcotics in Global History.* Berkeley: University of California Press, 2013.
Kinsella, Sharon. *Adult Manga: Culture and Power in Contemporary Japanese Society.* Honolulu: University of Hawai'i Press, 2000.
Kishimoto Shigenobu. *Chūryū no gensō.* Excerpted in *Riidingusu Sengo Nihon no Kakusa to fubyōdō* 2, ed. Hara Junsuke, 128–41. Tokyo: Nihon toshosentaa, 2008.
———. "Shin chūkankaisō-ron wa kanōka." *Asahi shinbun*, June 9, 1977, evening 3rd ed.
Kita Yasutoshi. *Saji Keiji to Kaikō Takeshi: Saikyō no futari.* Tokyo: Kōdansha, 2015.
Kitada Akihiro. *Zōho, kōkoku toshi, Tokyo.* Tokyo: Chikuma shobō, 2011.
Kitada Akihiro, Nogami Gen, and Mizutamari Mayumi, eds. *Cultural Politics 1960/70.* Tokyo: Serika shobō, 2005.
Kitahara Shigetoshi. *Rengōsekigun "Asama-sansō jiken" no shinjitsu.* Nagano: Hōzukishoseki, 1996.
Kitamura Mitsufumi. *Terebi wa Nihonjin o baka ni shitaka?* Tokyo: Heibonsha, 2007.
Kiridōshi Risaku. *Yamada Yōji no sekai: genfūkei o otte.* Tokyo: Chikuma shobō, 2004.
Kobayashi Nobuhiko. *Gendai shigo nōto.* Tokyo: Iwanami shoten, 1997.
———. *Okashina otoko: Atsumi Kiyoshi.* Tokyo: Shinchōsha, 2003.
Kobayashi Toshiaki. *Shutai no yukue.* Tokyo: Kōdansha, 2010.
Kōdoseichōki o kangaerukai. *Kōdoseichō to Nihonjin.* 3 vols. Tokyo: Nihon editaasukūru shuppanbu, 1985–1986.
Koenaki koe no kai. *Fukkokuban Koenaki koe no tayori.* 2 vols. Tokyo: Shisō no kagakusha, 1996.
Kōgo Eiki. "Kōdo keizaiseichō to media: Terebi no kakudai." In *Media shi o manabu hito no tameni*, ed. Ariyama Teruo and Takeyama Akiko, 309–40. Tokyo: Sekaishisōsha, 2004.
Kokumin seikatsu kenkyūjo. *Shōwa 42 nendo-ban: Kokumin seikatsu tōkei nenpō.* Tokyo: Shiseidō, 1967.
Kokuritsu rekishi minzoku hakubutsukan, ed. *Kōdo keizai seichō to seikatsu kakumei.* Tokyo: Yoshikawa kōbunkan, 2010.
Komatsu Sakyō. *Japan Sinks.* Trans. Michael Gallagher. New York: Harper & Row, 1976.
———. *Komatsu Sakyō jiden.* Tokyo: Nihon keizaishinbun shuppansha, 2008.
———. *Nihon chinbotsu.* 2 vols. Tokyo: Kōbunsha, 1973.
———. *Yomu tanoshimi kataru tanoshimi.* Tokyo: Shūeisha, 1981.
Konishi Makoto. "Naze ima uchigeba no kenshō ga hitsuyōka." In *Kenshō uchigeba*, by Iida Momo, Ikuta Ai, Kuriki Yasunobu, Kurusu Munetaka, and Konishi Makoto, 5–19. Tokyo: Shakaihihyōsha, 2001.
Konno Tsutomu. "Terebiteki shisō towa nanika." *Eiga hyōron* 24, no. 3 (1967): 40–49.
Kōno Hiromi. "Kōno Hiromi (35 sai)." In *Jinsei dokuhon terebi*, 213–14. Tokyo: Kawadeshobō shinsha, 1983.
Koschmann, Victor. *Revolution and Subjectivity in Postwar Japan.* Chicago: University of Chicago, 1996.

Koyama Ken'ichi. "Yama no bunkō no kiroku." *Hōsō bunka* 15, no. 6 (June 1960): 52–58.

Kunihiro Yōko. "Dankai no sedai: Terebi to seichō o tomonishi, oini mukau." In *Terebi to iu kioku: Terebi shichō no shakaishi*, ed. Hagiwara Shigeru, 77–99. Tokyo: Shin'yōsha, 2103.

Kunō Yasushi. *Asama-sansō jiken no shinjitsu*. Tokyo: Kawadeshobō shinsha, 2000.

——. *"Yodo-gō" jiken 122 jikan no shinjitsu*. Tokyo: Kawadeshobō shinsha, 2002.

Kurigami Kazumi. "Kare wa saigoniwa jibun ga messeiji ni natteshimatta." In *CM ni channeru o awaseta hi: Sugiyama Toshi no jidai*, ed. Baba Kei'ichi and Ishioka Eiko, 87–88. Tokyo: PARCO shuppan, 1978.

Kurosaki Isao. "Doshirōto 'teinen' kara no shuppatsu." *Shuppan kurabu dayori*, October 1, 2002.

Kusakabe Gorō. *Shinema no gokudō: Eiga purodyūsaa ichidai*. Tokyo: Shinchōsha, 2012.

Kushima Tsutomu. *Maboroshi bankoku hakurankai*. Tokyo: Shōgakukan, 1998.

*Kyojin no hoshi*. "Mezase eikō no hoshi." Disk 1. DVD. Tokyo: Kōdansha and TMS, 2001.

——. "Oriawanu keiyaku." Disk 16. DVD. Tokyo: Kōdansha and TMS, 2001.

Lacan, Jacques. *Écrits: A Selection*. Trans. Bruce Fink. New York: Norton, 1977.

Lee Young-Chea. "Sengo Nicchō kankei no shoki keiseikatei no bunseki: Zainichi Chōsenjin kikoku undō no tenkaikatei o chūshin ni." *Ritsumeikan hōgaku*, nos. 333 and 334 (2010): 33–58.

Lefebvre, Henri. *Everyday Life in the Modern World*. New Brunswick, N.J.: Transaction, 1990.

"Mainichi Design Awards, Kanendo jushōsha ichiran." http://macs.mainichi.co.jp/design/m/index.html#menu3.

*Mainichi shinbun*. "Naite, waratte, okotte: Saru Satō san 'ato' o nigosu," June 17, 1972, evening 4th ed.

Maki Yōko and Koyama Tetsurō. "Kare wa ikinuku tsumori datta: Maki Yōko san ni kiku." *Bungakukai* 44, no. 2 (February 1990): 286–92.

Manabe Hiroki. "Kōgai no 60 nen." *Asahi shinbun*, October 31, 2005, 13th ed.

Marotti, William. "Japan 1968: The Performance of Violence and the Theater of Protest," *American Historical Review* 114, no. 1 (February 2009): 97–135.

Matsuda Masao. *Teroru no kairo*. Tokyo: San'ichishobō, 1969.

Matsumoto Hideo. "Sasebo jiken to terebi hōdō." *Gendai no riron* (April 1968): 112–15.

Matsushima Toshiyuki. *Nikkatsu roman poruno zenshi*. Tokyo: Kōdansha, 2000.

Matsushita Keiichi. "Nihon ni okeru taishūshakairon no igi." *Chūōkōron* (August 1957): 80–93.

——. *Sengo seiji no rekishi to shisō*. Tokyo: Chikuma shobō, 1994.

——. "Taishū tennōsei ron." *Chūōkōron* (April 1959): 30–47.

——. "Taishūshakai no seiritsu to sono mondaisei." *Shisō*, no. 389 (November 1956): 1317–38.

Matsuyama Iwao. *Gunshū*. Tokyo: Yomiuri shinbunsha, 1996.

McDonald, Keiko Iwai. "The Yakuza Film: An Introduction." In *Reframing Japanese Cinema: Authorship, Genre, History*, ed. Arthur Nolletti Jr. and David Desser, 165–92. Bloomington: Indiana University Press, 1992.

McKee, Ann C., et al. "Chronic Traumatic Encephalopathy in Athletes: Progressive Tauopathy After Repetitive Head Injury." *Journal of Neuropathology & Experimental Neurology* 68, no. 7 (July 2009). https://academic.oup.com/jnen/article/68/7/709/2917002.

McLuhan, Marshall. *Understanding Media: The Extension of Man*. Cambridge, Mass.: MIT Press, 1964.

*Messeiji: Densetsu no CM direkutaa, Sugiyama Toshi*. TBS, 114 min. August 28, 2006.

Mikami Osamu. *1970 nendai ron*. Tokyo: Hihyōsha, 2004.

Minami Hiroshi and Shakai shinri kenkyūsho. *Shōwa bunka zoku 1945–1989*. Tokyo: Keisōshobō, 1990.

Mishima Yukio. *The Decay of the Angel*, The Sea of Fertility 4. Trans. Edward Seidensticker. New York: Vintage, 1990.

———. *Mishima Yukio zenshū*, 44 vols. Tokyo: Shinchōsha, 2000-06.

Miura Atsushi. *Dankai sedai no sengoshi*. Tokyo: Bungeishunjū, 2007.

———. *Kazoku to Kōfuku no sengoshi: Kōgai no yume to genjitsu*. Tokyo: Kōdansha, 1999.

Miyadai Shinji. *Owarinaki nichijō o ikiro: Ōmu kokufuku kanzen manyuaru*. Tokyo: Chikuma shobō, 2018.

Miyadai Shinji et al. *Sabukaruchaa shinwa kaitai*. Tokyo: Parco shuppankyoku, 1993.

Miyahara Teruo. *Jitsuroku! Shōnen magajin meisaku manga henshū funtōki*. Tokyo: Kōdansha, 2005.

Miyamoto Tsuneichi. *Miyamoto Tsuneichi Chosakushū 2*. Tokyo: Miraisha, 1967.

Miyazaki Isamu. *Shōgen sengo Nihon keizai*. Tokyo: Iwanami shoten, 2005.

Miyazaki Manabu. *Kindai yakuza kōteiron: Yamaguchi-gumi no 90 nen*. Tokyo: Chikuma shobō, 2007.

———. *Yakuza to Nihon: Kindai no burai*. Tokyo: Chikuma shobō, 2008.

Mizuki Shigeru. *Gegege no kakeibo*. *Mizuki Shigeru manga daizenshū* 102, 323–562. Tokyo: Kōdansha, 2018.

———. *Mizuki Shigeru manga daizenshū*. 109 vols. Tokyo: Kōdansha, 2013–2019.

———. "Terebi-kun." *Mizuki Shigeru manga daizenshū* 58, 5–36. Tokyo: Kōdansha, 2015.

Mochizuki Akira and Jinbo Shirō. *Sain wa V!* 4 vols. Tokyo: Shimanaka shoten, 2005.

Mori Masato. *Shōwa ryokōshi: Zasshi "Tabi" o yomu*. Tokyo: Chūōkōron shinsha, 2010.

Mori Tsuneo. *Jūgekisen to shukusei*. Tokyo: Shinsensha, 1984.

Morris-Suzuki, Tessa. *Exodus to North Korea: Shadows from Japan's Cold War*. Lanham, Md.: Rowman & Littlefield, 2007.

Motoki Masahiko. *Shūkanshi wa shinazu*. Tokyo: Asahi shinbun shuppan, 2009.

Mura Nunoe. *Gegege no nyōbo*. Tokyo: Jitsugyō no nihon sha, 2008.

Murakami Tomohiko. "*Ashita no Jō* no kinō, kyō, ashita." *Kinema junpō*, February 1, 1980, 119–21.

Murakami Yasusuke. "Shin chūkankaisō no genjitsusei." *Asahi shinbun*, May 20, 1977, evening 3rd ed.

Muramatsu Takeshi. "Terebi, kono shiseikatsu eno shinryakusha." *Taiyō* (September 1968): 126–27.

Nagai Katsuichi. "*Garo*" *henshūchō*. Tokyo: Chikuma shobō, 1987.

Nagamine Hidetoshi. *Tōdaisei wa donna hon o yondekitaka: Hongō, Komaba no dokusho seikatsu 130 nen*. Tokyo: Heibonsha, 2007.

Nagao Saburō. *Shūkanshi keppūroku*. Tokyo: Kōdansha, 2004.
Nagasaki Hiroshi. *Nihon no kagekiha: Sutairu no keifu*. Tokyo: Kaienshobō, 1988.
Nagasaki-shi shi hensan iinkai. *Shin Nagasaki-shi shi* 4. Nagasaki: Nagasaki-shi, 2013.
Nagata Hiroko. *Jūroku no bohyō*. 2 vols. Tokyo: Sairyūsha, 1982–1983.
——. *Watashi ikitemasu*. Tokyo: Sairyūsha, 1986.
——. Written statement. Matsuida Police Station May 6, 1972. Takazawa Collection, University of Hawaii.
Naikaku Chōsashitsu. *Rengōsekigun ni okeru ningen no kenkyū: "Rinchi jiken" o shikishita kanbu tachi*. Tokyo: Naikaku Chōsashitsu, 1972.
Naiki Toshio. "Kashihon manga." In *Manga no Shōwa shi: Shōwa 20-nen–55-nen*. Tokyo: Randamu Hausu Kōdansha, 2008.
Nakahira Takuma. *Naze shokubutsu zukan ka*. Tokyo: Chikuma shobō, 2007.
Nakajima Sadao. "*Nihon ansatsu hiroku* no koto." In *Kasahara Kazuo: Hito to shinario*, ed. Shinario sakka kyokai, 400–402. Tokyo: Shinario sakka kyōkai, 2003.
Nakano Midori. *Oyōfuku kuronikuru*. Tokyo: Chūōkōron shinsha, 1999.
Nakashibetsu-chō 50 nen shi hensan iinkai. *Nakashibetsu-chō 50 nen shi*. Nakashibetsu: Nakashibetsu-chō, 1995.
Nakauchi Isao. *Waga yasu'uri tetsugaku*. Tokyo: Nihon keizai shinbunsha, 1969.
Nakazawa Yuriko. "Ganso an-non zoku 2." In *Waga sedai, Shōwa 29 nen umare*, ed. Kawadeshobō shinsha henshūbu, 231. Tokyo: Kawadeshobō shinsha, 1987.
Namiki Shōkichi. *Nōson wa kawaru*. Tokyo: Iwanami shoten, 1960.
Nanba Kōji et al. *Zoku no keifugaku*. Tokyo: Seikyūsha, 2007.
Natsume Fusanosuke. *Manga no fukayomi, otona yomi*. Tokyo: Iisuto puresu, 2004.
Neitzel, Laura. *The Life We Longed For: Danchi Housing and the Middle Class Dream in Postwar Japan*. Portland, Me.: MerwinAsia, 2016.
NHK Aakaibusu bangumi purojekuto. *Yamano bunkō no kiroku*. Tokyo: Futabasha, 2004.
NHK hōdōkyoku Yodo-gō to rachi shuzaihan. *Yodo-gō to rachi*. Tokyo: Nihon hōsō shuppan kyōkai, 2004.
NHK hōsōbunka kenkyūjo. *Terebi shichō no 50 nen*. Tokyo: Nihon hōsō shuppan kyōkai, 2001.
NHK shuzaihan. *NHK supesharu Sengo 50 nen sonotoki Nihon wa*. Vol. 3, *Chisso Minamata kōjō gijutsusha-tachi no kokuhaku Tōdai Zenkyōtō 26 nenngo no shōgen*. Tokyo: Nihon hōsō shuppan kyōkai, 1995.
Nihon hōsō kyōkai. *Hōsō 50 nenshi, shiryōhen*. Tokyo: Nihon hōsō shuppan kyōkai, 1977.
——. *20 seiki hōsōshi* 1. Tokyo: Nihon hōsō shuppan kyōkai, 2001.
Nihon nōritsu kyōkai sōgō kenkyūjo. *Kurashi to keizai no deeta sōran 2005*. Tokyo: Seikatsu jōhōsentaa, 2005.
Nihon zōsen shinkō zaidan. *Zōsen fukyō no kiroku: Daiichiji sekiyukiki ni taiōshite*. Tokyo: Nihon zōsen shinkō zaidan, 1982.
"*Ningen Jōhatsu*: The World of Imamura Shōhei." http://www.cinemanest.com/imamura/home.html. Accessed September 17, 2017.
Nishii Kazuo, ed. *Rengōsekigun: "Ōkami" tachi no jidai, 1969–1975*. Shiriizu 20 seiki no kioku. Tokyo: Mainichi shinbunsha, 1999.

Nishijima Norio, ed. *Eizō hyōgen no orutanatebu: 1960 nendai no itsudatsu to sōzō.* Tokyo: Shinwasha, 2005.
Nishimura Tōru. "Kishu ryūritan." In *Orikuchi Shinobu jiten,* ed. Nishimura Tōru, 158–68. Tokyo: Daishūkan, 1988.
Nishiwaki, Hideo. *Nihon no akushon eiga.* Tokyo: Shakaishisōsha, 1996.
Nitta Masao. *Yamada Yōji: Naze kazoku o egaki tsuzukerunoka.* Tokyo: Daiyamondosha, 2010.
Nogami Tatsuo. "Ninkyō eiga wa kabuki." *Kinema junpō,* August 30, 1971, 56–57.
Noguchi Yukio. *Sengo keizaishi: Watashitachi wa dokode machigaeta noka.* Tokyo: Tōyō keizai shinpōsha, 2015.
———. *Shinpan 1940 nen taisei.* Tokyo: Toyō keizai shinpōsha, 2002.
Norimatsu Suguru. *Bokushingu to Daitōa: Tōyō senshuken to sengo Ajia gaikō.* Tokyo: Bōyōsha, 2016.
Ochiai Emiko. *The Japanese Family System in Transition: A Sociological Analysis of Family Change in Postwar Japan.* Tokyo: LTCB International Library Foundation, 1997.
Oda Mitsuo. *Kōgai no tanjō to shi.* Tokyo: Seikyūsha, 1997.
Ōe Kenzaburō. "Japan, the Ambiguous, and Myself." Nobel Lecture, December 7, 1994. http://www.nobelprize.org/nobel_prizes/literature/laureates/1994/oe-lecture.html.
Ogi Masahiro. "Banpaku eizō sōhihanron V." *Kinema junpō,* September 15, 1970, 44–47.
Ogimoto Haruhiko, Muraki Yoshihiko, and Konno Tsutomu. *Omae wa tadano genzai ni suginai: Terebi ni naniga kanōka.* Tokyo: Asahi shinbun shuppan, 2008.
Oginome Keiko. *Joyū no yoru.* Tokyo: Tōgensha, 2002.
Oguma Eiji. *1968.* 2 vols. Tokyo: Shin'yōsha, 2009.
Ōizumi Yasuo. *Asama-sansō jūgekisen no shinsō.* Tokyo: Shōgakukan, 2003.
Okabe Hiroyuki. *Hadaka no keizaigaku.* Tokyo: Shōkoten shobō, 1958.
Okazaki Takeshi. *Shōwa 30 nenndai no nioi.* Tokyo: Gakken, 2008.
Ōki Minoru. *Ōki Minoru zen shishū.* Tokyo: Chōryūsha, 1984.
Oku Kōhei. *Seishun no bohyō: Aru gakusei katsudōka no ai to shi.* Tokyo: Bungeishunjū, 1965.
Ōmiya Tomonobu. *Kin no tamago tenshoku rurōki.* Tokyo: Populasha, 2005.
Ono Hiroshi, "Gūzōkashita 'Wadatsumi zō.'" *Sekai* (August 1969): 223–25.
Ōno Shigeru. *"Sandei" to "Magajin."* Tokyo: Kōbunsha, 2009.
Ōsaka Iwao. "Nihon ni okeru tere-porittekusu no tenkai." *Sekai* 956 (December 2003): 191–209.
Ōsaki Norio. "Hakken sareta Nihon." In *Disukabaa, Disukabaa Japan Tōku e ikitai,* ed. Nariai Hajime and Shimizu Hiroko, 188–92. Tokyo: Tokyo Station Gallery, 2014.
Ōshima Nagisa. *Waga Nihon seishin kaizōkeikaku.* Tokyo: Sanpō, 1972.
Ōta Shizuki. "Hekichi no terebi chōsa." *Hōsō kyōiku kirokushū* 7 (1961): 85–111.
Ōtake Hideo. *Shinsayoku no isan: Nyūrefuto kara posutomodan e.* Tokyo: Tokyo daigaku shuppankai, 2007.
Ōtsuka Eiji. *Kanojotachi no Rengōsekigun.* Tokyo: Bungeishunjū, 1996.
Ōtsuka Eiji and Sasakibara Gō. *Kyōyō toshiteno manga, anime.* Tokyo: Kōdansha, 2001.
Ōyama Ken, Satō Dai, and Hayami Kenrō. *Danchi dan.* Tokyo: Kinemajunpōsha, 2012.
Oyamada Tomokiyo. *Matsunoya hikki.* Tokyo: Kokusho kankōkai, 1908.

Partner, Simon. *Assembled in Japan.* Berkeley: University of California Press, 1999.
——. "Brightening Country Lives: Selling Electrical Goods in the Japanese Countryside, 1950–1970." *Enterprise & Society* 1, no. 4 (December 2000): 762–84.
Ridgely, Steven C. *Japanese Counterculture: The Antiestablishment Art of Terayama Shūji.* Minneapolis: University of Minnesota Press, 2010.
Rony, Fatimah Tobing. *The Third Eye: Race, Cinema, and Ethnographic Spectacle.* Durham, N.C.: Duke University Press, 1996.
Ross, Kristin. *May '68 and Its Afterlives.* Chicago: University of Chicago Press, 2002.
Sadakane Hiroyuki. "Shōshitsu suru Banpaku, shōhi sareru toi—1970 nen, Osaka Banpaku ni tsuite." In *Cultural Politics 1960/70,* ed. Kitada Akihiro, Nogami Gen, and Mizutamari Mayumi, 156–72. Tokyo: Serika shobō, 2005.
Saishu Satoru. "Hitotsu no kekki: Watashi no Zenkyōtō." *Asahi kuronikuru shūkan 20 seiki 1969,* August 9, 1999, 8.
Saitō Ayako. "Takakura Ken no aimai na nikutai" In *Otokotachi no kizuna, Ajia eiga, homosōsharu na yokubō,* ed. Yomota Inuhiko and Saitō Ayako, 63–120. Tokyo: Heibonsha, 2004.
Saitō Jirō. *"Shonen janpu" no jidai.* Tokyo: Iwanami shoten, 1996.
Saitō Takao. *Kajiwara Ikki den: Yūyake o miteita otoko.* Tokyo: Bungeishunjū, 2005.
Sakaguchi Hiroshi. *Asama-sansō 1972.* 2 vols. Tokyo: Sairyūsha, 1993.
——. *Kashū ankoku seiki.* Tokyo: Kadokawa gakugei shuppan, 2015.
——. *Sakaguchi Hiroshi kakō.* Tokyo: Asahi shinbunsha, 1993.
——. *Tokoshi eno michi.* Tokyo: Kadokawa shoten, 2007.
——. *Zoku Asama-sansō.* Tokyo: Sairyūsha, 1995.
Sakaiya Taichi. *Dankai no sedai.* Tokyo: Bungeishunjū, 2005.
Sakamoto Hiroshi. *Heibon no jidai: 1950 nendai no taishū gorakushi to wakamono tachi.* Kyoto: Shōwadō, 2008.
Sakurai Tetsuo. *Haikyo no zanzō: Sengo manga no genzō.* Tokyo: NTT shuppan, 2015.
*Sandei mainichi.* "Rengōsekigun jōshin kokkyō yukino daihōisen," March 5, 1972, 16–21.
Sankei shinbun Sengoshi kaifū shuzai han, ed. *Sengoshi kaifū 2.* Tokyo: Sankei shinbun nyūsu saabisu, 1995.
Sano Shin'ichi. *Karisuma: Nakauchi Isao to Daiei no sengo.* Tokyo: Nikkei BP-sha, 1998.
——. *Miyamoto Tsuneichi no shashin ni yomu ushinawareta Shōwa.* Tokyo: Heibonsha, 2004.
Santō Kyōden and Miyazaki Shōzō. *Fukagawa Taizen.* Tokyo: Chinshokai, 1917.
Sartre, Jean-Paul. *Being and Nothingness.* New York: Philosophical Library, 1956.
Sas, Miryam. *Experimental Arts in Postwar Japan: Moments of Encounter, Engagement, and Imagined Return.* Cambridge, Mass.: Harvard University Asia Center, 2011.
Sasaki Morio. "Disukabaa Japan wa kokumin eno marusei kōgeki." *Shakaishugi* (December 1971): 142–47.
Sasaki Takeshi et al. *Sengoshi Daijiten, 1945–2004.* Tokyo: Sanseidō, 2005.
Satō Masa'aki. *Gekiga shishi 30 nen.* Moroyamamachi, Saitama: Tōkōsha, 1984.
Satō Tadao. *Nihon eigashi 3.* Tokyo: Iwanami shoten, 1995.
Satō Takumi. *Terebi teki kyōyō: Ichioku sō hakuchika eno keifu.* Tokyo: NTT shuppan, 2008.
Sawamiya Yū. *Shūdan shūshoku: Kōdo keizai seichō o sasaeta kin no tamago tachi.* Fukuoka: Genshobō, 2017.

Schivelbusch, Wolfgang. *Railway Journey: The Industrialization of Time and Space in the 19th Century.* Oakland: University of California Press, 1977.
Sedgwick, Eve K. *Between Men: English Literature and Male Homosocial Desire.* New York: Columbia University Press, 1985.
Seikatsu kagaku chōsakai. *Danchi no subete.* Tokyo: Seikatsu kagaku chōsakai, 1963.
Sekikawa Natsuo. *Suna no yōni nemuru: Mukashi sengo toiu jidai ga atta.* Tokyo: Shinchōsha, 1993.
Sekizawa Mayumi. "Kōdo keizaiseichō to chiikishakai." In *Kōdo keizaiseichō to seikatsu kakumei,* ed. Kokuritsu rekishi minzoku hakubutsukan, 41–70. Tokyo: Yoshikawa kōbunkan, 2010.
Shigekane Yoshiko. *Nyōbo no yuriisu.* Kōdansha, 1984.
Shigenobu Fusako. *Jūnenme no manazashi kara.* Tokyo: Hanashi no tokushū, 1983.
——. *Kakumei no kisetsu: Paresuchina no senjō kara.* Tokyo: Tōgensha, 2012.
——. *Ringo no ki no shitade anata o umōto kimeta.* Tokyo: Gentōsha, 2001.
——. "Saraba Rengōsekigun no dōshishokun: Beirūto yori aito kanashimi o komete." *Shūkan yomiuri,* April 15, 1972, 16–19.
Shiino Reinin. *Rengōsekigun jiken o yomu nennpyō.* Tokyo: Sairyūsha, 2002.
Shima Shigeo. *Bunto shishi: seishun no gyōshukusareta sei no hibi tomoni tatakatta yūjintachi e.* Tokyo: Hihyōsha, 1999.
Shima Taizō. *Yasuda kōdō, 1968–1969.* Tokyo: Chūōkōron shinsha, 2005.
Shimada Keizō. "The Adventures of Dankichi." In *Reading Colonial Japan: Text, Context, and Critique,* ed. Michelle M. Mason and Helen J. S. Lee, 245–70. Stanford, Calif.: Stanford University Press, 2012.
——. *Bōken Dankichi manga zenshū.* Tokyo: Kōdansha, 1975.
Shimada Shigetoshi. *Yodo-gō jiken 30 enme no shinjitsu.* Tokyo: Sōshisha, 2002.
Shimizu Isao. *Sazae san no shōtai.* Tokyo: Heibonsha, 1997.
Shimizu Masashi. *Tsuge Yoshiharu o yome.* Tokyo: Chōeisha, 2003.
——. *Tsuge Yoshiharu o yomu.* Tokyo: Gendai shokan, 1995.
Shimura Hiro'o. "Hen'yōsuru Discover America." *Senden kaigi* (January 1972): 42–49.
Shinano Tarō, ed. *Shinsayoku undō: Gokuchū shokan shū.* Tokyo: Shinsensha, 1994.
Shintani Takanori. "Denki sentakuki no kioku." In *Kōdo keizai seichō to seikatsu kakumei,* ed. Kokuritsu rekishi minzoku hakubutsukan, 113–33. Tokyo: Yoshikawa kōbunkan, 2010.
Shiomi Takaya. "Gokuchū no shidōsha Shiomi Takaya no shōgen." In *Shōgen Rengōsekigun,* ed. Rengōsekigin jiken no zentaizō o nokosukai. Tokyo: Kōseisha, 2013.
——. *Sekigunha shimatsuki: moto gichō ga kataru 40 nen.* Tokyo: Sairyūsha, 2003.
Shiota Ushio. *Tanaka Kakuei shikkyaku.* Tokyo: Bugeishunjū, 2002.
Shiozawa Shigeru. *Dokyumento terebi jidai: 25 nen no ningen dorama.* Tokyo: Kōdansha, 1978.
Shōgen Rengōsekigun jiken no zentaizō o nokosukai, ed. *Shōgen Rengōsekigin jiken.* Tokyo: Kōseisha, 2013.
Shōnai-machi. "Shōnai-machi no rekishi." https://www.town.shonai.lg.jp/gyousei/gaiyou/tyouseiyouran/rekishi.html.
*Shūkan asahi.* "Daiei no mise wa shōhisha no 'kaihōku' ya," October 27, 1972, 26–29.
——. "Shinbun kisha wa deteike!" June 30, 1972, 15–20.

———. "Ūman ribu mo taji taji 'joshi jakunen teinen-sei' no kabe," March 24, 1972, 114–16.
*Shūkan josei.* "Kabuki no minasan Junko o ibiranaide hoshii!" April 22, 1972, 40–43.
*Shōnen magajin.* "Shōgeki no Riki'ishi To'oru kokubetsushiki fan 700 nin nekkyō no tsudoi," April 19, 1970, 119–21.
*Shūkan manga sandei.* "Kūzen no zankoku shiin kōkai no uchimaku," June 2, 1965, 20–23.
*Shūkan myōjō.* "Naitei shita!? Kōtaishihi: Sonohito Shōda Michiko san no egao," November 23, 1958, 8–12.
*Shūkan posuto.* "Shufu kōrugaaru ga ichiban ōitoiu kōgai danchi," September 25, 1970, 36–39.
*Shūkan sankei.* "Asama jiken: Shōgakusei kara shufu made no uketomekata," March 27, 1972, 132–34.
*Shūkan shinchō.* "Happyōgo tōkakan," December 15, 1958, 28–34.
*Shūkan taishū.* "*Ashita no Jō* ni kaketa Kajiwara Ikki: Chiba Tetsuya shi no tatakai no ato," April 26, 1973, 34–36.
Shūkanshi kenkyūkai, ed. *Shūkanshi.* Tokyo: San'ichi shobō, 1959.
Shundō Kōji and Yamane Sadao. *Ninkyō eigaden.* Tokyo: Kōdansha, 1999.
Standish, Isolde. *Myth and Masculinity in the Japanese Cinema: Toward a Political Reading of the Tragic Hero.* London: Routledge, 2000.
———. *Politics, Porn and Protest: Japanese Avant-Garde Cinema in the 1960s and 1970s.* New York: Continuum, 2011.
Statistics Bureau of Japan. "Historical Data 4–1: Employed Person by Status in Employment—Whole Japan." http://www.stat.go.jp/english/data/roudou/lngindex.htm
———. "Motion Picture (1955–2005)." http://www.stat.go.jp/english/data/chouki/26.htm.
———. "Tatami-sū oyobi hitori Atari tatami-sū." http://www.e-stat.go.jp/SG1/estat/GL08020103.do?_toGL08020103_&tclassID=000001027434&cycleCode=0&requestSender=search.
Steinhoff, Patricia G. "Hijackers, Bombers, and Bank Robbers: Managerial Style in the Japanese Red Army." *Journal of Asian Studies* 48, no. 4 (November 1989): 724–40.
———. *Shi eno ideorogii: Nihon-Sekigunha.* Trans. Kimura Yumiko. Tokyo: Iwanami shoten, 2003.
———. "Three Women Who Love the Left: Radical Woman Leaders in the Japanese Red Army Movement." In *Re-Imaging Japanese Women,* ed. Anne Imamura, 301–24. Berkeley: University of California Press, 1996.
Sudō Hisashi. *Hajakensei no rōman.* Tokyo: San'ichi shobō, 1974.
Sudo Naoki. *Nihonjin no kaisō ishiki.* Tokyo: Kōdansha, 2010.
Suga Hidemi. *Kakumeitekina, amarini Kakumeitekina: 1968 nen no kakumei shiron.* Tokyo: Sakuhinsha, 2003.
———, ed. *1968.* Tokyo: Sakuhinsha, 2005.
———. *1968 nen.* Tokyo: Chikuma shobō, 2006.
*Sugiyama Toshi TVCM Works: ACC Awards 1961–1974.* DVD. Tokyo: Avex, 2010.

Suttmeier, Bruce. "Seeing Past Destruction: Trauma and History in Kaikō Takeshi." *positions* 15, no. 3 (Winter 2007): 457–86.
Tachibana Takashi. *Chūkaku vs. kakumaru*. 2 vols. Tokyo: Kōdansha, 1983.
———. "Tanaka Kakuei kenkyū: Sono kinmyaku to jinmyaku." *Bungeishunjū* (November 1974): 92–131.
Tachibanaki Toshiaki. "Marukei to kinkei: Kaikyū masatsu herashita 'mujun' no jinzai ikusei." *Asahi shinbun*, August 1, 2006, evening ed.
Tada Michitarō. "The Glory and Misery of My Home." In *Authority and the Individual in Japan: Citizen Protest in Historical Perspective*, ed. J. Victor Koschmann, 207–17. Tokyo: University of Tokyo Press, 1978.
———. "Tsukiai no arachi, danchi seikatsu." *Fujin kōron* (February 1961).
Tahara Sōichirō. *Nihon no sengo: Teinen o mukaeta sengo-minshushugi*. Tokyo: Kōdansha, 2005.
———. *Rengōsekigun to Ōmu: Waga uchinaru Arukaida*. Tokyo: Shūeisha, 2004.
———. "73 nen 12 gatsu 13 nichi nanika ga shinda." *Mondai shōsetsu* (November 1977): 340–64.
Takada Fumio. *Tadashii dankai no sedai hakusho*. Tokyo: Kōdansha, 1993.
Takagi Masayuki. *Shinsayoku 30 nen shi*. Tokyo: Dōyō bijutsusha, 1988.
Takaha Tetsuo. "Satsuei hōkoku: *Kazoku*." *Eiga satsuei*, no. 39 (1970): 9–11.
Takahashi Gorō. *Shūkanshi fūunroku*. Tokyo: Bungeishunjū, 2006.
Takahashi Mayumi. *Katararezaru Rengōsekigun: Asama-sansō kara 30 nen*. Tokyo: Sairyūsha, 2002.
Takahashi Tōru, Fujitake Akira, Okada Naoyuki, and Yufu Shōko. "Terebi to 'kodoku na gunshū.'" *Hōsō to senden: CBC repōto* 3, no. 6 (June 1959): 3–13.
Takahashi Yukiharu. *Karibu kai no "rakuen": Dominika imin 30 nen no kiseki*. Tokyo: Ushio shuppansha, 1987.
Takahei Masahito. *Kamagasaki Sekigun heishi Wakamiya Masanori monogatari*. Tokyo: Sairyūsha, 2001.
Takakura Ken and Wakita Takuhiko. "Eiga shinseikatsu, fan no koto." *Kinema junpō*, March 20, 1971, 78–81.
Takano Etsuko. *Nijussai no genten*. Tokyo: Shinchōsha, 1979.
———. *Nijussai no genten: Jōshō*. Tokyo: Shinchōsha, 1979.
———. *Nijussai no genten: Nōto*. Tokyo: Shinchōsha, 1980.
Takatori Ei. "Takamori Asao ni yoru *Ashita no Jō*." In *Ashita no Jō no jidai*, ed. Nerima kuritsu bijutsukan, 154–55. Tokyo: Kyūryūdō, 2014.
Takazawa Kōji. *Rekishi to shiteno shinsayoku*. Tokyo: Shinsensha, 1996.
———. *Shukumei: Yodo-gō bōmeishatachi no himitsukōsaku*. Tokyo: Shinchōsha, 1998.
———, ed. *Zenkyōtō gurafitii*. Tokyo: Shinsensha, 1990.
Takeda Izumo, Miyoshi Shōraku, and Namiki Senryū. *Kanadehon Chūshingura*. Tokyo: Iwanami shoten, 1937.
Takeuchi Osamu. *Sengo manga 50 nenshi*. Tokyo: Chikuma shobō, 1995.
Takigawa Hiroshi. *Kagekiha kaimetsu sakusen: Kōan kisha nikki*. Tokyo: Sanichi shobō, 1973.

Tamiya Takamaro. "Shuppatsu sengen." In *Zōho Sekigun dokyumento—sentō no kōjiroku,* ed. Sashō henshū iinkai, 92–101. Tokyo: Shinsensha, 1978.

Tanaka Kakuei. *Building a New Japan: A Plan for Remodeling the Japanese Archipelago.* Tokyo: Simul Press, 1973.

———. *Nippon rettō kaizōron.* Tokyo: Nihon kōgyō shinbunsha, 1972.

Tanaka Mitsu. *Inochi no onnatachi e: Torimidashi ūmanribu ron.* Tokyo: Kawadeshobo shinsha, 1992.

———. "Nagata Hiroko shikeishū no shini: Onna de arisugita kanojo." *Asahi shinbun,* February 26, 2011, 13th ed.

Tanaka Yoshihisa and Ogawa Fumiya, eds. *Terebi to Nihonjin: "Terebi 50 nen" to seikatsu, bunka, ishiki.* Tokyo: Hōsei daigaku shuppankyoku, 2005.

Tanikawa Kenji. "Sengo eiga ni okeru kanshū." In *Taishū bunka to media,* Sōsho gendai no media to jaanarizumu 4, ed. Yoshimi Shunya and Tsuchiya Reiko, 142–65. Kyoto: Mineruba shobō, 2010.

Tanizawa Ei'ichi. "Kaikō Takeshi no utsu." *Nihon byōsekigaku zasshi,* no. 64 (August 2002): 2–14.

———. *Kaisō Kaikō Takeshi.* Tokyo: Shinchōsha, 1992.

Tateishi Yasunori. *Matsushita Kōnosuke no Shōwa-shi.* Tokyo: Nanatsumori shokan, 2011.

Tatematsu Wahei. *Eiga shugisha, Fukasaku Kinji.* Tokyo: Bungeishunjū, 2003.

Tazawa Ryūji. "Chiba Tetsuya: Ashita no Jō ga watatta 1970 nen toiu hashi." in *Wakamono ga "Wakamono" datta jidai,* ed. Shūkan kinyōbi, 97–110. Tokyo: Kinyōbi, 2012.

Teikoku-shoin. "Tōkei shiryō: gunji hi." https://www.teikokushoin.co.jp/statistics/history_civics/index05.html.

Teranishi Jūrō. *Nihon no keizai shisutemu.* Tokyo: Iwanami shoten, 2003.

Terayama Shūji. "Darega Riki'ishi o koroshitanoka." *Nihon dokusho shinbun,* February 16, 1970, 8.

———. *Makeinu no eikō.* Tokyo: Kadokawa Haruki jimusho, 1999.

———. *Shin sho o suteyo, machi e deyō.* Tokyo: Kawade shobō, 1993.

*30 byō no sogekihei.* Terebi Asahi, 50:00. December 20, 1979.

Tichi, Cecelia. *Electronic Hearth: Creating an American Television Culture.* New York: Oxford University Press, 1992.

Tōei anime. "Anime *Gegege no Kitarō* 50 shūnen kinen." http://www.toei-anim.co.jp/kitaro/50th/.

Tomii Reiko. *Radicalism in the Wilderness: International Contemporaneity and 1960s Art in Japan.* Cambridge, Mass.: MIT Press, 2016.

Tominaga Ken'ichi. *Nihon no kindaika to shakai hendō.* Tokyo: Kōdansha, 1990.

———. "Shakai kaisōkōzō no genjō." *Asahi shinbun,* June 27, 1977, evening 3rd ed.

Tono'oka Akio. "Kansatsusha no hihyōsei: Betonamu sensō yori." *Kokubungaku: Kaishaku to kyōzai no kenkyū* 27, no. 15 (November 1982): 45–49.

Torrance, Richard. "The Nature of Violence in Fukasaku Kinji's Jingi naki tatakai (War Without a Code of Honor)." *Japan Forum* 17, no. 3 (2005): 389–406.

*Tosho shinbun.* "Konwaku suru kenryokushasō," May 29, 1965.

Toyohara Kikō and Chiba Tetsuya. *Chiba Tetsuya to Jō no Tatakai to seishun no 1954 nichi.* Tokyo: Kōdansha, 2010.

Tsubomatsu Hiroyuki. *Kotobukiya kopii raitaa Kaikō Takeshi*. Osaka: Taru shuppan, 2014.
Tsubouchi Yūzō. *1972: "Hajimari no owari" to "owari no hajimari."* Tokyo: Bungeishunjū, 2003.
Tsuchiya Yoshio. *Kurosawa saan! Kurosawa Akira tono subarashiki hibi*. Tokyo: Shinchōsha, 1999.
Tsuchiya Yuka. "Senryōki no CIE eiga (Natoko eiga)." In *Fumikoeru dokyumentarii*, Nihon eiga wa ikiteiru 7, ed. Kurosawa Kiyoshi, Yoshimi Shunya, Yomota Inuhiko, and Lee Bong-ou, 155–81. Tokyo: Iwanami shoten, 2010.
Tsuge Yoshiharu. *Hinkon ryokōki*. Tokyo: Shōbunsha, 1991.
——. *Tsuge Yoshiharu, shoki kessaku tanpenshū 1*. Tokyo: Kōdansha, 2003.
——. *Tsuge Yoshiharu zenshū*. 9 vols. Tokyo: Chikuma shobō, 1993–1994.
Tsuge Yoshiharu and Gondō Shin. *Tsuge Yoshiharu mangajutsu 2*. Tokyo: Waizu shuppan, 1993.
Tsuge Yoshiharu, Ōsaki Norio, and Kitai Kazuo. *Tsuge Yoshiharu Nagare gumo tabi*. Tokyo: Ōbunsha, 1982.
Tsuji Ichirō. *Watashi dake no hōsōshi*. Tokyo: Seiryūshuppan, 2008.
Tsunemitsu Tōru. *Shigusa no minzokugaku: Jujutsuteki sekai to shinsei*. Kyoto: Mineruba shobō, 2006.
Tsunoyama Sakae. *Jikan kakumei*. Tokyo: Shinshokan, 1998.
Tsurumi Shunsuke. *Kitai to kaisō*. 2 vols. Tokyo: Shōbunsha, 1997.
Tsuruta Kōji. "Boku to ninkyō eiga." *Kinema junpō*, March 20, 1971, 87–90.
Tsutsui Yasutaka. *Tsutsui Yasutaka zenshū*. 24 vols. Tokyo: Shinchōsha, 1983–85.
Turim, Maureen. *The Films of Oshima Nagisa: Images of a Japanese Iconoclast*. Berkeley: University of California Press, 1998.
Uchiyama Takashi. *Nihonjin wa naze kitsune ni damasarenaku nattanoka*. Tokyo: Kōdansha, 2007.
Ueda Yasuo. *Zasshi wa miteita: Sengo jaanarizum no kōbō*. Tokyo: Suiyōsha, 2009.
Uegaki Yasuhiro. *Heishitachi no Rengōsekigun*. Tokyo: Sairyūsha, 1984.
——. "Kaisetsu ni kaete: Uegaki Yasuhiro rongu intabyū." In *Rengōsekigun jiken o yomu nenpyō*, ed. Shiino Reinin, 133–56. Tokyo: Sairyūsha, 2002.
——. *Rengōsekigun 27 nen me no shōgen*. Tokyo: Sairyūsha, 2001.
——. Written statement. Sasanoi Police Station, April 21, 1972. Takazawa Collection, University of Hawaii.
Ueno Eishin. *Oware yuku kōfutachi*. Tokyo: Iwanami shoten, 1960.
——. *Shutsu Nippon ki*. Tokyo: Shakai shisōsha, 1995.
Ueno Kōshi. *Nikutai no jidai*. Tokyo: Gendaishokan, 1989.
——. *Sengo saikō*. Tokyo: Asahi shinbunsha, 1995.
Ui, Jun. "Minamata Disease." In *Industrial Pollution in Japan*, ed. Jun Ui, 103–32. Tokyo: United Nations University Press, 1992.
Ukai Masaki, Nagai Yoshikazu, and Fujimoto Ken'ichi, eds. *Sengo Nihon no taishūbunka*. Kyoto: Shōwadō, 2000.
Umeno Kenjirō, ed. *Kōrudo chein nenkan 1976*. Tokyo: Sankei maaketengu, 1976, 939.
Uryū Yoshimitsu. "Shōshitsu suru Banpaku, Shōhi sareru toi—1970 nen, Osaka Banpaku nitsuite." In *Cultural Politics 1960/70*, ed. Kitada Akihiro, Nogami Gen, and Mizutamari Mayumi, 114–34. Tokyo: Serika shobō, 2005.

Wakamatsu Kōji. "Yonaoshi no kikkake." *Shukan Gendai*, March 21, 1972, 122.

Wakatsuki Yasuo. *Gaimushō ga keshita Nihonjin*. Tokyo: Mainichi shinbunsha, 2001.

———. *Hatten tojōkoku eno ijū no kenkyū: Boribia ni okeru Nihon imin*. Tokyo: Tamagawa Daigaku shuppanbu, 1987.

Washida Koyata. *Shōwa shisōshi 60 nen*. Tokyo: San'ichi shobō, 1986.

Watanabe Daisuke. "Futsū no jikan no sugoshikata no seiritsu to sono henyō." In *Sōchūryū no hajimari: Danchi to seikatsu jikan no sengoshi*, ed. Watanabe Daisuke, Aizawa Shinichi, and Mori Naoto, 19–41. Tokyo: Seikyūsha, 2019.

Watanabe Ichie, Shiokawa Yoshinobu, and Ōyabu Ryūsuke, eds. *Shinsayokuundō 40 nen no hikari to kage*. Tokyo: Shinsensha, 1999.

Watanabe Osamu. "Kōdoseichō to kigyōshakai." In *Kōdoseichō to kigyōshakai*, ed. Watanabe Osamu, 7–126. Tokyo: Yoshikawa kōbunkan, 2004

Williams, Raymond. *Raymond Williams on Television*. Ed. Alan O'Conner. London: Routledge, 1989.

Yamada Shōji. "CM sakka no shi: Sugiyama Toshi no shi to tanjō." *Nihon kenkyū*, no. 29 (December 2004): 325–41.

Yamada Yōji. *Eiga wa omoshiroika*. Tokyo: Junpōsha, 1999.

———. *100 nen intabyū Yamada Yōji*, NHK BShi, November 15, 2007; DVD. Tokyo: NHK Enterprises, 2009.

———. "Synopsis: *Kazoku*." Tokyo: Shōchiku Ōtake Library, n.d.

Yamada Yōji, Baishō Chieko, Okamoto Hiroshi, Kawamoto Saburō, Suzuki Kenji, and Yamada Kōichi. "Yamada Yōji kantoku o kakomu *Kazoku* tōron." *Kinema junpō*, October 15, 1970, 30–36.

Yamadaira Shigeki. *Ninkyō eiga ga seishun datta*. Tokyo: Chikuma shobō, 2004.

Yamaguchi Masatomo. "Dōgu." In *Kōdo seichō to Nihonjin 2*, ed. Kōdo keizaiseichō o kangaeru kai, 61–104. Tokyo: Niho editaasukūru shuppanbu, 1985.

Yamamoto Akira. *Sengo fūzokushi*. Osaka: Osaka shoseki, 1986.

Yamane Sadao. *Tezuka Osamu to Tsuge Yoshiharu: Gendai manga no shuppatsuten*. Tokyo: Tōhoku shobo, 1983.

Yamane Sadao and Yonehara Hisashi. *"Jinginaki tatakai" o tsukutta otokotachi*. Tokyo: NHK shuppan, 2005

Yanagihara Ryōhei. "Torisu jidai no Kaikō-kun." In *Osaka de umareta Kaikō Takeshi*, Nanba Toshizō et al., 24–49. Osaka: Taru shuppan, 2011.

Yasko, Guy. "The Japanese Student Movement 1968–70: The Zenkyōtō Uprising." Ph.D. diss., Cornell University, 1997.

Yasuda Takeshi. *Mishima Yukio nichiroku*. Tokyo: Michiya, 1996.

Yasumi Akihito. "Kaisetsu: Dantei no ronri." In *Naze shokubutsu zukan ka*, by Nakahira Takuma, 299–308. Tokyo: Chikuma shobō, 2007.

Yomiuri shinbun shakaibu. *Rengōsekigun: Kono ningen sōshitsu*. Tokyo: Ushio shuppan, 1972.

Yomiuri shinbun Shōwa jidai purojekuto. *Shōwa jidai 30 nendai*. Tokyo: Chūōkōron shinsha, 2012.

Yomota Inuhiko. "Kokuchi to genjitsu." In *1968 2, Bungaku*, ed. Yomota Inuhiko and Fukuma Kenji, 13–50. Tokyo: Chikuma shobō, 2018.

———. *Shirato Sanpei ron*. Tokyo: Sakuhinsha, 2004.

Yonehara Hisashi and Yoshida Sadaji. "Manei, Uchida Tomu, soshite Fukasaku Kinji: Kikigaki kameraman Yoshida Sadaji." In *"Jinginaki tatakai" o tsukutta otokotachi*, ed. Yamane Sadao and Yonehara Hisashi, 88–119. Tokyo: NHK shuppan, 2005.

Yoshida Haruo. *Kaikō Takeshi: Tabi to hyōgensha*. Tokyo: Sairyūsha, 1992.

Yoshida Naoya. "Eiga to terebi dokyumentarii." In *Nihon eiga no mosaku*, Kōza Nihon eiga 6, ed. Imamura Shōhei, Satō Tadao, Shindō Kaneto, Tsurumi Shunshuke, and Yamada Yōji, 384–93. Tokyo: Iwanami shoten, 1987.

Yoshida Naoya and Shindō Kaneto. "Terebi no hōhō." In *Nihon eiga no mosaku*, Kōza Nihon no eiga 6, ed. Imamura Shōhei, Satō Tadao, Shindō Kaneto, Tsurumi Shunshuke, and Yamada Yōji, 368–83. Tokyo: Iwanami shoten, 1987.

Yoshikawa Hiroshi. *Kōdoseichō: Nihon o kaeta 6,000 nichi*. Tokyo: Yomiuri shinbunsha, 1997.

Yoshimi Shunya. *Banpaku to Sengo Nihon*. Tokyo: Kōdansha, 2011.

——. "Consuming America, Producing Japan." In *The Ambivalent Consumer: Questioning Consumption in East Asia and the West*, ed. Sheldon Gardon and Patricia L. Maclachalan. Ithaca, N.Y.: Cornell University Press, 2006.

——. *Hakurankai no seijigaku*. Tokyo: Chūōkōron, 1992.

——. *Koe no shihonshugi: denwa, rajio, chikuonki no shakaishi*. Tokyo: Kōdansha, 1995.

——. "Media ibento toshiteno Goseikon." In *Sengo Nihon no media ibento, 1945–1960*, ed. Tsuganesawa Toshihiko, 267–87. Kyoto: Sekaishisōsha, 2002.

——. "1964 Tokyo Olympics as Post-War." *International Journal of Japanese Sociology*, no. 28 (2019): 80–95.

——. *Shikakutoshi no chiseigaku: Manazashi toshiteno kindai*. Tokyo: Iwanami shoten, 2016.

——. "Terebi ga ie ni yattekita: terebi no kūkan, terebi no jikan." *Shisō*, no. 956 (December 2003): 26–48.

——. "Terebi o dakishimeru sengo." In *Taishū bunka to media*, ed. Yoshimi Shunya and Tsuchiya Reiko, 166–96. Kyoto: Mineruba shobō, 2010.

Yoshimoto Taka'aki. *Masu imeijiron*. Tokyo: Fukutake shoten, 1984.

——. *Waga tenkō*. Tokyo: Bungeishunjū, 1995.

——. *Yoshimoto Taka'aki zenchosakushū* 13. Tokyo: Keisōshobō, 1969.

Yoshioka Ei'ichi. *Kaikō Takeshi no bungakusekai: Kōsakusuru Ōeru no kage*. Tokyo: Alpha Beta Books, 2017.

Yui Tsunehiko, Yanagisawa Asobu, and Tatsuki Mariko. *Sezon no rekishi* 1. Tokyo: Libro Port, 1991.

Yuki Sōichi. *Dankai no sedai towa nandattanoka*. Tokyo: Yōsensha, 2003.

Yukino Kensaku. "Waga seishun no shisōhenreki." In *Shōgen Rengōsekigun*, ed. Rengōsekigin jiken no zentaizō o nokosukai. Tokyo: Kōseisha, 2013.

Zahlten, Alexander. *The End of Japanese Cinema: Industrial Genres, National Times, and Media Ecologies*. Durham, N.C.: Duke University Press, 2017.

Zenkyōtō hakusho henshū iinkai. *Zenkyōtō hakusho*. Tokyo: Shinchōsha, 1994.

# Index

1960s Japan, 94; conditions of, 168, 202; economic power of, 94; everyday life of, 9
Abe Kōbō, 152, 153
activists, 186, 229, 231–33; female, 231; non–Red Army, 232; political, 6, 230; radical, 230, 249; Red Army faction, 315n15; student, 212, 220, 248, 304n37, 311n43, 312n57; and sympathizers, 211; URA, 229; violent confrontation of, with authority, 196; youth, 8
advertisement, 134; as de-advertisement, 134; of experimental artists, 8; for household appliances, 34; IBM, 294n45; Panasonic, 19; Sanyō, 78, 79; for *Shūkan bunshun*, 75; for Suntory, 1, 146, 147; television, 259, 261; Tōshiba, 36, 37; for vacuum cleaner, 34, 36–38
agency, 148, 156, 157, 209, 313n61; of action 209, 223; autonomous, 143, 197, 211; creative, 134; genuine, 206, 208, 209, 222, 226; historical, 47, 199;

independent, 5, 173, 202, 221; individuality and, 227; masculine, 145, 166, 226, 265; newfound, 156; patriarchal, 108; political, 226; recovery of, 159; sense of, 45; transparent, 166; of violence, 241; of yakuza hero, 181, 184
agrarian communities. *See* communities
Agriculture Foundation Law (Nōgyō kihon hō), 30
agricultural land redistribution. *See* land reform
Akasegawa Genpei, 9
Akihito, Crown Prince, 74, 75, 79, 80, 283n70; wedding of, 74, 75, 81, 283n76
Akimoto Kei'ichi; Kaikō and, 144, 160, 161, 165, 295n1; photos of execution by, 297n27; at public execution, 150
Akiyama Shun; and danchi life, 79–81, 280n31
*Akuma kun* (*The Devil Boy*), 70
Akutagawa literary prize, 146, 147, 296n15

Akutagawa Ryūnosuke, 141
alienation effect (Brecht), 93
Amakasu Akira, 73
Amano Masako, 34
Amasawa Taijirō, 115
Americanization, 12
American soldiers, 190, 191, 305n49
an-non tribe (*an non zoku*), 135, 136
*an·an*, 135
Anderson, Benedict, 51
antihero 129, 174; anguished, 175
Aoto Mikio, 245, 247, 318n69
*Asahi Graph*, 130
*Asahi Journal*, 199, 282n50
Asaine Hideo, 224
Asama-sansō, 228–30, 234, 250, 253; hostage situation, 319n90
Ashida Terukazu, 149
Asia Pacific War, 12, 27, 50, 66, 145, 200, 264; catastrophe of, 226; defeat in, 148; deprivation during, 220; final phase of, 263, 276n78, 305n51, 313n59; and Kaikō, 145; and Komatsu, 263; and Tsuge, 115; unresolved memories of, 299n50; URA and, 319n90
Atsumi Kiyoshi; in *It's Tough Being a Man* series, *106*; in *Where Spring Comes Late*, 105–107
avant-garde culture, 8, 9, 269n19; cutting edge of, 10
"The Average" (Heikinteki; Ōki), 2

baby boomers, Japanese, 199
Baird, Bruce, 9
Bandō Kunio, 236, 245, 249; as Japanese Red Army member, 252; release of, from prison, 252
baseball, 200–202, 204–8, 210; American identity of, 208; culture, 203; managed, 203; passion for, 204, 206, 207; spiritual aspect of, 206
*Battles Without Honor and Humanity* (*Jinginaki tatakai*; Fukasaku), 174, 175, 183, 188–89, 196–198, 302n17, 306n60; characters in, 192; and conventions of yakuza film, 188, 193; and first-wave yakuza film, 191, 193, 196; and humor, 193; narrative structure of, 190; new looks of, 189; paradox in, 190; pessimistic outlook of, 195; and political conditions of, 1973 196; relationship to larger historical context, 194; return of yakuza hero in, 194; success of, 189; as Toei's response to political climate in early, 1970s Japan
*Battles Without Honor and Humanity: Deadly Fight in Hiroshima* (*Jinginaki tatakai: Hiroshima shitō-hen*; Fukasaku), 195
*Battles Without Honor and Humanity: Final Episode* (*Jinginaki tatakai: Kanketsu-hen*; Fukasaku), 194; and Kasahara, 306n64
*Battles Without Honor and Humanity: Police Tactics* (*Jinginaki tatakai: Chōjō sakusen*; Fukasaku), 195
*Battles Without Honor and Humanity* series (*Jinginaki tatakai*; Fukasaku), 175, 187, 194, 197
*Being and Nothingness* (Sartre), 77
Betsuyaku Minoru, 8
*Big Gambling Ceremony* (*Bakuchiuchi; Sōchō tobaku*; Yamashita), 175, 192, 302n17
*Bildungsroman*, 202, 226
black market, 188, 190, 191, 195
blender, 46; as symbol of consumerism, 46, 47, 49, 82, 138
*Blondie*, 12

[ 348 ] INDEX

blue-collar workers, 4, 25, 31, 32, 273n41, 291n7; and assimilation into body of regular workers, 32; as danchi residents, 285; demands of, 31; discrimination against, 273n42; in early postwar years, 31; and farmers, 4, 5, 46; children of, 46; white-collar workers and, 31, 45
bodily performance, 200, 217, 224, 227
body, 107, 151, 152, 166–68, 179, 207, 209, 217, 221, 222, 226, 240, 247; athletic, 15; average, of Ōki, 2; as connection to past, 299n50; dead, 247; destruction of, 222, 223, 226; disciplining of, 311n46; as enemy territory, 238; of executed Vietnamese high school student, 150; female, 108, 121, 123; growing, 312n58; of Hijikata, 9; hurt and fatigued, of Uegaki, 248; as interface between life and death, 167; of Kaneko, as site of ideological battle, 244, 245, 318n71; of Katō, 240; of Kojima, 238, 316n38; and ideal masculine self, 204; and historical conditions of postwar Japan, 209; neglected, 248; organ without, 217; and escape from quotidian life, 168; rebellion of, 166; of regular workers, 32; of Sakaguchi, 246; as site of resistance against consumer culture, 209, 211; as source of light, 217, 218; as spiritual root, 107; and tension with spirit, 209; unscathed, 194; upper, 207; of Vietnamese peasant, 154
bourgeoisie, 230
boxing, 209, 210, 213, 214, 216, 222, 224; as bodily dialectics, 213; and capitalism, 220; disciplinary regime of, 212; educational benefits of, 212; inherent violence of, 210–11; and language of capitalism, 216; as means of communication, 215, 224; modernization of, 210; old style of, 210; passion for, 220; physical language of, 213; postwar Japanese, 210; regime of, 222; world of, 16, 200, 210, 214; in *Tomorrow's Jō*, 212–16, 220, 224
*Brutal Tale of Chivalry* (*Shōwa zankyōden*; Saeki), 188
*Brutal Tale of Chivalry 2: The Chinese Lion and Peony Tattoo* (*Shōwa zankyōden 2: Karajishi botan*; Saeki), 178
*Brutal Tale of Chivalry 7: Hell Is a Man's Destiny* (*Shōwa zankyōden 7: Shinde moraimasu*; Makino), 176–80
*Brutal Tale of Chivalry* series (*Shōwa zankyōden*), 174, 179, 182, 184
*Building a New Japan* (*Nihon rettō kaizōron*; Tanaka), 256
Bund. *See* Second Communist League
Burakumin, 32, 274n55; and resident Koreans and yakuza, 306n61

Cahn, Alvin, 210
camera, 73, 75, 136, 139, 150; 16-mm film, 53; handheld, 99, 187–89; imaginary, 138; infrared, 284n78; lens of, 140; marked presence of, in Discover Japan posters, 136; gaze of, 77, 166; television, 19–21, 56, 74, 302n13
Campanis, Al, 203
campus activism, 45, 173
capitalism, 176, 178, 179; boxing and, 220; consumer, 6, 11; deleterious effects of, 179, 184; language of, 104, 179, 216, 222, 224; new phase of, in Japan, 130; as cause of social disintegration in yakuza film, 176; shady side of, 101; symptom of, 185; in *Tomorrow's Jō*, 217, 225

capitalist, 173, 176, 213, 216, 224, 312n53
Catholicism, 89, 285n3
Chiba Tetsuya, 215, 217, 223, 312n55; artistic vision of, 201; and assistants, 223, 313n64; and final scene of *Tomorrow's Jō*, 223, 313n64, 314n69; and Kajiwara, 200–202, 308n14, 309n15, 314n67; repatriation of, from Manchuria, 313n59
children, 62–64; city 60; in danchi, 80, 81; disadvantaged, 69; of Dorobu, 56, 57, 59, 60, 278n15; from single-parent households, 32; and television, 62, 66; as vanguard of emerging consumer society, 63
"Chōhachi's Inn" (Chōhachi no yado; Tsuge), 131
Chun, Jayson Makoto, 13
*chūryū* (middle stratum of society), 45–48
*chūryū ishiki* (consciousness of belonging to the middle social stratum of society), 47–49, 277n92
cities, 4, 26, 29, 30, 258; countryside and, 29, 38; employment in, 30; European, 300n56; major, 60, 255–257; midsize, 257; relocation to, 30; residents in, 61; in Tokyo area, 22
Civil Information and Education Section (General Headquarters), 60
class, 202, 209; adverse effects of, 204, economic, 202, 204, 208, 213, 214; lower, 309n26; weight, 209, 214, 215
class divide, 202, 204, 280n37
coal industry, 88, 91, 92, 285n4, 285n5, 285n7
"Cold Chain Recommendation," 41
cold chains, 41; Nakauchi and 276n83
Cold War geopolitics 26, 150

college, 42, 44, 46, 173, 304n37; and existing curricula, 43; junior, 42; private, 43
college campuses, 186, 199, 211
college students, 43, 184, 186, 228, 300n56
colonial project, 164
colonial subjects, Japanese representations of, 208
*Combat!*, 165, 269n26
commercialism, 117 118
commodity fetishism, 239
consumer culture, 3, 4, 7, 11, 12, 63, 131, 146, 169, 313n61; deleterious effects of, 10, 12; material conditions of, 223; outsider of, 69; resistance against, 209
consumer society, 3, 5, 8, 131, 143, 230, 248; critique of, 6; Daiei and, 40; emerging, 14, 28, 63, 276n85; encounter with, 117; epitome of Japan's, 247; escape from, 3, 130, 249, 255; establishment of, 229; fight against, 230; homogenous time of, 264; of Japan, 3, 12, 13, 46, 72, 82, 147, 247; Japanese masculinity and, 7; life inside, 40; mass, 3, 4, 14, 133, 143, 145, 173, 174, 198, 226, 229, 230, 249; and Oguma, 268n13; smooth surface of, 202; subjects of, 49; Sugiyama and, 261; symptoms of, 230; television and, 68, 69; URA and, 16; visual media and, 6
consumerism, 2, 3, 24, 40, 46, 230, 255, 256, 261, 264; blender as symbol of, 46; coercive power of, 3; cutting edge of, 261; Daiei and, 40; development of, 264; Japanese discomfort with, 265; effects of, 231, 255; explosive expansion of, 4, 256; fight against, 230; frenzy of, 79; as

hyperconsumerism, 169; metavision and, 16, 254; new media and, 256; promises and perils of, 63; urban cultural life and, 59; world of, 15, 46; zombies and, 313n61

consumers, 4, 12, 23, 28, 39–41, 49, 256, 276n75; desires of, 41; female, 135; Japanese, 173; as king, 78, 79; liberation of, 40; male, 7; media, 265; needs of, 40; primary identity as, 293n36

consumption, 3, 4, 14, 28, 41, 49, 62, 68, 139, 146, 264; alcohol, 260; domestic, 26; feminine, 6; frontier of, 135; habit of, 62; mass, 2, 6, 41; media, 130; national space of, 13, 25, 81; new circuit of, 4; passive, 200; pleasure of, 244; production and, 6, 22, 25, 26, 41, 51, 217; of U.S. culture, 14; of wealth, 257; Western values of, 64; world of, 261

corporation, 134; dependency on, 34; full-fledged members of, 34; Japanese, 30–33, 113, 184, 273n41, 273n45; large-scale, 28, 31–33

counternarrative, 4, 6

countryside, 28–30, 33, 38, 39, 53, 114, 140, 142, 256, 305n49; and cities, 38, 173; construction projects in, 29; depopulation and aging in, 256–57; economic opportunity in, 256; effects of, 264; as exotic tourist attraction, 143; residents of, 4, 256; transformation in, 28; urbanization of, 46

Daiei (supermarket chain), 39–41; 276n75

Daiei Film, 111; and yakuza film, 174

*danchi*, 51, 79; 280n30, 280n31; 2DK, 97; Akiyama and, 79–81; 285n91; and American-style living, 284n87; blue-collar workers and, 285n92; concrete structure of, 79; as cutting edge of modern living in Japan, 82; definition of, 284n85; everyday living in, 82; Hara and, 80, 82; Hibarigaoka, 79, 80; highly standardized space of, 62; homogenizing effects of, 285n92; housewives at, 82; prostitution at, 285n96; residents of, 82, 285n91; social meaning of, 284n85

*Danchi Wife* (*Danchi zuma: Hirusagai no jōji*, 1971), 82

darkness, 70, 96, 118, 123, 141, 142, 158, 159; of death, 164; depth of, 219; destructive, 166; and Kaikō, 169; and light, 168; of night, 129, 284n78; and symbolic representation, 164; television and, 79, 166

*Darkness in Ending Flowers* (*Hana owaru yami*; Kaikō), 169, 300n61

*Darkness in Summer* (*Natsuno yami*; Kaikō), 145, 166–68, 300n56, 300n57

*Dawn Over the Mountains* (*Yamano bunkō no kiroku*, 1959–1960), 54, 56–62

*dekasegi*, 29, 62, 256

Dentsū, 130, 131, 133, 134, 138, 293n28

department stores, 40, 276n77; Daiei and, 40; Japanese, 40; as part of exhibitionary complex, 279n20; in prewar Japan, 40; retail strategies of, 40

depopulation, 30, 257; in 1960s, 320n2; in 1970s, 321n2

*Discover Japan* (*Deisukabaa Japan*; magazine), 131, 132

Discover Japan campaign, 130, 131, 133–35, 138–40, 294n49; posters of, 136, 137, 138, 142; and provoke, 294n45; and Tsuge, 117, 118, 131, 140, 143; and young women, 293n35

*Distant Cry from Spring, A* (*Harukanaru yama no yobigoe*; Yamada), 109
documentary aesthetic, 92, 187
*Dodgers' Way to Play Baseball* (Campanis), 203
Domesticity, 205
Dorobu, 54–56, 58, 61, 70, 72, 75, 79; children of, 56, 57, 59, 60, 278n15

education, 24, 34, 43, 45, 46; and baseball, 206; high school, 34; higher, 42–46, 273n38; level of, 48; for masses, 42; middle school, 115, 142; of Ozuma Armstrong in *Star of the Giants*, 208; physical, 34; of Yabuki Jō in *Tomorrow's Jō*, 212
environmental destruction 20, 113, 184, 323n30
everyday life, 61, 62, 70, 72, 83, 88, 105, 101, 123, 129, 145, 152, 157, 158, 167, 168, 183, 317n65; in 1960s Japan, 9; changes in, 82; chores of, 127; deleterious effects of, 64; desire for, 63; façade of, 82; of film audience, 72; under high-growth regime, 87; in I-novel, 167; of Japan, 152; at Japan's geographical margins, 88; in post-1972 Japan, 254; private realm of, 168, 261; in recent past, 143; as site of constant struggle, 111; in Tokyo, 129; of yakuza film's audience, 179
execution; impending, of Sakaguchi, 253; of Revolutionary Left member, 236, 251, 318n77; of Vietnamese youth, 150, 151, 152, 154–58, 166, 296n5, 297n27
Expo '70, 10, 99–101, 108, 133, 263; Midori Pavilion at, 100; Mitsubishi Pavilion at, 100; multiscreen projection systems at, 100; multitrack audio systems at, 100; as television-like space, 100, 102

factual recording. See *jitsuroku*
family life, 81, 281n43, 285n92; male workers' absence from, 81; television and, 54, 64, 67
farmers, 29, 53, 54, 79, 109; blue-collar workers and, 46; dairy, 93; and *dekasegi*, 62; Dominican, 286n10; local, 289n49; tenant, 25, 26
Film Classification and Rating Committee (Eiga rinki kanri iinkai), 182
Franky, Lily, 100
freedom, 13, 92, 136, 148, 159, 182, 209, 210, 213, 214, 222, 223, 226; of action, 226; creative, 261, 308n9; perfect, 223, 224; promised land of, 95; ultimate, 226
free spirit, 214, 215, 220, 222; constraints on, 200; source of, 212; tension between free will and, 215, 222
From Gung-ho to Beautiful (Mōretsu kara byūtifuru e; advertisement campaign), 133, 134
frozen food, 41, 42, 276n85; Nakauchi's distaste for, 276n83
Fuji Junko, 180, 185; heteronormative identity of, 186; marriage of, 304n36; and Takakura, 185
Fujioka Wakao, 130, 138, 293n28; and de-advertisement (*datsu-kōkoku*), 134; and Discover Japan campaign, 130, 133, 135, 142; masculine identity of, 130; misogyny of, 134, 293n36; and Tsuge, 130, 131
Fujitake Akira, 76, 77, 79
Fukasaku Kinji, 188, 189, 193, 196; as director of *Battles Without Honor and*

*Humanity* series, 188, 189, 197, 305n48, 305n49; masculine ideal of, 307n68; rape allegation against, 307n68; reactions of, to URA's bloody purges, 196
Fukuda Takeo, 258
Fuller, Robert, 13
Furuhata Yasuo, 185
Furuhata, Yuriko, 9
future, 38, 67, 148; myth of a better, 226

*Gangster VIP* (*Burai yori daikanbu*; Masuda Toshio), 183
*Garo*, 12, 115, 116
gaze, 56, 77, 93, 139, 151, 153, 162, 166, 182, 217, 220, 279n20, 303n21; burning, of Hoshi Hyūma in *Star of the Giants*, 219; of camera, 77, 139, 166, 249; circular flow of, 56; of Shiraki Yōko in *Tomorrow's Jō*, 216, 220; and countergaze, 77, 159; critical and reflective, 58, 93; ethnographic, 140; imagined, 135, 156, 157, 160; invasive, 140; investigative, 59; media, 76, 77, 255; of modernization, 54; nostalgic, 179; of others, 62, 279n20; outside, 5, 60; of outsiders, 54, 168; public, 72; pure, 153, 297n31; self-reflective, 60, 114, 130, 143, 265; social, 54; sympathetic, of Yamada, 14, 114; of television, 50, 51, 54, 68, 71, 79, 83, 279n20; of Tsuge, 140, 141; ubiquitous, 79; undiscriminating, 160; universal, 54; voyeuristic, 73, 77
GDP, 50
*Gegege no Kitarō* (*Kitaro*; Mizuki), 70, 281n44
gender relations, 7, 33, 34, 49, 108, 243, 245, 304n36; inequality in, 7, 14, 31,
33, 34, 83; in postwar Japan, 7; reversal of, 289n48; Yamada and, 108, 289n49
gender trouble, 182
"Gensenkan Master" (*Gensenkan shujin*), 117–23, 125, 126, 129–31, 136, 139, 292n11, 292n12
Gini coefficient, 27, 28
glass: reflections on, 108; as transparent threshold, 94, 96, 97, 99, 103–105, 108
*Good Morning* (*Ohayō*; Ozu), 62–68, 76; 280n30
Gordon, Andrew, 33, 273n42, 273n45
gossip, 74, 282n57; celebrity 5, 73; community of, 71, 77; about imperial family, 75; media, 206; rumors and, 63; safe objects of, 74; sexuality and, 76; weeklies, 76
gun, 150, 163, 177, 191, 228, 232–35, 239, 281n37, 316n22; for battle of annihilation, 239; as fetish object, 239; against Japanese sword, 177; in possession of Revolutionary Left, 235; in possession of URA, 238, 239
GUN (artist collective), 9

Hamano Sachi, 7
handheld camera: in *Where Spring Comes Late* 99; in *Battles Without Honor and Humanity*, 187–89
Hara Takeshi, 79, 82
Hashimoto Kenji, 202
Hegelian Spirit, 157
*Heibon* (monthy), 73, 283n60
*heibon, shūkan* (*Weekly Heibon*), 73
heroes, 200; anticapitalist, 174; baseball, 205; body of, 227; cultural, 10, 11, 265; defiant, 11; eventual triumph of, 309n26; imaginary, 6; Japanese, 205; manga, 199; marginal identity of,

INDEX [ 353 ]

heroes (*continued*)
183; and struggles against mass consumption, 6; Tanaka as folk, 255; valorous and vulnerable, 7; young, 15, 200, 202. *See also* yakuza hero

heterosexual love, 182, 213, 224

heterosexual relations, 7, 205

high-growth economy, 4, 6, 23, 26, 28, 30, 40, 50–52, 70, 82, 101, 148, 176, 230, 260, 312n57; alternative to Japan under, 14; amenities of, 79; causes and effects of, 26; changes in higher education during, 42; changing lifestyle under, 273; dramatic transformation under, 50; early years of, 28, 81; euphoric influence of, 95; as giant blender, 46; ill effects of, 134; Japan before, 23; Japan under, 6, 14, 23, 24, 49, 50, 91, 93; late 1960s under, 91; life under, 93, 94, 96, 106; mass consumer society as direct outcome of, 229, 268n13; national drama of, 50, 82; pressure of, 94; rags-to-riches story of, 50; reach of, 94; reinvented gender roles and, 34; socioeconomic reality of, 5, 110; tail end of, 112, 267n5; television and, 23; Tokyo under, 149

high-growth era, 5, 19, 24, 26, 27, 30, 38, 79, 83, 114, 133, 254–57, 263, 264, 277n92; early years of, 46, 82; end of, 16; ethos of, 258; historical dynamics of, 268n13; optimism of Japan in, 16; paradigm shift of, 254; peak of, 209; production regime of, 9; radical socioeconomic changes during, 25; tail end of, 118, 200; Tokyo Tower as icon of, 256

high-growth regime, 16, 25, 38, 40, 49, 91, 93, 95, 101, 111, 113, 118, 142, 231, 200, 262, 264, 280n37; admission to, 42; alternative to, 83; battle against, 102; clean break from, 6; demise of, 255; economic benefits of, 26; independence from, 92; last piece of outside in, 183; life under, 49, 87, 168, 280n37; new national space under, 22, 51; Torajirō as outsider to, in *It's Tough Being a Man* series, 106

high school, 42, 56, 204; age cohort, 42; education, 34; student, 150, 252, 308n3

high-speed railway system, 133, 257

highway, 41, 257

Hijikata Tatsumi, 8–10; and *butoh* dance, 9

Hino Keizō, 147

historical conditions, 174, 208, 221, 226, 312n58; fetters of, 206; of postwar Hiroshima, 194; of postwar Japan, 16, 185, 195, 204, 209, 226, 275n65, 312n57; product of, 222

Hokkaido, 55, 87, 88, 91, 101, 106, 108, 109, 289n51, 296n17; Abashiri in, 124; Abashiri Prison in, 183; eastern 107; eastern coastal province of, 183; expansive land of, 107; ferry bound for, 105, 107; Nakashibetsu in, 89, 107

*Home from the Sea* (*Kokyō*; Yamada), 15, 87, 88, 109–14

homoeroticism, 182

homosocial bonds, 181, 182, 205, 224

Horikiri Naoto, 113

Hosaka Masayasu, 257

Hoshijima Ichirō, 185

hostage situation, 228, 250, 252

humanism, postwar Japanese, 148

*ichioku sō hakuchika*, 64; 280n33

Ikebe Ryō, 176, 184

Imamura Shōhei, 93, 287n18

income, 48; of agrarian household, 29; agricultural, 29, 256; of average household, 53; disposable, 28, 38; distribution of, 14, 25, 28; film-distribution, 111; of urban working households, 22, 280n34; new sources of, 62; of rural households, 29, 62, 256; urban landowners' rental, 27
inflation, 20, 26, 27, 258; and unemployment, 50
*Into a Black Sun* (*Kagayakeru yami*; Kaikō), 145, 153, 156–64, 166, 168, 296n6; ending of, 161, 164, 166; Kaikō's commentary on, 300n60; narrative of, 145, 154
Itō Kazuko, 248
*It's Tough Being a Man* television program (*Otoko wa tsuraiyo*; Yamada), 106, 288n47
*It's Tough Being a Man* film series (*Otoko wa tsuraiyo*; Yamada), 11, 83, 88, 106, 112, 113, 288n46, 290n66; and demise of yakuza film, 307n67

Japan National Railways (JNR), 15, 92, 114, 117, 130, 131, 133, 134, 293n30; image of, 297n35; stations of, 136–38
Japanese film industry, 175, 197; decline of, 65, 87, 174, 175, 283;
Japanese literature: contemporary, 148; postwar, 145
Japanese Red Army, 252, 320n96
Japanese uniqueness, discourse of, 47, 254
*Japan Sinks* (*Nihon chinbotsu*; Komatsu), 262, 263, 322n30
*jitsuroku* (factual recording), 188; as Tōei's marketing ploy, 189; style, 192, 193, 197
JNR. *See* Japan National Railways
*Josei jishin* (*Women's self*), 73, 75

*Kagayakeru yami*. See *Into a Black Sun*
Kaikō Takeshi, 12, 15, 143, 144, 149, 153, 154, 156, 158, 160, 161, 166–69, 289n51; command of English and French, 297n26; contemporary critics of, 150; criticism on, by Mishima, 152; criticism on, by Yoshimoto, 151–53; darkness trilogy of, 166, 168, 300n60; early career of, 146, 147; eulogy for, 148; and Japan's mass consumer society, 143; masculine project of, 143; and television, 165, 166; and television commercial, 134, 146, 168; and Tokyo, 149, 155; on Tokyo Olympics, 149; and travel, 143; as urban explorer, 149; and Vietnam, 15, 144, 145, 147–49, 297n33, 322n29; as war correspondent, 150, 152
Kajiwara Ikki, 15, 199–203, 205, 208, 210; and Chiba, 201, 202, 223, 308n14, 309n15, 309n19, 309n20; final scene of *Tomorrow's Jō* and, 223, 313n64
Kaneko Michiyo, 244–46; body of, as site of ideological battle, 244, 245; death of, 245, 318n71; Mori's condemnation of, 244; pregnancy of, 245
*kanri yakyū* (managed baseball), 203
*Kantō Hizakura Ikka* (Makino), 185
*Karajishi botan*, 184, 185; Mishima and, 301n7
Kara Jūrō, 10
Kasahara Kazuo, 188–90, 192, 194, 195, 197; on factual-recording style, 192, 193; and Fukasaku, 189
"Katoki sekai ron" (A thesis on the transitional phase of the world; Shiomi), 232
Katō Hidetoshi, 72

Katō Kazuhiko, 134
Katō Michinori, 252
Katō Yoshitaka, 239, 240, 246; beating of 240; younger brothers of 240, 249–52
Katsura Chiho, 112
Kawabata Yasunari, 138
Kawakami Tetsuharu, 203, 309n28
Kawasaki Noboru, 200, 201, 207, 219
Kawashima Tsuyoshi, 234; arrest of, 234; as leader of Revolutionary Left, 234; in prison, 316n35
Kishimoto Shigenobu, 47–49
Kitada Akihiro, 100
Kitai Kazuo, 130
Kobayashi Nobuhiko, 113, 185
Kojima Kazuko, 239, 240, 246; dead body of, 238
"Kokumin seikatsu ni kansuru yoron chōsa," 45
Komatsu Sakyō, 255, 262, 263, 289n51; Kaikō and, 322n29
Konno Tsutomu, 61
Korean residents in Japan, 32, 274n58
Korean War, 26, 91, 220, 221; economic impact of, on Japan, 295n3
Kotobukiya (present-day Suntory), 146, 296n7; PR team of 147
Kunihiro Yōko, 13
Kure City (Hiroshima), 110, 189, 190, 191, 193
Kurigami Kazumi, 260, 260
Kurosaki Isao, 73, 75
Kurosawa Akira, 188, 282n55, 306n60
Kusakabe Gorō, 185

labor movements, postwar, 32
land reform, 29
labor shortages, 28
labor unions, 21, 31, 145
*Laramie*, 13, 269n26

Latin America; emigrant communities in, 92, 286n11; migration to, 91
LDP. *See* Liberal Democratic Party
Liberal Democratic Party (LDP), 21, 27, 29, 32, 271n8, 274n58, 320n2; agricultural policies of, 28, 29, 256; agricultural sector's support for, 29; economic growth under, 27; economic policies of, 28, leaders of, 249; leadership election in 1972, 255, 256, 258; pro-Taiwan members of, 258; Tanaka faction in, 258; Tanaka's political rivals in, 258
liminal figure, 181, 209, 290n64
liminal identity, 210
liminal space, 129; prisons as, 183
*Liquor Heaven (Yōshu tengoku)*, 147
living dead. *See* zombies

machismo, 154
Makino Masahiro, 176
Mamada Takao, 48
*Man from Abashiri Prison, A*, series (*Abashiri bangaichi*), 123–24, 129, 174, 183
manga: editors of, 200, 201; experimental, 11, 12; readers of, 199, 200; rental books, 116, 291n7; in transition, 116; weeklies, 5, 70, 72, 199, 291n7, 307n1
manhood, 202; community of, 181; Japanese, 4, 6, 7
Mao Zedong, 40, 236
Marotti, William, 9
masculine drama, 4, 205, 219; of 1972 16
masculine identity, 14, 121, 158, 209, 298n41; of Fujioka, 130; injured, 209; of male danchi residents, 82; of male workers, 81; pursuit of, 15; recovery of, 121; working-class, 200
masculinist myth, 7, 11

masculinity, 7, 82, 154; crisis of, 8; of cultural heroes and would-be revolutionaries, 265; cultural reimagining of, 7; during high-growth era, 83; elusive, 143; imaginary state of, 118; Japanese, 7; recovery of, 123, 158
mass communication, 46
mass consumer society. *See* consumer society
mass consumerism. *See* consumerism
mass consumption; act of, 41; feminizing effects of, 6; world of, 2
mass culture, 317n65; narrative of, 121
masses (*taishū*), 10, 21, 40, 43, 44, 75, 77, 131, 146; everyday life of, 317n65; false consciousness of, 48; Tanaka as enabler of, 257
Matsushita Kei'ichi, 74, 75
Matsuzawa Yutaka, 9
McLuhan, Marshall, 50, 76
media environment, 76, 166, 168
media images, 5, 13, 145, 153, 166
Meiji period, 24, 111, 176, 178
metavision, 5, 16, 264
metavisuality, 52, 56, 60, 100; and mass consumerism, 254
methamphetamine (Philopon), 192, 305n51
Michiko, Princess, 74, 75, 79, 80; as symbol of national optimism, 74
middle class, 42; aspiring, 79; new, 48, 71; upper, 43
middle stratum consciousness. See also *chūryū ishiki*
middle stratum of society. See also *chūryū*
Ministry of Education, 60, 279n17
Ministry of Foreign Affairs, 92
Ministry of Labor, Women and Juvenile Bureau, 33

Mino Kōzō, 188, 305n48
Mishima Yukio, 152, 153, 175, 176, 276n75, 297n31; on *Big Gambling Ceremony*, 175, 176; death of, 319n90; and "Karajishi botan," 301n7; and *magajin*, 311n42; in yakuza film, 301n8
misogyny, 253; of Fujioka, 293n36
Mitsukoshi department store, 39, 40, 276n78
Miyadai Shinji, 5
Miyahara Teruo, 201, 311n42, 314n69
Miyamoto Tsuneichi, 52–54, 57, 62, 79
Mizuki Shigeru, 68, 70, 201, 292n15, 295n55; and Tsuge, 115, 116
modernization: of boxing, 210; disruptive effects of, 178; gaze of, 54; of Japan, 176, 181, 210; regime of, 25, 95
moral debt of Yabuki Jō in *Tomorrow's Jō*, 216, 223–25
Moriyama Daodō, 8, 294n43
Mori Tsuneo, 233, 235–42, 244, 245; arrest of, 247; confessions of, to police interrogators, 251; critical retrospective of, 242, 243; death of, 252, 261; defection of, from Bund, 237, 316n33; misogynistic attitudes of, 243; and Nagata, 239, 241, 242, 244, 247
Mukai Satoshi, 148
Mukōyama Shigenori, 246
Murakami Tomohiko, 224
Murakami Yasusuke, 45–48
Muramatsu Takeshi, 71

Nagata Hiroko, 234–36, 238–45; arrest of, 247; confessions of, 252; death of, 243, 253; death sentence of, 252–53; Mori and, 239, 242, 244, 247
Nakahira Takuma, 138

Nakano Midori, 136
Nakano Takeo, misogyny of, 253
Nakauchi Isao, 41, 276n80; and Mao Zedong's writing, 40; populist conviction of, 39, 40; reservations about cold chains of, 276n83
Nakazawa Yuriko, 136
Namekata Masatoki, 239, 246, 316n38
Nanba Kōji, 135
National Diet, 52, 278n3
national income per capita, 27
National Liberation Front, 15, 167, 298n44
national pension systems, 32
National Survey of Social Stratification and Social Mobility (SSM), 45, 48
*Natsuno Yami.* See *Darkness in Summer*
*New Battles Without Honor and Humanity* series (Fukasaku), 197
*New Battles Without Honor and Humanity: Boss's Last Days* (Fukasaku), 194
new left movements, 16, 229, 249, 251
New Life Movement (Shin seikatsu undō), 33
newspaper, 51, 211, 249, 253, 261
Newspaper Research Center (University of Tokyo), 74
NHK. See Nihon Hōsō Kyōkai
*Night and Fog in Japan* (Ōshima), 185
Nihon Hōsō Kyōkai (Japan Broadcasting Corporation: NHK), 19, 56, 57, 61, 65
Nikkatsu Studio, 10, 82, 111, 168
*Nippon Chivalry* series (*Nihon kyōkakuden*), 174, 184
Nippon Television Broadcast Corporation, 13, 22, 76, 165; executives of, 166; president of, 271n13, 300n54; and Yomiuri Giants, 203; and Yomiuri Shinbun, 203

Nixon, Richard, 20, 236; visit to China by, 249
Noguchi Yukio, 26
*Nonno*, 135, 136
North Korea, 211, 233, 234, 274n58; Red Army faction members in, 315n15
nostalgia, 114, 117, 131, 142, 143, 148; admixture of, and commercialism, 118; and existential angst, 11; objects of, 121, 123, 142; scene of, 120, 125; site of, 126; space of, 121; Tsuge and, 154

observer, 142, 154, 167; agency as 157; cynical, 149; frivolous status as, 155; Kaikō as, 152, 155; neutral, 166; opportunistic, 145; pessimistic, 81; powerful status as, 153; problematic status as, 159; sovereign position as, 162
Oguma Eiji, 8, 183, 263n13
oil crisis of 1973, 113, 258, 261–63
Ōki Minoru, 2, 3, 267n4
Okinawa, 55; reversion of, 19, 20, 323n31
Okuzawa Shūichi, 251
oppositional politics, 5, 9, 11, 16, 174, 196, 245
Organization of Petroleum Exporting Countries, 258
Ōshima Nagisa, 10, 11, 93, 112, 185
*Otoko wa tsuraiyo.* See *It's Tough Being a Man*
Ōtsuka Eiji, 242, 312n58
Ōtsuki Setsuko, 244, 246, 316n38
*Outlaw Killer* (*Hitokiri Yota*; Fukasaku), 188, 193
outside, 25, 164; geographical, 5, 100; last piece of, in regime of high-growth, 183; temporal, 5

outsider, 25, 139, 140; of consumer culture, 69; within corporate labor system, 33; to high-growth regime, 106; within Japan, 41, 290n64; masculine, 121; position as, 15; ownership rates; of refrigerator, 39, 67; of television, 39, 66, 67; of washing machine, 39, 67

Ōya Sōichi, 64

Ozaki Michio, 241, 246; beating of, 247, 317n51; death of, 318n77

Ozu Yasujirō, 62, 63, 65, 68; death of, 65; tongue-in-cheek perspective of, on television, 65; uneasiness of, with television's power, 67, 76, 280n37

Panasonic, 36, 40

Partner, Simon, 33, 272n29

patriarch, 88, 104, 178, 192; traditional, 111

patriarchal authority, 64, 65, 108

patriarchy; command of, 181; declining, 64; inflexible, 183; sense of indebtedness to, 181; vision of, 34

People's Republic of China, 26, 235, 298n39; Japan's relations with, 20, 258; Kaiko's visit to, 147; Nixon's visit to, 236, 249; U.S. relations with, 249

Piston Horiguchi, 210

Play, The (artist collective), 9

police, 52, 53, 182, 183, 211, 228, 229, 233–36, 241, 247–51, 311n44, 316n22, 316n23, 318n74, 319n86; confrontations with, 229, 241 320n104; bloody fight against, 241; and community relations, 249; extensive search by, for radical activists and sympathizers, 249; riot, 53, 186, 187, 211, 228, 248, 312n57;

security, 233; and television, 248; URA's clash with, 223, 228, 229, 250, 251; visual surveillance by, 248

political activism, 4, 8, 9, 82, 195, 196; of 1968 and 1969, 4; on campus, 45, 173; collapse of, 229; and popular culture, 8

popular culture, 4, 8, 9, 313n61; fantasy space of, 7–8; in late 1960s and early 1970s Japan, 11; and media, 12; Oguma and, 8; and politics, 15; production process for, 7; scholarly attention on, 9

poverty, 48, 66, 70, 115, 128, 139, 141, 142, 204, 281n37; of atomic bomb slum, 195; realism of, 139, 142

poverty line, 28, 272n24, 283n62

print media, 20, 21, 51, 70, 73, 271n10; and emergent national consciousness, 51; and television, 70

*provoke* (magazine), 138, 294n43, 294n45

pugilism. *See* boxing

quotidian life. *See* everyday life

*Railway Journey* (Schivelbusch), 94

Red Army faction (Kyōsandō Sekigunha), 211, 229, 231–37, 239, 241, 243–46, 316n21; Arab branch of, 252; criticism by, on Revolutionary Left, 242; joint training session of, with Revolutionary Left, 242; leadership of, 233; members of, in North Korea, 315n15; merger of, with Revolutionary Left, 221, 229, 317n42; and *Tomorrow's Jō*, 199, 210, 243; vertical command structure of, 231

*Red Peony Gambler* (Hibotan bakuto; Yamashita), 178, 180

*Red Peony Gambler* (*Hibotan bakuto*) series, 174, 182, 185, 303n30

refrigerators, 22, 38; ownership rates of, 39, 66, 67, 272n26
revolution, 187, 231, 238; communist 238; and death, 238; global, 231, 232, 238, 252; on national level, 231; prospect of, 186; pursuit of, 228
Revolutionary Left (Japan Communist Party Revolutionary Left Kanagawa Committee; Kakumei saha), 229, 231, 234–37, 239–46, 251, 315n17, 316n35; anti-U.S.-patriotism of, 231, 249; assault on police by, 241; female members of, 231, 242; joint training session of, with Red Army faction, 242; leaders of, 237; Maoist ideology of, 231; merger with Red Army faction, 211, 231, 317n42; mountain base of, 236; Nagata as leader of, 238; Sakaguchi's relations with, 247
revolutionary solider, 228, 239, 241, 244
"Right On, Overseas Edition" (Zubari kaigai-ban; Kaikō), 149
"Right On, Tokyo" (Zubari Tokyo; Kaikō), 149
Ritsumeikan University, 43; teaching conditions at, 44, 312n57
Rony, Fatimah Tobing, 60
royal wedding of 1959, 74, 75, 81, 283n76
"A Rustic Inn" (Riarizumu no yado; Tsuge), 117, 118, 131, 139–43

Sadakane Hiroyuki, 100
Saeki Kiyoshi, 178, 184, 188
Saigon: Kaikō's travel to, 144, 145; Kaikō's attraction to, 148; Majestic Hotel in, 165; public execution in, 150, 166
Saishu Satoru, 186
Saitō Ayako, 181
Saji Keizō, 146

Sakaguchi Hiroshi, 234–36, 241, 247, 248, 249, 252, 316n33; body of, 246; on death row, 253; death sentence of, 252–53; proposal of, for bases in China, 235; recollections of, 236, 240, 245, 246
Sakai Mutsuo, 146
Sakisaka Yasuko, 246
*Sandei mainich* (Weekly Mainichi), 72
Sano Mitsuo, 220
Saragi Tokuji, 232
Sartre, Jean-Paul, 77
Sas, Miryam, 8, 9
Satō Eisaku, 19, 20, 255
Schivelbusch, Wolfgang, 94
Science and Technology agency, Resources Council, 41
Second Communist League (Kyōsanshugisha dōmei; Bund), 231, 232; 237; Kansai faction of, 232, 237
Sedgwick, Eve, 181
seeing, 152; act of, 153, 154, 159, 161; action and, 152, 153, 155; active subject of, in Vietnam, 159; agent of, 77, 153; double consciousness of, and being seen, 60; ethically responsible agent of, 153; idealized and masculine notion about, 153; modern technology of, 79; new way of, 5, 79; private experience of, 54; proper way of, 153
seer, 15, 153, 155–157, 161, 190; cool, 163; omnipotent, 77; sovereign position of, 161, 162; superior position of, 162
self-reflectivity, 3, 52, 56. See also metavisuality
sexual desire, 134, 245; male, 134; never-to-be-satisfied, 126
sexual intercourse, 81, 120, 158, 168, 244; on screen, 10; with Vietnamese mistress, 158

Shibano Haruhiko, 235; death of, 235, 241
Shigenobu Fusako, 252
*shikan* 視姦, 155, 156
*shikansha* 視姦者, 155, 298n36
Shimizu Ikutarō, 50, 56
Shindō Ryūzaburō, 246
Shinoda Masahiro, 11, 112, 283n70
Shiozawa Shigeru, 260
Shiomi Takaya, 231–33, 238, 252
Shirai Yoshio, 210
Shirato Sanpei, 10, 291n8
Shōchiku Studios, 11, 88, 106, 111, 112; decline of Japanese film industry and, 111; executives of, 106; Yamada and, 106, 112, 288n46
Shōda Michiko. *See* Princess Michiko
*Shōnen magajin, Shūkan* (*Weekly Shonen Magazine*), 12, 70, 72, 199, 281n44, 313n63
*Shōnen sandei, Shūkan* (*Weekly Shonen Sunday*), 72
Shōriki Matsutarō, 13, 271n13
*Shūkan asahi* (*Weekly Asahi*), 72, 144, 149
*Shūkan bunshun* (*Weekly Bunshun*), 75, 282n50, 308m8
Shundō Kōji, 185, 305n48
social mobility, 40
social security system, 32
social stratification, 49, 271n15
softcore porn films, 7, 9, 82, 111, 168, 300n58
*sōkatsu* (self-criticism), 196, 229, 232, 239, 240–42, 244, 245, 252, 319n74
"The Spider Thread" (Akutagawa), 141, 295n53
SSM. *See* National Survey of Social Stratification and Social Mobility
Standish, Isolde, 9

*Star of the Giants* (*Kyojin no hoshi*), 15, 16, 199, 201–205, 209, 219, 226, 227, 308n8; as drama of homosocial bonds, 205; popularity of, 201–203
*Street Mobster* (*Gendai yakuza*; Fukasaku), 188, 193; hopeless story of, 196
subjectivity, 186, 208, 226, 305n52; autonomous, 145, 196, 209, 226; communist, 228, 238–41; concept of, 227; debates on, 314n70; general state of, 77; genuine, 208; political, 226; revolutionary, 223, 226, 238, 245, 317n65; self-reflective, 60; unfettered, 145
subjugation, 154
Sudo Naoki, 48
Suga Hidemi, 223
Sugawara Bunta, 190, 193, 194
Sugiyama Toshi, 255, 260, 261, 321n17; biographer of, 322n26; death of, 259–61, 322n26; friends and associates of, 260, 261; intense lifestyle of, 260; life and death of, 321n21; as message, 260; and Mobil Oil ad, 259, 260
Suntory, 1, 146, 296n7; and Kaikō, 168; products of, 147, 168; television commercial for, 1–3

Tachibana Takashi, 257
Tada Michitarō, 46, 79
Tahara Sōichirō, 261
Takada Fumio, 184
Takada Kōji, 194; Kasahara's collaboration with, 306n64
Takahara Hiroyuki, 243
Takaha Tesuo, 92, 93
Takakura Ken, 185, 302n15; in *Distant Cry from Springi*, 109; frustration of, with yakuza film, 304n33; and Fuji,

Takakura Ken (*continued*)
    185; in *Hell is a Man's Destiny*, 176; and Ikebe, 184; and Tsuruta, 193
Takamori Asao. *See* Kajiwara Ikki
Takano Etsuko, 43, 44, 277n89
Takeshita Noboru, 19
Tamiya Takamaro, 199, 211, 232, 233, 315n15
Tanaka Kakuei, 16, 254–58; arrest of, 258, charges of bribery and Foreign Exchange Management Act against, 258; as epitome of ethos of high-growth era, 258; as folk hero, 255; loyal supporters of, 257; as minister of post and telecommunications, 256; political style of, 257; popularity of, 257; resignation of, from premiership, 258; spectacular success of, in diplomacy, 258; and victory of, in LDP leadership election, 255
Tanaka Mitsu, 243; criticism by, on Nagata, 244; recollections of, 250
Tanaka Tokuzō, 174
Tatematsu Wahei, 173
tattoos, 179, 180, 183, 302n15, 306n57
television: affective impact of, 50; reach of, 165; black-and-white, 38, 39; broadcasting of, 21; color, 39, 40; and domestic space, 65; and educational research, 54–62; educational value of, 56; gaze of, 51; glow of, 103; introduction of, 6; and living room, 6, 73, 166, 228, 250, 253, 279n20, 282n55; as love, 61, 62, 75; ownership of, 28; police violence captured on, 248; power of, 57; primetime, 166; and regime of high growth, 93; and royal wedding, 74, 75; social benefits of, 67; as source of light, 79; transformative effects of, 53; transparency of, 21; and travel, 115;

two-dimensional world of, 103; war on, 165; and weeklies, 49, 77
television documentary, 56, 57, 63, 70, 93, 165, 166, 300n54, 302n13
*Television Scandal News* (*Terebi sanmenkiji*), 76
television stations, 283n62; commercial, 256, 314n2; in early years of operation, 13; under LDP pressure, 21, 249; NHK, 256
television viewers, 50, 71, 72, 248–50; early, 279n; gaze of, 68, 77; increase in, 72; radio listeners and, 53
tenant farmers, 25, 26, 29
Terabayashi Makie, 248
Teraoka Kōichi, 246
Terayama Shūji, 8, 10, 212, 215
Terebi-kun. *See* "The TV Boy"
*That Which Arrives from the Shores* (*Nagisa kara kurumono; Kaikō*), 158, 162, 299n49
*Theater of Life* (*Jinsei gekijō*; Uchida), 174
Tochigi Prefecture, 54, 55, 235
Tōei, 111, 174, 185, 187, 188, 195–97, 289n58; executives of, 304n36; president of, 304n36; theaters of, 303n25; and yakuza film, 176, 188
Tōhō, 111, 112
Tokyo Olympics (1964), 38, 149, 263
*Tokyo Story* (*Tokyo monogatari*, 1953), 64
Tomii, Reiko, 9
Tominaga Ken'ichi, 47, 48
*Tomorrow's Jō* (*Ashita no Jō*; Kajiwara and Chiba), 15, 16, 199, 201, 202, 209, 210, 213, 215, 226, 227, 308n8, 312n58; and class issues, 202; concepts of real men in, 202; ending of, 223; final episode of, 313n63; Mishima Yukio and, 311n42; planning stage for, 310; popularity of, 200, 202, 211, 220; readers of, 224; and Red Army

faction, 199, 210, 243; script of, 209; serialization of, 312n55; and *Star of the Giants*, 226, 227, 308n8; tomorrow in 224
Toshiba; advertisement for, 36, 38
*Tough Guy* (*Akumyō*; Tanaka), 174
*Tough Guy* (*Akumyō*) series, 174
Tōyama Mieko, 241–43, 246
tradition, 180, 183; authentic Japanese, 179, Japanese literary, 167; restrictive forces of, 15; security of, 180
traditional values, 181, 183, 191; hero's departure from, 181
transportation networks, 41
travel, 115, 130, 133, 143, 167; air, 92; dismal conditions of, 139; as extension of mass consumerism, 138, 139; fashion and 135; fantastical 142; long-distance, 59; and male sexual desire, 134; narcissistic vision of, 139; nature of, 132–33; as performative act, 131, 136, 138; railway, 133, 293n35; and search for self, 133, 135, 136, 167; television as rival of, 133; and Tsuge, 131
travel boom, 117; and Tsuge, 131, 139
Treasury of Loyal Retainers, The (Kanadehon Chūshingura; Takeda Izumo, Miyoshi Shōraku, Namiki Senryū), 177, 178
Treaty of Mutual Corporation and Security between the United States and Japan (1960; U.S.-Japan Security Treaty), 52, 319n86
Tsubouchi Yōzō, 1, 267n5
Tsuchiya Yuka, 60
Tsuge Yoshiharu, 11, 12, 115–18, 121, 124, 125, 127–31, 134, 138, 141–43, 158, 292n11, 292n12, 292n15, 292n16; alter ego of, 123; angst-filled travelers in works of, 117, 121, 143; autobiographical works of, 292n17; contemporary world of, 123; creative trajectory of, 295n56; and connection with past, 292n10; and self-negation, 116; earlier works of, 123, 129; early career of, 116, 291n7, 297n8; early life of, 115–17, 127–29, 291n4; fantasy of, 117, 126, 127, 129, 130, 140; fantasy world of, 117, 118, 123, 130, 158, 295n56; fast-growing fame of, 117; and Fujioka, 130, 31, 293n28; imaginary world of, 123; and Kitai, 130; and *A Man from Abashiri Prison*, 292n13; and nostalgia, 121, 125; portrayals of elusive masculinity by, 143; and poverty, 128; psychological issues of, 128; and Discover Japan campaign, 15, 130, 131, 143; and sea, 129, 293n24; search for spiritual home by, 148; self-reflective gaze of, 114; semiautobiographical works by, 143; special issue of *Garo* on, 115; and "Spider Thread," 295n35; split gaze of, 140; and travel boom, 131, 139; travel manga of, 143; working-class identity of, 116
Tsuruta Kōji, 193, 303n30; and Takakura Ken, 304n33
"The TV Boy" (*Terebi-kun*; Mizuki), 68–70, 281n44

Uchida Tomu, 174
Uchiyama Takashi, 30
Uegaki Yasuhiro, 237, 238, 247–48; hurt body of, 248; public appearance of, 253; incarceration of, 252–53
Ueno Eishin, 91, 92
*Under the Flag of the Rising Sun* (*Gunki hatameku motni*; Fukasaku), 188
unemployment benefits, 29, 62

United Red Army (Rengō sekigun), 6, 16, 211, 221, 230, 231, 237, 249, 252, 316n35; battle with police, 6, 223, 229, 250, 251; arrests of members of, 250; bloody purges by, 187, 195, 196, 239, 319n90; and consumer society, 230; crimes of, 229; formation of, 229, 231, 243, 318n74; future of, 236; gender dynamics within, 243; ideological discord within, 240; ideological struggle of, 16, 223; leaders of, 238, 244, 261; members of, 6, 223, 227–30, 234, 238, 246, 248, 249, 252, 253, 264, 317n65; military training camp of, 229; mountain bases of, 230, 232, 239; revolutionary ideas of, 241; Sakaguchi's involvement in, 245; self-criticism (sōkatsu) sessions of, 239; struggle of, against bourgeois, 248; training sessions of, 238, 239

United States, 12, 14, 20, 39, 47, 206, 234, 284n87, 294n49; ambivalent feelings toward, 13; bases in Japan, 144; Cold War policies of, toward Japan, 26; conciliatory popular representations of, 12; culture of, 14; dark history of slavery in, 206; economic assistance of, 26; as former enemy nation, 209; images of, 12; Japan's subjugation to, 319n90; as main source of Japanese values, 13; Mao Zedong's urge to stand against, 236; material power of, 205; military operations of, in Vietnam, 144, 295; number of television sets in, 39; perceptions of, 13; racial tensions in, 47; and reversion of Okinawa, 20; scientific power of, 210

universal health care, 32

universities, 43, 44, 46, 186, 272n25, 311n42; private, 43; public, 311n42

University of Tokyo, 74, 186, 199

URA. *See* United Red Army

USS *Enterprise*, 21, 248

utopia, 145, 164; antiestablishment, 211; dialectical, 213

vacuum cleaners, 36, 37, 66; ownership rates of, 67

Vietcong, 159, 160, 161, 163, 165

Vietnam, 144, 145, 147–49, 151–53, 157–59, 166–68, 297n32; as absolute outside, 168; central, 165; as consumable images, 153, 166; dearth of information about, in Japan, 150; death and destruction in, 145, 158; fast-growing popular interest in, 295n2; future of national liberation struggle in, 173; Kaikō's attraction to, 148, 150, 151; Kaikō's brush with death in, 167; Kaikō's experiences in, 145, 153, 295n1; Kaikō's reporting on, 147, 149; Kaikō's return to, 297n33; Kaikō's transition from Tokyo to, 149, 322n29; North, 144; people of, 145; reality in, 153, 158, 298n39; South, 144; transformative effects of, 149; transformation of, into consumable images, 186; U.S war in, 157

Vietnamese soldiers, 155, 162–64, 299n50, 299n52

Vietnamese women, 158

Vietnam War, 13, 26, 143–45; impact of, on Japan's economy, 295n3; Japanese corporations' involvement in, 184; Japan's movements against, 296n4; Kaikō's experiences in, 15; Nippon Television's three-part documentary on, 165

Vietnam War Report (*Betonamu senki*; Kaikō), 144, 150–52, 154, 156, 160, 161, 166
visual field, 4–7, 52, 77, 79, 138, 161, 162; traveler and, 142
visual media, 5, 6, 53
vomit, 217, 221
voyeur, 76, 77, 156, 297n31

Wakamatsu Kōji, 10, 229
*War Chronicle of a South Vietnam Marine Battalion* (*Betonamu Kaihei daitai senki*), 165
war experiences, 195, 220, 221
war generations, 209, 220, 221, 263
Washida Koyata, 157
washing machine, 38, 63, 65, 280n35; in danchi apartment, 80; ownership rates of, 39, 67
weeklies, 5, 14, 72–76, 267n5, 282n48, 282n50, 282n53; focus of, on the personal and quotidian, 51; gossip, 76, 282n57; manga, 72, 116, 199, 200, 307n1; photo exposé, 76, 77, 284n78; rise of, 73; and royal wedding, 74–76; television and, 49, 51, 71, 74, 77, 79
*Where Spring Comes Late* (*Kazoku*; Yamada), 87, 88, 92, 94, 97–99, 101–4, 106, 108, 109, 111, 112, 114, 146, 189; hopeful message of, 15
white-collar workers, 25, 28, 48, 273n41, 275n65, 285n92; and blue-collar workers, 28, 45; in large-scale corporations, 31
wildness (*yasei*), 212, 213, 215, 220, 222, 223; of Jō in *Tomorrow's Jō*, 212
window, 80, 108, 168; glass, 94, 99; television as, 54; train, 93, 94, 96, 97, 103–105
women, 7, 25, 31, 33, 34, 135, 253; exclusion of, from homosocial bonds, 205, 243; and manga industry, 268n8; in postwar Japanese family, 275n65; reinvented gender role for Japanese, 34; transformation of, into revolutionary soldiers, 242; and washing machine, 280n35; young, 74, 135, 143, 293n35
World War II, 150, 165

yakuza, 175; in Hiroshima, 194; and tattoos, 179; quotidian life of, 197
yakuza film, 8, 12, 15, 173, 111, 174, 180, 183–85, 190: cinematic conventions of, 174, 187, 188, 196; decline of, 186, 187; fans of, 174, 197, 198; first wave of, 15, 174–77, 179, 190–92, 193, 196; as kabuki-style performative art, 184; outlaw hero of, 173; overproduction of, 185; second wave of, 15; and student movements, 185
yakuza hero, 173–76, 179, 181, 184, 190, 193, 306n57; anguish of, 196; antithesis of, 194; arrest of, 183; chosen weapon of, 177; departure of, from traditional values, 181; evolution of, 193; final attack of, 179; forbearance of, 178; independence of, 184; as independent agent, 181; as itinerant gambler, 181; liminal status of, 181; lone, 173; marginal identity of, 183; moral actions of, 185; reinvention of, 187; in state of existential angst, 196; subjectivity of, 182; Torajirō as comedic incarnation of, in *It's Tough Being a Man* series, 106; valor and virility of, 191; as viewer par excellence, 194; violent act of, 182
yakuza world, 174, 180, 181, 185, 188, 191, 193, 197
Yamadaira Shigeki, 184, 185

Yamada Shōji, 260

Yamada Takashi, 232, 245, 246

Yamada Yōji, 11, 14, 87, 88, 91, 94, 95, 97, 105, 106, 108, 109, 114, 285n1; anxiety of, as filmmaker, 87, 112; critique by, of contemporary Japan, 83, 94; hopeful message of, 15; *It's Tough Being a Man series*, 83, 88, 106, 288n44; realistic visions of contemporary Japan, 88; nostalgic turn of, 290n66; optimism of, 87; as Shōchiku director, 106, 112, 288n46; and traditional gender relations, 108, 289n49; use of handheld camera by, 188; *Where Spring Comes Late*, 93, 94, 287n26

Yamaguchi Hitomi, 146

Yamamoto Akira, 12, 14

Yamamoto Jun'ichi, 244, 246

*Yamano bunkō no kiroku.* See *Dawn Over the Mountains*

Yamashita Kōsaku, 178

Yamazaki Jun, 246

Yamazaki Masakazu, 165

Yanagihara Ryōhei, 146

Yanagita Kunio, 61

"Yanagiya Master" (Yanagiya shujin), 117, 118, 121–27, 129–30, 139

Yasumi Akihito, 138

*Yojimbo* (Kurosawa), 188

Yom Kippur War, 258

Yomiuri Giants, 200, 203, 204, 206, 207

Yomiuri Shinbun, 13, 203

Yoshida Haruo, 162

Yoshida Naoya, 93

Yoshida Sadaji, 189, 197; camerawork of, 189

Yoshida Yoshishige (Kijū), 10, 11, 112

Yoshimi Shunya, 34, 67, 99

Yoshimoto Taka'aki, 230; and criticism of Kaikō, 151–53

Yoshino Masakuni, 244, 249, 252

Zahlten, Alexander, 9

zombies, 222; in materialist world, 223

GPSR Authorized Representative: Easy Access System Europe, Mustamäe tee 50, 10621 Tallinn, Estonia, gpsr.requests@easproject.com

www.ingramcontent.com/pod-product-compliance
Lightning Source LLC
Chambersburg PA
CBHW021930290426
44108CB00012B/788